International Assisted Reproductive Technology

STEPHEN PAGE

AMERICAN BAR ASSOCIATION
Family Law Section

Cover design by Amanda Fry/ABA Design

Printed in the United States of America.

28 27 26 25 24 5 4 3 2 1

A catalog record for this book is available from the Library of Congress.

Contents

Chapter 10 In Different Parts of the Same Country, Different Laws May Apply 247

Chapter 11 Insurance for International Parent Journeys 265

Updates and downloads are available at:
https://ambar.org/IART.

About the Author

Stephen Page is a dad through surrogacy and egg donation. He has also suffered infertility. He is a multiple award-winning Australian lawyer who has long specialized in assisted reproductive technology (ART), especially international ART. His clients have gone all over the world in order to become parents, including to 36 U.S. states and eight Canadian provinces, and to many other countries including Argentina, Brazil, Colombia, Georgia, Ghana, Greece, Iran, Kenya, Mexico, Nigeria, the Philippines, Russia, Sri Lanka, and Ukraine.

Stephen was admitted as a solicitor in 1987. Since 1988 he has advised in more than 1,900 surrogacy journeys for clients throughout Australia and in 37 other countries. He has been an accredited family law specialist since 1996.

In 2020 Stephen received the inaugural Pride in Law Award. In 2023 he received the Queensland Law Society President's Medal.

Stephen serves on a number of committees, including the American Bar Association's ART Committee, and as a board member of the Fertility Society of Australia and New Zealand.

Introduction

"The law concerning assisted reproduction, and the parenting consequences to those participating in that process, has been evolving for some time. In large part, the law has lagged behind the science of reproduction and the social forces that have arisen from the resulting family dynamics."[1]

It is a particular honour to write this book for the American Bar Association when I am not an American. I am an Aussie, pronounced Ozzie.

I did not expect, back in 1988 when I was a newly admitted solicitor in one of the suburbs of my city, beautiful Brisbane, in Australia that one client would change my life. She was my first surrogacy client. Since then I have advised in more than 1,900 surrogacy journeys for clients throughout Australia and at last count 37 countries, including of course the United States.

I was fortunate that my state, in reaction to the *Baby M* case[2] and the birth of Australia's first baby conceived through gestational surrogacy, Alice Kirkman,[3] was the only Australian jurisdiction to criminalize all surrogacy—no matter who did it, no matter how much was paid, no matter if it was traditional or gestational, and no matter where in the world it happened—the first place to do so. I say fortunate, because out of my duty to my clients I was forced to quickly learn where else surrogacy could be done. Conversations with new clients would go like this:

Clients: "We want to become parents through surrogacy."

Me: "That is an offense [and then describe the law.]"

Clients: "If we can't do surrogacy here, where can we do it?"

---

1. *Re* Family Law Act, 2016 B.C.S.C. 22.
2. 537 A.2d 1227 (N.J. 1988).
3. Maggie Kirkman et al., *IVF Surrogacy: A Personal Perspective*, Access Austl., https://access.org.au/?p=264 (last visited Apr. 29, 2024).

I could have merely said I didn't know. Instead, I took my duty to my clients seriously, and looked it up. In the early days this was especially difficult, as there were very few resources available on the internet. I had to make the effort to go to a law library and look it up.

Two more lessons were learnt quickly:

1. A ban on surrogacy does not work, unless politicians are prepared to police the nation's bedrooms—as traditional surrogacy can occur with at-home insemination.[4]
2. If barriers are put in place, intended parents, out of desperation to become parents as part of our biological urge to reproduce, will go elsewhere.

These are lessons that some legislators have not worked out—and make the lot of a lawyer practicing in this field the more interesting and the more complex.

When I saw that first client, I did not know, and could have scarcely believed, that I would suffer infertility, or that I would have a husband and then a daughter conceived through surrogacy. But these things have come to be. Life can be much more interesting than we plan it to be.

My first overseas surrogacy clients in the late 2000s had a simple request. They wanted to become parents. Their case, in its simplicity, speaks of the complexity of international ART. They were a gay couple who lived in China. Out of necessity they needed an egg donor and a surrogate. One man was Australian and one British. They undertook surrogacy in India, and wanted their child to live in Australia, and for the child to have both UK and Australian citizenship. After their journey started, the Indian government put before Parliament a bill that would have prevented them undertaking surrogacy in India.

As it turns out, changes in India did not happen for a few years yet. But always at the back of the mind was the thought—*this could happen now.*

This book is an attempt to give a practical guide for fellow lawyers to navigate international ART law—of course, surrogacy (the most complex form of reproduction, and in an international setting, the most complex form of surrogacy), but also the other ways that impact how people reproduce through ART internationally—egg, sperm, and embryo donation, and the interplay with adoption.

You may wonder, if you flip through this book, why there is a chapter on international legal architecture—and another one confined to Europe.

4. As occurred in my first surrogacy case, in 1988.

The simple answer is length—to make the chapters digestible to the reader. Most of the countries of Europe seemingly dislike surrogacy with a passion, which then explains why so many cases have ended up in the European Court of Human Rights. I have set these out at length as each has turned on its own facts—and they illustrate powerfully the attitude of the respondent countries towards surrogacy.

I want to thank my two secretaries, Grace White and Lisa Edwards, who have endured my efforts with relative patience during the period of writing this book, as well as my typist, Jenny Ehrlich. My husband Mitchell and daughter Elizabeth have had remarkable patience while I have been writing. Jeff Salyards at the American Bar Association has patiently waited for this book finally to be produced.

This book has been written on the lands of the Jagera and Turrbal peoples.

Given the scope of the book, it has been impossible to cover every country in the world, but I have tried to cover themes, and filled the book with data, to help. The desire to have this book done, rather than perfect, has meant that some topics, such as posthumous reproduction, sex selection, and mitochondrial donation, have been left out. Updates and downloads are available at: https://ambar.org/IART. If there is sufficient interest in this book, these will be covered in a second edition.

If you enjoy this book as much as I enjoy helping others become parents, you will enjoy this book greatly! Good luck!

Chapter 1

International Law Architecture (Other Than European Conventions)

"Everyone should be able to establish details of their identity as individual human beings, which includes the legal parent-child relationship."

Mennesson v. France[1]

When intended parents are pursuing an international assisted reproductive technology (ART) journey, they will need to traverse not only the law in the other country, but also the law at home and—in the midst of each of those countries' laws—any international law also affecting the journey.

Quite simply, there is very little international law architecture concerning an international surrogacy or ART arrangement.

Why Not Europe Here, Too?

I have written a separate chapter about Europe due to length. As seen in Chapter 2, there are both passive and active conventions and protocols in Europe that impact international ART. There have been numerous decisions of the European Court of Human Rights impacting international ART.

Any understanding of international legal architecture concerning ART, or the lack of it, must come back to fundamental concepts in Western law about parentage, as set out in Table 1.1. These maxims have been around since the time of Justinian, and underpin many countries' presumptions about who is a parent.

1. App. No. 65192/11, Eur. Ct. H.R. at 96 (2014).

Table 1.1. Parentage Maxims

Latin Maxim	Meaning
mater semper certa est	The mother is always certain. In other words, the woman who gave birth to the child is the mother.
pater est quem nuptiae demonstrant	The father is he who is married to the mother.

The struggle over the centuries was not to identify the mother—that was self-evident—but to identify the father. On their face, these maxims can be difficult to reconcile with who is a parent in a particular journey—for example, when there is a surrogacy journey. This manner of thinking in the maxims is the justification for holding that the surrogate is the mother—as seen in many European countries (as illustrated in European Court of Human Rights cases in Chapter 2).

A Hague Convention?

Due to a lack of international legal architecture, and at a time of the seeming rise of India as a surrogacy destination, the Hague Conference on Private International Law (HCCH) commenced in 2010 pursuing a convention concerning international surrogacy arrangements, and that of private international law concerning children. While governing international surrogacy arrangements formed the genesis of the project, it was soon realized that the parentage of many children, not born through international surrogacy arrangements, was not recognized internationally.

Until the 1970s, there were two types of children in the world—legitimate and illegitimate. In much of the world that distinction thankfully is now at an end. However, there are seemingly two types of children born in the world:

- Those conceived through sexual intercourse, whose parentage is recognized
- Those conceived through ART of some kind, whose parentage may or may not be recognized, or whose parentage is recognized in some countries but not in others

As of 2023, it is anticipated that there will, eventually, be such an instrument, and, if so, when it might be entered into, and its form.

There has been a broad dispute for some years that has slowed down the enactment of a convention. On the one hand, the United States has upheld the principles of reproductive autonomy and liberty,[2] including

2. As seen historically in such cases as *Skinner v. Oklahoma ex rel. Williamson*, 316 U.S. 535 (1942), and *Johnson v. Calvert*, 5 Cal. 4th 87 (1993).

that the parentage of intended parents through surrogacy is taken as given. On the other hand, much of Europe, opposed conceptually and in law to surrogacy, has cloaked itself in upholding the rights of the child—where the surrogate is identified as the mother.

It remains to be seen whether an international instrument can be drafted that meets these opposite world views—and that will be accepted by both U.S. and European countries.

In the absence of a specific Hague convention, it is necessary to look at whatever other international laws are in place.

Existing International Law

International law concerning international surrogacy arrangements falls into the obvious categories of private international law (such as Hague conventions) and public international law (such as United Nations [UN] conventions).

In planning the journey home, it is important not to fall foul of a relevant Hague convention. Planning should therefore be in place to ensure that, if possible, there is compliance.

International human rights conventions, such as the 1989 UN Convention on the Rights of the Child, or the European Convention on Human Rights are more passive in nature. They are only sought to be invoked once a problem has arisen. Nevertheless, they indicate how societies think. In the Americas, there is a clear statement by the Inter-American Court of Human Rights about reproductive freedom in the context of ART. In Europe, by contrast, the focus is on the rights of the child, with a particular focus on the genetic connection between the child and one of the couple. In broad terms in Europe, it seems that when there is no genetic connection, then the parentage of the child is more parlous.

The European cases make plain what should be obvious—when there is no genetic connection between both parents and the proposed child, greater care should be taken with planning the international journey, as the citizenship and parentage of the child may be at risk. They also make plain that if the couple then splits up, the nongenetic parent may not be recognized as a parent in the receiving country, even though that parent is recognized as a parent in the sending country.

History as to the Rights of the Child

In 1959 the UN General Assembly adopted the Declaration on the Rights of the Child. The declaration followed both the Geneva Declaration on the Rights of the Child of 1924 and the Universal Declaration of Human

Rights as well as other international statutes. The declaration is written in the language of 1959 (i.e., it is gendered—in referring to the child, it is *he*). There is a belief in the declaration as to the doctrine of tender years (i.e., infants should be in the care of their mothers, not their fathers), and the declaration has in any event been overtaken by the 1989 UN Convention on the Rights of the Child.[3] Nevertheless, it is a good place to start.

Principle 1 provides:

> The child shall enjoy all the rights set forth in this Declaration. Every child, without any exception whatsoever, shall be entitled to these rights, without distinction or discrimination on account of race, colour, sex, language, religion, political or other opinion, national or social origin, property, birth or other status, whether of himself or of his family.

Principle 2 provides:

> The child shall enjoy special protection, and shall be given opportunities of facilities, by law and by other means, to enable him to develop physically, mentally, morally, spiritually and socially in a healthy and normal manner and in conditions of freedom and dignity. In the enactment of laws for this purpose, the best interests of the child shall be the paramount consideration.

Principle 3 provides:

> The child shall be entitled from his birth to a name and a nationality.

Principle 6 provides:

> The child, for the full and harmonious development of his personality, needs love and understanding. He shall, wherever possible, grow up in the care and under the responsibility of his parents, and, in any case, in an atmosphere of affection and of moral and material security; a child of tender years shall not, save in exceptional circumstances, be separated from his mother. Society and the public authorities shall have the duty to extend particular care to children without a family and to those without adequate means of support. Payment of State and other assistance towards the maintenance of children of large families is desirable.

Principle 9 provides, relevantly:

3. G.A. Res. 1386 (XIV) (Nov. 20, 1959).

> The child shall be protected against all forms of neglect, cruelty and exploitation. He shall not be the subject of traffic, in any form. . . .

One must be careful with the declaration as to what it does not say. It does not say how children might be created. In 1959 sperm donation was rarely practiced. In vitro fertilization (IVF) had not yet been invented. It does not say as to who are a child's parents.

1961 Hague Infants Convention

Two years later, in 1961, the Hague Infants Convention commenced. Article 1 refers to the need to protect the person or property of a child having regard to the infant's *habitual residence*—a concept well known to Hague practitioners.

Articles 3 to 5 are the significant articles.

Article 3 provides:

> A relationship subjecting the infant to authority, which arises directly from the domestic law of the State of the infant's nationality, shall be recognised in all the Contracting States.

Article 4 provides:

> If the authorities of the State of the infant's nationality consider that the interests of the infant so require, they may, after having informed the authorities of the State of his habitual residence, take measures according to their own law for the protection of his person or property.
>
> That law shall determine the conditions for the initiation, modification and termination of the said measures. It shall also govern their effects both in respect of relations between the infant and the persons or institutions responsible for his care, and in respect of third persons.
>
> The application of the measures taken shall be assured by the authorities of the State of the infant's nationality.
>
> The measures taken by virtue of the preceding paragraphs of the present Article shall replace any measures which may have been taken by the authorities of the State where the infant has his habitual residence.

Article 5 commences:

> If the habitual residence of an infant is transferred from one Contracting State to another, measures taken by the authorities of

> the State of the former habitual residence shall remain in force insofar as the authorities of the new habitual residence have not terminated or replaced them.
>
> Article 13 commences:
>
> The present Convention shall apply to all infants who have their habitual residence in one of the Contracting States.

This convention is often forgotten. It is limited in scope in that the only contracting parties, with the exception of China (concerning only Macao), are all located in Europe, as outlined in Table 1.2.

Table 1.2. Contracting Parties to the 1961 Hague Infants Convention

Country
Austria
China (Macao special administrative region [SAR] only)
France
Germany
Italy
Latvia
Lithuania
Luxembourg
The Netherlands
Poland
Portugal
Spain
Switzerland
Türkiye

In 2015, the Nepal Supreme Court[4] issued an interlocutory injunction that stopped all surrogacy there. The court cited concerns about a lack of law in Nepal authorizing surrogacy (as it is authorized by a decision of the Cabinet, not by the enactment of any law or issue of any regulation), exploitation of Indian women (as the Cabinet decision banned Nepalese women from undertaking surrogacy, with the result that Nepalese women travelled to India to be surrogates, and Indian women travelled to Nepal

4. *See, e.g.*, *SC Quashes All Surrogacy Petitions*, MyRepublica (July 15, 2016), https://myrepublica.nagariknetwork.com/news/sc-quashes-all-surrogacy-petitions/.

to be surrogates), and a breach of the 1961 Hague Infants Convention by two countries whose citizens were intended parents through surrogacy in Nepal. Those two countries were the United States and Australia, neither of whom had ever signed the convention.

A month later, in reaction to the court's interlocutory injunction, the government banned surrogacy in Nepal.

1961 Hague Apostille Convention

This convention allows the recognition by certification or apostille of documents from another country. It is common to apostille documents to ensure that they are able to be recognized by the home country.

This convention allows the form of the document to be recognized, but does not deal with the substance. As seen in *Paradiso & Campanelli v. Italy*,[5] a decision of the European Court of Human Rights, discussed in Chapter 2, the limitations with this convention are that countries can still peek behind the document, notwithstanding that it has been apostilled, in order to find out the truth.

1980 Hague Child Abduction Convention

This convention is so often talked about that it would appear for some family law practitioners that it is the only Hague convention. It concerns civil aspects of international child abduction.

Whilst there have been many criticisms of this convention, it is widely applied, with 87 jurisdictions having contracted to the convention, even though many of those are not Members of the HCCH. This convention is remarkably widely in force in countries from Albania to Zimbabwe.

Significantly, some surrogacy destinations are contracting parties to the convention: Argentina, Brazil, Canada, Colombia, Cyprus, Georgia, Greece, Mexico, Russian Federation, South Africa, Thailand, Ukraine, and the United States.

This convention arises if a child is a habitual resident in country A that is a contracting country, and is either wrongfully removed, in breach of someone's rights of custody, from that country and taken to country B (which is also a contracting country), or rightfully removed, but wrongfully retained in country B. In the alternative, there are rights of access.

The presumption under the convention is that if someone has rights of custody, then ordinarily if there has been a wrongful removal to or wrongful retention in the other country, the child should be returned. There are discretionary issues for the court to consider in country B as

5. App. No. 25358/12 (Dec. 9, 2015).

to whether the child should be returned, but the general approach taken under the convention is that the child should be returned quickly.

Rights of custody are defined in Article 5:

> [These] shall include rights relating to the care of the person of the child and, in particular, the right to determine the child's place of residence.

The convention arises concerning international surrogacy arrangements or international ART typically in two scenarios:

1. Where the surrogate or her husband[6] remains a parent in the country that is the surrogacy destination—and the child has returned with the parents to their home country
2. Where one of the intended parents is not a parent in the home country, and that "parent" has then removed the child from that country to another Hague country

---

Scenario 1: Possible Action by the Surrogate

The intended parents undertake surrogacy in country A (such as the United States) and then return home (another contracting State) to country B. If the child is considered to be habitually resident at the time of birth in country A and there is a failure to terminate the parental relationship between the surrogate and her partner (if any) with the child, then the surrogate and her partner may still have rights of custody under the convention. Therefore, any removal of the child from country A to country B may be wrongful or, if it is with the consent of the surrogate and her husband for a limited time, then the retention may be wrongful.

Great care should be taken to ensure that any rights of custody that might exist on the part of the surrogate and her husband[7] are terminated before the child leaves the country. Although I am not aware of it ever occurring in practice, the nightmare scenario for parents is that they return to their country with their child after having undertaken surrogacy abroad, to discover that the surrogate has changed her mind—and wants the child returned to her country, where the child was born.

If the authorities in the receiving country take the view that the child was habitually resident in the country of birth, and there was a wrongful removal or retention, then great efforts may be made to ensure that the child is returned to the country of birth as quickly as possible.

---

6. Or spouse or partner.

7. Of course, this could, depending on the law of country A as to who is recognized as a parent, instead be the surrogate's wife or partner.

Habitual residence is commonly seen as a question of fact.[8]

There have been two decisions internationally, discussed later, that have both taken the view that habitual residence for a child born through surrogacy is the country in which the intended parents are habitually resident—but one could well imagine a court taking a different view—especially if the law of the country of birth makes plain that the surrogate is the mother of the child—and that the rights of custody still exist.

Confusingly, by contrast to the term *rights of custody*, the term that is used in the 1996 Hague Child Protection Convention is that of *parental responsibility*, which at its essence is the same concept as rights of custody under the 1980 Hague Convention. Article 1(2) of the 1996 Hague Convention provides:

> For the purposes of this Convention, the term "parental responsibility" includes parental authority, or any analogous relationship of authority determining the rights, powers and responsibilities of parents, guardians or other legal representatives in relation to the person or the property of the child.

The 1996 Hague Child Protection Convention is discussed later.

Habitual Residence

Two cases have decided habitual residence in the context of international ART, both determining that habitual residence of the child is the habitual residence of the intended parents.

The New Zealand Case: In re Application by L [2003] NZFLR 529

Mr. and Mrs. L. lived in New Zealand. Mrs. L.'s sister, Mrs. G., and Mr. G. lived in Queensland, Australia. Mrs. G. offered to be the surrogate for Mr. and Mrs. L.

Regulatory approval was obtained from the relevant New Zealand committee. Mrs. L. travelled to New Zealand, was implanted, and then flew home. She then gave birth in Queensland.

Mr. and Mrs. L. were at the birth. They cared for the baby from birth. When he was seven days old, they brought him back to New Zealand to live.

The question for the court was the habitual residence of the child. If the child's habitual residence was Australia, then under New Zealand law, which took up the 1993 Hague Intercountry Adoption Convention,

8. *E.g.*, Monasky v. Taglieri, 206 L. Ed. 2d 9 (2020).

the provisions of the 1993 Hague Convention would apply. The approval of the relevant departments in Queensland and New Zealand would be required before the adoption order could be made. Neither agency had been consulted by Mr. and Mrs. L.

The New Zealand department was of the view that New Zealand was the place of the child's habitual residence.

The court held that the child's habitual residence was New Zealand. Mr. and Mrs. L. were his caregivers right from birth, on the basis of the agreement reached by them with Mr. and Mrs. G. Accordingly, his residence in Australia could be temporary only, it always having been intended that, following his birth, he would travel to New Zealand with his genetic parents. The 1993 Hague Convention therefore did not apply, and there was nothing to prevent an adoption order being made. The adoption order was made.

Comment

If the court had formed the view that the habitual residence was in Australia, then an adoption order would never have been made, leaving the child in limbo.

In reaction to *In re Baby M*,[9] Queensland was the first jurisdiction in the world to criminalize surrogacy extraterritorially. See Chapter 4. What Mr. and Mrs. G. had done by entering into a surrogacy agreement in New Zealand was illegal under Queensland law.[10]

If Mr. and Mrs. L. or Mr. and Mrs. G. (or for that matter New Zealand authorities) had approached the relevant Queensland department, there is no question that it would have refused to provide consent, as it would have endorsed an act that the Queensland Parliament had made plain was illegal.

The case is also illustrative of the limits to criminalizing surrogacy, in that surrogacy still occurred in Queensland, despite it being illegal.

Baby Sara: Case C-490/20, VMA v. Sofia Municipality (2021)[11]

A child, Baby Sara, was born to two moms through IVF in Spain. The women lived in Spain. The birth mother was a Bulgarian citizen. Her wife was from Gibraltar, a British colony. The child could not take citizenship

9. 537 A.2d 1227 (N.J. 1988).

10. *Surrogate Parenthood Act 1988* (Qld) s 3; *repealed by Surrogacy Act 2010* (Qld). There remain offences in Queensland concerning overseas commercial surrogacy.

11. Case C-490/20, https://curia.europa.eu/juris/document/document.jsf;jsessionid=A02D8C1E1259AA90E63FC4F70FD7006F?text=&docid=239902&pageIndex=0&doclang=EN&mode=lst&dir=&occ=first&part=1&cid=116267.

from the non-biological mother. The women sought unsuccessfully to have their parentage recognized by the issue of a Bulgarian birth certificate. This was opposed by Bulgarian authorities.

The European Union Court of Justice started from the premise, confirmed by the Spanish government at the hearing, that the determination of parentage under Spanish private international law is linked to the child's habitual residence. As the women lived in Spain, then habitual residence of the child was in Spain. Under Spanish law, the parenthood of the wife of the biological mother was established.

The court held that the child's parentage was recognized in Bulgaria. See Chapters 2 and 7.

The practice of some countries, such as Australia, is to interview the surrogate prior to the grant of citizenship overseas for a child born through surrogacy in what are perceived to be higher risk countries. This practice has existed to minimize the possibility of child trafficking, but also to ensure that consent of the surrogate for the child to travel overseas permanently is clearly given, in part out of concerns arising from the 1980 Hague Convention.

Countries where Australian authorities, for example, would undertake these interviews include those in Table 1.3 (and accompanying notes). The list is not intended to be exhaustive. Several of these countries are no longer surrogacy destinations.

Table 1.3. Perceived Higher Risk Countries Where Surrogates Were Interviewed by Australian Authorities for Consent for the Child to Relocate Overseas

Country	Party to the 1980 Hague Convention?	Currently (2023) a Surrogacy Destination?
Cambodia	No	No
China	Yes, but only for Hong Kong SAR and Macao SAR	Yes, to a limited degree
Colombia	Yes	Yes
Cyprus	Yes	Yes
Georgia	Yes	Yes[12]

12. The Georgian Health Minister had announced that from January 1, 2024, international intended parents would be banned from accessing surrogacy in Georgia. As of April 16, 2024, the laws to effect this ban had not been enacted. *Surrogacy Services in Georgia*, Australian Embassy Türkiye, https://turkey.embassy.gov.au/anka/Surrogacy.html (last visited Apr. 16, 2024). Reports from Georgia suggest (as of May 2024) that the ban may not be enacted.

Country	Party to the 1980 Hague Convention?	Currently (2023) a Surrogacy Destination?
India	Yes	No
Mexico	Yes	Yes
Nepal	No	No
Thailand	Yes	Yes
Ukraine	Yes	Yes[13]

Cambodia banned surrogacy in 2016. Cambodia illustrates the risk of unregulated surrogacy destinations. Prior to the clampdown, surrogacy was a free-for-all in Cambodia. Thai surrogacy agents, restricted following the Thai baby farm and Baby Gammy saga, moved across the border, promoting surrogacy in Cambodia. For a brief period, everything flourished.

The clampdown was with immediate effect, resulting in pregnant surrogates, parents, and babies immediately going into hiding. The government said that it would prosecute those who engaged in surrogacy for undertaking human trafficking. It did so, including making an example of an Australian surrogacy promoter[14] (who had previously promoted surrogacy in Thailand), and who made the mistake of continuing to promote surrogacy in Cambodia after the government said that the country was closed. The government issued a decree denouncing the evils of surrogacy:

> Surrogacy, one of a set of services to have a baby by Assisted Reproductive Technology, is banned completely.[15]

The government also said in late 2016 that laws would be enacted shortly. It has not done so as of 2023, showing the gulf between law and practice that exists in some countries when it comes to surrogacy.

China[16] does not have a specific ban against surrogacy. Article 3 of the 2001 Administrative Measure for Assisted Reproductive Technology

13. Although surrogacy stopped in Ukraine in February 2022, following the invasion by Russia, by late in 2022 it had recommenced, even though the war has not ended.

14. Candace Sutton, *Aussie Mum of Six Locked Up in Cambodia's Notorious Prey Sar Prison*, News.com.au (Nov. 27, 2016), https://www.news.com.au/lifestyle/real-life/aussie-mum-of-six-locked-up-in-cambodias-notorious-prey-sar-prison/news-story/63dfbc06fe2cddd3b767b6df20fcd770 (discussing Tammy Davis-Charles).

15. Prakas, signed Oct. 24, 2016.

16. Hong Kong has laws concerning surrogacy.

forbids all medical institutions and medical staff form performing surrogacy procedures or commercializing fertilized eggs and embryos. Under Article 22, any breach of Article 3 is subject to a warning and a fine of up to 30,000 yuan. There can also be administrative sanctions and criminal punishments. The Ethical Principles of Assisted Reproductive Technology and Human Sperm Banks, subsection 5, part 3 prohibits staff from performing surrogacy procedures.

A feature of Chinese law is that the birth certificate is definitive proof of parentage. A Chinese birth certificate is different from a birth certificate in the United States, for example. In the former, the details on the birth certificate cannot be challenged, while in the latter courts will peek behind the birth certificate, in order to determine parentage.

The result is that unscrupulous Chinese doctors, fearful of being punished, undertake surrogacy, but do so in great secrecy. The intended parents do not know the identity of the surrogate, and rarely meet her, even at the birth. The intended parents, a heterosexual couple, are then named on the birth certificate as the parents.

Foreign governments are concerned that the child may have been trafficked. Children born to Australian intended parents in China (typically migrants from China originally) are at times denied Australian citizenship due to the secrecy of the process in China—because the surrogate is never able to be identified.

Cyprus illustrates how risky surrogacy can be for the child and the intended parents. Cyprus is divided in two: north and south. North Cyprus, ruled by Turk Cypriots, is not recognized by any other country, except Türkiye. The south is the Republic of Cyprus, recognized internationally. The two are divided by the UN buffer zone. IVF clinics that undertake surrogacy are located in North Cyprus. After the child is born in North Cyprus, which is essentially a zone with laws not recognized by any other place, other than Türkiye, the child is smuggled across the border, to then have its birth registered in the south, in the Republic of Cyprus.

Scenario 2: Nonrecognition of a Parent

Great care must be taken to ensure that the intended parents are recognized as the parents. Failure to have parentage recognized may result in a loss of protection in case the other parent abducts the child.

This arises when the intended parents have returned home, but only one of them is recognized as a parent in the country in which they have returned. Therefore, if one of the parties decides to remove the child from that country, country A, to take the child to country B to live, there may be no repercussions under the 1980 Hague Convention because the stay-at-home parent has no rights of custody.

This might occur most commonly where the stay-at-home parent has no genetic relationship with the child, or the couple are a gay couple. Either way, if the stay-at-home parent is not recognized as a parent in their home country, they do not have rights of custody under the 1980 Hague Convention, and cannot easily have the child returned.

Their journey to have the child returned to country A might be further complicated because they are not recognized as a parent in country B either.

In other words, the parent can come home from work one day to discover that their partner and child have left—and it is all over. The other parent has ensured that the child has been abducted from a country in which their partner had no rights of custody under the 1980 Hague Convention, and therefore could not seek the summary return of the child, and abducted to a country where the other parent may not be recognized as a parent either, making it almost impossible for the stay-at-home parent to have the child returned.

You may think that this sounds like academic theory, and that such cases would never arise in real life. They exist. I had such a case. My client was the parent who was not recognized in country A as a parent, being the nongenetic parent. The child was abducted by the other parent from country A to country B, both of which are Hague countries. Because my client was not a parent in country A, the 1980 Hague Convention did not apply.

My client struggled, in the absence of recognition of their parentage, to then take effective action concerning the child in country B. Eventually, due to the delays and inertia of the court system (not being the fast-tracked Hague system), and the difficulties and costs of international family law litigation, my client gave up.

Just because someone is a parent in the United States, for example, does not mean that they will be recognized elsewhere as a parent. The risk of nonrecognition, and its impact under the 1980 Hague Convention, illustrates the necessity for there to be some convention recognizing parentage—and for every intended parent who is undertaking an international surrogacy arrangement to obtain expert legal advice from lawyers in both countries.

See Chapter 8, Citizenship and Residence Are Not the Same.

1989 UN Convention on the Rights of the Child

This convention has been entered into by every country on earth, including Somalia—except the United States. This convention, like the other human rights conventions, is more a passive bystander than an active participant, unlike the various Hague conventions. The convention has been held in a decision of the European Court of Human Rights not to establish maternity for an intended mother through surrogacy who was not the genetic mother.[17]

Those countries outside the United States will typically look to this convention for setting out the basic rights of the child. Article 3.1 provides:

> In all actions concerning children, whether undertaken by public or private social welfare institutions, courts of law, administrative authorities or legislative bodies, the best interests of the child shall be a primary consideration.

This wording is deliberate. It does not say that the best interests of the child shall be *the* primary consideration, but *a* primary consideration (i.e., it is one of potentially several primary considerations).

Article 7.1 provides:

> The child shall be registered immediately after birth and shall have the right from birth to a name, the right to acquire a nationality and, as far as possible, the right to know and be cared for by his or her parents.

As with other international conventions, there is no definition of who is a *parent*. This has therefore made interpretation of this convention problematic, depending on who is looking at the convention. For example, in Germany, the surrogate, even a U.S. surrogate, is considered to be the mother and therefore must be on the birth certificate.

Article 7.1 provides:

> States Parties shall ensure the implementation of these rights in accordance with their national law and their obligations under the relevant international instruments in this field, in particular where the child would otherwise be stateless.

In countries where surrogacy is against public policy, courts are then left with a fait accompli—namely that to deny the child citizenship or other rights may result in the child being left stateless.

Article 8.1 provides:

> States Parties undertake to respect the right of the child to preserve his or her identity, including nationality, name and family relations as recognized by law without unlawful interference.

17. A.M. v. Norway, App. No. 30254/19 (Mar. 24, 2022).

Article 8 came about from the efforts of the Argentinian delegation. Argentina had previously been ruled by a junta. After capturing and torturing its opponents, many of them were disposed of by throwing them out of planes over the south Atlantic. Many of the opponents had babies. These babies were then given out to childless couples, perceived to be friendly to the regime, to raise as their own.

It is no surprise that when democracy returned to Argentina, there was great concern that the identity of children was upheld.

What is the identity of the child for the purposes of Article 8? How does the child relate to the intended parents and to the surrogate or her partner? This then brings out a debate about what is motherhood and who is a parent. Different perspectives occur by looking at the surrogacy transaction. Whilst in California,[18] for example, the intended parents are recognized as the natural parents of the child, based on intention, in other jurisdictions, who is recognized as a parent may be based upon genetics or who gave birth. It should never be assumed that the intended parents are recognized in both jurisdictions as the parents based on intention.

In the English case *A v. P (Surrogacy: Parental Order: Death of Applicant)*,[19] consideration was given as to Article 8 (and Article 8 on the right to privacy and family of the European Convention on Human Rights):

> The concept of identity includes the legal recognition of relationships between children and parents. In ZH (Tanzania) v Secretary of State for the Home Department UKFC 2011 4 Baroness Hale considered that the courts in this jurisdiction and decision makers had to have regard to the key principles of the [UN Convention on the Rights of the Child (UNCRC)], both in respect of article 8 of the [European Convention on Human Rights (ECHR)] and in its application decisions by authorities in this jurisdiction. . . . If the consequences of a purpose of construction of [the UK surrogacy statute] is that the child's identity with his biological father is preserved and the child's identity is linked to both Mr and Mrs A [the intended parents] the court may consider itself bound to arrive at such a conclusion on the combined reading of article 8 ECHR and article 8 of the UNCRC.[20]

---

18. Johnson v. Calvert, 5 Cal. 4th 87 (1993); *In re* Marriage of Buzzanca, 61 Cal. App. 4th 1412 (1998).
19. [2011] EWHC (Fam) 1738.
20. *Id.* [28].

Although the UN convention is not part of the domestic law of Australia (as Australia has signed the convention, but it is not part of the municipal law), nevertheless the approach as seen in the United Kingdom has also been adopted in Australia so far as domestic surrogacy journeys are concerned, at least in one case.[21]

However, the identity of the child may also be considered to be that which comes about by virtue of the court order, or is tied to the child's genetic origins, or is tied to the surrogate, as the woman who gave birth to the child.[22]

The difficulties with relying on the identity of the child are illustrated in several of the European Court of Human Rights cases in Chapter 2.

Article 16.1 provides:

> No child shall be subjected to arbitrary or unlawful interference with his or her privacy, family, home or correspondence, nor to unlawful attacks on his or her honour and reputation.

Article 35 provides:

> States Parties shall take all appropriate national, bilateral and multilateral measures to prevent the abduction of, the sale of or traffic in children for any purpose or in any form.

1993 Hague Intercountry Adoption Convention

This convention can apply to international ART journeys when adoption is part of the process of becoming parents, or is perceived to be, or may be a means of securing parentage. In some countries, such as New Zealand, the legislated process of becoming a parent through surrogacy is via adoption. In many countries that do not have specific laws concerning surrogacy, such as Kenya, the process of becoming parents is via adoption.

To have the other parent recognized, either via gamete donation (for example for lesbian couples) or surrogacy (as in Hawaii, for example) involves stepparent or second parent adoption.

One hundred and eight countries are contracting States for this convention.

---

21. *KRB & BFH v RKH & BJH* [2020] QChC 7. I appeared and cited *Re X* in my submissions.

22. Trans men of course can also give birth, but the argument is always presented as to the link between the child and its "mother" (i.e., the surrogate).

The convention can have an impact on parentage through international ART. See Chapter 13, Interplay of Adoption and Surrogacy.

1996 Hague Child Protection Convention

This convention seeks to clarify which place has jurisdiction with their relevant child protection authorities to take measures directed to the protection of the person or property of the child, and therefore determine which law is to be applied by such authorities in exercising their jurisdiction, and to determine the law applicable to parental responsibility.

This convention develops on what is set out in the 1961 Hague Children's Convention.

The convention allows for the registration of overseas child orders. Article 28 provides:

> Measures taken in one Contracting State and declared enforceable, or registered for the purpose of enforcement, in another Contracting State shall be enforced in the latter State as if they had been taken by the authorities of that State. Enforcement takes place in accordance with the law of the requested State to the extent provided by such law, taking into consideration the best interests of the child.

In a practical sense, if two countries are Parties to the 1996 Hague Convention as well as the 1980 convention, the 1996 convention can be a much more effective and quick method of return of the child. In essence, if the child is habitually resident in country A and is then removed to country B, then the jurisdiction of country A follows the child, until a point is reached at which it can be said that the child is habitually resident in country B.

Fifty-eight countries are Parties to this convention, including Argentina, Australia, Belgium, Brazil, Canada, China (Hong Kong and Macao only), Colombia, Cyprus, France, Georgia, Germany, Greece, Ireland, Japan, South Korea, the United Kingdom, and the United States.

Unlike the 1980 and 1983 Hague Conventions, a child does not have to be habitually resident in a contracting State to fall within the scope of the 1996 convention. For example, a child may have his or her habitual residence in a non-contracting State, but still fall within the scope of Article 6 (refugee children, internationally displaced children), while those whose habitual residence cannot be established, Article 11 (measures in cases of urgency), or Article 12 (provisional measures) of the 1996 convention may also apply.

One would think on reading Article 28 that it applies to international surrogacy arrangements. However, the convention does *not* apply to international surrogacy arrangements. Article 4(a) provides:

The Convention does not apply to—

1. The establishment or contesting of a parent-child relationship.

HCCH has published a practical handbook concerning the convention.[23] The practical handbook makes plain that international surrogacy arrangements are excluded from this convention:

> 3.33 This provision excludes from the scope of the Convention measures that are concerned with establishing or contesting the parentage of a particular child or children. Therefore, if an application is made to the authorities of a Contracting State to establish or contest the parentage of a particular child, those authorities will have to look to their non-Convention jurisdictional rules to assess if they have jurisdiction. Similarly, applicable law and the recognition of foreign decisions on this issue are matters left to non-Convention rules.
>
> 3.34 This exclusion extends to the question of whether the parties to the parent-child relationship, i.e., the child of the parent(s) if minor(s), require the authorisation of a legal representative to recognise the relationship. It will be for the non-Convention rules of a State to determine the answers to questions such as:
>
> - whether a child who is recognised must consent to such recognition and must be represented for this purpose if below a certain age;
> - whether a guardian ad litem must be designated to represented or assist the child in a lawsuit concerning the parent-child relationship; or
> - whether the underage mother of a child must herself be represented in connection with any declarations of recognition or consent of any proceedings concerning her child's status.

23. HCCH, Practical Handbook on the Operation of the 1996 Hague Child Protection Convention (2014).

However, the question as to the **identity** of the legal representative of the child concerned and as to whether, for example, the designation of that person results by operation of law or requires the intervention of an authority, falls with the scope of the Convention.

3.35 The exclusion in Article 4 a) of the Convention also extends to the status of a child born as a result of an international surrogacy agreement.[24]

American Conventions

1969 American Convention on Human Rights

Article 17. 2 provides:

> The right of men and women of marriageable age to marry and to raise a family shall be recognized, if they meet the conditions required by domestic laws, insofar as such conditions do not affect the principle of nondiscrimination established in this Convention.
>
> Article 17.4 provides:
>
> The law shall recognize equal rights for children born out of wedlock and those born in wedlock.
>
> Article 18 provides:
>
> Every person has the right to a given name and to the surnames of his parents or that of one of them. The law shall regulate the manner in which this right shall be ensured for all, by the use of assumed names if necessary.
>
> Article 19 provides:
>
> Every minor child has the right to the measures of protection required by his condition as a minor on the part of his family, society, and the state.
>
> Article 20.2 provides:
>
> Every person has the right to the nationality of the state in whose territory he was born if he does not have the right to any other nationality.

24. *Id.* §§ 3.33–3.35.

Article 24 provides:

> All persons are equal before the law. Consequently, they are entitled, without discrimination, to equal protection of the law.

The Inter-American Court of Human Rights has delivered several decisions concerning reproductive rights. The two most relevant are *Murillo v. Costa Rica* (2012) and *Brítez Arce v. Argentina* (2022).

Murillo v. Costa Rica[25]

The court overturned the ban on IVF in Costa Rica.

The law in Costa Rica required that a maximum of six eggs could be collected in a treatment cycle, that none of them could be frozen or discarded, but that all of them must be transferred to the patient's uterus. Fifteen babies had been born via IVF in Costa Rica before the Constitutional Chamber held that IVF could occur, provided that IVF did not endanger "the right to life from the moment of conception" (i.e., fertilization)—an effective ban. The State also encouraged the repudiation of those with infertility.

The case concerned IVF. The court helpfully laid out the history of IVF, including in Latin America:

> "The first birth of a baby resulting from in vitro fertilization occurred in England in 1978. In Latin America, the first baby born through in vitro fertilization and embryo transfer was reported in Argentina in 1984. Since the birth of the first person as a result of . . . ART was reported, five million people in the world have been born thanks to the advances in this technology." Furthermore, "each year, millions of ART procedures are performed. It is estimated that, in 2008, 1.6 million treatments resulted in the birth of 400,000 individuals between 2008 and September 2009" globally. In Latin America, "it is estimated that from 1990 to 2010, 150,000 individuals were born," according to the Latin American Register of Assisted Reproduction. . . . Costa Rica is the only State in the world that expressly prohibits IVF.[26]

The ban impacted several couples, who then sought relief. Costa Rica defined an "embryo" as a human being and person.

25. Preliminary Objections, Merits, Reparations, and Costs, Judgment, Inter-Am. Ct. H.R. (ser. C) No. 257 (Nov. 28, 2012), https://www.corteidh.or.cr/docs/casos/articulos/seriec_257_ing.pdf.

26. *Id.* paras. 66–67.

Among other arguments by Costa Rica were legal dilemmas associated with IVF:

1. There was no consensus about the status of frozen embryos, especially when the parents separate or divorce.
2. "'[T]he separation of the parents who have frozen their embryos can lead to the problem of forced paternity . . . if one of the parents demands the implantation of the embryo in spite of the separation or divorce.'"[27]
3. "'[IVF] poses a far-reaching problem with regard to the regulation of paternity,' in particular the problem of 'the paternity rights of the husband of the woman who under[went] a heterogeneous [IVF]—with genetic material from a man other than her husband or partner,' given that 'one of the essential factors to determine paternity is the determination of the genetic material.'"[28]

The court held:

> [T]he decision to have biological children using assisted reproduction techniques forms part of the sphere of the right to personal integrity and to private and family life. In addition, the way in which this decision is arrived at is part of the autonomy and identity of a person, in both the individual dimension and as part of a couple.[29]

The court considered Article 11 of the convention, which protects private and family life:

> Article 11 of the American Convention requires the State to protect individuals against the arbitrary actions of State institutions that affect private and family life. It prohibits any arbitrary or abusive interference with the private life of the individual, indicating different spheres of this, such as the private life of the family. Thus, the Court has held that the private sphere is characterized by being exempt from and immune to abusive or arbitrary interference or attacks by third parties or by public authorities. In addition, this Court has interpreted Article 7 of the American Convention broadly when indicating that it includes a concept of liberty in a broad sense as the ability to do and not do all that is lawfully permitted. In other words, every person has the right to

27. *Id.* para. 128.
28. *Id.*
29. *Id.* para. 272.

organize, in keeping with the law, his or her individual and social life according to his or her own choices and beliefs. Liberty, thus defined, is a basic human right, inherent in the attributes of the person, that is evident throughout the American Convention. The Court has also underscored the concept of liberty and the possibility of all human beings to self-determination and to choose freely the options and circumstances that give meaning to their life, according to their own choices and beliefs.

The scope of the protection of the right to private life has been interpreted in broad terms by the international human rights courts, when indicating that this goes beyond the right to privacy. The protection of private life encompasses a series of factors associated with the dignity of the individual, including, for example, the ability to develop his or her own personality and aspirations, to determine his or her own identity and to define his or her own personal relationships. The concept of private life encompasses aspects of physical and social identity, including the right to personal autonomy, personal development and the right to establish and develop relationships with other human beings and with the outside world. The effective exercise of the right to private life is decisive for the possibility of exercising personal autonomy on the future course of relevant events for a person's quality of life. Private life includes the way in which an individual views himself and how he decides to project this view towards others, and is an essential condition for the free development of the personality. Furthermore, the Court has indicated that motherhood is an essential part of the free development of a woman's personality. Based on the foregoing, the Court considers that **the decision of whether or not to become a parent is part of the right to private life** and includes, in this case, the decision of whether or not to become a mother or father in the genetic or biological sense.

The Court considers that this case addresses a particular combination of different aspects of private life that are related to the right to found a family, the right to physical and mental integrity and, specifically, the reproductive rights of the individual.

145. First, the Court emphasizes that, unlike the European Convention on Human Rights, which only protects the right to family life under Article 8 of this instrument, the American Convention contains two articles that protect family life in a complementary manner. In this regard, the Court reiterates that Article

11(2) of the American Convention is closely related to the right recognized in Article 17 of this instrument. Article 17 of the American Convention recognizes the central role of the family and family life in a person's existence and in society in general. The Court has already indicated that the family's right to protection entails, among other obligations, facilitating, in the broadest possible terms, the development and strength of the family unit. This is such a basic right of the American Convention that it cannot be waived even in extreme circumstances. Article 17(2) of the American Convention protects the right to found a family, which is also comprehensively protected in different international human rights instruments. For its part, the United Nations Human Rights Committee has indicated that the possibility of procreating is part of the right to found a family.

146. Second, the right to private life is related to: (i) reproductive autonomy, and (ii) access to reproductive health services, which includes the right to have access to the medical technology necessary to exercise this right. The right to reproductive autonomy is also recognized in Article 16(e) of the Convention for the Elimination of All Forms of Discrimination against Women, according to which women enjoy the right "to decide freely and responsibly on the number and spacing of their children and to have access to the information, education and means that enable them to exercise these rights." This right is violated when the means by which a woman can exercise the right to control her fertility are restricted. Thus, the protection of private life includes respect for the decisions both to become a mother or a father, and a couple's decision to become genetic parents.

147. Third, the Court emphasizes that, in the context of the right to personal integrity, it has analyzed some of the situations that cause particular distress and anxiety to the individual, as well as some serious impacts of the lack of medical care or problems of accessibility to certain health procedures. In the European sphere, case law has defined the relationship between the right to private life and the protection of physical and mental integrity. The European Court of Human Rights has indicated that, although the European Convention on Human Rights does not guarantee the right to a specific level of medical care as such, the right to private life includes a person's physical and mental integrity, and that the State also has the positive obligation to ensure this right to its citizens. Consequently, the rights to

> private life and to personal integrity are also directly and immediately linked to health care. The lack of legal safeguards that take reproductive health into consideration can result in a serious impairment of the right to reproductive autonomy and freedom. Therefore, there is a connection between personal autonomy, reproductive freedom, and physical and mental integrity. . . .
>
> [T]he right to private life and reproductive freedom is related to the right to have access to the medical technology necessary to exercise that right. The right to enjoy the benefits of scientific progress has been internationally recognized and, in the inter-American context, it is contemplated in Article XIII of the American Declaration and in Article 14(1)(b) of the Protocol of San Salvador. It is worth mentioning that the General Assembly of the United Nations, in its declaration on this right, described its connection to the satisfaction of the material and spiritual needs of all sectors of the population. Therefore, and in keeping with Article 29(b) of the American Convention, the scope of the rights to private life, reproductive autonomy and to found a family, derived from Articles 11(2) and 17(2) of the Convention, extends to the right of everyone to benefit from scientific progress and its applications. The right to have access to scientific progress in order to exercise reproductive autonomy and the possibility to found a family gives rise to the right to have access to the best health care services in assisted reproduction techniques, and, consequently, the prohibition of disproportionate and unnecessary restrictions, de jure or de facto, to exercise the reproductive decisions that correspond to each individual.[30]

The court held that conception was the act of pregnancy, not fertilization:

> "[C]onception" cannot be understood as a moment or process exclusive of a woman's body, given that an embryo has no chance of survival if implantation does not occur.[31]

The court considered embryo personhood, in the process considering the American Convention, the Universal Declaration of Human Rights, the International Covenant on Civil and Political Rights (ICCPR), the Convention on the Elimination of All Forms of Discrimination against

30. *Id.* paras. 142–147, 150 (emphasis added) (citations omitted).

31. And, in doing so, echoed my case *LWV v LMH* [2012] QChC 26, which came to the same conclusion. *Id.* para. 187.

Women (CEDAW), the UN Convention on the Rights of the Child, the European Convention on Human Rights, and the African Charter on Human and People's Rights. The court held that the absolute protection of the embryo cannot be alleged, annulling other rights, and that its protection was instead gradual and incremental according to its development.[32]

The court highlighted the differences in how IVF is regulated:

> Although IVF is performed in many countries, this does not necessarily mean that it is regulated by law. In this regard, the Court notes that the comparative legislation on assisted reproduction techniques submitted by the parties (Brazil, Chile, Colombia, Guatemala, Mexico, Peru and Uruguay) reveals that there are norms that regulate some practices in this area. The Court notes that, for example: (i) human cloning is prohibited in Chile and Peru; (ii) the laws of Brazil, Chile and Peru prohibit the use of assisted reproductive techniques for purposes other than human procreation; (iii) Brazil stipulates that the ideal number of eggs and pre-embryos to be transferred may be no more than four, to avoid increasing the risk of multiple births, and prohibits the use of procedures "aimed at embryonic reduction" and the commercialization of biological material is a crime, and (iv) there are different types of regulations on cryopreservation.
>
> For example, Chile prohibits the freezing of embryos for deferred transfer, while Brazil and Colombia allow the cryopreservation of embryos, spermatozoids and eggs. In addition, some countries, such as Argentina, Chile and Uruguay, are trying to take measures so that assisted reproduction treatments will be covered by State health care programs and policies.
>
> 256. The Court considers that, even though there are few specific legal regulations on IVF, most of the States of the region allow IVF to be practiced within their territory.[33]

The court ordered that reparations be paid to the affected couples, and that Costa Rica was to end the ban on IVF, regulate IVF, and allow IVF through its social security system, based on nondiscrimination.

The significance of *Murillo* cannot be understated:

1. In the Americas, at least, there is a recognized right to procreate.

32. *Id.* paras. 263–264.
33. *Id.* para. 255.

2. Similarly (including drawing on similar conventions in Europe and Africa), there is the right to take advantage of scientific progress when it comes to forming a family.
3. The right to procreate is part of the right to privacy and family life. By comparison, as seen in Europe, the right to family life is seen to exist only when the family already exists, and that it requires a genetic connection to exist, at least to one of the parents.
4. Embryos are not people, and therefore do not have human rights upon their creation.
5. Conception occurs upon pregnancy and not before.

***Brítez Arce v. Argentina*[34]**

The court declared that those who are pregnant have the right to be protected from obstetric violence. The court ordered restitution to the family, in the case of a pregnant Argentinian woman who died from inadequate medical treatment. The court noted the Inter-American Convention on the Prevention, Punishment, and Eradication of Violence against Women, known as the Convention of Belém do Pará (1994), but the convention applied after the events in question.[35] The court nevertheless took the contents of the convention into consideration for the purposes of characterizing obstetric violence.[36] The court defined "obstetric violence" as:

> (A) form of gender-based violence . . . exercised by health care providers against pregnant women, during access to health services that take place during pregnancy, childbirth and postpartum, which is expressed mostly, but not exclusively, in a dehumanizing, disrespectful, abusive or negligent treatment of pregnant women; in the denial of treatment and full information on the state of health and applicable treatments; in forced or coerced medical interventions; and in the tendency to pathologize natural reproductive processes, among other threatening manifestations in the context of health care during pregnancy, childbirth and postpartum.[37]

The court held:

---

34. Merits, Reparations, and Costs, Judgment, Inter-Am. Ct. H.R. (ser. C) No. (Nov. 16, 2012), https://www.corteidh.or.cr/docs/casos/articulos/seriec_474_ing.pdf.
35. *Id.* para. 76.
36. *Id.*
37. *Id.* para. 68.

> [W]omen have the right to live a life free of obstetric violence and States have the obligation to prevent it, punish it and refrain from practicing it, as well as to ensure that their agents act accordingly. . . . States have the obligation to provide adequate, specialized and differentiated health services during pregnancy, childbirth and within a reasonable period after childbirth, to guarantee the mother's right to health and prevent maternal mortality and morbidity [under international law].[38]

1988 Protocol of San Salvador

Article 3 provides for an obligation of nondiscrimination.

Article 15 sets out the right to the formation and protection of families. Article 15 provides relevantly:

> 1. The family is the natural and fundamental element of society and ought to be protected by the State, which should see to the improvement of its spiritual and material conditions.
> 2. Everyone has the right to form a family, which shall be exercised in accordance with the provisions of the pertinent domestic legislation.
> 3. The States Parties hereby undertake to accord adequate protection to the family unit and in particular:
>   a. To provide special care and assistance to mothers during a reasonable period before and after childbirth; . . .

1994 Inter-American Convention on International Traffic in Minors

In addition to trafficking of minors, the convention[39] covers, under Article 3,

> the civil aspects of the wrongful removal, transfer, or retention of minors internationally, not dealt with by other international conventions on this subject.

Article 2 provides that the convention

> shall apply to any minor who is habitually resident in a State Party or is located in a State Party at the time when an act of international traffic occurs in respect of him or her.

---

38. *Id.* para. 77.

39. Organization of American States, Inter-American Convention on International Traffic in Minors, Mar. 18, 1994, O.A.S.T.S. No. 79.

The definitions in Article 2 make plain in the context of surrogacy; that if parentage is not firmly established before the child leaves the country of birth, or consent is given by the parent for the child to be removed permanently, then the convention may apply. The three key definitions in Article 2 are:

> "International traffic in minors" means the abduction, removal or retention, or attempted abduction, removal or retention, of a minor for unlawful purposes or by unlawful means.
>
> "Unlawful purpose" includes, among others, prostitution, sexual exploitation, servitude or any other purpose unlawful in either the State of the minor's habitual residence or the State Party where the minor is located.
>
> "Unlawful means" includes, among others, kidnaping, fraudulent or coerced consent, the giving or receipt of unlawful payments or benefits to achieve the consent of the parents, persons or institution having care of the child, **or any other means unlawful** in either the State of the minor's habitual residence or the State Party where the minor is located.

Given the interplay between adoption and surrogacy, a payment to a surrogate for her expenses might be seen as being a payment for adoption, and therefore unlawful. If the surrogate (and her husband) is the parent, and the surrogate's consent is not obtained, then the removal might be an unlawful means.

Therefore, if

1. intended parents in the United States enter into a surrogacy agreement with a surrogate in another American country; and
2. the surrogate is the parent in the other American country; and
3. the child is born in the other American country; and
4. the surrogate refuses to consent to the child being removed from that country, but the intended parents take the child back to the United States anyway; then

because the child was at least located in the other country at birth (if not habitually resident), and the surrogate's consent was not obtained, the convention may apply.

European Conventions

The significance of European conventions and agreements cannot be understated for residents living anywhere in Europe, or anywhere in the

European Union. Given the many decisions by the European Court of Human Rights, in particular, European conventions have their own chapter, Chapter 2.

Other Conventions

Other international conventions that may be relevant are:

- Optional Protocol on the Convention on the Rights of the Child on the Sale of Children, Child Prostitution, and Child Pornography
- Palermo Protocol—the Protocol to Prevent, Suppress, and Punish Trafficking in Persons, Especially Women and Children, supplementing the UN Convention against Transnational Organized Crime
- 1954 UN Convention Relating to the Status of Stateless Persons

Other rights that may be impacted include:

- The right to health (Article 25 of the Universal Declaration of Human Rights, Articles 10(2), 12(1), and (2) of the International Covenant on Economic, Social, and Cultural Rights (ICESCR), Articles 12(1)–(2), 14(2) of CEDAW, and Article 24(1)–(2) of CRC), including the right to reproductive health
- The right to decide the number of spacing of one's children (Article 16(1) of CEDAW), including the right to reproductive self-determination and the right to make family planning choices
- The right to privacy (Article 17(1)–(2) of ICCPR and Article 16(1)–(2) of CRC), including the right to decide freely and without arbitrary interference with one's reproductive functions
- The right to equality and nondiscrimination (Article 2 of the Universal Declaration of Human Rights, Article 2(1) of ICCPR, Article 2(2) of ICESCR, Articles 1, 3, 11(2) of CEDAW, and Article 2(1), (2), (5) of CRC), including the right to nondiscrimination in the area of life and reproductive health
- The right to education and information (Article 10 of CEDAW), including the right to education regarding sexual and reproductive matters free from discrimination and the right to receive information about one's state of health, the right to be informed about one's rights and responsibilities in matters of sexuality and reproduction, risks, and effectiveness of birth control methods, and implication of pregnancy

- The right to be free from practices that harm women and girls (Articles 2(f) and 5(a) of CEDAW, Article 24(3) of CRC), including the practices and traditions that harm women's and girls' reproductive rights
- The right to benefit from scientific progress (Article 27(1) of the Universal Declaration of Human Rights, Article 7 of ICCPR, and Article 15 of ICESCR), including progress in the area of human reproduction, and not to be the subject of experimentation in the same area.

Take Away

1. There is a general lack of international law concerning parentage of children born through ART.
2. However, existing conventions, such as the 1980 and 1993 Hague Conventions, may apply to the journey in question.
3. The right to procreate is seen as part of the legal landscape in the Americas—but as seen in Chapter 2 is not recognized as a concept in Europe.
4. As always, if intended parents are proposing to undertake international ART, it is absolutely vital that expert lawyers in both countries are engaged so that they can obtain the right advice.

Chapter 2

European Conventions and Protocols

In addition to international conventions, Europe has a series of conventions and protocols that impact international assisted reproductive technology (ART) in various ways. They are:

1. European Convention on Human Rights
2. European Union (EU)
3. Brussels II Revised
4. European human tissue directive

I also cover:

5. Next steps?

European Convention on Human Rights

This convention, entered into in 1950, applies to all European countries, from Azerbaijan to Iceland, whether or not they are part of the EU.

Although every country in Europe, with the exceptions of the Vatican City (Holy See), and possibly also the breakaway state in Moldova, Transnistria, and North Cyprus, is a signatory to the European Convention on Human Rights, many, but not all, are also Members of the EU, as seen in Table 2.1. For a comparison of same-sex parenting in Europe see Table 7.2 in Chapter 7.

Table 2.1. Membership of the EU

European Jurisdiction	Member of EU?
Albania	No
Andorra	No
Armenia	No
Austria	Yes
Azerbaijan	No

European Jurisdiction	Member of EU?
Belarus	No
Belgium	Yes
Bosnia and Herzegovina	No
Bulgaria	Yes
Croatia	Yes
Cyprus	Yes
• North Cyprus[1]	In legal theory, yes; in practical effect, no
Czechia	Yes
Denmark	Yes
• Faroe Islands	No
• Greenland	No, special association
Estonia	Yes
Finland	Yes
France	Yes
Georgia	No
Germany	Yes
Gibraltar	No
Greece	Yes
Hungary	Yes
Iceland	No
Ireland	Yes
Italy	Yes
Kosovo	No
Latvia	Yes
Liechtenstein	No
Lithuania	Yes
Luxembourg	Yes
Malta	Yes
Moldova	No
• Transnistria[2]	No

1. Cyprus has been partitioned since 1974. North Cyprus is only recognized by Türkiye.

2. Transnistria is a breakaway, unrecognized state within Moldova. The Council of Europe considers it Russian occupied.

European Jurisdiction	Member of EU?
Monaco	No
Montenegro	No
The Netherlands	Yes
North Macedonia	No
Norway	No
Poland	Yes
Portugal	Yes
Romania	Yes
Russia	No
San Marino	No
Serbia	No
Slovakia	Yes
Slovenia	Yes
Spain	Yes
Sweden	Yes
Switzerland	No
Türkiye	No
United Kingdom	No
• Guernsey, Alderney, and Sark	No
• Isle of Man	No
Vatican City	No

The convention was the brainchild of Sir Winston Churchill, and sought, through a body called the Council of Europe, to have common human rights rules throughout Europe.

Two key provisions, in the context of international ART, are Article 8, the right to respect for private and family life, and Article 14, prohibition of discrimination.

Aside from surrogacy, discussed later in detail, the convention has arisen in other ways in ART:

- A complete ban on pre-genetic testing (then only in Italy, Switzerland, and Austria—with proposals in Switzerland to allow this testing in some ways) was a violation of Article 8 rights.[3]

3. Costa & Pavan v. Italy, App. No. 54270/10 (Feb. 11, 2013), https://hudoc.echr.coe.int/eng?i=001-112993; R.R. v. Poland, App. No. 27617/04 (Nov. 28, 2011), https://hudoc.echr.coe.int/eng?i=001-104911.

- There was no right for a jailed murderer and his wife to access artificial insemination.[4]
- There was no right to egg and sperm donation through in vitro fertilization (IVF).[5]

The European Court of Human Rights has been keen, where necessary, to uphold the human rights of a child born overseas, but not to uphold the parentage of a person where the child was born through international surrogacy. The court has drawn a distinction between parentage via operation of law, and parentage through the making of a foreign court order, although not consistently. It is essential, when reading the court's surrogacy judgments, to go first to see if there is a judgment concerning the particular country—for example, France. It is then necessary to turn to the specific facts of that case.

While there have been broad themes, each case has turned on its own facts. To take a too broad approach, such as that the court has upheld the parentage of children born through surrogacy abroad when there has been a foreign court order establishing parentage, would be a mistake. Sometimes it has done so—but not always. The court has looked at the public policy setting of each State. It has focused on the practical impact of the law in each State upon the rights of the child. The focus has been on the rights of the child, not that of the intended parents.

From *Mennesson v. France* (2014) onwards:

> [T]he Court has made a clear distinction between the situation of the child and that of the intended parents. It did not enshrine the right to a child under article 8 of the Convention, but it did emphasize the right of the born child to his or her identity. It considers that "whenever a child's situation is at stake, the best interests of the child must take precedence."[6] Failure to recognise a parent-child relationship between a child and his or her intended parents is a source of legal uncertainty for the child and

4. Dickson v. United Kingdom, App. No. 44362/04 (Dec. 4, 2007), https://hudoc.echr.coe.int/eng?i=001-73360.

5. SH v. Austria, App. No. 57813/00 (Nov. 3, 2011), https://hudoc.echr.coe.int/eng?i=001-98048.

6. Mennesson v. France, App. No. 65192/11, ¶ 81 (Sept. 26, 2014), https://hudoc.echr.coe.int/eng?i=001-145389; Advisory Opinion, No. P16-2018-001, ¶ 38 (Apr. 10, 2019).

has highly detrimental effects on his or her identity in society.[7] Advisory Notice No. P16-2018-001 further added:[8] "[t]he issue in the context of the recognition of a parent-child relationship between children born as a result of surrogacy and the intended parents actually goes beyond the question of the identity of those children. Other essential aspects of their privacy are at stake when it comes to the environment in which they live and develop and the persons who are responsible for meeting their needs and ensuring their well-being."[9]

The court has made a distinction, it appears, in international surrogacy between when parentage was obtained by way of operation of law (where parentage is not recognized by the court) and that where it was obtained by way of court order (where parentage is more likely, but not always, to be recognized).

There is also a seeming distinction between when there is a genetic link between parent and child (which will more likely result in parentage being recognized) and when there is not (when the more likely outcome is that parentage will not be recognized).

The other theme running through the case law is as to the practical impact on the child. If there is little practical impact on the child—so the child can go about his or her business going to school, having medical treatment, and the like—then the court is less likely to feel a need to override the country's laws that deny recognition of the parentage. However, if there is a direct practical impact on the child, as seen in *Mennesson* and *Labassee v. France*, for example, where the child was not entitled to an identity, then the court is much more inclined to act.

Finally, if the effect of setting aside the impugned actions would be to adversely impact the child, then the court is less likely to want to do so, as seen in *Paradiso & Campanelli v. Italy*, for example.

I have set out the significant cases from the court, as they describe key principles, illustrate the discretionary jurisdiction involved, and also illustrate, by the names of the respondent countries, negative attitudes to surrogacy in particular, and in some cases LGBTQIA+ people, by those countries.

---

7. DB v. Switzerland, App. No. 58817/15, ¶ 88 (Feb. 22, 2023), https://hudoc.echr.coe.int/eng?i=001-220955; *Mennesson*, App. No. 65192/11, ¶¶ 96, 98, 99; Advisory Opinion, No. P16-2018-001, ¶ 40.

8. Advisory Opinion, No. P16-2018-001, ¶ 45.

9. *DB*, App. No. 58817/15, ¶ 6 (Krenc, J.).

It seems clear that there is no convention right of access to artificial insemination[10] or IVF using donated gametes.[11]

Mennesson v. France, App. No. 65192/11 (2014); Labassee v. France, App. No. 65941/11 (2014)

These were parallel judgments.

Mr. and Mrs. Mennesson underwent surrogacy in California that resulted in the birth of twins. The children were conceived from Mr. Mennesson's sperm and eggs from a donor. The surrogacy agreement specified that the surrogate was not paid a fee, but was paid for her expenses. A California pre-birth order established Mr. and Mrs. Mennesson's parentage.

Similarly, Mr. and Mrs. Labassee underwent surrogacy in Minnesota, which resulted in the birth of a girl. She was conceived from Mr. Labassee's sperm and eggs from a donor. Minnesota state court made orders, the effect of which was that Mr. and Mrs. Labassee were shown on the birth certificate as the only parents.

French authorities refused to register the children's details in the French register of births, deaths, and marriages as surrogacy was suspected.

The Mennesson children travelled to France as U.S. citizens travelling under their U.S. passports. French authorities commenced an investigation of the parents, alleging that they had made false representations infringing the civil status of the children. As those laws did not have extraterritorial effect (see Chapter 4), the investigation was ended.

The Mennessons and the Labassees proceeded through the French courts, ultimately ending up before the European Court of Human Rights. It was argued that the actions by French authorities to refuse to recognize the family was an interference in their rights to family life, in breach of Article 8. The Mennessons argued that the interference was not in accordance with the law, and was therefore not justified.

The government submitted that the interference had been "in accordance with the law." They observed in that connection that Article 167 of the Civil Code, which was a public-policy provision, provided that any reproductive or gestational surrogacy agreement was null and void, and that the Court of Cassation had observed that the principle of inalienability of the human body and civil status, which were also a matter of public policy, precluded the attribution of the status of father or mother by contract and precluded giving effect to a parent-child relationship provided for in surrogacy agreements. The fact that those judgments concerned the

10. Dickson v. United Kingdom, App. No. 44362/04 (Dec. 4, 2007).

11. SH v. Austria, App. No. 57813/00 (Nov. 3, 2011).

validity of adoption orders made following a surrogacy arrangement carried out on French territory did not affect their relevance in this case. Surrogacy agreements contravened public policy. The Mennessons could not have been unaware of the prohibition on surrogacy arrangements under French law when they entered into the agreement, or of the difficulties likely to arise subsequently.

The court stated that the mere fact that the public prosecutor's office in *Mennesson* itself requested registration of the California order, in order to then request that the entry be annulled, cannot lead the court to conclude that the aim pursued by the interference in question did not appear among those listed in the second paragraph of Article 8. Nor, however, is it convinced by the government's assertion that the aim was to "prevent disorder or crime." The government had not established that where French nationals have recourse to a surrogacy arrangement in a country in which such an agreement is legal that this amounts to an offence under French law.

The reason France refused to recognize a legal parent-child relationship between children born abroad as the result of a surrogacy agreement and the intended parents was that it sought to deter its nationals from having recourse to methods of assisted reproduction overseas that were prohibited in France and aimed, in accordance with its perception of the issue, to protect children and surrogate mothers. Accordingly, the court accepted that the government may consider that the interference pursued two of the legitimate aims listed in the second paragraph of Article 8 of the convention: the "*protection of health*" and "*the protection of the rights and freedoms of others*."

The Mennessons submitted that an additional factor was that the interference did not allow the pursued aim to be achieved, since it did not deprive the children of the legal parent-child relationship with the mother and father recognized under California (or Minnesota) law and did not prevent the applicants from living together in France. Their effective and affective family life was "legally clandestine." This was particularly shocking in the case of Mr. Mennesson, who was deprived of recognition of the legal parent-child relationship with the children by the refusal to record the particulars of the children's birth certificates in the French register of births, marriages, and deaths even though he was their biological father and there was nothing to prevent that relationship from being officially recorded. What was more, the applicants had no other possibility of having the parentage established.

The potential outcomes for the children were worse: without recognition of a legal parent-child relationship, the children did not have

French nationality, did not have a French passport, had no valid residence permit (even if, as minors, they could not be deported), and might find it impossible to obtain French nationality and thus be ineligible to vote and ineligible for unconditional leave to remain in France; they could also be prevented from inheriting from Mr. and Mrs. Mennesson. If Mr. Mennesson died or should Mr. and Mrs. Mennesson separate, then Mrs. Mennesson would be deprived of any rights in respect of the children, to their and her own detriment. In order to carry out administrative tasks for which French nationality or an official legal parent-child relationship were required (registration of the children for social-security purposes, enrolment at the school canteen or outdoor centre, or applications for financial assistance from the Family Allowances Office), they had to produce the U.S. birth certificates together with an officially sworn translation in order to prove that the children were theirs, and the success of their application depended on the goodwill of the person dealing with it.

The court held that recourse to a surrogacy arrangement raises sensitive ethical questions. It also confirmed that States must in principle be afforded a wide margin of appreciation, regarding the decision not only whether or not to authorize this method of assisted reproduction but also whether or not to recognize a legal parent-child relationship between children legally conceived as the result of a surrogacy arrangement abroad and the intended parents.

However, an essential aspect of the identity of individuals is at stake where the legal parent-child relationship is concerned. The margin of appreciation afforded therefore needed to be reduced.

Moreover, the solutions reached by the legislature—even within the limits of this margin—are not beyond the scrutiny of the court. It fell to the court to examine carefully the arguments taken into consideration and leading to the solution reached, to determine whether a fair balance had been struck between the competing interests of the State and those directly affected by that solution. In doing so, it must have regard to the essential principle according to which, whenever the situation of a child is in issue, the best interests of that child are paramount.

The court considered that a distinction between the Mennessons' (and Labassees') right to respect for their family life, and that of the children. As the children did not have French civil-status documents or a French family record book they were obliged to produce—non-registered—U.S. civil documents accompanied by an officially sworn translation each time access to a right or a service required proof of the legal parent-child relationship, and were sometimes met with suspicion, or at the very least incomprehension, on the part of the person dealing with the request. The Mennessons referred to difficulties encountered when registering the children with social security, enrolling them at the school canteen or an outdoor centre, and applying to the Family Allowances Office for financial assistance.

A consequence that under French law the children did not have a legal parent-child relationship with Mr. or Mrs. Mennesson (or Mr. and Mrs. Labassee) was that the children had not been granted French nationality. This complicated travel as a family and raised concerns—be they unfounded, as the government maintained—regarding the children's right to remain in France once they attained majority and accordingly the stability of the family unit. To be added to that was the uncertainty of what may happen if Mr. Mennesson were to die, or the couple to separate.

The court held that there was a fair balance provided for the private lives of Mr. and Mrs. Mennesson, and Mr. and Mrs. Labassee.

However, the children were in a position of legal uncertainty. An essential aspect of the identity of the children was at stake. Everyone should be able to establish details of their identity as individual human beings, which includes the legal parent-child relationship. An essential aspect of the identity of individuals is at stake where the legal parent-child relationship is concerned. While Article 8 does not guarantee a right to a particular nationality, nationality is an element of a person's identity. The children's right to respect for their private life was substantially affected, which took on a special dimension when one of the intended parents was the biological parent. Any step to formally recognize Mr. Mennesson as the parent would fall foul of the Court of Cassation's approach. There had been a contravention of the children's right to respect for their private life.

Advisory Opinion, No. P16-2018-001 (2019)

The Court of Cassation sought an advisory opinion from the European Court of Human Rights about the Mennessons.

The Court of Cassation asked:

1. By refusing to enter in the register of births, marriages, and deaths the details of the birth certificate of a child born abroad as the result of a gestational surrogacy arrangement, in so far as the certificate designates the "intended mother" as the "legal mother," while accepting registration in so far as the certificate designates the "intended father," who is the child's biological father, is a State Party overstepping its margin of appreciation under Article 8? Should a distinction be drawn according to

whether or not the child was conceived using the eggs of the "intended mother"?

2. If yes to either of the two questions above, would the possibility for the intended mother to adopt the child of her spouse, the biological father, this being a means of establishing the legal mother-child relationship, ensure compliance with the requirements of Article 8?

A 17-member bench held that the effect of Article 8 required that domestic law provide a possibility of recognition of a legal-parent child relationship with the intended mother, designated in the birth certificate and legally established abroad as the legal mother. That recognition does not require an entry in the register of births, deaths, and marriages, but could be achieved by another prompt and effective method, such as adoption of the child by the intended mother.

The case highlighted the difference of approach *within* Europe as to surrogacy. The court compared 43 European countries other than France. Surrogacy was permitted in only nine of the 43 countries, surrogacy appeared to be tolerated in another ten, and was explicitly or implicitly prohibited in the other 24. In 31 of the countries, including 12 in which surrogacy was prohibited, it was possible to establish paternity by the intended father based on genetics.

In 19[12] of the 43 countries, including seven that prohibited surrogacy arrangements,[13] it was possible for the intended mother to establish maternity of a child born through a surrogacy arrangement to whom she is not genetically related.

The procedure for establishing or recognizing a legal parent-child relationship between children born through a surrogacy arrangement and the intended parents varies from one State to another, and several different procedures may be available within a single State. The avenues available include registration of the foreign birth certificate, adoption, or court proceedings not involving adoption. In particular, registration of the foreign birth certificate is possible in 16[14] of the 19 Member States surveyed in which surrogacy arrangements are tolerated or permitted and

12. Albania, Andorra, Armenia, Azerbaijan, Belgium, the Czech Republic, Finland, Georgia, Germany, Greece, Luxembourg, the Netherlands, Norway, Russia, Slovenia, Spain, Sweden, Ukraine, and the United Kingdom.

13. Finland, Germany, Luxembourg, Norway, Slovenia, Spain, and Sweden.

14. Albania, Andorra, Armenia, Azerbaijan, Belgium, Georgia, Greece, Moldova, the Netherlands, the Republic of North Macedonia, Poland, Portugal, Romania, Russia, Ukraine, and the United Kingdom.

in seven[15] of the 24 States that prohibit surrogacy at least insofar as the certificate designates an intended parent with a genetic link to the child. It is possible to have a legal parent-child relationship established or recognized by means of court proceedings not involving adoption in the 19 States that permit or tolerate surrogacy arrangements and in nine of the 24 States that prohibit them. Adoption is possible in five of the States that permit or tolerate surrogacy arrangements[16] and in 12 of the 24 States that prohibit them,[17] particularly in respect of parents who are not genetically related to the child.

Paradiso & Campanelli v. Italy, App. No. 25358/12 (2015)

This case is an illustration of a country removing a child from the intended parents—due to concerns about surrogacy—and succeeding.

Ms. Paradiso and Mr. Campanelli were a married couple who had infertility issues. After eight cycles of IVF in Italy, they underwent surrogacy in Russia, using Mr. Campanelli's sperm and an egg from a donor. Ms. Paradiso said that she took Mr. Campanelli's sperm with her to Russia. Surrogacy is illegal in Italy. The child was born in Russia. Parentage via surrogacy under the Russian Family Code is, with the consent of the surrogate, by operation of law. Ms. Paradiso went to Russia, and following the consent of the surrogate, then registered the birth of the child on the basis that Ms. Paradiso and Mr. Campanelli were the parents. The birth certificate did not mention surrogacy.

The birth certificate was then apostilled in accordance with the 1961 Hague Apostille Convention. Ms. Paradiso then went to the Italian consulate in Moscow, notifying the consulate that she and Mr. Campanelli were the parents. There was no mention of surrogacy. The child was then given permission by Italian authorities to travel to Italy.

The following day, Ms. Paradiso and the child arrived in Italy. Mr. Campanelli then sought that the particulars of the birth be registered in Italy.

Almost immediately after their arrival in Italy, Italian authorities commenced an investigation out of concern that they were contravening adoption laws. About two months after the return, an Italian court ordered that a DNA test be carried out. About one month later, the test results revealed that Mr. Campanelli was not the genetic father.

---

15. Austria, Finland, Germany, Iceland, Malta, Norway, and Türkiye.

16. Albania, Belgium, the Czech Republic, the Netherlands, and Portugal.

17. Bulgaria, Croatia, Estonia, Finland, Germany, Iceland, Luxembourg, Norway, Slovenia, Spain, Sweden, and Türkiye.

When the child was six months old, given the genetic testing, an Italian court ordered that the child be removed from Ms. Paradiso and Mr. Campanelli. The removal occurred almost immediately. The biological parents of the child were unknown. As there was nothing to prove the allegation that the sperm had been taken to Russia, the Italian court found that this was not a case of surrogacy, as there was no genetic relationship between Ms. Paradiso and Mr. Campanelli and the child.

Ms. Paradiso and Mr. Campanelli were unsuccessful in seeking to adopt the child, as an alternative to having their parentage recognized. There were serious suspicions by Italian authorities that offences had been committed as to egg and sperm donation, which was banned in Italy under the Medically Assisted Reproduction Act, and as to adoption under the International Adoption Act. Ms. Paradiso had put about a rumour that she was pregnant; she had gone to the consulate and implied that she was the natural mother; she had then admitted that the child had been born to a surrogate; she had stated to the carabinieri that Mr. Campanelli was the biological father, although the DNA tests had disproved this. She had been very vague as to the identity of the genetic mother; the documents concerning the surrogate motherhood stated that both of them had been seen by the Russian doctors, although Mr. Campanelli had not been in Russia. The documents about the birth did not have a precise date. All that was known was that the child had been born and that he had been handed over to Ms. Paradiso against payment of almost €50,000. Accordingly, the hypothesis that the applicants had conducted themselves illegally with a view to having the particulars of the birth certificate entered in the register of births, marriages, and deaths and to circumventing the Italian legislation appeared, in the view of the European Court of Human Rights, to be sound.

The child was subsequently placed in foster care with the intention of being adopted out.

Ms. Paradiso and Mr. Campanelli submitted that it had been impossible to obtain recognition of the legal parent-child relationship established abroad and about the removal and placement measures decided by the Italian courts. They alleged that there had been a violation of Articles 6, 8, and 14 of the European convention, and also of the 1961 Hague Apostille Convention and of the United Nations Convention on the Rights of the Child.

The court found that they lacked standing to act on behalf of the child:

> [T]he applicants have no biological ties with the child. Irrespective of the question of whether the birth certificate drawn up in

> Russia had legal effect in Italy, and if so, what effect, the child had been placed under guardianship . . . and had been represented by the guardian in the domestic proceedings. The proceedings to have the parent-child relationship recognised in Italy were unsuccessful and the child has a new identity and a new birth certificate. The applicants were also unsuccessful in the proceedings to adopt the child. The procedure to have the child adopted by another family is underway and the child has already been placed in a foster family. No signed form of authority has been submitted authorising the applicants to represent the child's interests before the Court. This implies that, from a legal point of view, the applicants do not have standing to represent the minor's interests in the context of judicial proceedings. In those circumstances, the Court considers that the applicants do not have standing to act before the Court on behalf of the child.[18]

Italy submitted that the apostille on the birth certificate did not prevent Italian authorities from verifying the truthfulness of the documents. Given that there was no genetic link, the birth certificate was inaccurate. Even supposing that there had been interference with the applicants' right to respect for their private and family life, it had been compatible with Article 8, since it had been in accordance with the law and corresponded to the aim of protecting the child, and was necessary in a democratic society. Given the authorization to adopt that they had obtained, the applicants had been in a position to adopt a child, especially since the bilateral agreement concluded between Italy and Russia in 2008 had opened the way for 781 adoptions in 2011 alone. Lastly, the government noted that there was no European consensus in the area of gestational surrogacy.

The court held that, prior to the child being removed from their care, the applicants had acted as parents towards the child, and therefore there was a de facto family life between them. Article 8 applied.

Article 8 protected both family and private life. The latter included, to a certain degree, the right to establish relationships with others. There seemed to be no reason of principle why the notion of "private life" should be taken to exclude the determination of a legal or biological relationship between a child born out of wedlock and his natural father. The court had previously held that respect for private life requires that everyone should be able to establish details of their identity as individual human beings

18. Paradiso & Campanelli v. Italy, App. No. 25358/12, ¶ 49 (Dec. 9, 2015).

and that an individual's entitlement to such information is of importance because of its formative implications for his or her personality. Mr. Campanelli sought to establish, by judicial means, whether he was the natural father. His request for recognition of the paternity that had been legally established abroad was coupled with a search for the biological truth, seeking to determine his links with the child. Consequently, there was a direct link between the establishment of paternity and his private life. The facts of the case accordingly fell within the ambit of Article 8.

Under Article 5 of the 1961 Hague Apostille Convention, the only effect of the apostille is to certify the authenticity of the signature, the capacity in which the person signing the document has acted, and, where appropriate, the identity of the seal or stamp that the document bears. The explanatory note to the aforementioned convention indicates that the apostille does not attest to the truthfulness of the content of the original document. This limitation on the legal effects deriving from the Hague convention was intended to preserve the signatory States' right to apply their own choice-of-law rules where they are required to determine the probatory force to be attached to the content of the certified document. The Italian courts did not base their decisions on the foreign birth certificate but chose to apply the Italian legislation on the legal parent-child relationship.

The Youth Court's application of Italian law derived from the choice-of-law rule according to which paternity is determined by the national law of the country in which the child was born. Given that the child was born from gametes of unknown donors, the child's nationality was not established. In this situation, the court considered that the domestic courts' application of Italian law resulting in the finding that the child had been abandoned could not be viewed as arbitrary. The court noted that the measures in respect of the child, taken by Italian courts, were based on the provisions of domestic law. Therefore, interference was in accordance with the law.

Given that Russian law did not require the child to have a genetic link with at least one of the intended parents, and the difference with the law in Italy, it was not necessary to establish whether there was extensive harmonisation of surrogacy laws in Europe.

The court said that it was called upon to examine a case in which a Russian company—which employed the lawyer representing the applicants—accepted a sum of money from the applicants; it purchased gametes from unknown donors; it found a surrogate mother and implanted the embryos in her; it handed the child over to the applicants; it assisted them in obtaining the birth certificate. To explain this process more clearly, the lawyer indicated that it was entirely possible to circumvent the requirement to have a genetic link with one of the future parents by purchasing the embryos, which thus became "one's own" embryos. Irrespective of any ethical considerations as to the actions of the company, the consequences of those actions had been very serious for the applicants, especially if it is borne in mind that Mr. Campanelli was certain that he was the child's biological father and that it had not been shown that he was not acting in good faith.

The court found that Italy's response was disproportionate, resulting in a breach of Article 8:

- The mere fact that the child would have developed closer emotional ties with his intended parents had he stayed with them for longer is not sufficient to justify his removal.
- The fact that there were open criminal proceedings against the applicants was irrelevant, as the proceedings had not been determined. The applicants would have only been legally disqualified from adopting if they had been convicted—which had not occurred.
- Although the applicants had been approved by Italian authorities as to be suitable to adopt, the Italian court found that the applicants were incapable of bringing up and loving the child on the sole ground that they had circumvented the adoption legislation, without any expert report having been ordered by the courts.
- The child had received a new identity *two years* after the application had been made for the registration of his birth in Italy. This "lack of existence" had a significant impact on administrative matters: it was unclear under what name the child was to be registered for school, for vaccination records, or for residence. The lack of identity was with the aim of preventing the applicants from discovering the child's whereabouts. It is necessary, however, to ensure that a child is not disadvantaged on account of the fact that he or she was born to a surrogate mother, especially in terms of citizenship or identity, which are of crucial importance under Article 7 of the United Nations Convention on the Rights of the Child.

However, because the child had undoubtedly developed emotional ties with his foster family, there was no obligation on the part of Italy to return him.

Italy was ordered to pay the applicants €20,000 damages and €10,000 costs.

D v. France, App. No. 11288/18 (2020)

The intended parents, husband and wife, underwent surrogacy in Ukraine. They were the genetic parents. The child was conceived and born in 2012. Ukraine issued a birth certificate in which the husband and wife were named as the parents. The local public prosecutor in France refused to register the wife as the mother, as she had not given birth. An application to court for transcription of a foreign civil status act (as opposed to an action for recognition or establishment of parentage) was successful in overcoming the objections of the prosecutor.

However, on appeal, in 2017, the wife was ordered to be removed from the birth certificate. The only exception in France to the rule of *mater semper certa est* (the mother is always certain) was that of adoption. Therefore, the intended mother could not be named on the birth certificate. It was held by the court that there was not an interference with the child's right to privacy, because the child was in the household of his father and his father's wife, and there could in due course be an adoption in favour of the father's wife.

The European Court of Human Rights held that, given the differences of establishing parenthood between that in California seen in *Mennesson*—where orders were obtained—and that in *D*—from Ukraine, where parentage was obtained by operation of law—that it was permissible for France to insist that the husband be shown on the birth certificate as the father, but not the wife as the mother.

H v United Kingdom, App. No. 32185/20 (2020)

The risks of surrogacy when there is not a binding agreement (as seen in countries such as the United Kingdom, Australia, and New Zealand) are illustrated by this case. A and B were a gay couple who wanted to be parents through surrogacy. They entered into a surrogacy arrangement with the surrogate, C, and her husband, D. A child, H, was conceived and born from A's sperm and an egg from a donor.

The arrangement broke down. Under UK law, C and D were recognized as the parents. In order for A and B to be recognized as the parents, a parental order transferring parentage from C and D to A and B needed to be made. That order can only be made by consent. C and D did not initially tell A and B of the birth. Due to the refusal of C and D to consent, a parental order could not be made. Orders had been made granting A and B parental responsibility of H, and for H to live with them.

H's birth certificate stated that her parents were C and D. H, through B as her litigation guardian, sought that the birth certificate reflect that

A was her father, and that the UK Human Fertilisation and Embryology Act 2008 breached her right to respect for her private life under Article 8.

The government said that there was no breach. It could not be assumed that genetic parental relationships took precedence over other parental relationships. If this were the case, the egg donor would have been registered as H's mother instead of C. In addition, on account of her age, H's own view of her private identity was neither known nor ascertainable. The case was distinguishable from the surrogacy cases previously considered by the court because there was no clear and exclusive father-child relationship between A and H. On the contrary, four people regarded themselves as her parents, and three as her father.

Finally, the government argued that H was provided with absolute certainty as to her legal parentage from birth; C and D were her legal parents and this fact could only be changed by order of the domestic courts. There was no international contradiction in H's identity, since she was not recorded as being the daughter of A in any other country. Moreover, this was not a case in which she could not or would not know of the genetic link between herself and A.

In the alternative, the government submitted that any interference with H's right to respect for her private life was justified. It was not in dispute that any interference was in accordance with the law, or that it pursued the legitimate aims of protecting health and protecting the rights of freedoms of others by ensuring legal certainty and clarity as to whom the law treated as parents; ensuring that donors of gametes used in the process of assisted procreation were not treated as legal parents; and ensuring that surrogacy arrangements were not enforceable in domestic law. As complex social and ethical issues were concerned, on which there was no European consensus, the State had a wide margin of appreciation. Furthermore, the legislation in this area had been reviewed by Parliament and was the subject of very considered legislative objectives.

In the government's view, if there was any duty on the State at all, it was to provide for the possibility of legal recognition of the relationship between A and the applicant; how that recognition was realized was a matter for the State. In the present case, the State had provided multiple possibilities for legal recognition, including parental orders and parental responsibility orders. A was not eligible for the former, but had been granted the latter with the consequence that he had full parental responsibility for the applicant.

The court dismissed the application, on the basis of accepting the government's submissions. Any interference with H's right to respect for her private life might flow from the automatic recognition of D, not A, on the birth certificate, and any interference was very limited indeed.

The court said that there was no evidence to support the applicant's claim that there was an "unarguable international consensus" in favour of recognizing the biological father on the birth certificate. The court approved the approach taken by the United Kingdom to make clear who were the parents, given the possibility of there being five people who could be the parents—the parties, and the egg donor.

The court held that the child's best interests may include fundamental components other than the legal recognition of the intended parents, such as protection against the risks of abuse that surrogacy arrangements may have.

Fjölnisdóttir v. Iceland, App. No. 71552/17 (2021)

Valdís Fjölnisdóttir and Eydís Agnarsdóttir were a female married couple. They underwent surrogacy in California, where a son was born to them in 2013 with both donor eggs and sperm. The child was not genetically related to either of them.

A court order had been made in California declaring them to be the parents. A birth certificate then issued in California stating that they were the parents. The child then obtained a U.S. passport and moved with them back to their home in Iceland.

They were unable to register the child in Iceland. Icelandic authorities stated that as the child had been born in the United States to a surrogate then Icelandic legal provisions on a child's parentage were not applicable, and the child was not automatically entitled to citizenship under the Icelandic Citizenship Act.

Government authorities considered that as the surrogate was the mother, the child was an unaccompanied minor, and took the child into State care. A legal guardian was appointed. By agreement, the child initially was allowed to remain in the care of the couple.

In 2015, in the midst of their legal battles, the law changed in Iceland, which enabled the child to obtain Icelandic citizenship. The couple then divorced. The agreement with the State that the child be in their care became invalid as a result.

By 2019, the Supreme Court had ordered that the child be permanently fostered by Ms. Fjölnisdóttir and her spouse, but spend equal time with Ms. Agnarsdóttir and her spouse.

In 2013 the couple had applied to adopt the child. State authorities had put that application on hold, while the registration proceedings remained on foot.

In 2014 they were advised by the government that the surrogate was the mother, and as it appeared that she was married, her husband was the father. Thus, the surrogate's and her husband's consent were required for the adoption. State authorities required proof that the surrogate and her husband had not received a fee or benefits in relation to the consent, including pay for loss of income (see Chapter 13). The couple responded, saying that the surrogate was single, and that no payments had been made in connection with the consent for adoption within the meaning of section 14 of the Adoption Act.

Once they divorced, the couple discontinued the adoption application.

In 2016, the district court rejected the application for registration. The district court found that in accordance with the fundamental principles of Icelandic family law, the woman who gave birth to a child was considered its mother. Consequently, the first and second applicants could not be considered the child's parents. The district court also noted that the principles of private international law generally did not require a State to recognize a decision rendered by the authorities of another State if it was manifestly incompatible with the fundamental legal principles of the former State, even if the decision was compatible with the laws of the latter.

Noting that surrogacy was unlawful in Iceland, and punishable by fines or up to three months' imprisonment in the event of a violation within Icelandic jurisdiction, the district court found that recognizing as parents those who were resident in Iceland but went abroad for the purposes of surrogacy would create a legal loophole around the ban on surrogacy. The district court therefore found that Iceland had a legitimate reason to refuse to recognize parentage established abroad in such circumstances.

As for the third applicant/child's right to respect for his private and family life, the district court recognized that "family life" had been established between the three applicants, and that the authorities' refusal to register the child as the couple's son in the national register had interfered with his private and family life. However, that interference had served the aim of upholding the ban on surrogacy and thereby protecting the interests of others, namely preventing women from being pressured into carrying children for others and ensuring that children could seek information about their heritage. The district court noted that the authorities had taken steps to ensure the child's best interests and to counteract the difficulties that the applicants had experienced as a result of the refusal to register the third applicant, by allowing the child to be fostered by the women to preserve the family bond between them, and by granting him a residence permit and subsequently citizenship.

The district court also discussed the adoption application. It noted that special rules applied to the adoption of a child by its foster parents, in accordance with which a child could be adopted without the approval of its biological parents if this was clearly in the child's best interests. Accordingly, the district court considered that the adoption application would probably have been approved if the couple had not divorced.

In light of these considerations, the district court found that the interference with private and family life caused by the refusal to register the third applicant had been necessary to protect morality and the rights of others, and that it had been accompanied by sufficient counterbalancing efforts to alleviate the negative effects of the refusal. The child's best interests, although of paramount importance, could not override the fundamental legal principles of parentage.

The appeal to the Supreme Court was dismissed. That court found that the effect of Icelandic law about parentage presumptions meant that only the woman who gave birth to a child conceived by artificial fertilization could be considered its mother under Icelandic law.

Under section 5 of Act No. 55/1996 on Artificial Fertilisation and the Use of Human Gametes and Embryos for Stem Cell Research, surrogacy was prohibited.

The couple and child then applied to the European Court of Human Rights. They were unsuccessful. The Icelandic government said that the women could have applied to adopt the child, either as individuals or with their new spouses.

The applicants submitted that although surrogacy was illegal in Iceland, the ban on surrogacy did not apply extraterritorially, and that they had gone through the surrogacy process in California in full accordance with the law of that state. Further, the best interests of the child had not been sufficiently taken into account by the authorities. After all, the couple had been screened as suitable to be foster carers. The failure to recognize their parentage meant that the child did not have inheritance rights, and caused the women to live in a state of uncertainty, which had caused them anguish and distress, forcing them to maintain a position as foster parents and foster child.

The government submitted that there had been extensive national and political debate on the subject of surrogacy in the country. This had included a working group on surrogacy appointed by the Minister of Health, whose 2010 report had concluded that surrogacy should not be legalized. Following a successful parliamentary proposal in 2011, a bill legalizing altruistic surrogacy with a biological link to one of the intended parents had been introduced in Parliament twice, but had not been voted on. The government therefore submitted that adoption was the only available avenue for intended parents to have their relationship with a child born by way of surrogacy recognized as a parent-child relationship.

The government submitted that Article 8 of the convention did not guarantee the right to found a family or the right to adopt. They furthermore reasoned that the State should enjoy a wide margin of appreciation when deciding on matters concerning surrogacy and assisted reproduction techniques, particularly in cases such as the present one, where there was no biological link between the child and the intended parents. The government emphasized that domestic law placed a ban on surrogacy, which the applicants should not be allowed to circumvent by arranging surrogacy abroad.

The government reasoned that the applicants had not been through any official screening process in Iceland, such as those in place for adoption procedures, and the fact that the surrogacy in this case had been commercial in nature had created a risk of the surrogate mother and the child being exposed to exploitation and abuse. They submitted that the ban on surrogacy excluded the possibility that a woman who gave birth to a child could relinquish her natural status as its mother, and prevented a woman from being pressured to allow her body to be used to bear a child with whom she must then sever all ties. They also submitted that the ban on surrogacy protected children's right to know about their origins, as children born by way of surrogacy would face difficulties in seeking information about their biological parentage.

The court followed *Paradiso & Campanelli*, holding:

> The provisions of Article 8 do not guarantee either the right to found a family or the right to adopt. The right to respect for "family life" does not safeguard the mere desire to found a family; it presupposes the existence of a family, or at the very least the potential relationship between, for example, a child born out of wedlock and his or her natural father, or the relationship that arises from a genuine marriage, even if family life has not yet been fully established, or the relationship between a father and his legitimate child even if it proves, years later, to have had no biological basis, or the relationship that arises from a lawful and genuine adoption.[19]

The court held that the requirements of "family life" had been fulfilled on the particular facts. The court took account of the long duration

19. Fjölnisdóttir v. Iceland, App. No. 71552/17, ¶ 57 (May 18, 2021).

of the first two applicants' uninterrupted relationship with the child, the quality of the ties already formed, and the close emotional bonds forged with the child during the first stages of his life, reinforced by the foster care arrangement adopted by the national authorities and not contested by the government before the court.

Applying *Mennesson* and *Paradiso & Campanelli*, the court found the refusal to recognize the first and second applicants as the child's parents pursued the legitimate aim of protecting the rights and freedoms of others, because the ban on surrogacy served to protect the interests of women who might be pressured into surrogacy, as well as the rights of children to know their natural parents.

The court noted the government's submission that either the first or the second applicant may still apply to adopt the child, as individuals or together with their new spouses. Although mindful of the practical problems that might arise due to the fact that only one of the first two applicants can be permitted to adopt the child, the court took this possibility into account in its holistic examination of the necessity of the interference, in particular as regards the Article 8 rights of the child, the third applicant.

Considering all of the above, in particular the absence of an indication of actual, practical hindrances in the enjoyment of family life, and the steps taken by the respondent State to regularise and secure the bond between the applicants, the court concluded that the nonrecognition of a formal parental link, confirmed by the judgment of the Supreme Court, struck a fair balance between the applicants' right to respect for their family life and the general interests that the State sought to protect by the ban on surrogacy.

Hájovský v. Slovakia, App. No. 7796/16 (2021)

This case is an illustration that even when there are no laws about surrogacy, society might deeply disapprove of surrogacy, and of the extraordinary efforts and delays in obtaining justice. The initial events occurred in 2005, but justice was not obtained until 16 years later.

In 2005 Mr. Hájovský, aged about 64, and his "*alleged partner*" put an anonymous notice in a national newspaper seeking a surrogate. Surrogacy was not regulated in Slovakia.

A television reporter pretended to be the surrogate, and then met Mr. Hájovský. She secretly filmed the meetings. Her story, about buying a child, was then broadcast on national television with Mr. Hájovský's details. The report said that he was part of a group seeking to sell children overseas, something that Mr. Hájovský denied.

A national newspaper then followed up the story with "Trade in unborn children," both in print and online, and displayed pictures of Mr. Hájovský from the television story. This was without his consent. The article stated that Mr. Hájovský had made his sister impersonate his wife and that, having lived for a long time in the United States, he had only recently acquired Slovak citizenship. The article also mentioned the role of doctors who were allegedly ready to help with the assisted reproduction and the falsification of documents. The article ended by stating that although trafficking of unborn children was illegal in Slovakia, the applicant and his fake partner would probably escape justice and would not be punished because there was no legislation that would enable their actions to be prosecuted.

Mr. Hájovský sued the television station and won.

He then sued the newspaper publisher—and lost—because the article aimed to inform readers about questions of public interest, the issue of assisted reproduction being extremely sensitive and somewhat controversial; that he had attracted public and media attention by publishing his advertisement, thus excluding the relevant facts from his private sphere; and that the article in question contained only true information that had already been broadcast on public television. The appellate court allowed the photographs to be used for news reporting without his previous consent, and found that his actions were legally unacceptable and morally reprehensible.

Mr. Hájovský appealed. The matter was remitted. The remittal court stated that Slovak law did not allow surrogacy, and that any contract conflicting with the principle that a child's mother is the woman who gave birth to that child, would be invalid as being contrary to good morals. Moreover, the commercial aspect of the surrogacy raised serious ethical questions, which was undoubtedly one of the reasons why the advertisement had aroused so much interest in the media and among the public; and the issue of surrogacy was a matter of legitimate public interest upon which the press was called to inform the public. In the court's view, the article in question did not contain any harsh or vulgar expressions, and was not only critical about the manner in which Mr. Hájovský had tried to obtain a child but also about the actions of other people who were to have been involved in the process of assisted reproduction. There was no doubt that the article and the criticisms contained in it had a factual basis and relied on true and uncontested facts. Therefore, publication of the article did not amount to an unjustified interference with Mr. Hájovský's rights, which were in that case overridden by the defendant's right to freedom of expression.

Concerning the publication of the pictures, to which he had not consented, the appellate court referred to a legal exemption, enabling pictures to be used without the consent of the person concerned, for the purposes of news reporting. The term "news reporting" covered not only informing about facts of public interest but also assessing those facts in a critical manner. Although the article containing Mr. Hájovský's pictures concerned his private life, his private life was touched upon as a secondary issue (to illustrate his motives), the core theme—and a matter of public interest—being the manner in which Mr. Hájovský had tried to obtain a child by offering a financial reward through surrogacy, which was not allowed under Slovak law. The publication of the article with the pictures was also considered topical, given that it had occurred two days after the television broadcast and thus covered the subject at a time when the public were hearing information about Mr. Hájovský's actions. The pictures served the purpose of confirming the trustworthiness of the information published, all the more so because the subject of the article was unusual. The fact that it was published in the so-called tabloid press did not as such exclude it from the news reporting exemption, since the decisive factor was the manner in which the topic had been approached; in the present case, neither the content of the article nor the pictures were intended to create scandal about or to ridicule the applicant.

That court also observed that the author of the article had assessed the trafficking of unborn children in Slovakia as being illegal, while quoting the statement of a third party that the trafficking of unborn children could not be prosecuted because of the absence of relevant legislation. This amounted to a contradiction since an action that was not regulated by the criminal law could neither be contrary to that law nor subject to punishment; nevertheless, a surrogacy contract would be invalid from the perspective of family law. According to the court, it was necessary to take into account the fact that the article had been written by a journalist and published in a newspaper designed for a wide public, which required the acceptance of even simplified or distorted allegations; in the present case, the abovementioned contradiction amounted to a lack of precision that did not have any impact on the applicant's personality rights, given that the substance of the information relied upon in the article was true.

Mr. Hájovský relied on Article 8, as to the respect for his private life. He did not contest that the publisher could legitimately publish an article about surrogacy in order to initiate a public debate, but he argued that there had been no pressing social need to illustrate that topic using his own story, which disclosed his identity and private aspects of his life. The publication of his pictures had not, in any manner, contributed to a discussion about surrogacy; its only goal had been to create a scandal about him, cause a sensation, and increase the number of readers.

The court agreed, given that Mr. Hájovský had placed his advertisement anonymously, was not a public figure, could not have expected to be recorded or reported on in a public manner, and did not voluntarily cooperate with the media, and no effort had been made to protect his privacy, such as masking or blurring his face.

S-H v. Poland, App. Nos. 56846/15 and 56849/15 (2021)

Mr. S and Mr. H were a same-sex couple living in Israel. They had dual United States and Israeli citizenship. Mr. H was also a Polish citizen. The couple underwent surrogacy in California. Twins were born. The twins were conceived from the sperm of Mr. S and an egg from a donor. The couple were declared by the California court to be the parents.

The couple and children then travelled to Israel, where they lived.

The children were Jewish, whose ancestors, Polish Jews, had been killed in the Holocaust. When the children were almost two, Mr. S sought confirmation from Polish authorities of the children's Polish citizenship. The authority sought the parents' marriage certificate, documents relating to the recognition of paternity, as well as citizenship of the mother.

In response, a certified copy and one translated into Polish of the judgment were provided. The children's lawyer refused to provide any further material, and asked authorities to issue a decision based on the material at hand.

The authorities then sought a copy of the children's Polish birth certificates in order to determine their filiation and family relationship with Mr. S and Mr. H. Their lawyer declined to do so, saying that all relevant information had been provided, and asking for a decision to be made.

The applications were refused. The authority noted that the Polish birth certificates had not been supplied. He held that, under Polish laws, a child's mother was the woman who had given birth. The Polish system did not allow for the concept of surrogacy. Therefore, the authority found that the surrogate was the mother (i.e., the woman who had undertaken to conceive and give birth to them). The refusal resulted in the children's applications for citizenship by descent being refused.

On the basis of the presumption of paternity under Polish law, the surrogate's husband was found to be the father.

On administrative review, the first instance decision was upheld. The couple were directed to institute proceedings under Article 1148 of the Code of Civil Procedure in order to determine whether the California court order was to be recognized in Poland. The couple did not. The

Minister determined that, in any event, transposing the California order into Polish law would contravene the principles of the Polish legal system.

After an unsuccessful appeal to an administrative court, the couple appealed to the Supreme Administrative Court. Their appeal was dismissed. In the words of the European Court of Human Rights:

> The court noted that for the determination of Polish citizenship, the children's genetic link to Mr S. was of no relevance: a child who had one Polish parent and one foreign parent acquired Polish citizenship at birth. However, the court observed that the term "parent" carried a legal meaning. Pursuant to the relevant provisions of the Family and Custody Code, a child's mother was the woman who had given birth to that child. If the child was born during her marriage there was a legal presumption that the child's father was the mother's husband. This presumption could only be rebutted by bringing an action for denial of paternity.
>
> The court further held that surrogacy agreements were not recognised in the Polish legal system as they ran counter to the principles of community life. It also noted that the Polish legal system had not attributed parental rights to "so called partner relationships". For that reason, accepting the judgment of the Superior Court of California would have been against public policy principles (*klauzula porządku publicznego*). Likewise, the applicants' birth certificates could not have any legal effect. These certificates indicated Mr S. as the applicants' father and Mr H. as the applicants' mother/parent. Since the certificates indicated the two men as parents, and by that confirmed the surrogacy agreement, they ran counter to the basic principles of the Polish legal system. Mr S. could not therefore be considered to be the applicants' parent. Lastly, the court noted that the cases of *Mennesson* and *Labassee* related to different sets of facts.[20]

The children then applied to the European Court of Human Rights. They sought to rely on Article 8 (right to private and family life) and Article 14 (no discrimination) of the European Convention on Human Rights.

Their application was dismissed.

As to Article 8, the court stated:

> [I]n order to reach the conclusion that a complaint is compatible *ratione materiae* with Article 8 of the Convention, the measure

20. S-H v. Poland, App. Nos. 56846/15 and 56849/15, ¶¶ 23–24 (Dec. 9, 2021).

> complained of must attain a certain level of seriousness and be carried out in a manner causing prejudice to personal enjoyment of the right to respect for one's private and/or family life (ibid., §§ 110–14). Conversely, once a measure is found to have seriously affected the applicant's private life, the complaint is to be deemed compatible *ratione materiae* with the Convention.
>
> The Court notes that the concept of "private life" is a broad term not susceptible to exhaustive definition. It covers the physical and psychological integrity of a person. It can therefore embrace multiple aspects of the person's physical and social identity which includes the legal parent-child relationship . . .; an essential aspect of the identity of individuals is at stake where the legal parent-child relationship is concerned (see *Mennesson v. France*, no. 65192/11, §§ 46, 96, ECHR 2014 (extracts), and *Labassee v. France*, no. 65941/11, §§ 38, 75, 26 June 2014).
>
> Moreover, while the provisions of Article 8 do not guarantee the right to acquire a particular nationality or citizenship, the Court has previously stated that it cannot be ruled out that an arbitrary denial of citizenship might in certain circumstances raise an issue under Article 8 of the Convention because of the impact of such a denial on the private life of the individual . . . .[21]

The first question the court had to determine was whether the refusals affected the children's private life. In order to answer that question, the court engaged a "*consequence-based approach . . . to examine whether the impugned decisions had sufficiently serious negative consequences for the applicants.*"[22]

The court considered it needed to look at the practical obstacles concerning the children. Although the family were considering moving to Europe, no firm evidence had been given. It did not appear that such a move was imminent. The children were settled in Israel with the couple, and enjoyed U.S. and Israeli citizenship. They had never lived in Poland. The decisions made by Polish authorities did not render them stateless. The applicants did not alert the court to any negative consequences or practical difficulties that they might encounter in their chosen country of residence, resulting from the Polish courts' refusal to confirm the acquisition of Polish citizenship. The children could benefit, in the State where they lived, from the legal parent-child relationship with their biological

21. *Id.* ¶¶ 63–65.
22. *Id.* ¶ 67.

father where the recognition of that relationship was not put into doubt. The actions of Polish authorities did not leave the children in a legal vacuum.

The court distinguished *Mennesson* and *Labassee*, because although authorities in this case had also refused to give effect to the foreign birth certificates establishing the legal parent-child relationship, that link was recognized in Israel, where they lived. Unlike *Mennesson*, *Labassee*, and *Fjölnisdóttir*, so far the family has not had to overcome any practical obstacles on account of the Polish authorities' decisions.

The court held:

> Even taking into account their complaint that the domestic authorities determined de novo their legal parentage in accordance with the principles of Polish family law, considering that they do not live in Poland, the Court is unable to find any factual basis for concluding that there has been an interference with the right to respect for family life in the present case.[23]

The court held that Article 14 is not a substantive provision, with no independent existence. As the complaint was dismissed as to Article 8, therefore Article 14 cannot apply either.

AM v. Norway, App. No. 30254/19 (2022)

This case is an illustration of the seeming priority in Europe given to genetic parenthood (as opposed to who intended to be a parent) and, likewise, who is the mother of the child. It is an extraordinary case where a woman suffering infertility necessarily became a parent through surrogacy in the United States. The U.S. order was not accepted by the court to establish parenthood of the woman. The child was not to have an ongoing relationship with her. The case paints a clear picture about why overseas judgments establishing parenthood should be upheld (but may not be), including, if necessary, by a Hague convention.

A husband and wife in Norway sought to conceive naturally. When that failed, they tried IVF. When that failed, they tried surrogacy in the United States. Their first attempt failed. Their relationship gradually deteriorated. They divorced. However, they both were still interested in proceeding with surrogacy in the United States.

The husband formed a new relationship. Nevertheless, the former husband and wife continued to try surrogacy in the United States. In 2013 the parties entered into a surrogacy agreement in Texas with a surrogate.

23. *Id.* ¶ 74.

She was implanted with an embryo composed of the former husband's sperm and an egg from an anonymous donor.

Consistent with the Texas Family Code, a court in Bexar County declared the parties to be the parents. The parties were then named on the birth certificate as the parents. Following the birth, the child stayed with the intended mother. The intended father visited daily. This pattern continued after their return to Norway.

Norwegian authorities accepted that the intended father was the father, based on his acknowledgment of paternity.

The parties agreed in writing to shared responsibility. They disagreed about how fast the arrangement should move to a 50/50 arrangement. Over time, the parenting arrangements broke down.

By this time, the father's new partner became pregnant. A meeting between the parties, the father's partner, and Norwegian authorities failed to resolve the matter.

Three months later, the father decided that the child should stay with him and not see the intended mother.

The intended mother then sought unsuccessfully to be recognized as the mother of the child.

Trial Court

The trial court found the type of surrogacy was illegal in Norway. It was nonetheless a fact that some Norwegian nationals travelled to other countries to have a child through surrogacy, as the parties had done. The fact that surrogacy was not legal in Norway did not deny the child and the social parent the possibility of achieving a safe legal framework for their relationship. However, it was clear that complicated legal and practical issues could arise in some cases, for example concerning the establishment and transfer of parentage, parental responsibility, citizenship, issuing of passports, and immigration. The fact that at least two countries' legal systems were involved could give rise to conflict between the legal rules of different countries, which further complicated the matter. If a conflict arose between the biological parent and the intended parent before the intended parent's legal relationship with the child had been established, the conflict became even more complex.

The court held that under section 2 of the Children Act, the surrogate was the mother, as she was the birth mother, notwithstanding that the surrogate had no genetic or biological relationship with him, and in principle no legal relationship with him under Norwegian law. There was no authority under Norwegian law for the social mother under a surrogacy arrangement to have legal maternity transferred from the biological mother to herself.

The only way of fixing the problem was by adoption—which required the consent of the father. He refused to consent.

The intended mother unsuccessfully sought to rely on a temporary Surrogacy Act—which the court found had expired before she would have been eligible, and required the intended parents to have a shared wish to raise the child together.

The court noted that regardless of what the applicant and others could think about the father's choice to cut off contact between the intended mother and the child, it seemed as though the child had been living in a safe, adequate environment since then, with his father, his stepmother, and with his half-sibling and other family members.

The Appeal

The appellate court took the same approach as the trial court.

The intended mother invoked her status as a mother in the United States, submitting that her parentage there had to be recognized in Norway, despite Norwegian statutes to the contrary. Refusing recognition of the U.S. court decision would, she submitted, be in contravention of the United Nations Convention on the Rights of the Child, the European convention, and the constitution. In her opinion, those sources of law had to be given independent significance in the application of Norwegian national law. She had argued that neither the Dispute Act, the Children Act, nor the Adoption Act could be interpreted to mean that Norwegian legal provisions prevented recognition of the U.S. court decision. Moreover, she had maintained that the best interests of the child were the fundamental point of departure under the Convention on the Rights of the Child, the constitution, and the Children Act.

The appellate court found that none of the international conventions provided an independent basis for her claim for maternity. In that court's view, the application of the law in the case before it—which was based on the provisions of the Children Act and the Adoption Act—was not in contravention of the constitution, the European convention, or the Convention on the Rights of the Child. The court agreed with the government that the conventions could not be a factor in the interpretation when applying the provisions of Norwegian law. As had been argued by the government, the Norwegian rules were unequivocal and not in contravention of conventions by which Norway was bound.

The intended mother submitted that it was also in the child's best interests to have two parents from birth on, and that having the intended mother as the child's legal and actual mother was the best thing for him.

She had maintained that it was a fundamental part of a child's identity to know who the intended mother was in surrogacy cases as per Article 8 of the United Nations Convention on the Rights of the Child.

The appellate court said that in surrogacy cases the child had two biological parents from birth on, namely the surrogate mother and the legal father. The child's biological parents were known, and the child's right to know its biological origin and identity was therefore safeguarded. (It did not explain how the egg donor fit into this pattern.) The legislature had considered and explicitly decided against parentage for the intended parent in surrogacy cases, which was not in contravention of the child's best interests.

Nor did the court find that the right to respect for private and family life pursuant to Article 8 of the European convention, and the constitution, had been violated. The convention did not give intended parents an independent basis for establishing parentage or family life. In *Mennesson*, the court had concluded that there had been no violation of the right to family life or the intended parents' right to private life. The only right violated had been the child's right to respect for private life. The intended parents in that case had been married when the surrogacy agreement was entered into and when the U.S. court decision that recognized them as parents was pronounced. They were still married when the court pronounced judgment in the case—14 years later. The facts of that case were different.

The Supreme Court of Norway summarily dismissed the intended mother's appeal.

European Court of Human Rights

A third-party intervenor submitted that in reaching a conclusion about the recognition of legal parentage in surrogacy cases, the best interests of the child always had to be accorded the primacy required by the United Nations Convention on the Rights of the Child, in particular Article 3. The court had to take this approach under Article 53 of the European convention. They further submitted that, if it was accepted that the recognition of the legal parentage of the intended parents in surrogacy cases was analogous to cases of adoption, then the appropriate United Nations convention (Article 21) was paramountcy.

The court could not find that the rules applied in the case would generally pose problems under Article 8 of the convention or that Norway would be in breach of that provision for not having recognized the intended mother's parenthood because the surrogacy arrangement had been carried out in the United States and she had been registered as the child's parent there.

While the court found that the father's treatment of the intended mother was particularly harsh, this could not be attributed to the authorities. The court found that there was no violation of Article 8.

DB v. Switzerland, App. No. 58817/15 (2023)

In 2010 a gay couple living in Switzerland underwent surrogacy in California. A child was conceived from sperm of the second applicant, and an egg from an anonymous donor. A pre-birth order declared that both the men were the parents.

After the child's birth, the child travelled to Switzerland. The couple had a registered partnership. The child obtained Swiss citizenship due to the genetic relationship with the second applicant.

The parties sought to have the first applicant recognized in Switzerland as a parent. Birth authorities refused to register the birth or to recognize the California judgment. Matters then seesawed on appeal.

Federal Supreme Court

The court held that the prohibition of all forms of surrogacy required a rigid position of refusing to recognize the resulting nongenetic parent-child relationship and of holding that the manifest circumvention of the law led to a breach of public policy. In its view, denying a violation of the public policy would have obliged law enforcement authorities to accept as a fait accompli a parent-child relationship established by a fraud of the law, which would have encouraged assisted reproduction tourism and rendered the national ban on surrogacy largely ineffective.

The manner in which the parent-child relationship had been established could not be disregarded. The use of surrogacy in California in order to circumvent the Swiss ban constituted a fraud on Swiss law. The court upheld the Californian judgment concerning the parent-child relationship between the child and his genetic father, but refused to recognize the link established by the American courts between the child and the nongenetic father.

In its view, the child's situation was sufficiently protected by the Swiss legal system and complied with the child's best interests. The child had always lived with the couple, so that they formed a family community protected by Article 8. The child's removal from his family environment was not justified. The child had acquired Swiss nationality and, therefore, was not at risk of statelessness. His U.S. nationality, however, was in a state of legal uncertainty as a result of the nonrecognition of the nongenetic father's parentage. As the genetic child of the second applicant, he had been registered in the civil registry and bore the latter's surname. If the second applicant had been unable to attend, the child would not have been deprived of any legal relationship with the first applicant, as the registered partnership granted the first applicant certain rights and duties of assistance.

While They Were Waiting

The applicants filed with the European Court of Human Rights in 2015. In 2018, same-sex adoption was allowed in Switzerland. They applied to adopt the child that day. Later that year the child was adopted by the first applicant. In 2021 equal marriage laws were enacted in Switzerland.

The government, not surprisingly, sought the dismissal of the application. The applicants noted that adoption was granted eight years after the child's birth. Until then, they had been forced to live in uncertainty and suffer inconvenience because the first applicant and child were not related.

The court held that Article 8 applied to the family, both as to private life for the child, and family life for all three.

The *applicants* claimed that if surrogacy had already taken place and the child had been born, it was no longer justified, in the light of the best interests of the child, to claim that the child is intended to protect it against abstract commercialization. Full recognition of the foreign judgment (i.e., the judgment establishing the parent-child relationship between the child and the two fathers) should take precedence, by virtue of the real and concrete interests of the child. Consequently, the interference with the applicants' protected rights does not pursue any legitimate aim. The first applicant had no right of representation in respect of his son for eight years. With the child in day care, kindergarten, and school, the first applicant would have faced serious difficulties because he had no decision-making power. Similarly, he could have travelled abroad with the child only with the prior consent of the second applicant.

The *government* claimed that foreign judgments are not recognized in Switzerland if they are manifestly incompatible with Swiss public policy. Surrogacy was prohibited in Switzerland. This was motivated by protection of the woman and of the child. The protections for the child in Switzerland were consistent with the United Nations convention, and the European convention.

One *intervenor*, Polish Catholic organization Ordo Iuris, said that there was great reluctance in Europe to include anyone other than biological parents in birth certificates.

Another *intervenor*, Alliance Defending Freedom International, stated that the majority of European countries prohibit surrogacy and that it is up to each to decide how to regulate this issue, which raises ethical, moral, psychological, social, and legal questions; and that the practice of surrogacy can lead to the commercialization and trafficking of human beings and jeopardizes the dignity and safety of women and children.

The court accepted that the refusal to recognize the U.S. order was in accordance with Swiss law. Switzerland's refusal to recognize a parent-child relationship between children born abroad as a result of surrogacy and the intended parents stemmed from the desire to discourage its nationals from resorting outside Switzerland to surrogacy when it is prohibited at home, in order, according to its perception of the problem, to protect the children and the surrogate mother. The court therefore accepted that the interference in question pursued two of the legitimate aims listed in the second paragraph of Article 8 of the convention: "*the protection of health*" and "*the protection of the rights and freedoms of others*."

The court considered that the refusal to recognize the birth certificate lawfully drawn up abroad, without providing for alternative methods of recognition of the relationship between the nongenetic father and child, did not pursue the best interests of the child. In other words, the general and absolute impossibility of obtaining recognition of the relationship between the child and the first applicant for a significant period of time constituted a disproportionate interference with the child's right to respect for his private life protected by Article 8. As a result, Switzerland, in the circumstances of the case, exceeded its discretion by failing to provide for such a possibility in good time. Accordingly, there had been a violation.

However, in applying *Mennesson*, the brief allegations, as to the difficulties encountered by parents in crèches, kindergartens, and schools, are not sufficiently substantiated and, in any event, do not appear to be serious enough to be regarded as a disproportionate interference with the aims pursued, namely the prohibition of surrogacy. The court concluded that the practical difficulties that the applicants might have encountered in their family life in the absence of the recognition in Swiss law did not exceed the limits imposed by compliance with Article 8 of the convention.

KK v. Denmark, App. No. 25212/21 (2022)

The intended parents, a husband and wife, lived in Denmark and underwent gestational surrogacy in Ukraine. The genetic parents of the child were the husband and an anonymous egg donor. In order to undertake surrogacy in Ukraine, the intended parents must be a heterosexual married couple, in which at least one of them has a genetic connection with the child.

The intended parents met these criteria. As a result, when twins were born, they were recognized, by operation of Ukrainian law, as the parents. The children obtained Danish citizenship due to the genetic connection with the intended father.

Under Danish law[24] either the birth mother or the genetic mother was the parent of the child. As a result, the surrogacy agreement in Ukraine that the surrogate was not a parent had no legal effect in Denmark. She remained the legal parent.

In order to enable the parentage of the intended mother to be recognized, the intended mother sought a stepparent adoption in Denmark. As she had only lived with the children in Denmark for 16 days after they returned to Denmark, that application was refused.

Although the process of surrogacy in Ukraine did not involve adoption, the Supreme Court of Denmark found that the payment of €32,265 to the Ukraine clinic, which included a payment to the surrogate, and for her consenting to the stepparent adoption, amounted to an illegal payment for adoption. The court considered the two decisions in *Mennesson*, but held that as the Adoption Act contained an absolute ban on anyone paying for an adoption, the application was refused.

The majority of the Supreme Court held:

> [W]hereas one should not prevent surrogacy arrangements not involving payment, agreements on the "delivery of a child" against payment seemed in conflict with the fundamental principles of our society. In this context, it is provided that it should not be possible to buy and sell unborn children, that infertility problems should not become actual "trading" in children and that in connection with agreements involving payment, there is a risk that a woman who chooses to give birth to a child for another may be influenced more by the payment offered than by the best interests of the child when choosing the "parents" of her child. It is also clear from the legislative history that making it punishable to enter into agreements on paid surrogacy had been considered, but that it had been concluded that it was probably rules barring entering into agreements rather than the threat of punishment which would counter such agreements being made.[25]

---

24. Children Act § 30.
25. K.K. v. Denmark, App. No. 25212/21, ¶ 16 (Dec. 6, 2022).

The court distinguished *Mennesson*, because no payment was made to the surrogate in that case, and focussed on general deterrence against commercial surrogacy, despite the "vital interests" of the children, who had lived with the intended mother all their lives, stating:

> It must, therefore, give rise to some doubt about how the court finds that the interests of the individual children affected in concrete cases should weigh against the interests underlying section 15 of the Adoption Act. These interests generally aim to discourage commercial surrogacy arrangements and to protect children against being turned into a commodity, including preventing the surrogate mother from caring more about what payment she is offered for the child than about the best interests of the child when selecting "parents" of that child. To this is added the interest in countering the exploitation of vulnerable women in commercial surrogacy arrangements.[26]

The majority concluded that Article 8 did not have an impact, because the children had Danish citizenship at birth and could therefore live in Denmark. Shared custody implied that the intended mother had a duty to care for the children and that in the event of separation or divorce, she would be able to retain custody. The children could be provided for under her will, and for inheritance tax purposes they would "*be in the same position as if they were her children.*"[27]

The *application to the European Court of Human Rights* was unsuccessful. The court noted that the Adoption Act was intended to ban facilitating surrogacy agreements, as set out in the travaux préparatoires to the 1986 Amending Act:

> Agreements on the "delivery of a child" against remuneration seem to conflict with the fundamental principles of our society. It ought to be impossible to buy or sell children, and this also applies to unborn children. Infertility problems should not become actual "trading" in children. To this is added that in connection with agreements involving remuneration, there is a risk that a woman who chooses to give birth to a child for another person may be influenced more by the payment offered than by the best interests of the child when choosing the "parents" of that child.[28]

26. *Id.*
27. *Id.*
28. *Id.* ¶ 20.

The Adoption Act enacted the 1996 Hague Child Protection Convention in 1997. In doing so, the stated purpose was:

> It is proposed that section 15 of the Adoption Act be amended to ensure that it complies with the prohibition against remuneration in Article 4(c)(3) and (d)(4) of the Hague Convention, whilst at the same time providing for the Convention's fundamental interest in preventing trafficking in children and unethical procedures.[29]

While the 1996 convention contained basic rules about adoption, the Adoption Act was seen as having wider application. Following the Supreme Court decision, Danish authorities considered that the section no longer applied as containing an absolute ban on stepparent adoption through commercial surrogacy. However, the relevant Ministry was also seeking to amend the Adoption Act to bring it into line with the Supreme Court decision—but had put matters on hold in light of the appeal.

The court held that the effect of the Children Act was that the Ukrainian surrogate was deemed the mother under Danish law, even though she was not deemed a parent under Ukrainian law. Danish international private law established that parenthood for an intended parent, which is established in another country, is not recognized in Denmark because recognition is manifestly contrary to public policy. A Danish advisory body had considered that surrogacy reduced the female body to a "*cocoon for the production of an individual.*"[30]

The court noted the 1993 Hague Convention, the 1989 United Nations Convention on the Rights of the Child, and the European Convention on the Adoption of Children.

The court did not find any violation of the respect for family life, as there were no particular obstacles or practical difficulties in enjoying family life together.

However, the court found that the refusal of Danish authorities to allow the adoption meant there was a de facto refusal of the parent-child relationship, which had extended over seven years, during all of which time the children recognized the intended mother as their mother. Danish authorities had not struck a fair balance between the interests of the children in obtaining a legal parent-child relationship with the intended mother and the abstract concept of the rights of others who in general and in the abstract risked being negatively affected by commercial surrogacy.

29. *Id.* ¶ 22.
30. *Id.* ¶ 30.

There had therefore been a violation of the children's right to respect for their private life.

C v. Italy, ECtHR Application 47196/21 (2023)

A heterosexual couple from Italy underwent surrogacy in Ukraine. An embryo was implanted, from the sperm of the intended father and an egg from an anonymous donor. A girl was born in Ukraine. The Ukrainian birth certificate, in accordance with the Ukrainian Civil Code, recognized that the girl's parents were the Italian couple.

Italian authorities refused to register the birth, as it was contrary to public policy.

The Court followed the principles laid out in *Mennesson*, *Labassee*, *D v. France*, and its Advisory Opinion. Accordingly, Article 8 required that domestic law provide a possibility of recognition of the legal relationship between a child born through a surrogacy arrangement abroad and the intended father where he was the biological father. The lack of such a possibility entailed a violation of the child's right to respect for his or her private life as guaranteed by Article 8.

The choice of means by which to permit recognition of the legal relationship between the child and the intended parent fell within the States' margin of appreciation. There was no consensus in Europe about recognition of the legal relationship between the child and an intended parent through surrogacy. An individual's identity was less directly at stake where the issue was not the very principle of the establishment or recognition of his or her parentage, but rather the means to be implemented to that end. In addition, in the absence of recognition of a legal relationship between a child born through a surrogacy arrangement carried out abroad and the intended parent, it was in the child's interest that any legal uncertainty as to his or her identity within society in terms of establishing his or her parentage be as short-lived as possible.

In that connection, there was a duty to exercise exceptional diligence when a person's relationship with his or her child was at stake, as the passage of time might result in a de facto determination of the matter.

Each Contracting State had to equip itself with legal instruments that were adequate and sufficient to ensure compliance with the positive obligations imposed on it under Article 8 of the Convention, including the duty to exercise exceptional diligence when a person's relationship with his or her child was at stake.

It was of no concern to the Court by which means the parentage of a child born through a surrogacy arrangement abroad was established or recognized (partial or full registration of the details of the foreign birth certificate, full or simple adoption, fresh establishment of the legal relationship in the child's country of residence), but it had to verify that the decision-making process of the child's State of residence, seen as a whole, adequately ensured the protection of the interests at stake. It was thus paramount that the procedure laid down by domestic law for establishing parentage could be implemented promptly and effectively, in accordance with the child's best interests, so that he or she was not kept for a lengthy period in a position of legal uncertainty.

In order to ensure a "prompt" and "effective" result in accordance with the child's best interests when it came to establishing a legal parent-child relationship between a biological parent and a child born through a surrogacy arrangement abroad: (1) the decision-making process had to be sufficiently focused on the child's best interests and, to that end, free of excessive formalism and apt to further those interests irrespective of any procedural flaws; (2) the domestic courts were required to cooperate with the parties by pointing to the legal solutions available, irrespective of their specific requests.

By a majority of six to one, the Court held that Italian authorities had failed to fulfil their positive obligation to the child's right to respect for her private life. Italy was ordered to pay €15,000 in respect of nonpecuniary damage.

The Court unanimously dismissed the application concerning the establishment of the legal parent-child relationship between the child and the intended mother.

The Court had to determine whether the refusal to recognize the legal relationship between the child and her intended mother, as established by the foreign birth certificate, was compatible with the child's right to respect for her private and family life.

While Italian law did not allow for transcription of the birth certificate details concerning the intended mother, it nevertheless afforded her the possibility of legally recognizing the child by adoption.

According to the Plenary Court of Cassation, adoption allowed courts to assess the requirements of Article 8 and the child's best interests. That review would be carried out on the basis of prerequisites that each State could establish in accordance with its margin of appreciation, for instance by requiring a relationship between the two parents and the involvement of the intended parent in the parental project through specific acts.

The Court found that the desire to have a parent-child relationship recognized between the applicant and the intended mother was not generally and absolutely impossible to satisfy.

As a result, by refusing to enter the details of the applicant's foreign birth certificate in the relevant civil register insofar as it designated the intended mother as her mother, the respondent State had not, in the circumstances of the present case, overstepped its margin of appreciation.

The EU

An effect of the EU is that EU citizens can move freely within the EU. As seen in Chapter 7, there are differing rules in European jurisdictions about how same-sex parentage is recognized. An ongoing issue when families move internationally is whether parentage, recognized in jurisdiction 1, will be recognized in jurisdiction 2.

Two decisions of the Court of Justice of the European Union have enabled the recognition of parentage of lesbian couples across EU countries, provided that they are recognized in jurisdiction 1, which is an EU Member. In both cases, a lesbian couple had ART in Spain, where their parentage was recognized.

Baby Sara

Baby Sara was conceived and born in Spain through ART to a lesbian couple. Her mothers came from Bulgaria and Gibraltar. Neither were of Spanish descent. Spanish citizenship as a result was refused.

Under the British Nationality Act, a child is not eligible for British citizenship by descent from a Gibraltar-born parent.

Sara's mothers then sought to register the birth in Bulgaria. Bulgarian authorities did not recognize the Spanish birth certificate, because same-sex unions are not recognized in Bulgaria, and two people of the same sex cannot be registered as the parents on a child's birth certificate.

Various directives of the EU allow the right of citizens of the EU and their family members to move and reside freely within Member States.

Bulgaria was opposed to recognizing both mothers as the parents. The Court of Justice of the European Union stated:

> The rules on parentage determine the family relationships which are at the heart of family law. They represent the essence of the conception which the Republic of Bulgaria is seeking to protect as its national identity. . . . The definition of a family and its members is of fundamental importance for the State community. Hence, the obligation to transcribe the Spanish birth certificate

would even lead to prejudging to whom the Republic of Bulgaria must grant nationality.[31]

However, families come in all shapes and sizes:

> Admittedly, it could be argued, and with good reason, that the legal recognition of other forms of family life would not have any negative impact on the conception of the "traditional" family which the Republic of Bulgaria is seeking to protect, but would leave it completely untouched. . . .
>
> However, on the other hand, it should be noted that a significant number of the obstacles to the applicant's freedom of movement . . . can be removed by recognising the family relationships established in Spain for the sole purpose of applying secondary EU law on the free movement of citizens. Thus, the recognition of her daughter as her "direct descendant" . . . and the recognition of her wife as her "spouse" . . . . would have the effect of enabling them to reside in the territory of the Bulgarian State together with the applicant.[32]

The court held:

> Since the obligation to recognise the family relationships established in Spain for the sole purpose of applying secondary EU law on the free movement of citizens does not alter the conceptions of parentage or marriage in Bulgarian family law, nor does it lead to the introduction of new conceptions in that law, it must be considered that a refusal to recognise the applicant and her wife as the child's parents for those purposes goes beyond what is necessary to safeguard those objectives.
>
> It must therefore be concluded that . . . Bulgaria may not refuse to recognise the applicant and her wife as the child's parents for the sole purpose of applying secondary EU law on the free movement of citizens on the ground that Bulgarian law does not provide for the institution of marriage between persons of the same sex or for the maternity of the wife of the biological mother of a child.[33]

---

31. Case C-490/20, VMA v. Sofia Mun., ECLI:EU:C:2021:1008, ¶ 105 (Dec. 14, 2021).

32. *Id.* ¶¶ 107–108.

33. *Id.* ¶¶ 114–115.

Baby Sofia

Baby Sofia was conceived and born through ART in Spain to two mothers, Kashka from Poland and Sinéad from Ireland. The Spanish birth certificate named both mothers, but did not issue identity documents, as children of foreigners are not automatically entitled to Spanish citizenship.

Poland refused to issue identity documents for Baby Sofia.

Applying the *Baby Sara* case, the Court of Justice of the European Union said:

> [The relevant directive] requires the Polish authorities to issue an identity card or a passport to [Sofia] regardless of whether the Spanish birth certificate for that child has been transcribed into the Polish register of civil status. Therefore, in so far as Polish law requires the birth certificate to be transcribed before a Polish identity card or a Polish passport is issued, that Member State cannot rely on its national law as justification for refusing to draw up such an identity card or such a passport for [Sofia]. . . .
>
> Such a document, whether alone or accompanied by others, where appropriate by a document issued by the host Member State of the child concerned, must enable a child in [Sofia]'s situation to exercise the right to move and reside freely within the territory of the Member States, guaranteed in Article 21(1) [Treaty on the Functioning of the European Union (TFEU)], with each of the child's two mothers, whose status as parent of that child has been established by their host Member State during a stay. . . .
>
> It is important, furthermore, to note that the rights which nationals of Member States enjoy under Article 21(1) TFEU include the right to lead a normal family life, together with their family members, both in their host Member State and in the Member State of which they are nationals when they return to the territory of that Member State. . . .
>
> It is common ground that . . . the Spanish authorities lawfully established that there was a parent-child relationship, biological or legal, between [Sofia] and her two parents, [Kashka] and [Sinéad], and confirmed this in the birth certificate issued in respect of the child of those two parents. [Kashka] and [Sinéad] must, therefore, pursuant to Article 21 TFEU, as parents of a citizen of the Union who is a minor and of whom they are the primary carers, be recognised by all Member States as having the right to accompany that

child when her right to move and reside freely within the territory of the Member States is being exercised. . . .

Consequently, since [Sofia] has, according to the findings of the referring court, Polish nationality, the Polish authorities are required, as are the authorities of any other Member State, to recognise that parent-child relationship for the purpose of permitting that child to exercise without impediment, with each of her two parents, her right to move and reside freely within the territory of the Member States as guaranteed in Article 21(1) TFEU.

In addition, in order to enable [Sofia] to exercise her right to move and reside freely within the territory of the Member States with each of her two parents, [Kashka] and [Sinéad] must have a document which mentions them as being persons entitled to travel with that child.

The obligation for a Member State to issue an identity card or a passport to a child who is a national of that Member State, who was born in another Member State and whose birth certificate issued by the authorities of that other Member State designates as the child's parents two persons of the same sex, and, moreover, to recognise the parent-child relationship between that child and each of those two persons in the context of the child's exercise of his or her rights under Article 21 TFEU and secondary legislation relating thereto does not require the Member State of which the child concerned is a national to provide, in its national law, for the parenthood of persons of the same sex, or to recognise, for purposes other than the exercise of the rights which that child derives from EU law, the parent-child relationship between that child and the persons mentioned on the birth certificate drawn up by the authorities of the host Member State as being the child's parents. . . .

[A] national measure that is liable to obstruct the exercise of freedom of movement for persons may be justified only where such a measure is consistent with the fundamental rights guaranteed by the Charter. . . .

In the situation with which the main proceedings are concerned, the right to respect for private and family life guaranteed in Article 7 of the Charter and the rights of the child guaranteed in Article 24 thereof, in particular a child's right to have his or her best interests taken into account as a primary consideration in all actions relating to children, and a child's right to maintain on a regular basis a personal relationship and direct contact with both his or her parents, are fundamental.

Accordingly, the relationship between the child concerned and each of the two persons with whom she leads a genuine family life in the host Member State and who are mentioned as being her parents on the birth certificate drawn up by the authorities of that Member State is protected under Article 7 of the Charter.

In addition, since Article 24 of the Charter, as the Explanations relating to the Charter of Fundamental Rights . . . note, represents the integration into EU law of the principal rights of the child referred to in the Convention on the Rights of the Child, which has been ratified by all the Member States, it is necessary, when interpreting that article, to take due account of the provisions of that convention. . . .

In particular, Article 2 of that convention establishes, for the child concerned, the principle of non-discrimination, which requires that the rights set forth in that convention, which include, in Article 7 thereof, the right to be registered immediately after birth, the right to a name and the right to acquire a nationality, be ensured in respect of that child without there being discrimination against the child in that regard, including discrimination on the basis of her parents' sexual orientation.

In those circumstances, it would be contrary to the fundamental rights which are guaranteed to that child under Articles 7 and 24 of the Charter for her to be deprived of the relationship with one of her parents when exercising her right to move and reside freely within the territory of the Member States or for her exercise of that right to be made impossible or excessively difficult in practice on the ground that her parents are of the same sex. . . .

Having regard to all of the foregoing, the answer to the question referred is that Articles 20 and 21 TFEU, read in conjunction with Articles 7 and 24 of the Charter and Article 4(3) of Directive 2004/38, must be interpreted as meaning that, in the case of a minor child who is a citizen of the Union and whose birth certificate, issued by the authorities of a Member State, designates as that child's parents two persons of the same sex, the Member State of which that child is a national (i) is obliged to issue to that child an identity card or a passport without requiring the prior transcription of a birth certificate of that child into the national register of civil status, and (ii) is obliged to recognise, as is any

> other Member State, the document from another Member State that permits that child to exercise without impediment, with each of those two persons, his or her right to move and reside freely within the territory of the Member States.[34]

Brussels II Revised

Starting in 1998, with the Brussels I Regulation, the EU moved to ensure that there be EU rules on jurisdiction, recognition, and enforcement of judgments in matrimonial matters and matters of parental responsibility. This then was quickly replaced with what became known as Brussels II in 2000. The intent was to supplement the 1980 and 1996 Hague Conventions.

In 2000, France sought that Brussels II be extended to ensure that there be mutual enforcement of judgments on rights of access to children.

This culminated in 2003 with Brussels II Revised,[35] which extended Brussels II accordingly. However, Brussels II Revised does not extend to establishment of parenting. Recital (10) provides:

> This Regulation . . . does not apply to the establishment of parenthood, since this is a different matter from the attribution of parental responsibility, nor to other questions linked to the status of persons. . . .

European Human Tissue Directive

This directive[36] applies to all human tissue, including gametes, in the EU. The objective of the directive is to have high standards of quality and safety for human tissues and cells, in order to ensure a high level of protection of human health.[37] The definition of "tissue" includes gametes, but it is unclear if it includes embryos:

---

34. Case C-2/21, Praw Obywatelskich v. K.S., ECLI:EU:C:2022:502, ¶¶ 39–52 (June 24, 2022).

35. Council Regulation (EC) No. 2201/2003 of 27 November 2003 concerning Jurisdiction and the Recognition and Enforcement of Judgments in Matrimonial Matters and the Matters of Parental Responsibility, Repealing Reglation (EC) No. 1347/2000, 2003 O.J. (L 338) 1.

36. Directive 2004/23/EC, of the European Parliament and of the Council of 31 March 2004 on Setting Standards of Quality and Safety for the Donation, Procurement, Testing, Processing, Preservation, Storage, and Distribution of Human Tissues and Cells, 2004 O.J. (L 102) 48.

37. *Id.* art. 1.

> "[T]issue" means all constituent parts of the human body formed by cells.[38]

As sometimes seen with the definitions of "donor" and "donation," there are circular definitions. Therefore, while the directive might be thought to apply relevantly only to donations to others, it will also catch those who are using their gametes in ART.

"Donor" is defined as meaning "every human source, whether living or deceased, of human cells or tissues."[39] "Donation" is defined as meaning "donating human tissues or cells intended for human applications."[40]

As would be expected, there is a requirement for traceability, including for imports and exports from other countries,[41] and when exported from the EU to IVF clinics and banks in other countries that are accredited or licensed.[42]

The intention is to ensure that donors are voluntary and unpaid, and only that compensation is provided to make good the expenses and inconveniences related to the donation. Each EU country can set their own rules but must report to the EU every three years.[43]

As of mid-2023, the relevant committee of the European Parliament proposed updating the directive. However, these proposed changes[44] do not appear to change the substance of the directive.

Subject to national laws that may require disclosure of the identity of a gamete donor, donation is anonymous.[45]

The directive states that the European Commission shall establish EU standards for the quality of donated tissue.[46] The relevant standard

38. *Id.* art. 2.
39. *Id.*
40. *Id.*
41. *Id.* art. 9.1.
42. *Id.*
43. *Id.* art. 12.
44. *Draft Report on the Proposal for a Regulation of the European Parliament and of the Council on Standards of Quality and Safety for Substances of Human Origin Intended for Human Application and Repealing Directives 2002/98/EC and 2004/23/EC* (Jan. 18, 2023), https://www.europarl.europa.eu/doceo/document/ENVI-PR-738661_EN.pdf.
45. Directive 2004/23/EC, *supra* note 36, art. 14.
46. *Id.* art. 16.1.

precludes the use of donor gametes or embryos (where the recipient is other than the partner of the donor) where the donor tests positive for HIV.[47]

The effect is to preclude HIV-positive men (even with an undetectable viral load) from providing their sperm in the EU, or creating embryos in the EU, even if it is with the intention of shipping overseas, such as to the United States.

There is one variation, and one (as of late 2023) upcoming exception.

The Variation: Denmark

Denmark has a variation to the testing regime. However, the likely impact is the same. The European Centre for Disease Prevention and Control has said:

> A guidance document issued by the Danish health authorities[48] states:
>
> > "Sperm donation may take place regularly every week or several times a week over a longer coherent period of time. In such cases, the Danish Patient Safety Authority accepts that blood sampling is performed at the time of the first donation, and subsequently at least every three months. The concurrent donor should be asked every three months about possible changes in relation to risk behaviour. It is a prerequisite that a quarantine period of 180 days is applied, with subsequent retesting of the donor. If the blood donations sample is subject to additional tests for HIV, [hepatitis B virus] and [hepatitis C virus] by [nucleic acid test], retesting after 180 days can be omitted."
>
> The Danish Patient Safety Authority's reason for adopting this approach (blood samples taken and tested at least every three months and not at each time a donor produces a sample of sperm) significantly reduces the amount of diagnostic work: taking blood samples each time a donor produces a sample of sperm may not be practicable and acceptable. In practice, non-partner sperm donors are requested to provide two to three sperm samples per week over the course of several weeks.

47. Commission Directive 2006/17/EC of 8 February 2006 Implementing Directive 2004/23/EC of the European Parliament and of the Council as Regards Certain Technical Requirements for the Donation, Procurement, and Testing of Human Tissues and Cells, art. 3.2, 2006 O.J. (L 330M) 162.

48. VEJ no. 9356 of 26/05/2015, at 57.

> The Danish Patient Safety Authority concludes that their procedure for non-partner sperm donation and donor blood sampling will prevent the transmission of the infectious diseases tested for.[49]

Proposed Change: United Kingdom

Following Brexit, the UK government announced in late 2023 that it would introduce a bill so that HIV-positive egg and sperm donors who have an undetectable viral load will be able to proceed with ART. The change will impact on lesbian couples undertaking reciprocal IVF, and, among others, gay couples undertaking surrogacy—as genetic intended parents through reciprocal IVF or surrogacy are considered to be donors.

Next Steps?

If the European Parliament moves in any direction, it may seek to make surrogacy abroad harder for those living in the EU.

A proposed anti-trafficking amendment by two European Parliament committees in October 2023 targeted surrogacy. The proposed changes included:

> In order to tackle the steady increase of the number and relevance of offences concerning trafficking in human beings committed for purposes other than sexual or labour exploitation, it is necessary to include forced marriage, including those involving children, surrogacy and illegal adoption in the forms of exploitations explicitly listed in the Directive and to ensure that the Member States address within their national legal systems the widest range of forms of exploitation, insofar as these fulfil the constitutive elements of trafficking in human beings. . . .
>
> Surrogacy exposes both [mother and child] to high risk of exploitation—due to the lack of harmonised or clear rules banning this practice at international level—and to unscrupulous commercialization. This situation causes a significant increase in demand for trafficking in human beings and must be taken into account when identifying and combating this phenomenon. . . .

---

49. European Centre for Disease Prevention and Control, Technical Report: Laboratory Testing of Non-Partner Sperm Donors—An Assessment of Potential Risks Involved in Changing the Current Testing Protocols for HIV, Hepatitis B, and Hepatitis C (2018), https://www.ecdc.europa.eu/sites/default/files/documents/Testing-non-partner-sperm-donations.pdf.

The regulation of surrogacy in some Member States has made it possible to register minors who have been taken from their parents with the intention of selling them and making them victims of human trafficking networks. . . .

In order to clarify a legal uncertainty in the definition of trafficking in human beings, this Directive adopts a broader concept of what it should be considered than under Directive 2011/36/EU and Framework Decision 2002/629/JHA, and therefore includes additional forms of exploitation. The contract, usually called surrogacy, through which a natural or legal person agrees with a woman that she will carry a child for the purpose of handing it upon birth, regardless of the name and terms and conditions of such contract, is considered human trafficking, both of the woman who carries or is to carry the child and of the child. . . .

In accordance with the European Parliament resolution of the 21st of January 2021 on the EU Strategy for Gender Equality (2019/2169(INI)), in its paragraph 32, which "acknowledges that sexual exploitation for surrogacy and reproductive purposes or purposes such as forced marriages, prostitution and pornography is unacceptable and a violation of human dignity and human rights". In accordance with the European Parliament resolution of the 10th of February 2021 on the implementation of Directive 2011/36/EU on preventing and combating trafficking in human beings and protecting its victims (2020/2029(INI)), in its paragraph 28, that classifies surrogacy as a Traffic in Human Beings. In accordance with the European Parliament resolution of 5th of May 2022 on the impact of the war against Ukraine on women (2022/2633(RSP)), that "underlines the serious impact of surrogacy on women, their rights and their health, the negative consequences for gender equality and the challenges stemming from the cross-border implications of this practice, as has been the case for the women and children affected by the war against Ukraine; asks the EU and its Member States to investigate the dimensions of this industry, the socio-economic context and the situation of pregnant women, as well as the consequences for their physical and mental health and for the well-being of babies; calls for the introduction of binding measures to address surrogacy, protecting women's and newborns' rights".[50]

50. *Amendments 29–294: Draft Report Amending Directive 2011/36/EU on Preventing and Combating Trafficking in Human Beings and Protecting Its Victims* (July

In light of that inflammatory language, it is not surprising that there was a subsequent press release by the lead Members of the European Parliament:

> Last week, the Women's Rights and Civil Liberties committees adopted Parliament's draft position on the revision of the rules of combating trafficking in human beings. It focuses on prevention, boosting protection and support to victims, as well as tackling the crime more effectively.
>
> There have been claims that the text would entail a general ban on surrogacy. This is not the case. The adopted text only addresses surrogacy for reproductive exploitation in the context of trafficking. The explicit reference to "surrogacy for reproductive exploitation" would ensure that if a woman is recruited by being threatened to become a surrogate for the purpose of reproductive exploitation, she would be considered a victim of trafficking and benefit from the rights under these rules, while the traffickers would be prosecuted.
>
> Only when all the elements of trafficking occur—conduct, means and purpose—is it considered an offence, as defined in the 2011 rules, otherwise it cannot be considered a trafficking case. . . .
>
> Lead [Member of the European Parliament (MEP)] for the Women's Rights and Gender Equality Committee Maria Eugenia Rodriguez Palop (The Left, Spain) added:
>
> > "The proposal is very clear and legally sound—this is not about criminalising surrogacy but about including surrogacy in the context of trafficking, where reproductive exploitation has taken place. We are therefore solely talking about victims of this crime. Also, there are many other issues the proposal tackles, and numerous measures to assist, support and protect victims are at stake."
>
> Lead MEP for the Civil Liberties, Justice and Home Affairs Committee Malin Björk (The Left, Sweden) concluded:
>
> > "The text does not ban surrogacy in general, but it would criminalise surrogacy in the context of trafficking. For surrogacy to be an offence under the directive, all elements of

7, 2023), https://www.europarl.europa.eu/meetdocs/2014_2019/plmrep/COMMITTEES/CJ01/AM/2023/10-05/1282466EN.pdf.

> the crime constituting trafficking have to be present. This means that only surrogacy carried out through the use of force, threat or coercion would fall under the directive."[51]

In April 2024, the European Parliament voted to amend an existing anti–human trafficking directive to include further categories of trafficking, including "the exploitation of surrogacy."[52]

A possibility is that all or almost all international surrogacy for EU residents will cease. Another is that some of the exploitative behaviour seen in recent surrogacy scandals will be targeted. Lawmakers will have seen news reports only two months before from Greece, where there were arrests of eight of the ten staff at an IVF clinic in Crete. Greek authorities charged the owner and medical director and seven other staff at Mediterranean Fertility Institute in August 2023 with trafficking of donors and surrogates, including from the republic of Georgia, and IVF-related fraud.

Let's see.

Take Away

1. Each European country should be considered separately as to what rules may apply to international ART.
2. Generally, surrogacy is frowned upon in Europe—but not everywhere.
3. Parentage of children born in an EU country to lesbian couples (if they are recognized as the parents in the country of birth) is recognized throughout the EU, but there remain barriers to recognition.
4. Extreme care should be taken with the European Court of Human Rights jurisprudence when it comes to surrogacy, as decisions are often based on local factors, and the facts of the case at hand. Check as to the country involved first, then the specific local

51. *EU Parliament: Surrogacy Only Criminalised in the Context of Trafficking under New Proposals*, Insight EU Monitoring (Oct. 12, 2023), https://ieu-monitoring.com/editorial/eu-parliament-surrogacy-only-criminalised-in-the-context-of-trafficking-under-new-proposals/418169.

52. European Parliament legislative resolution of 23 April 2024 on the proposal for a directive of the European Parliament and of the Council amending Directive 2011/36/EU on preventing and combating trafficking in human beings and protecting its victims (COM(2022)0732 – C9-0431/2022 – 2022/0426(COD)), https://www.europarl.europa.eu/doceo/document/TA-9-2024-0310_EN.html.

laws impacted. How the child's parentage is established abroad (judgment or operation of law) may make a difference. Whether there is a genetic link between the intended parents and the child may also make a difference.

5. Exporting gametes from the EU remains difficult for HIV-positive people, although there is a glimmer of light in the United Kingdom.

Chapter 3

Where Do Intended Parents Go?

This chapter focuses on where intended parents go for their surrogacy journeys.

There are a limited number of countries in which surrogacy is readily available. The global leader has always been seen as the United States. Other countries have in the past been hotbeds for the undertaking of surrogacy—which was then shut down, sometimes very quickly—for example, India, Nepal, Thailand, and Cambodia. More recently, other countries where surrogacy for heterosexual couples has been available have closed their doors to international intended parents—Russia and Georgia.[1]

Countries That Have a Liberal Surrogacy Regime

These countries are:

The United States

I am indebted to Dean Hutchison for making the comment some years ago that intended parents from overseas see the journey to the United States as being a journey to the United States for surrogacy, whereas it is a journey to 51 different places for surrogacy.

Ukraine

When Russia invaded Ukraine in February 2022, in vitro fertilization (IVF) clinics and surrogacy agencies stopped functioning. Within about a year of the invasion, surrogacy in Ukraine recommenced. In recent years, Ukraine has been the second largest surrogacy destination after the United

1. As of June 2023, the Health Minister announced that laws would be enacted by January 1, 2024, banning international parents from undertaking surrogacy in Georgia. As of May 2024, the ban had not commenced. Reports from Georgia indicate that the ban will not be proceeding.

States, and is available to heterosexual married couples only, where at least one of them has a genetic connection with the child. Nevertheless, surrogacy in Ukraine has been brisk, as seen in the videos from the largest surrogacy provider there, which showed a nursery full of babies born in Ukraine but stuck there due to the pandemic, and as seen with videos of children being bunkered down following the Russian invasion.

Surrogacy in Ukraine is governed by the Ukrainian Family Code by which the intended parents are recognized as the parents by operation of law upon the birth of the child. It is highly recommended that the intended parents are in Ukraine by the time the child is born so that they can execute the necessary consents for registration.

There have been reports of questionable practices by some surrogacy agencies in Ukraine. I have certainly seen some Ukrainian surrogacy agreements that mandated that the surrogate have a C-section. That does not appear to be common.

Canada

The payment of a fee to the surrogate under Canadian law is an offence under the Assisted Human Reproduction Act. Surrogacy thrives in Canada, although it is of a much smaller scale than that in the United States. Who is a parent varies province by province. See Chapter 12.

Mexico

Mexico is a federation of 31 states. It is possible, at least in Mexico City and in Jalisco State, to have pre-birth orders recognizing the intended parents as the parents. It is unclear whether pre-birth orders can be obtained throughout Mexico.

Surrogacy is banned in two states: Coahuila and Querétaro. Surrogacy is regulated in two states: Sinaloa and Tabasco. In the other 27 states, there is a lack of regulation about surrogacy—hence the warning by the U.S. Embassy. See Chapter 10.

Colombia

Surrogacy has become popular in Colombia in recent years. There is no regulation. The Supreme Court has raised concerns about the lack of regulation, as seen in Chapter 6.

The common practice is that upon the birth of the child, the intended genetic father is shown as the father on the birth certificate, and the surrogate as the mother. A subsequent court order is then obtained to remove the surrogate as the mother and to have the other intended parent (male or female) in the surrogate's place.

Argentina

Surrogacy is practiced in Buenos Aires where, by operation of law, the intended parents are recognized as the parents upon the birth of the child. See Chapter 10.

Georgia

The republic of Georgia allowed heterosexual couples to undertake surrogacy there, where they were recognized by operation of law upon the birth of the child under the Georgia Health Code as the parents of the child—much in the same way as Ukraine or Kazakhstan. In June 2023, the Health Minister of Georgia announced that laws would be enacted and in force so that by January 1, 2024, surrogacy for foreign intended parents would be banned. By April 2024, the proposed laws had been presented to Parliament, but not enacted, and it would appear that the ban is not proceeding.

Russia

Russia allowed surrogacy for foreign intended parents provided that they were heterosexual married couples, as seen in the case of *Paradiso & Campanelli v. Italy*.[2] See Chapter 2. Despite the restrictions under Russian law, nevertheless, some surrogacy promoters promoted foreign single intended parents or gay couples to undertake surrogacy in Russia.

Surrogacy has not been available for foreign intended parents since 2022.

More Restricted Availability

Hong Kong

In theory, surrogacy can occur in Hong Kong. The Human Reproductive Technology Ordinance specifically allows for the licensing of IVF clinics to provide surrogacy services for heterosexual married couples. In reality, no clinic has ever been licensed. Hong Kong couples go overseas. They then put themselves potentially in peril in committing a breach of extraterritorial surrogacy laws, which ban overseas egg, sperm, and embryo agreements and commercial surrogacy. See Chapter 4.

South Korea

South Korea is illustrative of there being no laws on surrogacy. One may think therefore that surrogacy is widely available, and that anything goes. By contrast, surrogacy in South Korea is difficult to undertake.

2. App. No. 25358/12 (Dec. 9, 2015).

Surrogacy only rarely occurs. When I visited the largest IVF clinic in Asia, in Seoul, in 2019, I was told that the clinic had only undertaken two surrogacy journeys—both between sisters. The process of transferring parentage was via adoption. The clinic was concerned that if it undertook surrogacy more broadly, then, as the preeminent and largest clinic, that other clinics would follow, causing a rush and therefore requiring severe government intervention. It was decided, instead, to take a very cautious approach and only permit through the clinic any surrogacy that was between sisters. Even surrogacy between mother and daughter was not permitted by the clinic.

India

Surrogacy is available in India to heterosexual couples or to single women—if the surrogacy arrangement is altruistic. What has been unclear has been whether surrogacy in India is available to Overseas Citizens of India (OCI). India does not recognize dual citizenship. When Indians migrate—and take up citizenship elsewhere—they lose Indian citizenship. However, they gain OCI status, which, while they are not citizens, gives them some special status in India, for example in the ownership of land.

Australian data shows that seeking to prevent Australians from going overseas for commercial surrogacy backfired, as the numbers of Australian intended parents going to India skyrocketed, and then gradually declined, as India made it harder and harder for foreigners, and in particular Australians, to undertake surrogacy there.

With the passage of the Surrogacy (Regulation) Act, 2021, one would have expected that the number of foreign births would have crashed to zero. At least for Australian intended parents, it would appear that the number of births via surrogacy in India is increasing, albeit off a low base. The only possible explanation is that the intended parents (who must be Australian citizens, as the data concerns Australian citizenship by descent) must be OCIs. This therefore seems to illustrate that Indian authorities are allowing OCIs to access surrogacy in India.

For some years, I have obtained data from the Australian government under freedom of information. Australia seems unique in the world in collating data for the number of applications for citizenship by descent by those born overseas through surrogacy. The data is then broken down into where the child was born.

While the data has an Australian focus, it is also illustrative of wider trends. Table 3.1 shows the number of children born in India who applied for Australian citizenship by descent between 2009 and 2023. The data is collated on a fiscal year basis (i.e., from July 1 of one year until June 30 of the following year).

Table 3.1. Australian Surrogacy Births via India 2009–2022[3]

Year	No. of Births
2009	<10
2010	<10
2011	<10
2012	227
2013	191
2014	108
2015	74
2016	54
2017	14
2018	<5
2019	<5
2020	<5
2021	0
2022	<5
2023	5

The two most significant years are 2012 and 2023. In 2012, the number of Australian children born increased from fewer than ten (which was then the smallest number used for privacy purposes, now it is five), to 227.

The reason for that extraordinary outcome is an own goal in public policy. In 2010, New South Wales joined Queensland and the Australian Capital Territory in criminalizing surrogacy extraterritorially. See Chapter 4. When New South Wales did so, the government did not engage in any prior consultation. There was no public report suggesting the change. The change was not even part of the bill before Parliament. Instead, the change was by way of a surprise amendment by the Minister. The bill quickly became law.

There was a firestorm of publicity. Many couples who did not know until then that they could be parents through surrogacy, suddenly became

3. Australian Department of Home Affairs, Applications for Citizenship by Descent of Children Born via Surrogacy (obtained by author under freedom of information applications).

aware. Media reports and community seminars highlighted the role of India. Voila! An extraordinary increase in the number of Australian children born in India.

From 2012, steps taken by the Indian government limited the abilities of foreigners, including Americans and Australians, to undertake surrogacy there. At first, the Indian government took administrative action, requiring foreign intended parents to make plain to Indian authorities that surrogacy was legal back home. India had made this move following children not being able to return home to their parents' countries in Europe.

Then in 2014, news reports came about concerning an Australian couple, Mr. and Mrs. Farnell, who had undertaken surrogacy in Thailand—but only one of the children, Baby Pypah, had travelled with them to Australia to live. The other, Baby Gammy, was kept by the surrogate, Mrs. Chanbua, in Thailand. The Baby Gammy saga, as it became known, then revealed that Mrs. Chanbua had falsified her age, and that she had always wanted a boy—neither of which was known by the Farnells, and that Mr. Farnell was a convicted child sex offender. This was something that Mrs. Chanbua only became aware of through the world's media.

Hot on the heels of the Baby Gammy saga, in 2014 came reports that an Australian couple had undertaken surrogacy in India, had twins, but did not take one of them because it was the "wrong" gender.

Not surprisingly, India reacted by specifically restricting *Australians'* access to surrogacy. Again, not surprisingly, the number of Australian surrogacy births in India kept dropping. Prior to the enactment of the 2021 act, the only Australians undertaking surrogacy in India were OCIs.

By 2022, the number of births of Australian children in India via surrogacy had dropped to zero. But then, in 2023, the number increased to five. While a very small number, this number of births could only have happened if Australian citizens who are OCI undertook surrogacy in India. In turn, this seems to indicate that Indian authorities will allow OCIs to undertake surrogacy there, at least if they are from Australia.

New Zealand

New Zealand allows surrogacy, both domestically and internationally, but by way of an adoption process. Gestational surrogacy in New Zealand must be approved by an ethics committee. Traditional surrogacy therefore does not need, and usually does not have, that approval. The New Zealand Law Commission has recommended a wholesale rewriting of surrogacy law in New Zealand, so that there is an auto-recognition model of the intended parents in noncontroversial cases. Laws to that effect are yet to be enacted.

The Philippines

A conservative Catholic country, the Philippines is the only country other than the Holy See to ban divorce. Surrogacy is unregulated. It has been estimated by the Philippines Society for Reproductive Medicine that in recent years 50 children a year have been born through surrogacy in the Philippines.

The Philippines is illustrative of two points:

1. There is no ability to transfer parentage from the surrogate to the intended parents. Subject to overseas laws allowing termination of parental rights, the surrogate forever remains a parent—and one of the intended parents is not recognized.
2. Filipino authorities are very concerned about child trafficking. Intended parents should take extreme care that they are not caught up in efforts by the State to stamp out child trafficking.

I have received anecdotal reports that hospitals are falsely naming the intended mother on the birth certificate—with potential criminal charges for those concerned.

Thailand

Surrogacy is available in Thailand to heterosexual married couples, if one is a Thai citizen, the surrogacy arrangement is altruistic, and the surrogate is a relative.

Although previously popular, restrictions came about in 2014 in reaction to the Baby Gammy saga and the Thai baby farm. See Chapter 18.

One would think that with those restrictions, all surrogacy for foreigners would have stopped. However, surrogacy has continued to occur for Australians there. Whilst Australia is a multicultural country, and there are certainly migrants in Australia from Thailand, the number of Australian births via surrogacy in Thailand is out of proportion to the number of Thai migrants in Australia.

Media reports and statements by clients show porous borders in Indochina. It is not uncommon for the sperm to be supplied to a clinic in Cambodia, with a Thai egg donor travelling to a clinic in Laos to donate, and a Thai surrogate travelling to that clinic in Laos to become pregnant—and then giving birth, at the option of the intended parents in the close country of their choice, which has been Thailand, China, or Malaysia.

Marketing by agents has typically been on non-English communications, typically on WeChat to Chinese-language intended parents.

Table 3.2 shows that surrogacy in Thailand, at least for Australian intended parents, has continued, despite the above restrictions. As India tightened supply, Australians went to Thailand instead—accounting for the big increase between 2012 and 2014. After the law changed in 2014, the numbers have decreased. However, children have continued to be born to Australian intended parents, consistent with those media and client reports.

Table 3.2. Australian Births via Surrogacy in Thailand 2010–2023[4]

Year	No. of Births
2010	< 10
2011	< 10
2012	< 10
2013	23
2014	91
2015	97
2016	19
2017	12
2018	9
2019	10
2020	11
2021	8
2022	6
2023	6

The United Kingdom

Surrogacy is available in the United Kingdom to intended parents regardless of sexuality or relationship status. The surrogacy must be altruistic. It is a criminal offence to pay someone to negotiate the terms of the surrogacy agreement. A post-birth parental order is made. The United Kingdom does not recognize overseas surrogacy orders, which necessitates intended parents who have obtained foreign orders to then obtain a parental order in the United Kingdom.

The Law Commissions of England and Wales and of Scotland have recommended that the law be changed to allow auto-recognition of parentage at birth, but this is yet to eventuate.

4. *Id.*

The United Kingdom is a net exporter of intended parents, at least partly due to the inability of intended parents to be able to find an egg donor and/or surrogate.

Vietnam

Surrogacy is available in Vietnam to heterosexual couples only. Nevertheless, some underground surrogacy happens in Vietnam, as it does in many other countries, including for single men and gay couples.

Self-evidently, if surrogacy occurs other than in accordance with local law, it may be very difficult for the child's parentage to be recognized in the intended parents' country.

Wild West

There are other countries, described in broad terms by the former Chief Justice of the Family Court of Australia, John Pascoe, Officer of the Order of Australia and Commander of the Royal Victorian Order, as the "*Wild West*," where, in essence, anything goes. These may be countries where surrogacy is a criminal offence, at least by the doctor (such as China—but surrogacy nevertheless occurs). There are countries where there are simply very few, if any, rules concerning surrogacy, and seemingly anything goes. These countries include:

- **Malaysia**. As set out in Chapter 6, surrogacy is available to non-Muslim intended parents—but there will be no transfer of parentage from the surrogate, who will remain on the birth certificate as the mother. Most IVF clinics in Malaysia will not undertake surrogacy—and are devoted to providing IVF only to heterosexual, married couples.
- **Cyprus**. Cyprus is divided between the Republic of Cyprus in the south, with a largely Greek population, and the breakaway Northern Republic of Cyprus, which is only recognized by Türkiye. North Cyprus has a primarily Turkish population. Surrogacy in Cyprus occurs by IVF being undertaken by a clinic in North Cyprus (and therefore occurring in a jurisdiction that is not recognized anywhere other than Türkiye), where by virtue of the contract and traditional presumptions of parentage, the biological father and surrogate are named on the birth certificate as the parents.
- **Kenya**. As seen in Chapter 13, surrogacy in Ghana, Nigeria, and Kenya occurs but is based on adoption law. There have been reports of surrogates in Kenya seeking to extort the intended parents prior to the transfer of parentage occurring.

But Where Do Intended Parents Go?

There are no international figures that give us guidance. Whilst we hear that the United States is the biggest destination and Ukraine is the second biggest destination, no international authority has compiled figures. The best figures that I have seen have been provided by the Australian Department of Home Affairs, which I discussed earlier.

Australia is reputed to have the highest population proportionally of migrants or first-born generation citizens, at 51 percent. Approximately 85–89 percent of Australian children born overseas via surrogacy have been born in one of the significant well-known surrogacy destinations, but the balance is born in many other countries—many of which are not seen as surrogacy destinations.

What I have seen in practice is that many Australian intended parents who have migrated from their country of origin to Australia, not being able to undertake surrogacy in Australia, have travelled to their country of origin to undertake surrogacy there. The countries that I have seen Australians return to include Bangladesh, Brazil, Canada, China, Ghana, Greece, India, Iran, Kenya, New Zealand, Nigeria, Russia, South Africa, Sri Lanka, Thailand, Ukraine, the United States, and Vietnam.

Table 3.3 shows the variety of countries in which children have been born via surrogacy. Many of these countries are not known surrogacy destinations. Known surrogacy destination countries are shaded in gray.

Table 3.3. Australian Overseas Surrogacy Births July 1, 2018–June 30, 2023[5]

Country	2018	2019	2020	2021	2022	2023
Afghanistan						<5
Australia			<5[6]			
Bangladesh	<5					
Belarus				<5		
Brazil		<5		<5		<5

5. *Id.*

6. I don't know how, in one year, a child born via domestic surrogacy was added to the foreign list. However, I was aware of a case where twins were to be born on behalf of an Australian couple to a surrogate in Canada. The intended parents did not have newborn insurance. One of the children needed to be operated upon at birth in order to survive. The intended parents enabled the Canadian surrogate to fly to Australia, so that the children were born in Australia—and so that the costs of medical care for those children was borne by the Australian taxpayer.

Country	2018	2019	2020	2021	2022	2023
Cambodia	<5					
Canada	26	14	34	28	21	22
China	<5	5	9	<5		<5
Colombia				5	7	12
Cyprus					<5	<5
Czech Republic				<5	<5	
Egypt						<5
Ethiopia			< 5			
Georgia	9	16	20	27	7	33
Ghana	<5				<5	<5
Greece	<5	<5	<5	26		7
Guatemala			<5			
Hong Kong	<5					<5
Hungary				<5		
India	<5	<5	<5		<5	5
Iran	<5		<5	<5	<5	<5
Iraq		<5				
Jamacia		<5				
Kazakhstan		<5				
Kenya	<5	5	<5	<5		<5
Lebanon			<5			
Malaysia	<5	<5				
Mexico		<5	6	9	<5	14
Namibia			<5			
New Zealand		<5		<5	<5	

The data from the department stretches back to 2009.

The department used to say that the numbers were fewer than ten for privacy reasons but in 2015, changed that to fewer than five for privacy reasons.

Australia, like every country other than Türkiye, does not recognize the Republic of North Cyprus. Before the Turkish invasion in 1974, the Republic of Cyprus extended over the whole island. Australia deems the child to be born in the Republic of Cyprus, even if the child is born in the north. Some children born through surrogacy in North Cyprus are reported to have been smuggled across the United Nations Line of Control that divides North Cyprus from the Republic of Cyprus, so that their birth is recorded in the Republic of Cyprus and therefore recognized internationally.

Country	2018	2019	2020	2021	2022	2023
Nigeria		<5	<5		<5	<5
Pakistan		<5			<5	<5
Poland					<5	
Russian Federation		<5	7	5	<5	
South Korea					<5	
South Sudan				<5		
Sri Lanka		<5				<5
Thailand	9	10	11	8	6	6
Türkiye					<5	
Ukraine	32	61	50	38	49	43
United Arab Emirates		5				
United Kingdom	<5	<5	<5	<5	<5	<5
United States	67	95	120	76	99	68
Vietnam	<5		<5			
Total of Overseas Births	**170**	**232**	**275**	**223**	**213**	**236**

What Does the Australian Data Tell Us?

One obvious feature is that children have been born in countries where surrogacy is not allowed, or that do not appear to be obvious surrogacy destinations.

It is apparent that in recent years, the *United States* has remained the most popular destination, as seen in Table 3.4. Whether that remains the case, with the significant rise in costs, remains to be seen.

Table 3.4. Australian Surrogacy Births in the United States 2009–2023[7]

Year	No. of Births
2009	<10
2010	0
2011	15
2012	19

7. Australian Department of Home Affairs, Applications for Citizenship by Descent of Children Born via Surrogacy (obtained by author under freedom of information applications).

Year	No. of Births
2013	27
2014	57
2015	57
2016	49
2017	66
2018	67
2019	95
2020	120
2021	76
2022	99
2023	68

Again, the message is the same although not as dramatic as India. The move to criminalize extraterritorial commercial surrogacy in some Australian states has not worked. Consistent with world trends, the United States is the most popular market.

Ukraine has been a consistent surrogacy destination. Surprisingly, the numbers have kept up despite the pandemic. It will be interesting to see as to the number of births in future years, following the Russian invasion. One might have thought, in the aftermath of the invasion, that there were more children born in other European countries, as pregnant Ukrainian surrogates fled overseas. The data only reveals that fewer than five children, possibly one child, were born in each of the Czech Republic and Poland in the year ended June 30, 2022, and none in those countries in the year ended June 30, 2023.

Table 3.5 shows the number of Australian children being born via surrogacy in Ukraine between 2009 and 2023.

Table 3.5. Australian Births via Surrogacy in Ukraine 2009–2023[8]

Year	No. of Births
2009	<10
2010	0
2011	<10
2012	<10
2013	0

8. *Id.*

Year	No. of Births
2014	<10
2015	<5
2016	<5
2017	11
2018	32
2019	61
2020	50
2021	38
2022	49

The gradual rise with Ukraine is also consistent with it being the second most important surrogacy destination worldwide.

In *Canada*, for example, prior to 2016 the numbers were always fewer than ten or fewer than five. From 2015, Canada has remained a popular destination, as seen in Table 3.6.

Table 3.6. Australian Surrogacy Births in Canada 2009–2023[9]

Year	No. of Births
2009	0
2010	0
2011	<10
2012	<10
2013	<10
2014	<10
2015	<5
2016	5
2017	16
2018	26
2019	14
2020	34
2021	28
2022	21
2023	22

9. *Id.*

Even with pandemic restrictions, Canada has remained popular with Australians.

Similarly, with *Georgia*, one sees that prior to 2016 there were no surrogacy births of Australians in Georgia and they then commenced in 2016. Georgia has been a popular destination for Australians since then. It is considerably cheaper to undertake surrogacy there than, say, the United States. Table 3.7 shows Australian surrogacy births in Georgia between 2009 and 2023.

Table 3.7. Australian Surrogacy Births in Georgia 2009–2023[10]

Year	No. of Births
2009	0
2010	0
2011	0
2012	0
2013	0
2014	0
2015	0
2016	<5
2017	8
2018	9
2019	16
2020	20
2021	27
2022	7
2023	33

Another illustration of waves of surrogacy is that of *Mexico.* As set out in Chapter 18, Mexico was popular in the state of Tabasco until, following the exploits of Rudy Rupak and others, surrogacy there was banned to foreigners. See also Chapter 10. In more recent years, Mexico has again been promoted as a surrogacy destination, as reflected in the figures, as seen in Table 3.8.

10. *Id.*

Table 3.8. Australian Surrogacy Births in Mexico 2009–2023[11]

Year	No. of Births
2009	0
2010	0
2011	0
2012	0
2013	0
2014	0
2015	<5
2016	11
2017	6
2018	0
2019	<5
2020	6
2021	9
2022	<5
2023	14

In 2023, the highest number of Australian children via surrogacy were born in Mexico. In part, this is due to marketing to Australians of Mexico as a viable destination. In part, it is a reaction to the high and rising costs in the United States. Mexico is cheap by comparison.

Colombia has only been marketed to Australians in recent years. Only a small proportion of the births there are estimated to be for Australian intended parents. Prior to 2020, there were no Australian children born via surrogacy in Colombia. Now the number is rising, as illustrated in Table 3.9.

Table 3.9. Australian Births via Surrogacy in Colombia 2021–2023[12]

Year	No. of Births
2021	5
2022	7
2023	12

It is illegal in *China* for doctors to undertake surrogacy. Nevertheless, surrogacy continues there. Marketing to Australian intended parents

11. *Id.*
12. *Id.*

has typically occurred via Chinese social media, such as WeChat. Surrogacy for Australians stopped in China with China's closure to outsiders during the pandemic, but has restarted, as seen in Table 3.10.

Table 3.10. Australian Surrogacy Births in China 2009–2023[13]

Year	No. of Births
2009	<10
2010	0
2011	0
2012	0
2013	0
2014	0
2015	0
2016	<5
2017	8
2018	<5
2019	5
2020	9
2021	<5
2022	0
2023	<5

There are close links between the *United Kingdom* and Australia. It is not uncommon for Australian intended parents residing in the United Kingdom to undertake surrogacy there, albeit in small numbers. Those small, but consistent numbers, are seen in Table 3.11.

Table 3.11. Australian Surrogacy Births in the United Kingdom 2009–2023[14]

Year	No. of Births
2009	0
2010	0
2011	0
2012	<10
2013	<5
2014	<5

13. *Id.*
14. *Id.*

Year	No. of Births
2015	<5
2016	<5
2017	<5
2018	<5
2019	<5
2020	<5
2021	<5
2022	<5
2023	<5

Two alternative destinations are Kenya and Iran. Kenya has been promoted for surrogacy for single women and heterosexual couples. Australians who go to Iran are heterosexual couples who migrated from Iran. Table 3.12 shows a comparison of the number of births in each country, each of which commenced in 2018.

Table 3.12. Australian Surrogacy Births in Kenya and Iran 2018–2023[15]

Year	Births in Kenya	Births in Iran
2018	<5	<5
2019	5	0
2020	<5	<5
2021	<5	<5
2022	0	<5
2023	<5	<5

As the figures illustrate, intended parents, at least from Australia, go all over the globe to undertake surrogacy.

Other Countries

While most of the places that Australians go, as stated, are known surrogacy destinations, small numbers go to other countries. In the past, Australian children have also been born via surrogacy in:

- Afghanistan
- Argentina

15. *Id.*

- Bangladesh[16]
- Belarus
- Brazil[17]
- Cambodia[18]
- Cyprus[19]
- Czech Republic
- Egypt
- Ethiopia
- Ghana
- Guatemala
- Hong Kong[20]
- Hungary
- Iraq
- Italy[21]
- Jamaica
- Kazakhstan
- South Korea
- Lebanon
- Malaysia
- Namibia
- Nepal[22]
- New Zealand
- Nigeria
- Pakistan[23]
- Panama
- Papua New Guinea[24]
- South Africa
- Switzerland
- Türkiye
- United Arab Emirates
- Vietnam

---

16. Parentage is established via adoption.
17. Through the requirements of the regulated system.
18. But not since the flow-on from the banning of surrogacy in late 2016, with no births since 2018.
19. See the Wild West section in this chapter.
20. Where surrogacy is not legal.
21. Where surrogacy is not legal.
22. While surrogacy was permitted to foreigners.
23. Where surrogacy is illegal.
24. Where surrogacy is governed by adoptions, but only for locals.

The Roller Door Comes Down

A feature of international surrogacy since 2010 has been at various stages a crisis with surrogacy in one or a number of countries. There have then been two reactions to that crisis. The reaction in places like the United States where there have been allegations of human trafficking by lawyers has been to enforce the law, as happened with California attorney Theresa Erickson and Maryland attorney Hilary Neiman and agent Carla Chambers from Las Vegas, all of whom were sentenced to jail.

Similarly, when there have been clear cases of surrogacy fraud, the book has been thrown at individuals too, such as Allison Layton in California and Greg Blosser, owner of the Surrogacy Group, in Maryland.

The alternative approach, as seen repeatedly in developing countries, is to shut the door, with an immediate impact on surrogates who may be pregnant, intended parents who are either halfway through their journey or have come to that country to collect their child, and the child concerned. We have seen this with the roller doors coming down fast in the countries listed in Table 3.13.

Table 3.13. Countries That Slammed the Door Shut on Surrogacy

Country	When Did It Shut the Door on Surrogacy or Drastically Alter Availability?	Comment
India	2012, 2014, 2016, and, finally, 2021	The first three were by administrative fiat, the last by legislation.
Thailand	2014	Post-Baby Gammy—see Chapter 18; Thai baby farm—see Chapter 18.
Nepal	2016	Interlocutory and then final injunction made by the Supreme Court, then legislation. Surrogacy in Nepal was never allowed by legislation, but by Cabinet decision.
Tabasco, Mexico	2016	Following the adventures of Rudy Rupak—see Chapter 18. In 2021, the Supreme Court opened up surrogacy in Tabasco to gay couples and foreigners—see Chapter 10.
Cambodia	2016	The government decreed overnight that surrogacy was henceforth illegal, it would enact laws to that effect (but it has never done so), but it would charge those engaging in surrogacy with human trafficking offences (and then did so). See Chapter 18.

Escape from Ukraine

Two weeks before the Russian invasion I was contacted by Australian intended parents who had a pregnant surrogate in Ukraine. I was asked about whether the surrogate could come to Australia or what other country would be the best for the surrogate to give birth. I was pessimistic. I took the view that the Russians were likely to invade. My view was to get the surrogate out. I did not care where she got out to, as long as she was safe. From there, she could potentially go somewhere else. The evident places to avoid as a starting point were either Russia or Belarus.

The intended parent came back to me saying that the surrogate didn't want to move because she didn't think that the Russians would invade. They had threatened this many times before. She didn't go.

Even a day before the Russian invasion, I had the same conversation with another intended parent. My clear advice was to get the surrogate out.

Many pregnant surrogates did not believe that there would be an invasion. They remained in Ukraine at the time the Russians invaded. Babies were born in Ukraine at that time through surrogacy. There was then pandemonium. Embryos, eggs, and sperm were shipped overseas, sometimes in the backs of cars, to get them to safety out of Ukraine, driving via back roads to ensure that parents' genetic material was safe. Some clinics moved out of Ukraine altogether, fearful of the implications of war.

Pregnant surrogates were brought into the company of seasoned security guards, who had previously been soldiers, to smuggle them across the border. The same happened with babies and intended parents. Surrogates then gave birth in countries where surrogacy is not recognized, such as Poland. These were challenges visited upon intended parents, surrogates, babies—and the lawyers and agents assisting.

One afternoon in 2014, I was asked by a new client about a proposed surrogacy agreement in Ukraine. Aside from my expressed concern that an offence might be committed as to commercial surrogacy, the agreement provided that it was mandatory for the surrogate to have a C-section. I said that the surrogate's bodily autonomy had been stripped away, which it should not have been.

I also warned about the security situation in Ukraine. My client told me that she was still "95 percent convinced" that she would still sign up with the Ukrainian agency. She had a definite case of baby lust. Desperate to have a child, she was blinded by the risks.

The following morning, she called me. She said, "*In light of your warning about the security situation in the Ukraine, and that plane being shot down last night* [Malaysia Airlines flight MH17], *we decided not to go to Ukraine. You were right!*" My warning had been even more prescient than I could have imagined.

If you have clients who are going to these countries, always keep an eye on what is happening.

Take Away

While necessarily limited in scope, the Australian data shows that Australians go to known surrogacy destinations, but also go elsewhere. There is a lack of data about where nationals of other countries, such as U.S. citizens, undertake surrogacy.

The usual criteria to determine where intended parents go for surrogacy (aside from those who go back to their home country) would be these:

1. What is the cost? For those not going to the most expensive destination, the United States, cost is usually a determinative factor.
2. Is surrogacy available for them there? A gay couple, for example, would not go to Ukraine.
3. Is the country reasonably close, such as one plane flight away? Therefore, intended parents in Europe would be going to Ukraine much more than intended parents coming from Australia, for example.
4. How long does the process take? If surrogates are available now or close to now, then that will make that destination much more tempting.
5. Has the destination been marketed online, via social media, or at seminars?

If you ever have the opportunity to try to convince clients to go to a safer jurisdiction, than a risky jurisdiction, try to do so. The fact that surrogacy may have happened "safely" in the place they propose does not make it safe. Information they may have gleaned from the internet or from self-interested surrogacy promoters will mean nothing to them if the government in that country decides to pull down the roller door halfway through their journey.

Chapter 4

What Is Legal There May Be Illegal Here and Vice Versa

When I was thinking of the name of this chapter, I also thought of a couple of other names, *You say surrogacy, I say child trafficking*, or *Legal today, jail tomorrow.*

One of the assumptions made by intended parents, surrogacy agency owners, and lawyers is that in broadly similar societies, there are broadly similar laws about surrogacy and assisted reproductive technology (ART). That assumption may be completely wrong.

In much of Europe, for example, to undertake surrogacy is a criminal offence. Therefore, undertaking surrogacy overseas may be lawful, because no offence is being committed at home, but the ability to bring the baby back home may be extremely difficult or constrained.

I have said elsewhere in this book not to assume, and wherever possible to work with a counterpart in the country in which your client resides or of which your client is a citizen. Nothing beats what the late Anne-Marie Hutchinson, Order of the British Empire, Queen's Counsel (Honorary), called *"boots on the ground experience."*

A greater difficulty is that in some jurisdictions, what is considered to be good practice turns out to be a criminal offence back where they live or where they have come from. On some occasions, what they might be doing where they are living now, although not a criminal law of where they live, may be the criminal law of where they come from.

I cannot emphasize enough the need for the intended parents to get that legal advice from the other place, and for the lawyer in the destination country to understand the differences, and where possible to accommodate them.

There are two sets of laws that give my clients great grief. For some reason, despite its small size, Australia seems to specialize in making the legal journey for intended parents through surrogacy overseas particularly difficult.

Where Did Comity Go?

The fundamental concept underlying conflicts of law is the comity principle: your laws might be different to mine, but I will respect them anyway. Related to that concept is that my criminal laws only apply here, and do not apply anywhere else. And if I am going to put in place criminal laws, these laws will be legislated, and therefore accessible to all.

There are three exceptions to this comity principle. They are:

- Long-arm laws, which stretch out the criminal jurisdiction of the place to somewhere else
- Extraterritorial laws, which specifically apply an offence committed by someone here to something done there (even though the thing being done is legal there). Some places have *both* long-arm laws and extraterritorial laws.
- When a country is silent about what the law is, or says that there is a law in place (but there is not)—and applies some other law to the transaction

In this chapter, I outline:

- The effect of long-arm laws
- The application of extraterritorial laws
- An example where what the country has said it is going to do is not consistent with what it has done

Long-Arm Laws

It is not my intention to take you, the reader, through some of the obscure features of Australian law because they are Australian law—but because they contain traps for the unwary—and illustrate the point.

Australia, like many other jurisdictions, makes it an offence to engage in commercial egg, sperm, or embryo donation. In each Australian jurisdiction, typically there are two offences that apply, a bigger offence relating to paying an egg, sperm, or embryo donor a commercial amount, which attracts typically a penalty of up to 15 years imprisonment, and a small offence dealing with payment for human tissue, which typically attracts a penalty of six months imprisonment.

In most Australian jurisdictions, there is a long-arm law that specifically applies that jurisdiction's criminal laws somewhere else. The nature of these long-arm laws varies with each jurisdiction. In general terms, however, if the elements of the offence are committed in the home jurisdiction, then the offence can be committed even though the contract is overseas. An example of how these laws work in practice is seen with the example of Thel and Libby.

Thel and Libby

Thel and Libby live in Sydney. They have contracted with an egg donor agency in California to help find them an egg donor. The agency presents them with a contract, which is sent to them either by email (with the expectation that they will print off the PDF copy, sign it, scan it, and email it back) or by electronic means (such as DocuSign). They sign it and send it back. The amount payable to the donor is $15,000—which would be considered to be a commercial amount in New South Wales.

On the face of it, Thel and Libby may have committed two offences in New South Wales, though their actions are lawful in California—an offence punishable by up to 15 years imprisonment, and another offence punishable by up to six months imprisonment.

Under the Human Cloning for Reproduction and Other Prohibited Practices Act 2003 (New South Wales [NSW]), section 16, it is an offence to intentionally give or offer valuable consideration to another person for the supply of a human egg, human sperm, or a human embryo where the maximum penalty of imprisonment is for 15 years, although there is an exception for reasonable expenses.

Under the Crimes Act 1900 (NSW) section 10C, if *part* of the offence is committed in New South Wales or the *effect* of the offence occurs in New South Wales, then the offence is committed in New South Wales.

Therefore, if offer and acceptance occur in New South Wales or money is withdrawn from an account in New South Wales to pay the donor directly in California, then a very serious offence, punishable by up to 15 years imprisonment, can be committed.

Under the Human Tissue Act 1983 (NSW):

> A person must not enter into, or offer to enter into, a contract or arrangement under which any person agrees, for valuable consideration, whether given or to be given to any such person or to any other person—
>
> > (a) to the sale or supply of tissue from any such person's body or from the body of any other person. . . .
>
> Maximum penalty—40 penalty units or imprisonment for 6 months, or both.

There are two exceptions under that act:

> (2) Subsection (1) does not apply to or in respect of the sale or supply of tissue if the tissue has been subjected to processing or treatment and the sale or supply is made for the purpose of enabling the tissue to be used for therapeutic purposes, medical purposes or scientific purposes.

> (3) Subsection (1) does not apply to or in respect of a contract or arrangement providing only for the reimbursement of any expenses necessarily incurred by a person in relation to the removal of tissue in accordance with this Act.

The definition of *tissue* includes not only eggs or sperm and possibly embryos, but also would appear to include breastmilk. It is common in a U.S. surrogacy agreement to provide compensation for the surrogate providing colostrum or breastmilk.

Again, the Crimes Act 1900 (NSW) section 10C is a long-arm law that provides that if *part* of the offence occurs in New South Wales or the *effect* of the offence occurs in New South Wales, then the offence is committed in New South Wales.

One of the founding fathers of Australia, who largely wrote the Australian Constitution and became the first Chief Justice of Australia, Sir Samuel Griffith, was responsible for writing the Queensland Criminal Code (which was subsequently copied interstate). He expressed the view about why there was a need for long-arm laws. He said:

> In consequence, perhaps, of the insular position of England, the common law appears to contain no provision as to the punishment of an offender in a case where several acts or events are necessary to constitute an offence, and where some only of these acts or events occur within the jurisdiction, the rest occurring out of the jurisdiction; such, for instance, as the case of a man who, standing in Queensland territory, shoots a man standing in New South Wales. . . .[1]

He went on to say that the Queensland Criminal Code that he was drawing up was designed to cope with cases like that, cases that involved a man standing in one state who shoots somebody in another or in cases where somebody does something that has an effect in another state or vice versa.

As an example of a jurisdiction that, in general terms, does not have a long-arm law of the very description of Sir Samuel Griffith is that of Victoria, illustrated in the case of *Ward v The Queen*.[2] Mr. Ward was standing on a cliff in northern Victoria near the bank of the Murray River. The Murray River forms the boundary between the Australian states of New South Wales and Victoria. When Mr. Reid was standing

1. Quoted by Mr. Wells MLA, Queensland Legislative Assembly, Parliamentary Debates [Hansard] 685 (Sept. 7, 1988).
2. [1980] HCA 11, (1980) 142 CLR 308.

down beneath the cliff at the water's edge fishing, Mr. Ward shot him and killed him. Mr. Ward was charged and convicted of murder in Victoria.

He was subsequently acquitted by the High Court because, as it turned out, Mr. Ward was in the state of Victoria, whereas Mr. Reid was in the state of New South Wales. Victorian criminal law did not extend beyond the Victorian boundary.

The Special Case of Western Australia

Western Australia almost deserves a chapter on its own concerning surrogacy. Like other Australian states, Western Australia criminalized surrogacy in reaction to the *Baby M* case.[3]

By 2008 things had moved on. Whether or not there were going to be surrogacy laws became a central issue in the election between the two parties. The first law enacted after the election was the Surrogacy Act 2008 (Western Australia [WA]). Heterosexual married couples who had been unable to have children had spoken loud and clear to the media about how rough their lives were in not being able to become parents. As the government was concerned about the approach to be taken with surrogacy, surrogacy became extraordinarily narrowly strictly defined. The only people who can access surrogacy in Western Australia are heterosexual couples, single women, and lesbian couples. Single men and gay couples cannot. Who knows where non-binary, transgender, intersex people fall in the Western Australian scheme of things.

The surrogacy must be altruistic and here there are great limits. What is altruistic surrogacy is broadly described as being noncommercial (i.e., the surrogate is not paid a fee and the surrogate is not out of pocket). She is entitled to have her reasonable expenses met. Yet on the face of the act in Western Australia, a surrogate cannot be paid for travel and accommodation. To put Western Australia to scale, it has a population of about 2.5 million but is Australia's largest state, about the size of India. Its capital city, Perth, is described as the most isolated city on the planet.

Not only must there be a written agreement signed by all parties and the surrogacy arrangement be altruistic, there must be independent legal advice on both sides. Any donor of genetic material must be known (which then greatly restricts the availability of surrogacy) and the donor and partner must also be parties to the surrogacy arrangement and counselling and independent legal advice.

3. *In re* Baby M, 537 A.2d 1227 (N.J. 1988).

The surrogacy arrangement, with in effect the legal advice given to all parties, must then be provided to the state regulatory authority, which can only consider the application for surrogacy after a minimum cooling off period of three months. It is no surprise that to put the application together for approval, in vitro fertilization (IVF) clinics typically charge A$10,000.

It is also therefore no surprise that for every child born in Western Australia through surrogacy, approximately 20 are born overseas. It is a crime in Western Australia to provide a service knowing that the service is to facilitate a surrogacy arrangement that is for reward: punishable by up to five years imprisonment or a fine. The service offence, much like that in Hong Kong, deters Western Australian legal practitioners from giving advice to Western Australian residents about undertaking surrogacy overseas, even to altruistic surrogacy regimes such as Canada. Intended parents living in Western Australia must obtain legal advice from lawyers not in Western Australia.

Carmen and Colin

Carmen and Colin are a Western Australian couple. They decide to undertake surrogacy in Canada. They run a real risk of committing an offence under Western Australia's Surrogacy Act 2008 (WA) of entering into a surrogacy arrangement that is for reward. While the surrogacy agreement in Canada is altruistic, among the expenses that the surrogate is entitled to be paid are expenses that on its face would be criminal offences in Western Australia:

- Reimbursement of travel and accommodation
- Snow shovelling

In every Canadian surrogacy agreement, without fail, there is a provision for snow shovelling. Apparently, it has snowed on rare occasions in Western Australia. There is no allowance under the Surrogacy Act 2008 (WA) for expenses relating to snow shovelling. A provision for snow shovelling alone would mean that the surrogacy arrangement in Canada is, to use the Western Australian jargon, "*a surrogacy arrangement that is for reward*" with all the criminal consequences that might flow from that.

Colin and Carmen will need to obtain legal advice from an Australian lawyer who does not practice in Western Australia. They will need to ensure that they do not commit any element of the offence in Western Australia.

In the Baby Gammy case (see Chapter 6) it was argued that the intended parents had committed the offence by sending money to the surrogacy agency in Thailand, and sending instructions to that agency.

Extraterritorial Surrogacy Laws: The Queensland Disease

I write this book in Brisbane, the capital of Queensland. Sadly, Queensland has been the innovator for extraterritorial laws concerning surrogacy, the first of which was enacted in 1988. These laws in effect make it illegal in the place where the person lives—even though it concerns an overseas surrogacy arrangement, where the arrangement is legal.

Back in 1988, in reaction to the *Baby M* case in New Jersey,[4] Queensland enacted the Surrogate Parenthood Act 1988, which criminalized all forms of surrogacy (whether altruistic or commercial, gestational or traditional), whether within Queensland or anywhere outside Queensland if undertaken by anyone who was ordinarily resident in Queensland.

"Ordinarily resident" is a question of fact.

The enactment of an extraterritorial law concerning surrogacy was criticized at the time. As one member of Parliament said:

> A Parliament that constantly enacts provisions that it cannot enforce will bring itself into disrepute. How precisely will the Government enforce a provision that says that something that is legal in another State, but is illegal in Queensland, will be illegal nevertheless? How does the Government intend to override the laws of another State? How will the people be apprehended, unless they return to Queensland? It does not make sense. The Government does not have the apparatus to do that. Does it intend to send Queensland Police down to Victoria, South Australia or wherever it is to make sure that Queensland law is not contravened? The law is not enforceable. Worse than that, it cannot be made universal. If a Government takes a proposition such as this one that imports extraterritoriality; if it says, "Queenslanders have no right to do this and, what is more, they have no right to do it anywhere"; and if other States do exactly the same, what will happen is that one State will have legislated that a person has a right to do something and then he has the right to do it anywhere and another State will have legislated that a person does not have a right to do something and that it cannot be done anywhere. How will that work? That will lead to legal chaos. It just cannot be made universal. . . .

4. *Id.*

> Queenslanders are not children who are to be told, "not only will you not do what is against the law of Queensland when you are in Queensland, but also you will not do what is in accordance with the law in other States when you go to other States." Queenslanders cannot be treated like that. It is not as if a father is saying to his child, "yes, son, you can take the car out, but come home at 10 o'clock and make sure you don't drive it anywhere in the meantime." That is not the sort of situation that we are in. We are dealing with adults. We are dealing with Queenslanders who have every right to make up their minds to be law-abiding citizens in whatever place they choose.
>
> How will we identify them if they act in breach of this legislation? The Bill says that if they are ordinarily resident in Queensland, they can be caught by this provision. If people live in Queensland and go to New South Wales, how will we know? Will we send members of the police special branch down to catch people who are breaching Queensland laws? I repeat that I am not merely talking about the clause in this Bill, because it will come forward. . . . How will they be identified as Queenslanders? Will they be branded or will they have to wear a black arm band? It does not make sense.
>
> This clause is a paternalistic clause and one that is against every principle of law, both common law and statute. It is a principle that is an insult to the intelligence of the people of Queensland.[5]

Nevertheless, the bill was enacted.

That germ of an idea that originated in Brisbane was repeated in the Surrogacy Act 2010 in Queensland, which makes it a criminal offence to enter into a commercial surrogacy arrangement or to make payment under a commercial surrogacy arrangement anywhere in the world—if the person concerned is ordinarily resident in Queensland.

New Zealand researchers have described extraterritorial surrogacy laws as a "*failed experiment*."[6] That description is apt. No one has ever

---

5. Mr. Wells MLA, Queensland Legislative Assembly, Parliamentary Debates [Hansard] 685–86 (Sept. 7, 1988).

6. Debra Wilson & Julia Carrington, *Commercialising Reproduction: In Search of a Logical Distinction between Commercial, Compensated, and Paid Surrogacy Arrangements*, 21 NZBLQ 178, 186 (2015). *See also* SOUTH AUSTRALIAN LAW REFORM INSTITUTE, SURROGACY: A LEGISLATIVE FRAMEWORK—A REVIEW OF PART 2B OF THE FAMILY RELATIONSHIPS ACT 1975 (SA) § 12.3.1 (Report 12,

been prosecuted for undertaking commercial surrogacy overseas. As the statistics bear out, the laws have not deterred intended parents from undertaking surrogacy overseas.

That Queensland idea has been copied.

Australian Capital Territory

In 2004, the next in line was the Australian Capital Territory (ACT), which is where the Australian capital of Canberra is situated. The Parentage Act 2004 makes it a criminal offence to engage in commercial surrogacy overseas for someone who is ordinarily resident in the ACT.

No one has ever been prosecuted for undertaking commercial surrogacy overseas.

Hong Kong

In 2007, Hong Kong copied the Queensland approach with amendments to the Human Reproductive Technology Ordinance. Surrogacy is lawful in Hong Kong if it is altruistic, provided for a heterosexual couple, and by a clinic licensed in Hong Kong. No clinic has ever been licensed. Therefore, in reality, surrogacy cannot lawfully occur in Hong Kong. Four applications by clinics to be licensed have been refused and one application was withdrawn. If anyone wishes to undertake surrogacy, they must go abroad.

It is an offence under the ordinance to use donated gametes in a surrogacy arrangement. That offence appears to apply only in Hong Kong. Hong Kong has clear extraterritorial laws concerning egg, sperm, or embryo donation. Section 16(1) and (3) of the ordinance provides:

> (1) No person shall—
>
> (a) **whether in Hong Kong or elsewhere**, make or receive any payment for the supply of, or for an offer to supply, a prescribed substance intended to be used for the purposes of any reproductive technology procedure, embryo research or surrogacy arrangement;

2018); House of Representatives Standing Committee on Social Policy and Legal Affairs, Parliament of the Commonwealth of Australia, Surrogacy Matters: Inquiry into the Regulatory and Legislative Aspects of International and Domestic Surrogacy Arrangements ¶¶ 1.70–1.71, 1.112–1.113 (2016), *cited by* New Zealand Law Commission, Issues Paper 47: Review of Surrogacy, NZLC IP47, at 1.15 (2021).

(b) seek to find a person willing to supply for payment a prescribed substance referred to in paragraph (a);

(c) initiate or negotiate any arrangement involving the making of any payment for the supply of, or for an offer to supply, a prescribed substance referred to in paragraph (a); or

(d) take part in the management or control of a body of persons corporate or unincorporate whose activities consist of or include the initiation or negotiation of any arrangement referred to in paragraph (c). . . .

(3) In this section, "prescribed substance" means—

(a) a gamete or embryo; or

(b) fetal ovarian, or fetal testicular, tissue. (emphasis added)

This is a clear extraterritorial law.

Section 17(1) provides:

(1) No person shall—

(a) **whether in Hong Kong or elsewhere**, make or receive any payment for—

(i) initiating or taking part in any negotiations with a view to the making of a surrogacy arrangement;

(ii) offering or agreeing to negotiate the making of a surrogacy arrangement; or

(iii) compiling any information with a view to its use in making, or negotiating the making of, surrogacy arrangements;

(b) seek to find a person willing to do any act which contravenes paragraph (a);

(c) take part in the management or control of a body of persons corporate or unincorporate whose activities consist of or include any act which contravenes paragraph (a); or

(d) carry out or participate in any act in furtherance of any surrogacy arrangement where he knows, or ought reasonably to know, that the arrangement is the subject of any act which contravenes paragraph (a). (emphasis added).

Therefore, there is a clear extraterritorial ban in Hong Kong on surrogacy. Intended parents to become parents must go overseas and then in the process they are at risk of committing criminal offences.

Section 17(1)(d) makes it quite plain, in effect, that lawyers in Hong Kong cannot give advice to their clients "*in furtherance of any surrogacy arrangement*" where the lawyer, in effect, is aware that it is a commercial arrangement.

Therefore, Hong Kong intended parents are often flying blind until they come home. They cannot even get advice that the arrangement is illegal, other than in general terms that it is illegal.

According to Hong Kong colleagues and clients of mine from Hong Kong, when the parent then returns with the child to Hong Kong and applies for the relevant permit or visa, the Hong Kong waltz is then undertaken:

- **Step 1**. The parent discloses to the Hong Kong authorities that the child has been born through surrogacy. No one wants to commit the offence of lying to the government.
- **Step 2**. The Hong Kong authorities (if they are being polite) ask through the lawyer for the parent to attend at the police station for an interview. If they are being impolite, they come to the person's home and arrest them to take them to the station for an interview.
- **Step 3**. The interview occurs. After providing the identifying information, the parent claims the right to silence at which point the interview ceases and there is no prosecution.

The process is a farce. No one has ever been prosecuted, let alone convicted.

New South Wales

In 2010, this idea of extraterritorial surrogacy laws spread to New South Wales. Like other Australian states, New South Wales was in the process of undertaking a surrogacy review and having laws to allow noncommercial surrogacy. Nowhere in that process was there ever any discussion about any extraterritorial laws concerning commercial surrogacy. Then, at the third reading stage in Parliament (the debates already having occurred, this stage being only to move the bill and any proposed amendments), the relevant Minister stood up and moved an amendment to the bill to criminalize commercial surrogacy extraterritorially. Anyone who entered into a commercial surrogacy arrangement (as defined by what became the Surrogacy Act 2010 [NSW]) who was ordinarily resident in or domiciled in New South Wales commits an offence punishable by a fine of up to A$110,000 or two years imprisonment or both.

The bill quickly passed. Members of Parliament told me that they felt that they had no option. They wanted surrogacy laws in place. If they objected to the change, there was every chance no surrogacy law would be enacted.

There was community outrage. There was then a media firestorm in response. The law still took effect, but the anger was palpable by those who were halfway through their surrogacy journeys, and were now told what they were doing, once legal, was now illegal, and by those who were contemplating soon becoming parents.

The first impact was an amendment to regulations under the new act that in effect meant that if anyone had signed up with an overseas surrogacy agency by the commencement of the new act, what they were doing was lawful, even though it may well be commercial surrogacy. There was a gold rush at that point for overseas surrogacy agencies with New South Wales. Residents rushed to the doors to sign up in order to be able to go overseas ahead of the ban.

The resultant publicity meant that there was a pushback from the community and, following that, there was the founding of a community organization in Australia promoting surrogacy. I heard from many intended parents during this period who had been childless up to that point and were despairing about whether they would ever become parents. The resultant publicity meant that for the first time they were hopeful, becoming aware of surrogacy—and then proceeding to go overseas.

The result was astounding. The purpose of the amendment was in effect to stop New South Wales residents going to India for surrogacy. There was great concern about the potential exploitation of Indian surrogates. It was seen that the way to deter New South Wales residents from going there was to make it against the law to do so. The firestorm of publicity had the opposite effect, as demonstrated by Australian data.

No one has ever been prosecuted in New South Wales under this law.

The New South Wales law has the greatest reach of them all, as the offence is committed either by someone being ordinarily resident in New South Wales, or being domiciled in New South Wales.

I have undertaken freedom of information searches of the Australian Department of Home Affairs. When a child is born overseas through surrogacy and applies for citizenship, the Australian department keeps a record, not only of the number of births overseas through surrogacy, but also where the child was born.

In the period between 2009 to 2015, these were the number of Australian surrogacy births overseas, as shown in Table 4.1.

Table 4.1. Australian Surrogacy Births Overseas from 2009–2015[7]

Year Ended June 30	Number of Births
2009	10
2010	<10
2011	30
2012	266
2013	244
2014	263
2015	246

Ever since then, the number of Australian births overseas via surrogacy has typically been above 200. The dramatic period was between 2010, when there were fewer than ten births overseas, to 266 in 2012 (as highlighted in the table).

When the analysis is done of where those births occurred, they were primarily in India. The reduction in the number of births in India was because of changes in rules in India, not because of any changes to the rules or enforcement of the rules in New South Wales or other Australian jurisdictions, as seen in Table 4.2.

Table 4.2. Number of Australian Children Born via Surrogacy in India 2009–2015[8]

Year Ended June 30	Number of Births
2009	<10
2010	<10
2011	<10
2012	227
2013	191
2014	108
2015	74

As I stated, no one, whether in any of the three Australian jurisdictions or in Hong Kong, has ever been prosecuted for undertaking commercial surrogacy overseas. There has been plenty of criticism of these

7. Australian Department of Home Affairs, Applications for Citizenship by Descent of Children Born via Surrogacy (obtained by author under freedom of information applications).

8. *Id.*

laws. Nevertheless, there appears no appetite to repeal them. They remain a feature of the landscape, making it a legal minefield for intended parents undertaking surrogacy overseas.

As of April 2024, there is a bill to update the ACT's surrogacy laws. The bill does not propose to repeal the extraterritorial laws. A Parliamentary committee, in reviewing the bill, has recommended that those laws be reviewed. The bill has not been enacted.

Italy

As of April 2024, there is a bill before the Italian Senate to criminalize overseas surrogacy by Italian citizens. What started in Queensland has been exported to two other Australian jurisdictions, Hong Kong, and now Italy. These surrogacy journeys are not limited to commercial surrogacy. It is seen that they are being particularly targeted at gay couples. It is seen that in Italy with heterosexual couples that the woman will claim that she is pregnant overseas and everyone turns a blind eye. It is certainly quite a different process in Australia to that in Italy, namely that when bringing your baby home in Australia you must, like in Hong Kong, be honest with the government about how your child was born. Those who try to hide that their child was born through surrogacy (out of fear of prosecution) will find themselves in much greater difficulty, such as the citizenship application for their child being unsuccessful, if they lie to the Australian government.

Italians living overseas hold Italian citizenship. It is unclear if the extraterritorial surrogacy law applies to them.

Ireland

The Health (Assisted Human Reproduction) Bill 2022, which as of May 29, 2024, had completed Dáil Éireann, fifth stage, proposes to criminalize overseas commercial surrogacy[9] for those who are Irish citizens or are ordinarily resident in Ireland, if the act is an offense under the law of the place where the act was committed.[10]

9. Clause 93.
10. Clause 117.

Türkiye

In 2010, Türkiye banned IVF clinic personnel from referring their patients overseas for gamete or embryo donation,[11] but that law was repealed in 2014.[12]

John and Jan

It was a bright Saturday morning. Jan was in the kitchen baking cakes. John was out in the garden digging away. Life was pleasant and heavenly. The flowers were in bloom and the bees were buzzing.

Into this veritable paradise walked three plain clothes detectives from the local Child Protection Investigation Unit, "*Morning! We are here to talk with you about child trafficking—oh, and commercial surrogacy.*"

The couple, who almost died of shock, found to their horror that the Australian government agency responsible for tracking money laundering had traced money that they had sent to a surrogacy agency in Ukraine at a time before the 2022 invasion. Money was being funnelled through Ukraine as a means of sending it to Russia in breach of the United Nations sanctions. The anti-money laundering agency had referred the matter to police for investigation as to possible child trafficking and/or commercial surrogacy.

The couple stammered through their first interaction with police. The lead officer asked, "*Do you have a child?,*" to which the response in stammered English was, "*No, no, no, no.*" The couple then explained that they had sent money over for "*medical treatment.*" They were asked, "*Have you engaged in commercial surrogacy?*" Again, the response was, "*No.*"

Subsequently, I spoke with the police, who were much more interested in saving children and concerned about child trafficking. When it became clear that there was no child trafficking and that this was a childless couple who were seeking medical assistance, the police largely lost interest. On supply of documents by me to show that they were engaged in medical treatment, no further action was taken by police.

Jack and Ann

Jack and Ann were farmers. They had endured many seasons of hard weather, which was clearly evident on their faces. They decided to travel from Australia to Canada to undertake surrogacy. Canada, like Australia, is an altruistic surrogacy jurisdiction. They found their surrogate themselves, not through an agency. They made arrangements to stay for several

11. Regulation on Assisted Reproductive Treatment Practices and Assisted Reproductive Treatment Centers, Official Gazette, Mar. 6, 2010, No. 27513, art. 10(5).

12. Regulation on Assisted Reproductive Treatment Practices and Assisted Reproductive Treatment Centers, Official Gazette, Sept. 30, 2014, No. 29135.

weeks with the surrogate at her home in the lead up to and after the birth of the child. In exchange, they agreed with the surrogate that they would fly her and her boyfriend to Australia, spend a week together on holiday, and then, in effect, enable the surrogate and her boyfriend to have a holiday in sunny Queensland to see the Great Barrier Reef.

All that came to pass and then things went wrong. The husband, who was weather-beaten and as a result looked ancient, went to Australian government authorities to obtain a different kind of visa from the one that he had obtained for the child. During the course of that, he explained his error and his course of conduct with his wife in undertaking surrogacy in flying the surrogate back.

Seeing this apparently very old man give this explanation, departmental officers were immediately concerned that the couple were engaged in human trafficking. Within the hour, the surrogate and her boyfriend were arrested.

The following day, I was contacted by child protection officials. I was asked, when the case was explained to me, whether this was human trafficking and, with that, commercial surrogacy, causing the surrogate and her boyfriend to come out from Canada to Australia or not. My response was that the story of this couple seemed to ring true: "*No one has a valet service for babies through surrogacy.*" The couple and surrogate and her boyfriend subsequently were not charged. The clear message that I received was that authorities, whilst concerned about offences to do with commercial surrogacy, were much more concerned about the potential for human trafficking.

The Child with the Big Feet: New South Wales

The old skit from *Sesame Street* was that one of these things is not like the others. Clients of mine, one or both of whom were Australian, have lived in cities such as London, Tokyo, New York, and Sydney. The difference between those cities is that if they were living in Sydney, there was no question that they would be the subject of the Surrogacy Act 2010 (NSW). The worrying news is that even if they are living in one of those other cities, they may still be the subject of those laws and have the potential at least of committing an offence back in New South Wales. None of those other places seeks to impose its surrogacy laws on people living in Sydney.

Whether those laws are constitutionally valid is beside the point. They are on the statute books and the potential at least is for an offence to be committed.

The relevant offence in New South Wales is entering into or offering to enter into a commercial surrogacy arrangement.

The offence is committed by a person who is ordinarily resident or domiciled in New South Wales. The courts have held that "ordinarily resident" is a question of fact. Is the person living as a matter of fact (i.e., ordinarily resident) in New South Wales? There has certainly been case authority saying that someone can be ordinarily resident in two places at the same time. This is seen frequently in the Australian context by what are called fly-in/fly-out workers who have their home in one state and then fly across the country to work in a mine or industry in another state, and then do this on a rotating basis every week or two weeks. But what of someone who is domiciled? "Domiciled" of course is a legal concept as to the person's permanent place of abode and it may be domicile of origin or domicile of choice.

I will give an illustration of the point.

Bill and Ben in New York

Bill is a confident young professional. An Australian citizen, born in Sydney, Bill has lived in New York for five years under a work permit. Before that, Bill always lived in Sydney.

His husband Ben is also an Australian citizen. Ben came to New York to live with Bill. Ben has managed to obtain a green card. Ben was born in Sydney and lived there all his life, until the move to New York.

Bill and Ben propose to enter into a gestational carrier agreement with a carrier from Florida. Her fee is $45,000.

Bill is at risk of committing an offence of entering into a commercial surrogacy arrangement in New South Wales—because he remains domiciled there. Bill is not domiciled in New York, but by virtue of birth retains domicile of origin in New South Wales.

Ben is permanently resident in New York. Therefore, his domicile has shifted to New York. He is no longer domiciled in New South Wales. Ben is not at risk of committing the offence in New South Wales.

Taking that example a bit further, before they enter into the gestational carrier agreement, Bill and Ben move to Hong Kong.

Bill and Ben in Hong Kong

Bill enters Hong Kong under a temporary work visa. Ben enters Hong Kong under a dependency visa, by virtue of his relationship with Bill.

To add complication, Ben now discovers that he also holds Italian citizenship.

Bill and Ben propose to enter into the gestational carrier agreement.

Bill may well commit an offence under New South Wales law, as he remains domiciled in New South Wales. In addition, he may well commit an offence under Hong Kong law.

Ben similarly may commit an offence under each of New South Wales and Hong Kong law. If the law before the Italian Senate is enacted, he may also—as an Italian citizen—commit an offence under that law.

Both Long-Arm *and* Extraterritorial Laws

As we have seen in Hong Kong, extraterritorial laws can apply to *both* commercial egg donation and surrogacy. In the three Australian jurisdictions that have extraterritorial laws concerning surrogacy, *there are also* long-arm laws. Most of the time an intended parent may easily be committing a breach of the law due to their extraterritorial provisions. However, in some cases, there will be concern about a breach of a long-arm law. This particularly came to the fore during the pandemic.

Pasteur's Pandemic

Pasteur was a migrant from an Asian country who obtained Australian citizenship. To be close to family, he returned back to his country of origin and became a permanent resident there. In the middle of the pandemic, he found himself in Sydney. He wanted to become a parent again through surrogacy, and to undertake this journey in the United States.

The first difficulty was that under the Surrogacy Act 2010 (NSW) if he were *ordinarily resident* in New South Wales and entered into a commercial surrogacy arrangement, he would commit an offence. He was not ordinarily resident in New South Wales. He was stuck in New South Wales temporarily during the pandemic, as he was not allowed to return back to the Asian country in which he lived.

The second issue was whether he might be committing an offence because he was *domiciled* in New South Wales. Although Pasteur had obtained Australian citizenship, because he was a permanent resident of the other country, he was not domiciled in New South Wales.

However, that was not the end of the matter. He was still subject to the long-arm laws[13] by which if *part* of the act that was the offence was committed in New South Wales or the *effect* of the act that was the offence was committed in New South Wales then he committed the offence, which in this case was to enter into or to offer to enter into the commercial surrogacy arrangement.

13. *Crimes Act 1900* (NSW) s 10C.

But That's Not All—The Adoption Sting in the Tail

In Chapter 13, I cover the interplay between surrogacy and adoption.

But I want to touch on it in this chapter because, at least in my country, there are universal laws that make it a criminal offence to pay a mother for the child. That all makes sense. One would hope that there are many laws like those around the world. Australia, for some reason, has decided to apply these laws overseas. An example is the state of Victoria. Victoria does not have long-arm laws concerning egg donation or human tissue or long-arm or extraterritorial laws regarding surrogacy. One might then be mistaken in thinking that a Victoria resident can undertake surrogacy. If the surrogacy involves adoption, then an offence might be committed.

The Adoption Act 1984 (Victoria) is an illustration of the point. It is an offence to make payment for a child. The offence is stated broadly under section 119(1):

> (1) Subject to this section, any person who (whether before or after the birth of the child concerned) makes, gives or receives, or agrees to make, give or receive, a payment or reward for or in consideration of—
> (a) the adoption or proposed adoption of a child;
> (b) the giving of consent, or the signing of an instrument of consent, to the adoption of the child;
> (c) the transfer of the possession or custody of a child with a view to the adoption of the child; or
> (d) the making of arrangements with a view to the adoption of a child—shall be guilty of an offence and liable—
> (e) in the case of a body corporate, to a penalty of not more than 500 penalty units; or
> (f) in any other case, to a penalty of not more than 100 penalty units or to imprisonment for not more than 2 years or both.

Section 116, which applies to section 119, provides:

> This Part does not apply in respect of acts occurring outside Victoria, but, unless otherwise expressly provided, does apply in respect of acts done in Victoria in relation to adoption of children in, or children adopted in, any other State or a Territory or a country outside the Commonwealth and the Territories.

How this may apply to surrogacy is that in some regimes, adoption is the method of undertaking surrogacy. Three examples suffice:

- Places whereby the second intended parent becomes a parent through a second parent or step-adoption involving surrogacy—for example, Minnesota, Iowa, and Hawaii
- Places where an intended parent becomes a parent through adoption where there is no genetic link between the intended parent and the child—for example, Florida
- Places where adoption is the method of surrogacy approval—for example, New Zealand

Great care must be taken to ensure that the intended parents do not accidentally touch the tripwire of an adoption offence, whilst thinking they are in the clear after having not committed offences relating to egg donation or surrogacy.

The Parallel Universe—Cambodia

Following the Baby Gammy saga and the Thai baby farm (see Chapter 18) intended parents in relatively small numbers, at least from the West, went to Cambodia. The real growth area for intended parents for surrogacy in Cambodia, according to industry insiders that I spoke to, was Chinese intended parents travelling to Cambodia. Sometimes, they were single men who either identified as gay or, those who, because of the effects of the one child policy and the disproportionate number of men in Chinese society as compared to women, were never able to find a partner.

Business was booming to such an extent, and travel agents from China were able to bring in so many intended parents to Cambodia, that Chinese travel agents started to demand of IVF clinics in Cambodia when the surrogates would be induced—to comply with the travel bookings of the intended parents!

It's not surprising that it all fell apart. In late 2016, Cambodia in reaction to this burgeoning business decided that surrogacy had to stop. The Cambodian government announced that hence forth all surrogacy was illegal in Cambodia and that laws would be passed to regulate surrogacy. Those laws have still not passed. Nevertheless, those who engage in surrogacy in Cambodia are at risk of being convicted of human trafficking.

The Cambodian government decided to make an example of someone. That person was Tammy Davis-Charles, an Australian nurse and surrogacy promoter, who had previously promoted surrogacy to Westerners in Thailand. Even after the Cambodian government announced not to come to Cambodia for surrogacy, Davis-Charles's website continued to extol the virtues of surrogacy in Cambodia. That was not unusual to see.

When there have been previous surrogacy crises and the roller doors have come down, those who have made decent money out of promoting surrogacy to foreigners have continued to promote undertaking surrogacy in that country, despite surrogacy being banned. For example, in 2014 when India closed its doors to Australians, some IVF clinics in India were still promoting their wares to Australians. One couple spent $35,000 in this period creating embryos in India and then discovered they couldn't be used in India. They couldn't be sent anywhere. They had wasted their money to no purpose—to create embryos sitting in a freezer in a clinic on the other side of the world that couldn't be used for anything.

Tammy Davis-Charles was arrested in November 2016, shortly after the change of views by the Cambodian government about a month after Cambodian authorities similarly banned commercial surrogacy. Phnom Penh Court convicted her and two Cambodian staff members, Samrith Chakriya and Penh Rithy, of acting as intermediaries between adoptive parents and pregnant women and fraudulently obtaining documents, such as birth certificates.

Davis-Charles, who had set up her agency, Fertility Solutions PDG, had received at least $50,000 to facilitate surrogacy arrangements, with Cambodian women receiving $10,000 to carry a baby through surrogacy. Of the 23 surrogates she provided care for, 18 were carrying children for Australians. She was sentenced to 18 months after having spent nine months in pre-trial detention.

On May 22, 2017, Davis-Charles was freed. However, 43 pregnant Cambodian women, carrying babies mainly for clients in China, had been arrested. They too were convicted of human trafficking offences. In June 2018, 32 pregnant Cambodian women allegedly carrying babies for clients in China were also arrested in Phnom Penh.

Those babies born before January 8, 2018, were allowed to be taken out of Cambodia if the intended parents received municipal court permission. Those removing surrogate babies born after that date faced up to 14 years imprisonment for human trafficking.

Babies were smuggled out of Cambodia via road through Thailand in the period between October 2016, when the commercial surrogacy ban came into effect, and 2017.

The Cambodian women were told by the court that they had a choice after they gave birth to the children—that they could raise the child (of which they had no genetic connection) or they could go to prison.

Filipino women who had flown to Cambodia were sent back to the Philippines. It was also believed that they were involved in what was seen to be commercial surrogacy in Cambodia.

Despite all the noise made by the Cambodian government about having the law about surrogacy, Cambodia has never, since 2016, enacted a law concerning surrogacy. It has instead relied on laws concerning fraud, adoption, and human trafficking. A proclamation was made about surrogacy with the intent of there being laws enacted to prohibit commercial surrogacy. The Cambodian government was acting in a legal vacuum, which really says it all about the practice of surrogacy in Cambodia.

It cannot be emphasized enough that intended parents should only be going to a jurisdiction that:

1. Welcomes them—a jurisdiction that, for example, persecutes gay men should never be considered as a place for gay men to undertake surrogacy
2. Has sound regulation of and quality standards for its IVF industry
3. Has secure human rights protocols to ensure that everyone concerned has their human rights protected: the intended parents, the donor, the surrogate, and above all the child, among others
4. Has, if needed, clear laws able to be enforced with firm, fair, and transparent judicial oversight

At the time of writing this chapter, eight staff members from a fertility clinic in Greece have been arrested on allegations of human trafficking and fraud. Many international intended parents, including those from my home country, Australia, went to that clinic and have been caught up in the mess. It would appear that that clinic was an appropriate place to undertake surrogacy but, nevertheless, there has been an implosion with all the resulting damage to all concerned—particularly to the intended parents who are worried that they have lost their life savings and do not know if they can become parents again and surrogates who are left isolated, unsupported, and stranded.

If you are a lawyer who advises clients about going overseas, your clients will probably ask you for a recommendation about where to go. It may be that you then say that you can't give any recommendation. For many clients that will feel as though you are letting them down. Alternatively, you may, with highly qualified advice, give them advice about certain parameters. So as far as Greece is concerned, one would have thought that Greece was a safe destination for surrogacy:

- It is subject to the European Convention on Human Rights.
- Surrogacy was specifically regulated under the Greek Civil Code.
- Treatment for IVF cannot commence for a surrogacy journey unless there has been judicial approval first.
- Judicial approval requires a wait of between four and eight months before coming to court after the papers are filed, with a further delay after the judge has consulted a panel of colleagues.
- There is a regulator of the IVF industry.
- That clinic had been operating for 30 years and had an apparently very good reputation.

Take Away

1. Is there a reputable lawyer who can give you reliable advice in the other place? See Chapter 9.
2. How is IVF practiced in that other country?
3. Is single embryo transfer the norm?
4. Are clinics in that other country the subject of regulation or is their registration up-to-date?
5. Is there a strong human rights framework (or not) in that other country?
6. Does the judiciary appear independent?
7. Are there any extraterritorial or long-arm laws that might apply to this journey?
8. As far as you can ascertain, what are the laws concerning egg donation, surrogacy, and parentage in the other country?
9. How will the baby come home?
10. What happens if something goes wrong?
11. Is the country overall safe? Does it have security issues?

Chapter 5

Language Mangling

George Orwell is famous, among other works, for his six rules of writing, which emphasize keeping language simple and to the point. Regrettably, these rules seem to have been ignored at times in this area.

Much of assisted reproductive technology (ART) occurs in countries where English is not the main language. Even where it is, there may be different terms for the same concept. This can make the journey particularly interesting and frustrating.

The world of in vitro fertilization (IVF) is full of jargon. Trying to get your head around the jargon at times can make your head hurt, but still no closer to what you thought. I have a large vocabulary. I thought I knew my way around the jargon, until one day I had to speak at an IVF clinic's national conference. A previous speaker was talking in so much scientific jargon that I had no idea what she was saying. I wanted to know what the words were that she was describing. Therefore, I quickly entered them into my phone and then I Googled them. I particularly wanted to see if they were in the Scrabble Dictionary. Not that I play Scrabble often. I wanted some broad measure to see if the words she was using were widely recognized and *if* I happened to put one of those words on the board, amongst all the arguments, I would triumph!

One of the words that the speaker used was *trophectoderm.* When I looked "trophectoderm" up on https://scrabblewordfinder.org/ the page said: "Not a valid word." Then when I looked up the meaning of "trophectoderm" online, I got this definition from Merriam-Webster which says it all:

> Trophectoderm
>
> Noun troph·ec·to·derm/ ˌtrōf-'ek-tə-ˌdərm/
>
> Medical definition of trophectoderm: trophoblast: the outer layer of the mammalian blastocyst after differentiation of the ectoderm, mesoderm, and endoderm and the outer layers continuous with the ectoderm of the embryo.

I then realized what it was. "Derm" is of course to do with the skin. *Trophectoderm* is in effect the skin of the embryo. Bingo!

A helpful place to help you decode terms is the International Committee for Monitoring Assisted Reproductive Technologies (ICMART) international glossary.[1] However, although the glossary is extremely helpful, it is not the last word. By way of two examples:

- While the rest of the world talks of surrogates, the glossary talks of gestational carriers.
- ICMART, and more recently the American Society for Reproductive Medicine, have adopted a wider definition of "infertility," which essentially includes anyone who needs to do ART. By contrast, the World Health Organization remains steadfast in the traditional definition—requiring a heterosexual couple to be unsuccessful at conception after multiple attempts over 12 months.

I have set out some terms that have caused me grief at times, as listed in Table 5.1. I apologize in advance if you know the terms!

Table 5.1. Meaning of Some Commonly Used Terms

Term	Meaning/Comments
Altruistic surrogacy	In the words of a politician, where the surrogate is not out of pocket, but does not profit. However, what is—and is not—altruistic surrogacy is in the eye of the beholder, or in the definitions used by legislatures. Even within noncommercial surrogacy regimes, what is deemed altruistic (and therefore lawful and good) and what is deemed commercial (and therefore unlawful and bad) can vary greatly. What is clearly altruistic in one noncommercial surrogacy regime can be deemed commercial surrogacy in the noncommercial surrogacy regime next door. The devil is in the details.
ART, assisted reproductive treatment, assisted reproductive technology, artificial reproductive technology	Depending on who you listen to and where you are depends on which variation on a theme is used. Sometimes ART is taken to include artificial insemination, and sometimes not.
Arranged parents	The term in Western Australia for intended parents.
Birth mother	Surrogate.

1. *The International Glossary on Infertility and Fertility Care*, ICMART, https://www.icmartivf.org/glossary/a-d/ (last visited Mar. 26, 2024).

Term	Meaning/Comments
Birth parent	Surrogate and surrogate's partner, and sometimes someone else defined by law as a parent of the child at birth.
Blastocyst	A 5- or 6-day-old embryo. Clinicians will usually implant a blastocyst rather than a 3-day-old embryo, as the blastocyst is more advanced and therefore more viable.
Commercial substitute parent agreement	The term used for commercial surrogacy in the Australian Capital Territory.
Commercial surrogacy	Where the amount paid to a surrogate is deemed to be a commercial amount, and therefore illegal. Compensated surrogacy may or may not be commercial surrogacy. Commercial surrogacy may be gestational or traditional surrogacy.
Commissioning parents	Hopefully this term will go to the scrapheap of history. A term that some in the IVF industry have used for intended parents, which was then taken up in some legislation (and is now being written out of legislation).
Compensated surrogacy	Where the surrogate is compensated for her efforts. It may be gestational or traditional. It may be commercial or not.
Conception	When the child is conceived or created. This is such a controversial term that ICMART has not defined it. Commonly seen to be the commencement of a viable pregnancy (i.e., after implantation, and not fertilization of the embryo[2]). However, some laws define conception as being the act of fertilization.
Cryopreservation	When the eggs, sperm, and embryos are frozen in liquid nitrogen. Issues that arise internationally occur when the genetic material is thawed accidentally in transit, or when the vitrification of the genetic material (when the genetic material is snap frozen so that it has a glass like nature to it) is undertaken poorly, resulting in unusable genetic material being shipped.
Embryo	The common term of an egg fertilized by sperm, though the terms used in the United States sometimes refer to zygote or to the embryo before it is securely implanted.
Fresh embryo transfer/frozen embryo transfer	The terms are self-evident. More and more, frozen embryo transfers are being used, as pregnancy rates are similar to, or higher than, fresh embryo transfers in most cases—but individual doctors and clinics have their own approaches.

2. *E.g.*, LWV v LM*H* [2012] QChC 26.

Term	**Meaning/Comments**
Gestational carrier	Gestational surrogate.
Gestational carrier agreement	Surrogacy agreement, surrogacy arrangement.
Gestational surrogate, gestational surrogacy	Where the surrogate is not the genetic parent.
Hatching/assisted hatching	When the IVF clinic assists the embryo's shell to be broken to enable hatching to occur.
ICSI	Intracytoplasmic sperm injection—where the embryologist chooses what appears to be the viable sperm, snips off the tail, and injects it directly into the egg. It contrasts with traditional IVF where up to 200,000 sperm are placed in a petri dish with the egg, in the hope that one will fertilize. Some research indicates slightly higher risks for the child when ICSI is used rather than traditional IVF. ICSI has been used for infertile men. It is now the most popular method of IVF with surrogacy.
Oocyte	Egg.
Parent	The person at law who is the parent of the child. May or may not be the genetic parent, and may be the surrogate or surrogate's partner—depending on the law of the place.
Parentage order	The order recognizing the intended parents as the parents, either by declaration or transfer of parentage.
Parental order	The UK version of a parentage order.
Parenting order	An order determining parenting arrangements for a child, such as parental responsibility, custody, and the like.
PGD, PGS, PGT	Variations on a theme—pre-implantation genetic diagnosis, screening, and treatment. In essence this involves removing a few cells from the blastocyst to check for genetic abnormalities. The techniques can also identify the gender of the embryo—if the laws of the place allow that.
Quarantine	The length between when an embryo is created and when it can be implanted. The traditional quarantine period specified by the American Society for Reproductive Medicine is 6 months, which was the period to confirm that HIV was not present. Different clinics use different timeframes—from zero to 6 months, and commonly at 3 to 4 months.
Spermatozoa	Sperm.
Substitute parents	Intended parents.

Term	Meaning/Comments
Surrogate/surrogacy	A person who is pregnant for the intended parents and delivers the child to them. The surrogate can be gestational or traditional, and be altruistic, noncommercial, compensated, or commercial.
Surrogate mother	Surrogate.
Traditional surrogacy	Where the surrogate is the genetic parent. Pregnancy may occur through artificial insemination (including at home), sex, or through IVF.

Take Away

1. Where possible try to avoid using jargon.
2. Some jargon will inevitably creep in as it might be a medical term, or a term defined by law.
3. What is being described may be known to you by another term.

Chapter 6

Beware Cultural and Religious Differences

"But for their acted-on intention, the child would not exist."[1]

It might seem an obvious thing to say, but different countries view the world differently. In the context of surrogacy and assisted reproductive technology (ART), there are enormous differences about how the world is seen. The view is seen most starkly between the perspective of America, which although cognisant of the rights of the child, emphasizes the right to reproduce, and that of Europe, which is particularly concerned about surrogacy—and emphasizes the rights of the child.

Interestingly, the Supreme Courts of Mexico and Colombia, while proclaiming the right to reproduce, have also emphasized the rights of the child. In the words of the Supreme Court of Mexico:

> [Surrogacy] has been the subject of questioning in the field of bioethics and legal doctrine, on its ethical and legal validity, since it is considered an attack on the dignity of people, implying that the woman's body and the baby's parentage are the matter of a transaction between parties and trade; as well as for disdaining the bond or bonds that are generated between the baby and the pregnant mother during pregnancy, which is not only biological, but also psycho-affective and full of emotions. Therefore, it is indicated that it implies the use of poor mothers for rich ones, or the exploitation of women, even in cases where the use of this technique is not due to infertility or inability to get pregnant, but simply to avoid discomfort of pregnancy.
>
> However, there are also those who defend their practice under certain conditions, on the main basis of the right to procreation

1. Johnson v. Calvert, 5 Cal. 4th 87, 93 (1993).

> and the access to new technologies for human reproduction, as well as the defense of the right to self-determination of the people and their privacy; added to the idea of solidarity between couples who need to go to surrogacy to achieve having a child, with the woman who agrees to help them realize that purpose.
>
> In this sense, several countries prohibit surrogacy in any case, with the consequence that maternity is attributed to the pregnant mother; There are others that admit that as long as it is altruistically non-profit, and there are others in which it is considered admissible even for commercial reasons, with a regulation in all cases.[2]

It is important, when looking at the world, not to think that others see the way that your jurisdiction does. In a broad sense, America stands for the idea of reproductive freedom, whereas Europe stands for the idea of protection of the child and motherhood.

These separate ideas result in different outcomes. In the United States, for example, the emphasis on reproductive freedom has slowly moved to an intent model of determining who is a parent, as seen in a California case. Therefore, it is a feminist idea that women can take control of their bodies and be paid to be surrogates. Why should they be denied that?

Similarly, it is argued in America that paying egg donors is to give the donors choice—and is from a feminist perspective.

By contrast, in Europe, the emphasis on the surrogate as the mother, and the child as born from the mother, results in the prohibition of surrogacy—or if the view of the Supreme Court of Mexico is right—the view is taken that surrogacy ought to be prohibited—and as a consequence maternity is attributed to the pregnant mother.

The view is taken that surrogacy is dehumanizing of women, who are often considered to be poor and vulnerable. It is said that the feminist ideal is to protect women—by preventing them being paid to be surrogates or, in some cases, preventing them being surrogates in any circumstances. Similarly, it is argued that children born through surrogacy are commodities, and that donors who are compensated are commodified and exploited.

2. Amparo en Revisión, Suprema Corte de Justicia de la Nación [SCJN], Noviembre de 2018, 553/2018, párrafos 21–23.

The Right to Reproduce

The fundamental view in the United States is that there is a right to reproduce. This is best illustrated in the 1942 U.S. Supreme Court case *Skinner v. Oklahoma*[3] where Justice Douglas, in the context of a eugenics law in Oklahoma, said:

> We are dealing here with legislation which involves one of the basic civil rights of man. Marriage and procreation are fundamental to the very existence and survival of the race. The power to sterilize, if exercised, may have subtle, far-reaching and devastating effects. In evil or reckless hands, it can cause races or types which are inimical to the dominant group to wither and disappear. There is no redemption for the individual whom the law touches. Any experiment which the State conducts is to his irreparable injury. He is forever deprived of a basic liberty.[4]

That view was not expressed in the context of ART. Nevertheless, the dominant view from American colleagues is that there is a fundamental right to reproduce. As seen in Chapter 1, why shouldn't everyone who can take advantage of scientific and medical progress, and decide the spacing and number of their family?

Consistent with this right to reproduce, jurisprudence in the United States has moved towards an intention-based model of who is a parent. That sentence, of course, is a generalization, given the diversity within the United States, but nevertheless, an intention-based model was discussed in two seminal decisions by the Supreme Court of California and the California Court of Appeal, respectively. American ART lawyers will be very familiar with these cases. Nevertheless, they remain powerful statements of the right to reproduce—and who should be recognized as a parent, an approach not seen in Europe.

In *Johnson v. Calvert*,[5] a 1993 decision of the Supreme Court of California, Anna Johnson was paid $10,000 by Mark and Crispina Calvert to be their surrogate. An embryo comprising their genetic material was implanted into Anna. A child was conceived and born. The surrogacy arrangement broke down.

The issue before the court was which of the two women was the mother. Under statutory presumptions, each of Crispina, who was the

3. Skinner v. Oklahoma, 316 U.S. 535 (1942).
4. *Id.* at 541.
5. 5 Cal. 4th 87.

genetic mother, and Anna, who was the birth mother, was presumed to be the mother.

The court then had to consider what was the point of the transaction. Was it to implant an embryo into Anna so that she could be a parent? Or was it to implant an embryo so that Mark and Crispina could be the parents?

The clear intention of the parties was so that Mark and Crispina could be the parents. Based on intention, they were held to be the natural parents:

> Because two women each have presented acceptable proof of maternity, we do not believe this case can be decided without enquiring into the parties' intentions as manifested in the surrogacy agreement. Mark and Crispina are a couple who desired to have a child of their own genes but are physically unable to do so without the help of reproductive technology. They affirmatively intended the birth of the child, and took the steps necessary to effect in vitro fertilization. But for their acted-on intention, the child would not exist. Anna agreed to facilitate the procreation of Mark's and Crispina's child. The parties' aim was to bring Mark's and Crispina's child into the world, not for Mark and Crispina to donate a zygote to Anna. Crispina from the outset intended to be the child's mother. Although the gestative function Anna performed was necessary to bring about the child's birth, it is safe to say that Anna would not have been given the opportunity to gestate or deliver the child had she, prior to implantation of the zygote, manifested her own intent to be the child's mother. No reason appears why Anna's later change of heart should vitiate the determination that Crispina is the child's natural mother.
>
> We conclude that although the Act recognizes both genetic consanguinity and giving birth as means of establishing a mother and child relationship, when the two means do not coincide in one woman, she who intended to procreate the child—that is, she who intended to bring about the birth of a child that she intended to raise as her own—is the natural mother under California law.[6]

Anna also argued that the contract was void because it breached California laws criminalizing the payment for adoption, as it was a pre-birth waiver of her parental rights. The court rejected that argument:

---

6. *Id.* at 93.

> We disagree. Gestational surrogacy differs in crucial respects from adoption and so is not subject to the adoption statutes. The parties voluntarily agreed to participate in in vitro fertilization and related medical procedures before the child was conceived; at the time when Anna entered into the contract, therefore, she was not vulnerable to financial inducements to part with her own expected offspring. As discussed above, Anna was not the genetic mother of the child. The payments to Anna under the contract were meant to compensate her for her services in gestating the fetus and undergoing labor, rather than for giving up "parental" rights to the child. Payments were due both during the pregnancy and after the child's birth. We are, accordingly, unpersuaded that the contract used in this case violates the public policies embodied in Penal Code section 273 and the adoption statutes. For the same reasons, we conclude these contracts do not implicate the policies underlying the statutes governing termination of parental rights.[7]

The approach taken by Anna has been commonly seen in Europe. The response has been commonly seen in the United States. In the words of the court:

> Anna and some commentators have expressed concern that surrogacy contracts tend to exploit or dehumanize women, especially women of lower economic status. Anna's objections center around the psychological harm she asserts may result from the gestator's relinquishing the child to whom she has given birth. Some have also cautioned that the practice of surrogacy may encourage society to view children as commodities, subject to trade at their parents' will.
>
> We are all too aware that the proper forum for resolution of this issue is the Legislature, where empirical data, largely lacking from this record, can be studied and rules of general applicability developed. However, in light of our responsibility to decide this case, we have considered as best we can its possible consequences.
>
> We are unpersuaded that gestational surrogacy arrangements are so likely to cause the untoward results Anna cites as to demand their invalidation on public policy grounds. Although common sense suggests that women of lesser means serve as

7. *Id.* at 96.

> surrogate mothers more often than do wealthy women, there has been no proof that surrogacy contracts exploit poor women to any greater degree than economic necessity in general exploits them by inducing them to accept lower-paid or otherwise undesirable employment. We are likewise unpersuaded by the claim that surrogacy will foster the attitude that children are mere commodities; no evidence is offered to support it. The limited data available seem to reflect an absence of significant adverse effects of surrogacy on all participants.[8]

This intention-based approach was developed further in the 1998 California Court of Appeal decision in *In re Marriage of Buzzanca*.[9] John and Luanne Buzzanca had entered into a contract with a surrogate. An embryo, not composed of their genetic material, was implanted into the surrogate. It is unclear from the judgment whether they had created the embryo from donor egg and donor sperm, or if the embryo was a donor embryo. A child, Jaycee, was ultimately born.

In the words of the court:

> After the fertilization, implantation and pregnancy, Luanne and John split up, and the question of who are Jaycee's lawful parents came before the trial court.
>
> Luanne claimed that she and her erstwhile husband were the lawful parents, but John disclaimed any responsibility, financial or otherwise. The woman who gave birth also appeared in the case to make it clear that she made no claim to the child.
>
> The trial court then reached an extraordinary conclusion: Jaycee had no lawful parents. First, the woman who gave birth to Jaycee was not the mother; the court had—astonishingly—already accepted a stipulation that neither she nor her husband were the "biological" parents. Second, Luanne was not the mother. According to the trial court, she could not be the mother because she had neither contributed the egg nor given birth. And John could not be the father, because, not having contributed the sperm, he had no biological relationship with the child.
>
> We disagree. Let us get right to the point: Jaycee never would have been born had not Luanne and John both agreed to have a fertilized egg implanted in a surrogate.[10]

---

8. *Id.* at 97.
9. 61 Cal. App. 4th 1412 (1998).
10. *Id.* at 1412.

Following *Johnson v. Calvert*, the court held that Luanne and John were the parents:

> Just as a husband is deemed to be the lawful father of a child unrelated to him when his wife gives birth after artificial insemination, so should a husband and wife be deemed the lawful parents of a child after a surrogate bears a biologically unrelated child on their behalf. In each instance, a child is procreated because a medical procedure was initiated and consented to by intended parents. The only difference is that in this case—unlike artificial insemination—there is no reason to distinguish between husband and wife.[11]

The influence of this intention model of who is a parent has rippled out from California, including overseas.

Parentage by Intention/Genetics

Mexico

In *Amparo 553/2018*, the Supreme Court of Mexico held that a gay couple who had undertaken surrogacy in Yucatan were the parents, and that the surrogate was not.

The court held that Article 4 of the constitution protected the organization of the family, and provided the right of every person to decide freely and responsibly about the number and the spacing of children (in much the same way as the Convention on the Elimination of All Forms of Discrimination against Women has done for women, and the right to take advantage of scientific progress, seen in the International Covenant on Economic, Social, and Cultural Rights—see Chapter 1).

The concept of family is not identified by or limited to a single type of family, but in the context of a democratic state of law in which plurality is its essence, it must be understood that the constitutional norm is a reference to the family as a social reality, and therefore protects all its forms and manifestations as an existing reality.

Among the ways in which a family can take place is made up of a same-sex couple, who have rights to marry. The right to decide freely, responsible and informed about the number and spacing of their children, corresponds to the sphere of freedom and private life of people, for which there should be no arbitrary interference by the State, and which includes the right to decide to procreate a child. Consistent with the approach by

11. *Id.* at 1413.

the Inter-American Court of Human Rights (see Chapter 1), Article 11 of the American Convention on Human Rights regards the right to private life and family, in the sense that it constitutes the right of every person to organize, in accordance with the law, their individual and social life according to their own options and convictions, and that the decision to be a mother or father or not is part of the right to private life. It includes the decision to be a mother or father in the genetic or biological sense—that is, their reproductive rights.

The court noted that the Inter-American Court has recognized the right to ART (*Murillo* v. *Costa Rica*—see Chapter 1), concerning infertile heterosexual couples.

Same-sex couples have the same issue, as they cannot reproduce without the use of ART. Because Article 1 of the American Convention requires no discrimination, then the right to homosexual couples must be recognized to access advances in ART and to become fathers or mothers through these methods.

The consent to submit to ART always has as its starting point the element related to the intent that people have who wish to undertake ART. When within a marriage ART is consented to, one of the fundamental factors to determine the filiation of the children born is the intention of the parents, which is the desire to assume a child as one's own although biologically it is not, and, with this, all the responsibilities derived from filiation.

Such an approach is consistent with the mother's husband or common-law husband being found to be the father. The intention to parent in such a case can be given expressly or tacitly.

The approach, as seen in *Johnson v. Calvert*, about poor women being exploited, was also raised in this case. Surrogacy, it was argued, was considered an attack on the dignity of people, by implying that the woman's body and the parentage of the baby are matters of transaction between parties and trade, as well as disdaining the bond generated between the baby and the pregnant mother during the pregnancy, which is not only biological, but also psychological-affective and full of emotions. Therefore, it is pointed out that it implies the use of poor mothers by rich ones, or the exploitation of women, even in cases where the use of surrogacy is not due to infertility or the impossibility of pregnancy, but simply to avoid the inconvenience of pregnancy.

The Supreme Court stated that there are those who defend surrogacy under certain conditions, on the main basis of the right to procreation and the access to new technologies in human reproduction, as well as the defense of the right to self-determination of people and their privacy, added to the idea of solidarity between the couples who need to resort to surrogacy in order to have a child, with the woman who agrees to help them achieve that purpose.

The court noted the variation in approaches around the world to surrogacy—from outright prohibition—with the consequence that maternity is attributed to the surrogate, to others where altruistic surrogacy is permitted, and those where commercial surrogacy is permitted.

The court noted that surrogacy represents a reality contributed by the advances of science that affects the traditional conception that until now has been established around family relationships, mainly kinship and affiliation with children, and the rights of maternity and paternity, since it can give rise to various situations and conflicts between the parties involved, which makes its regulation imperative.

Therefore, there could be up to three mothers for the baby—the one who wishes to have it, the one who donates the egg, and the one who gestates it. In the state of Yucatan, there was no regulation about children born through ART. However, the absence of regulation should not be erected as an impediment to the recognition, protection, and enforcement of the fundamental rights of individuals.

The court held that, provided that the surrogate was an adult and had capacity, then parentage was determined by the intention of those seeking to be parents, along with the concurrent intention of the pregnant woman to the same effect.

The court held that the right to an identity under Article 8 of the United Nations Convention on the Rights of the Child included the right of a child to know his or her biological parents, which contributes to a better integral development of the child, and ultimately to promote a higher interest. Sometimes, the coincidence between biological and legal affiliation is not always possible.

When establishing the filiation of children, the purposes to fulfill in order to satisfy the best interests of the child that could come into conflict include:

- Allowing the minor to know his or her biological origin
- Maintaining relationships with the minor and the biological family
- Protecting the stability of relationships with relatives
- Protecting established identified filiation
- Guaranteeing the fulfillment of obligations derived from filiation that are necessary for the child's proper development

The point about the historical approach about determining paternity—before DNA tests, it was not possible to be certain about the biological link. Three approaches were taken to solve this:

1. The presumption of paternity
2. Acknowledgment of paternity
3. Care of the child

Each of these was trying to establish biological truth. That a man was the husband of the mother, recognized him as such, or behaved as a father is considered an indication that the biological link existed. However, none of these approaches guaranteed that there was a biological link.

Similarly, the development of ART makes it no longer possible to establish with certainty that the woman who gave birth to the child has a genetic link to it.

With acknowledgment, the rights and obligations of parenthood are assumed derived from paternity, regardless of whether there is a biological link.

Possession of the status of a child is not only an indication of paternity, but is also an instrument to legally recognize a factual situation that does not correspond to biological reality when such recognition is most beneficial to the child.

The gay married couple had entered into a gestational surrogacy agreement with a single surrogate. It was agreed that the gay couple would be the parents and that the surrogate would not be the parent of any child conceived from an embryo created from the sperm of one of the men and an egg from an anonymous donor.

Parentage of the couple was determined based on intention and their acknowledgment that they were the parents. To do so was considered in the child's best interests. It was fundamental that the couple intended to be the parents and that the surrogate consented to this.

The 2021 Case

In 2021, the Supreme Court ruled that human rights under the Constitution of Mexico applied also to foreigners. Therefore, laws in Tabasco that prevented foreigners and gay couples form undertaking surrogacy were invalid. A gay couple from Europe who had undertaken surrogacy in Tabasco were therefore recognized as the parents.

As of Mid 2024

Pre-birth orders recognizing both intended parents are made in both Jalisco State and Mexico City. Some attorneys are insistent, however, that the surrogate be named on the birth certificate, along with the genetic father.

It is important to take care with the choice of attorney and where surrogacy is to occur in Mexico, as surrogacy is banned in several states. See more in Chapter 4.

The U.S. Embassy in Mexico said in June 2024:

> There is no legal framework to protect foreigners or same-sex couples who pursue surrogacy in Mexico, despite agencies and clinics promoting Mexico as a safe, legal destination for commercial surrogacy. Surrogacy agreements between foreign and/or same-sex intending parents and gestational mothers are not enforced by Mexican courts. Intending U.S. citizen parents have suffered administrative and legal impediments in documenting children born through surrogacy. Some parents have been delayed weeks to months in Mexico while waiting for court decisions on parental rights and custody. Although the citizenship of the child might be straightforward, citizenship does not confer custody. Custody and parental rights are subject to Mexican law. Mexican surrogacy law is incomplete and open to wide interpretation.
>
> Be wary of agencies/clinics that guarantee the legality of surrogacy in Mexico or fail to explain the risks. Clinics that offer "VIP" packages such as expedited embassy/consulate appointments, tailored delivery dates, or birth documents that omit the gestational mother are often operating outside the boundaries of Mexican law. Although it is exceedingly rare, the gestational mother could enforce her parental right at any point during the surrogacy process regardless of signed and notarized contracts with the intending parents or the agency, causing possible long and unexpected delays in documenting your child's citizenship. Make sure you understand Mexican law, which recognizes the gestational mother as the child's legal parent with full parental rights and mandates that the gestational mother be listed on the Mexican state-issued birth certificate. Be aware that individuals who attempt to circumvent local law risk criminal prosecution. Mexican authorities have made arrests stemming from surrogacy cases.[12]

12. U.S. Mission to Mexico, *Surrogacy and Art in Mexico*, U.S. Embassy & Consulates Mex. (June 23, 2024), https://mx.usembassy.gov/surrogacy-art-and-dna-testing/.

Colombia

T-968/09 (2009)[13]

The Constitutional Court recognized parenthood through surrogacy, based on biology, but it also appears in part to be based on intention. Solomon, a citizen of Colombia, and his wife, Rachel, a citizen of the Dominican Republic, lived in the United States. They agreed with a Colombian woman, Mrs. Sarai, for her to be their surrogate. Three attempts, using embryos of the intended parents' genetic material, were unsuccessful. Attempts with donor eggs were also unsuccessful.

Solomon persuaded Mrs. Sarai to try again, as a traditional surrogate but using in vitro fertilization (IVF) with his sperm. He visited her frequently. However, the parties never lived together or had a relationship. In return, he promised her a "*good economic position so that she would have the child and that the child would be raised by the two of them.*"[14] Mrs. Sarai said that they tried natural conception once, unsuccessfully.

Solomon and Mrs. Sarai went to a second IVF clinic. They said that they were a couple.

IVF occurred, followed by implantation of four embryos, resulting in a twin pregnancy. Solomon paid Mrs. Sarai what was described as a "*large sum*," with monthly payments during the pregnancy, and a significant amount at the end of the pregnancy.

Twin boys were born. As Mrs. Sarai suffered from preeclampsia, she had to stay in the hospital. She registered the children in her name. Solomon was in the United States at the time of the births. Mrs. Sarai had hidden from the father that the children had been born.

During the nine months that the twins were in Mrs. Sarai's care, the father did not provide them with food or medical assistance, even though they had already been registered by him.

The children developed influenza and were then taken into state care. The father then sought that the children live with him in the United States. A court authorized their removal from Colombia. The father removed the children to the United States. A subsequent order to revoke the authorization did not result in the children's return.

A lower court found that there was a contract between Solomon and Mrs. Sarai as to traditional surrogacy, obliging her to deliver the fruit resulting from the couple to Solomon and Rachel. Surrogacy was not recognized under the law, as surrogacy was neither legal nor illegal, as

13. Corte Constitucional [C.C.] [Constitutional Court], diciembre 18, 2009, Sentencia T-968/09.

14. *Id.* I.1.

there was no code or law prohibiting it. Children were born with equal rights under the constitution and therefore the genetic mother is a mother in the case of a surrogacy contract. Mrs. Sarai was therefore the mother.

The Constitutional Court held:

> The family, society and the State have the obligation to assist and protect the child in order to ensure his or her harmonious and integral development and the full exercise of his or her rights, which take precedence over the rights of others.
>
> This enhanced protection of children's rights, according to constitutional jurisprudence, is based on three main reasons: (i) their situation of fragility vis-à-vis the world, to a greater or lesser degree depending on their personal development; (ii) it is a way of promoting a democratic society in which its members know and share the principles of freedom, equality, tolerance and solidarity; and (iii) it is a way of correcting the deficit of political representation suffered by children in our political system, as they cannot participate directly in the legislative debate. . . .
>
> This preferential treatment of the child as a relevant legal interest, which implies adopting "a form of determinate behavior, a duty to be, which delimits both state and private action in matters involving them," finds clear support and recognition in contemporary international law through the so-called principle of the best interests of the child, first enshrined in the 1924 Geneva Declaration on the Rights of the Child, and later reproduced in other international instruments such as the Universal Declaration of Human Rights, the 1959 Declaration of the Rights of the Child, the International Covenant on Civil and Political Rights and the [United Nations] Convention on the Rights of the Child.[15]

The court was concerned that it act in the best interests of the child, based on domestic law, Articles 3.1 and 3.2 of the United Nations Convention on the Rights of the Child, and consistent with the approach of the Inter-American Court of Human Rights. Further, there needed to be a balance between the rights of children and the rights of their parents, on the basis that the rights of the child prevail.

In a similar view to that of the Supreme Court of Mexico:

15. *Id.* II.3.

> [I]n a plural society, there cannot be a single and exclusive concept of family, identifying the latter only with that arising from the marriage bond.[16]

Children had a right to have a family and not be separated from it, which is directly related to their right to receive love and care in order to develop fully and harmoniously. Further:

> [M]easures that result in the separation of a child from his or her biological family are appropriate only when the circumstances of the case clearly indicate that the family is unfit to fulfil its basic functions in relation to the best interests of the child and that the suitability of a particular family group is determined by careful consideration of the particular circumstances of each case and by applying, among other things, the following criteria:
>
> (1) (i) the existence of clear risks to the life, integrity or health of the child,
> (ii) a history of physical, sexual or psychological abuse in the family, and
> (iii) all forms of abandonment, physical or moral violence, kidnapping, sale, sexual abuse, labor or economic exploitation, and hazardous work.
>
> (2) Other compelling grounds, including the inadequacy of a certain family group, but also on a case by case basis, for example, giving the child up for adoption or of having delegated the day-to-day care of a minor to persons other than his or her parents.
>
> (3) There are circumstances the verification of which is not sufficient, in itself, to justify a decision to separate the child from his or her biological family, for example, where the biological family is poor, or when its members do not have a basic education, or when one of its members has lied to the authorities in order to recover the child, or when one of the parents or relatives has a bad temper (without having abused the child, or in any of the circumstances constituting domestic violence).[17]

The court held:

16. *Id.* II.5.
17. *Id.*

> In the Colombian legal system there is no express prohibition for the execution of this type of convention or agreement. However, with regard to assisted reproduction techniques, which include surrogacy or surrogate motherhood, legal doctrine has considered that they are legally legitimate, by virtue of article 42-6 of the Constitution, which provides that "Children born in or out of wedlock, adopted or procreated naturally or with scientific assistance, have equal rights and duties."[18]

The court described that there was a "*regulatory vacuum*" of surrogacy and called for comprehensive regulation.

The *effect of the decision* is that where there is a biological link between parent and child, then the basis for parenthood is established. Commonly the intended genetic father will be recognized on the birth certificate in Colombia, along with the surrogate. Post-birth, a declaration will be obtained that the surrogate is not a parent. If there is a second intended parent, that intended parent will then be added to the birth certificate.[19]

The Constitutional Court in *T-275-22* (2022) upheld the ability of an intended, genetic father, Mr. Mauritius, through surrogacy to obtain paternity leave. The single surrogate, Lorena, chose not to take part in the proceedings.

The court noted that it had repeatedly warned of the need to regulate surrogacy. Since 2016, according to the judgment, there have been nine bills before the legislature to either prohibit surrogacy for profit, or to regulate ART. None of them have passed.

Another bill in 2023 similarly failed.

Argentina

Surrogacy in Argentina relies on statute and regulations. The Argentine Civil and Commercial Code recognizes procreative intent as a basis for filiation in ART. Parentage arises from intent, regardless of the genetic link.

Buenos Aires recognizes parentage through surrogacy. If the regulations are complied with, the intended parents (couples or singles, irrespective of marital status, gender, or sexuality) are recognized as the parents on the birth of the child by operation of law, whether or not there is a genetic link.[20]

---

18. *Id.*

19. As of May 2024, the delay in obtaining the declaration is between six and 18 months.

20. As of May 2024, there have been reports of significant delays in obtaining birth certificates for children born in Buenos Aires via surrogacy to foreign intended

The relevant regulation provides:

As a precautionary measure, the births of minors born through highly complex Assisted Human Reproduction Techniques, known as gestational surrogacy, are authorized to be registered under the following conditions:

1) That they are minors born in the Autonomous City of Buenos Aires by gestational surrogacy;
2) That the procreative intent of the parents has been expressed in a previous, free and informed manner;
3) That the gestational carrier has previously and duly expressed that she does not have procreative intent; and
4) That the registration must be made as a precautionary measure, and the data of the gestational carrier must be recorded in the file.[21]

Some requirements are:

- The ART can occur in Argentina or overseas.
- The child must be born in Buenos Aires.
- Each of the intended parents and the surrogate must execute informed consent (or lack of it, respectively), notarized, before implantation. One Argentine attorney requires the intended parents to execute their informed consent in Buenos Aires, out of concern that otherwise it is not valid.[22]

Parentage by Pre-Conception Order

Greece

Noncommercial surrogacy is available in Greece to single women and to heterosexual couples. Under Greek Civil Code Article 1458, a preconception order is made by a court. The order not only authorizes treatment to occur, but the effect of the order is that by operation of law the intended parents are the parents, and the surrogate is not.

parents. It is suggested that this is due to concerns raised by officials at the large number of foreigners undertaking surrogacy there, a factor not considered when the regulations were written.

21. Regulation No. 93/DGRC/17, Oct. 13, 2017, *as amended by* Regulation No. 103/DGRC/17, *as amended by* Regulation No. 122/DGRC/20, sec. 1.

22. As of June 2024, there have been reports of delays in birth certificates issuing to children born to foreign intended parents. It has been asserted that the delays are caused by officials concerned about the number of foreign intended parents undertaking surrogacy.

Israel

Noncommercial surrogacy is available to heterosexual married couples, gay couples, or single men or women. Under the Embryo Carrying Agreements Act,[23] surrogacy agreements must be approved by the Committee for the Approval of Embryo Carrying Agreements. These can cover surrogacy arrangements both in Israel and abroad. Among the many requirements are that the surrogate is of the same religion as the intended parents, although some latitude can be given if both the surrogate and the intended parents are not Jewish. There must be a genetic link between one of the intended parents and the child. The intended parents must be residents of Israel.

Under section 10 of the act, upon birth of the child, the intended parents are the parents of the child by operation of law.

Data from the Israeli Department of Health[24] reveals that between 1996 and 2017, 231 children were born to surrogates, of whom about 30 were born from multiple births. About 75 percent of the surrogates were aged in their 30s. Thirty-two percent of surrogates held an academic degree, of which 9 percent held a master's degree or doctorate. Two-thirds of the surrogates were married and one-third were single.

South Africa

Noncommercial surrogacy is available to singles or couples, at least one of whom is domiciled in South Africa. There must be a genetic link with at least one of the intended parents. Court approval is required before treatment commences. The court approval is to validate the surrogacy agreement.

Children's Act section 297 provides:

> (1) The effect of a valid surrogate motherhood agreement is that—
> (a) any child born of a surrogate mother in accordance with the agreement is for all purposes the child of the commissioning parent or parents from the moment of the birth of the child concerned;
> (b) the surrogate mother is obliged to hand the child over to the commissioning parent or parents as soon as is reasonably possible after the birth;

23. Also translated as the Gestational Carrier Agreements Law.

24. *Surrogacy in Israel*, Gov'T Isr., https://www.gov.il/en/service/embryo-carrying (last updated Mar. 21, 2024).

(c) the surrogate mother or her husband, partner or relatives has no rights of parenthood or care of the child;

(d) the surrogate mother or her husband, partner or relatives have no right of contact with the child unless provided for in the agreement between the parties;

(e) subject to sections 292 and 293, the surrogate motherhood agreement may not be terminated after the artificial fertilisation of the surrogate mother has taken place; and

(f) the child will have no claim for maintenance or of succession against the surrogate mother, her husband or partner or any of their relatives.

(2) Any surrogate motherhood agreement that does not comply with the provisions of this Act is invalid and any child born as a result of any action taken in execution of such an arrangement is for all purposes deemed to be the child of the woman that gave birth to that child.

Post-Soviet States: Parentage by Operation of Law

Georgia, Kazakhstan, and Ukraine

In each of these post-Soviet States, the intended parents—by process of law—are the parents of the child at birth, and the surrogate is not. The requirement in each is that the intended parents are a heterosexual, married couple who have a medical need.

Article 143 of the *Georgian* Health Code provides:

1. In vitro fertilisation shall be allowed:
   a) to treat infertility, if there is a risk of transmitting a genetic disease from the wife or the husband to the child, using the gametes or embryo of the couple or a donor, if a written consent of the couple has been obtained;
   b) if a woman does not have an uterus, by transferring the embryo obtained as a result of fertilisation to the uterus of another women ("surrogate mother") and growing it there; obtaining a written consent of the couple shall be obligatory.
2. If a child is born, the couple shall be deemed as parents, with the responsibilities and authorities proceeding from this fact;

> the donor or the "surrogate mother" shall not have the right to be recognised as a parent of the born child.

In June 2023, the Georgian Health Minister announced that there would be laws enacted in Georgia to ban international intended parents from January 1, 2024. As of April 2024, the relevant legislation was introduced to Parliament but not yet enacted. Part of the reason for doing so appears to have been the huge growth in surrogacy demand in Georgia. Part of it may have been to align Georgia with Russia—which banned international intended parents in 2022. Part may also have related to the Ozturk family. See Chapter 18. As of May 2024, reports from Georgia indicate that the government is not seeking to proceed with the proposed ban.

As of late 2023, with the continued capacity restrictions in Ukraine, and the pending closure in Georgia, *Kazakhstan* was seen as a new destination for surrogacy. Article 54 of the Kazakhstan Family Code provides:

> 1. A surrogacy contract shall be concluded in a written form in compliance with requests of the civil legislation of the Republic of Kazakhstan and shall be subject to be notarized.
> 2. Conclusion of surrogacy contract shall admittedly suggest parental rights and obligations of spouses (customers) to a child, born [as] a result of application of assisted reproductive methods and technologies.
> 3. Contemporaneously with the surrogacy contract, spouses (customers) shall conclude a contract with a healthcare organization, applying assisted reproductive methods and technologies, which will provide the relevant services.

Article 59.1 and .2 provides:

> 1. Spouses (customers) shall be recognized as the parents of a child, born as a result of assisted reproductive methods and technologies on the basis of the surrogacy contract.
>
>   In case of birth of two and more children in a result of application of such methods and technologies or according to the surrogacy contract, spouses (customers) shall incur liability for each born child in equal measure.
> 2. A wife (customer), concluded the surrogacy contract shall be registered as the mother of a child after his (her) birth in the medical birth certificate.

The second largest international surrogacy destination, *Ukraine*, shut down following the Russian invasion in February 2022. As of 2023, it had restarted—even when the bombs and missiles were still dropping.

Article 123 of the Ukrainian Family Code requires that there is a genetic link between one of the spouses and the child. It provides:

1. If the wife is fertilized by artificial procreation techniques upon written consent of her husband, the latter is registered as the father of the child born by his wife.
2. If an ovum conceived by the spouses is implanted to another woman, the spouses shall be the parents of the child.
3. Whenever an ovum conceived by the husband with another woman is implanted to his wife, the child is considered to be affiliated to the spouses.

As seen in Chapter 2, while a person or couple may, by operation of law, be identified as the parents of the child in the country of the child's birth, without a court order it may mean that they are not recognized as the child's parents in the home country—because the surrogate is identified there as the mother.

Russia

International intended parents can no longer (as of December 2022) access surrogacy in Russia. In a similar manner to Georgia, Kazakhstan, and Ukraine, the intended parents become parents by operation of law. A key difference between Russia and the other post-Soviet States is the requirement that the surrogate consent. There have been anecdotal reports of surrogates refusing to consent or seeking to extort the intended parents.

As seen in Chapter 2, with the case of *Paradiso & Campanelli v. Italy*,[25] where Russia recognizes the intended parents as the parents, they may not be recognized at home.

Article 51.4 of the *Russian* Family Code provides:

> Married persons who have given their consent in written form to the artificial fertilization or to the implantation of the embryo, shall be written down in the Register of Births if a child is born as a result of the application of these methods, as this child's parents.
>
> The married persons who have given their consent in written form to the implantation of an embryo in another woman for bearing it, may be written down as the child's parents only with the consent of the woman who has given birth to the child (of the surrogate mother).

25. App. No. 25358/12 (Dec. 9, 2015).

Presumption of Parentage by Contract

Brazil

In the absence of laws regulating surrogacy, surrogacy is governed by guidelines from the Federal Medical Council.[26] The guidelines require surrogacy to be altruistic,[27] and either when the intended mother has a medical need, or the intended parents are part of a same-sex marriage. The surrogate must be a family member.

Parentage is established by contract.

Iran

Although California and the Islamic Republic are as far away from each other as it is possible to be, Iran has taken a similar approach to that of California.

The traditional view held about Islam is that it bans surrogacy. A typical example is from neighbouring Pakistan, where the Sharia Court of Appeal held that surrogacy ought to be banned.

Surrogacy was first discussed at the Muslim World League's Islamic Fiqh Council in 1985, resulting in the view that surrogacy ought to be banned. The Fiqh Council of the Organization of the Islamic Conference concluded in 1986 that surrogacy was permissible only between heterosexual married couples under certain conditions.[28] The Islamic Fiqh Council determined that the five prohibited forms of ART were:

1. Egg donation
2. Sperm donation
3. Gestational surrogacy
4. Embryo donation or dual donation (i.e., egg and sperm donation)
5. Where a man has two wives, and the egg from one is implanted into the other

The council permitted two forms of IVF under Sunni Islam:

1. IVF, comprising the husband's sperm and the wife's egg, with the embryo implanted into the wife
2. Artificial insemination of the wife using the husband's sperm

In countries where sharia law affects Muslim people, but does not directly affect others, such as Malaysia, surrogacy is banned for Muslims but not for non-Muslims.

26. RCFM No. 2.121/2015.

27. As commercial surrogacy is considered uterus trafficking. CONSTITUIÇÃO FEDERAL [C.F] [CONSTITUTION] art. 199(4).

28. Shrabana Chattopadhyay, *Permissibility of Surrogacy in Islamic Law* (2020), https://ssrn.com/abstract=3952492 (last visited Mar. 29, 2024).

Iran, of course, is not Sunni but Shia. Surrogacy thrives in Iran, along with egg donation, provided it is for heterosexual married couples. Surrogates also need to be married.

Rather than rely on a court order to establish parentage, surrogacy in Iran is based on contract. Under the contract, the clear intent is that the intended parents, who are a heterosexual, married couple, are to be the parents, and that the surrogate and her husband are not. Reliant on the contract, which is made under the Iranian Civil Code of 1928, the intended parents are recognized automatically as the parents upon birth of the child. They are then registered as the parents on the birth certificate.

There appears to be a need for a genetic link between one of the intended parents and the child. The use of egg donors in surrogacy is common.

While it is said by some that surrogacy is "rent a womb," this concept is taken literally in Iran. The surrogate is named on the contract as lessor, and the intended parents as lessees. It is because of this status that the intended parents have the status of parents upon birth of the child.

Sri Lanka

Until recently, the process of surrogacy in Sri Lanka has been by way of adoption. Not surprisingly, this has been a very slow method of establishing parenthood.

The ongoing economic crisis in Sri Lanka, exacerbated in 2022 with the country running out of foreign reserves and, as a result, short of oil, medicine, and food, among other things, has caused a change in approach.

As of 2023, establishing parenthood in Sri Lanka, similar to that in Iran, is achieved by contract. Surrogacy is available to heterosexual married couples, where at least one of them has a genetic relationship to the child. By virtue of the contract, the intended parents are recognized as the parents upon the birth of the child. The intended parents can choose to simply be named on the birth certificate as the parents, or undertake the process of adoption. The latter will take several months, but gives certainty that the intended parents are the parents. There are risks for some foreign intended parents under the laws of their home jurisdiction if they undertake adoption in Sri Lanka. See Chapter 13.

Uruguay

Similarly to Brazil, surrogacy is established by contract.[29] The intended mother must have a medical need, as assessed by the ART Commission. Surrogacy must be altruistic. The surrogate must be a close relative.

---

29. Human Assisted Reproductive Treatment-Regulation Law No. 19167 art. 25 (2013).

The European View

As the Supreme Court of Mexico noted in 2018,[30] those countries that prohibit surrogacy attribute maternity to the pregnant mother. This view reflects the broad European view. It is that the surrogate and her rights are inviolate. This view was expressed by the then-United Nations Special Rapporteur on the Sale and Sexual Exploitation of Children, Including Child Prostitution, Child Pornography, and Other Child Sexual Abuse in a note to the secretariat in 2018 where the Special Rapporteur said:

> International and regional human rights instruments protect the right to "found a family" or the right to "respect for . . . private and family life." The language of a "right to procreate" is used in some national legal systems, though this terminology is not found in international human rights instruments. On bases such as these, it is sometimes argued that all adults are entitled to create a family and raise children. However, it is recognized that there is no "right to a child" under international law. A child is not a good or service that the State can guarantee or provide, but rather a rights-bearing human being. Hence, providing a "right to a child" would be a fundamental denial of the equal human rights of the child. The "right to a child" approach must be resisted vigorously, for it undermines the fundamental premise of children as persons with human rights.[31]

It was an approach that fit the description by the Supreme Court of Mexico of places that prohibit surrogacy. In her paper, the Special Rapporteur relied on the 1989 United Nations Convention on the Rights of the Child and in particular the optional protocol to the Convention on the Rights of the Child on the Sale of Children, Child Prostitution, and Child Pornography, and on the Trafficking of Persons Protocol of 2000.

The Special Rapporteur's view that there was no international law on the right to reproduce was wrong, as seen in Chapter 1.

The Special Rapporteur said that under the optional protocol:

> Surrogacy arrangements constitute sale of children whenever the surrogate mother or a third party receives "remuneration or

30. Amparo en Revisión, Suprema Corte de Justicia de la Nación [SCJN], Noviembre de 2018, 553/2018, página 23.

31. *Report of the Special Rapporteur on the Sale and Sexual Exploitation of Children, Including Child Prostitution, Child Pornography, and Other Child Sexual Abuse Material*, U.N. Doc. A/HRC/37/60, at 64 (Jan. 15, 2018).

any other consideration" in exchange for transferring the child. There are three elements in the definition of sale of children:

(a) "remuneration or any other consideration" (payment);
(b) transfer of a child (transfer); and
(c) the exchange of "(a)" for "(b)" (payment for transfer).[32]

In her view:

1. A pre-birth order (as is commonly seen in the United States and other countries such as in Mexico, Greece,[33] and South Africa) amounted to the sale of a child.
2. A binding surrogacy contract (as is commonly seen in a number of jurisdictions, such as much of the United States, and several jurisdictions where there is noncommercial surrogacy—such as Canada, Greece, and South Africa), whereby the intended parents become the parents of the child, amounted to the sale of a child.
3. Payment to the surrogate of greater than her reasonable expenses amounted to the sale of a child.

The then-Special Rapporteur's view is typified by this paragraph:

> The legal fiction of the "never-a-mother" gestational carrier is a legal concept which is used to justify denial of the surrogate mother's rights. Once the surrogate mother is reduced, during pregnancy, to a never-a-mother gestational carrier acting for the benefit of intending parents, the door is open to enforcing contracts that purport to alienate her rights and freedoms (e.g. the right to health and the right to freedom of movement).[34]

This "never a mother" view is the view commonly seen in the United States, Mexico, Argentina, Greece, Israel, South Africa, Georgia, Kazakhstan, Russia, Iran, and Sri Lanka—that the intended parents are the parents upon the birth of the child—and that the surrogate is not.

Further:

> Some claim that intending parents cannot buy "their own" children. However, intending parent(s) at a minimum are paying

32. *Id.* at 42.
33. Pre-conception order in each of Greece and South Africa.
34. *Report of the Special Rapporteur on the Sale and Sexual Exploitation of Children, Including Child Prostitution, Child Pornography, and Other Child Sexual Abuse Material*, *supra* note 31, at 57.

> for exclusivity, so that they will not have to share parentage and parental responsibility with the surrogate mother. In order to achieve this exclusivity, intending parent(s) pay the surrogate mother to release and transfer legal parentage and parental responsibility, as well as to physically transfer the child.
>
> The premise that the child is automatically the child of the intending parent(s) is also flawed. It is often the contract or the arrangement that is the basis for parentage in commercial surrogacy jurisdictions, and the contract explicitly or implicitly includes a transfer . . . .[35]

In addition:

> In general, the provisions relating to the transfer of the child are of the essence of the agreement, without which the intending parents would neither enter into the agreement nor pay the surrogate mother. Hence, although commercial surrogacy includes the sale of services, it also usually includes the sale of the child.
>
> Some try to evade the prohibition on sale of children by inserting into surrogacy agreements a provision stating, in substance, that the parties agree that all payments are for services and none are for the transfer or sale of the child. However, the prohibition on sale of children cannot be avoided by contracts arbitrarily relabelling the sale of children as something else, when in substance the arrangement includes the sale of children.[36]

At the time, the then-Special Rapporteur was considering whether or not there should be a United Nations convention outlawing all international surrogacy, other than that which she saw as noncommercial, where the surrogate could decide post-birth whether or not to relinquish the child.

Ultimately, she did not press for an international convention, acknowledged that there was a right to procreate, pressed for the Hague Conference on Private International Law to do more to protect the human rights of the surrogate and the child—and was actively involved in writing the Verona Principles, discussed later.

That manner of thinking is based in part, it is said, on the United Nations Convention on the Rights of the Child. See Chapter 1 for a discussion of the convention.

35. *Id.* at 58.

36. *Id.* at 60–61.

Part of this thinking in Europe appears derived from the age-old thinking to identify the father since the time of the Emperor Justinian: the mother is always certain.[37] Certainly, there appears to be a religious influence as to who is a parent, which is then reinforced by a view taken of the United Nations Convention on the Rights of the Child. This then comes down to who is considered to be the parent. If the surrogate, by having given birth, is considered to be the parent, then the child's rights automatically attach to the parent, not to the intended parents.

As seen in Mexico and Colombia, for example, despite their concerns about surrogacy, the courts have focused on the best interests of the child, while reconciling the legitimate rights and concerns of the intended parents and the surrogate. The approach commonly seen in Europe (illustrated in Chapter 2) is that the surrogate remains the mother. The fact that she may have agreed not to be the mother, and that under the law of the place where surrogacy occurred—for example, in the United States—she is not the mother, seems beside the point.

Public policy of most European countries is opposed to surrogacy and for upholding the rights of the child and the surrogate.

In the Netherlands, for example, although a U.S. birth certificate will reflect that the intended parents are the parents, that will be rejected. The thinking in the Netherlands is that the surrogate, being the mother, must necessarily be on the birth certificate. Article 8 provides:

1. States Parties undertake to respect the right of the child to preserve his or her identity, including nationality, name and family relations as recognized by law without unlawful interference.
2. Where a child is illegally deprived of some or all of the elements of his or her identity, States Parties shall provide appropriate assistance and protection, with a view to re-establishing speedily his or her identity.

That article came about following events in Argentina. The junta that then ruled Argentina had the practice of torturing its opponents and then flying them over the South Atlantic, pushing the opponents to their death. Their babies were then given away to "*deserving*" childless couples associated with the regime. Not surprisingly, after democracy returned to Argentina, the Argentinian delegation was insistent that there be this article to ensure that the child's right to an identity be established as part of international law.

---

37. "*Mater semper certa est.*"

This right to an identity has been interpreted by some in Europe as relating to genetics and by some as relating to the surrogate, or both. As seen in Mexico and Colombia, the right to an identity includes those who are in reality the child's family—the intended parents—not the legal fiction of the surrogate.

Rarely in Europe, this right to an identity has been identified as relating to the intended parents. Article 8 was considered in England as including a positive obligation that requires the State to ensure that de facto relationships are recognized and protected by law. It required the court to provide protection on the rights of children, which are real and effective and not theoretical and illusory. Family life for the child came about because the child lived with both intended parents. The child was biologically related to the intended father and perhaps the intended mother. The effect of not making an order transferring parentage to the intended parents would be an interference with that family life in that the factual relationship will not be recognized by law. A further relevant consideration is that family life is not only a matter of fact and degree, but also the significance of legal relationships. If an order were not made, there would be no legal connection between the child and his deceased biological father. Protection of the right to family life presupposes the factual existence of family life. Once that is established, the State must facilitate and protect that right.[38]

Further:

> The concept of identity includes the legal recognition of relationships between children and parents. In ZH (Tanzania) v Secretary of State for the Home Department UKSC 2011 4 Baroness Hale considered that the courts in this jurisdiction and decision makers had to have regard to the key principles of the [United Nations Convention on the Rights of the Child (UNCRC)], both in Respect of article 8 of the [European Convention on Human Rights (ECHR)] and in its application to decisions by authorities in this jurisdiction. If the consequences of a purpose of construction of [the statute] is that the child's identity with his biological father is preserved and the child's identity is linked to both [the intended parents] the court may consider itself bound to arrive at such a conclusion on the combined reading of Article 8 ECHR and Article 8 of the UNCRC.[39]

38. A v. P (Surrogacy: Parental Order: Death of Applicant) [2011] EWHC (Fam) 1738, [2012] 2 FLR 143 [28].

39. *Id.*

As seen in Chapter 2, this idea of public policy being against surrogacy has been used time and again by countries not to recognize children of their citizens who have been born overseas through surrogacy.

The opposition to surrogacy, at least in part, comes from religion. Italy has proposed to ban all international surrogacy. See Chapter 4.

We have seen in Chapter 2 that the following countries banned surrogacy, and their nation's highest courts sought to withhold recognition of parentage to children born overseas through surrogacy, based on this public policy:

- France
- Iceland
- Italy
- Norway
- Switzerland

Each of the highest courts in Germany and Italy, while emphasizing the public policy against surrogacy, have taken differing approaches to whether parentage of a child born overseas will be recognized at home.

Germany

The Supreme Court of Germany[40] recognized the parentage of a child born through surrogacy in the United States.

A German gay couple underwent surrogacy in California with a single surrogate. The men obtained an order in California recognizing them as the parents. German authorities refused to register the men as the child's parents. Paternity was established, as the genetic father was recognized as a parent under German law. If the surrogate had been married, that would have been denied, as the surrogate's husband would have been recognized as the father.

Lower Court's Approach

Surrogacy was banned in Germany under Civil Code section 1591, Embryo Protection Act section 1(1) no. 7, and Adoption Mediation Act section 13c.

A lower court was scathing about surrogacy. The intention of the legislature is to protect the human dignity of the women and children concerned. The legislature took the view that surrogacy agreements disregarded the essential interests of the children thus created, since the importance of

40. Bundesgerichtshof [BGH] [Federal Court of Justice] Dec. 10, 2014, XII ZB 463/13.

development in the womb for the development of the child's personality and the significant contribution of the biological and psychological relationship between the pregnant woman and the child to that development were disregarded. That particular relationship prohibits the assumption of pregnancies as a kind of service. In addition, the protection of the women and children concerning health and psychological risks after childbirth should be ensured. The rejection of surrogacy is therefore to be regarded as a fundamental value decision and core of German law. It is prohibited for women to accept the burdens of pregnancy out of economic necessity and to make the child to be conceived the subject of a "commercial transaction." It cannot be argued that these are purely general preventive considerations, because in the present case, too, the mother and child were actually exposed to precisely those risks—insofar as it is advocated that the question of public policy infringement should be answered exclusively or primarily in the best interests of the child.

It was said that registration had been rightly refused because the nongenetic father was neither the father nor the mother of the child.

A sole registration of the genetic father was to be rejected as only incomplete notarization. The judgment of the Superior Court was not to be accepted with regard to the parent-child relationship between the nongenetic father and the child. Recognition would lead to a result that is manifestly incompatible with essential principles of German law. Admittedly, the reservation of recognition under public policy law is to be interpreted restrictively and limited to exceptional circumstances. An application could only be considered if the result of the recognition contradicted the basic ideas of German regulations and the concepts of justice contained therein to such an extent that it appeared intolerable according to domestic ideas. According to those assessments, however, there was a breach of public policy.

The ruling of the Superior Court is intended to establish a legal parent-child relationship solely on the basis of the surrogacy contract. The judge establishes the parent-child relationship between the child and the intended parents by judgment or order, without any further hearing or evidence, whereas in the absence of such a judicial act, the surrogate mother is entered on the birth certificate as the mother and, where appropriate, her husband as the father. A parent-child relationship established in this way is not only alien to German law, but is also intolerably contrary to essential principles of German law. German law recognizes a parent-child relationship only on the basis of parentage or adoption. Parenthood on the basis of a surrogacy contract could not be established under German law.

German law only recognized parentage through descent or adoption, and provides that the surrogate is the mother of the child.

According to the considerations made by the legislature with regard to the Adoption Mediation Act, the problem of involuntary childlessness for the assessment of surrogacy is countered by the drastic interference in the personality of the children born in this way, but also of the women used for the realisation of these interests, and equally by the influence on the mother-child relationship that begins with pregnancy. This special kind of relationship of unborn life with the mother prohibits the assumption of pregnancies as a kind of service, since the close personal relationship between the pregnant woman and the child, which is essential for the development of the child, can hardly be established under these circumstances.

It is no less important to ensure that the affected women and children are protected against health and psychological hazards after childbirth. In the case of children, it is above all a matter of an undisturbed search for identity and a secure family assignment; in the case of women it is a matter of excluding inhumane conflicts from taking over pregnancies as a service and not least possible disputes about the surrender of the child. Finally, special conflicts on the occasion of surrogacy could arise if, after the birth of a disabled child, the intended parents did not want to take over the child, if the surrogate mother did not want to separate from the child after the birth, or if the question of an abortion arose during pregnancy.

The court held that a foreign court decision that legally determines kinship between a child and his or her parents, as the California decision had done, can be fully recognized in Germany.

Any consideration of whether a foreign court decision is contrary to German public policy (*ordre public*) must take into account the human rights guaranteed by the European Convention on Human Rights. A foreign judgment assigning parenthood to a child's intended parents—rather than to the surrogate mother as provided by German law—does not automatically constitute a breach of German public policy if at least one of the intended parents is genetically related to the child. This also applies where the foreign court decision awards parenthood to the registered civil partner of the genetic father of the child, as well as the genetic father.

The decision of the California court would have been recognized in Germany if it had a legal or merely declaratory effect. In contrast to a mere registration or notarization of the relationship, the decision is based on a substantive examination (consistent with *Johnson v. Calvert*—see earlier in this chapter), which, in addition to the validity of the surrogacy agreement, also deals with the status sequence associated with it. Thus, a declaratory decision is also subject to procedural recognition. It has a corresponding legal effect and, if there are no obstacles to recognition, is binding in Germany.

The California court rightly assumed its international jurisdiction to decide the case. International jurisdiction under German law was linked to the nationality of the child, mother or father, or their habitual residence. The California jurisdiction arose because the surrogate was habitually resident in California, irrespective of the (effective) nationality and habitual residence of the child. Recognition was not precluded by any violation of public policy.

The child's right would be infringed if a legal status already established by another court's decision were to be abolished, which includes cases of surrogacy abroad. The court also relied on Article 3 of the United Nations Convention on the Rights of the Child, stating that the child's best interests must always be given preference in all decisions concerning the child.

A foreign judgment is not incompatible with this rule if the German judge—if he had decided the case—had come to a different conclusion on the basis of mandatory German law (prohibition of *révision au fond*). Rather, the decisive factor is whether the result of the application of foreign law in the specific case is in such strong contradiction to the basic ideas of the German regulations and the concepts of justice contained therein that it appears intolerable in the German view. The primary objective of the right to recognize a decision is to maintain the international consistency of decisions and—especially in matters relating to civil status—to avoid so-called limping legal relationships. The refusal of recognition on the grounds of violation of public policy is limited to exceptional cases.

With regard to the parenthood of the genetic father, a violation of public policy is ruled out for the simple reason that an application of German law would lead to a result consistent with the decision of the California Superior Court. On the basis of his acknowledgment of paternity declared before the German consulate, the genetic father would also be the father of the child concerned under German substantive law. Recognition was not excluded on the basis of the existing paternity of another man, as the surrogate was single, and the surrogate consented to the recognition. As a result, the decision of the California Superior Court does not violate public policy with regard to the nongenetic father either. Whether a foreign court decision that establishes a parenthood of the intended parents based on the surrogacy agreement is compatible with German public policy is controversial.

The fact that a foreign decision in the case of surrogacy assigns the legal parental status to the intended or ordering parents does not in itself result in a violation of German public policy, at least if an intended parent—unlike the surrogate mother—is genetically related to the child.

When deciding on the maternity of the genetic or biological mother in the sense of family law, the decisive factor must be that only the woman giving birth has a physical and psychosocial relationship with the child during pregnancy and during and immediately after birth.

The court followed the decisions of the European Court of Human Rights in *Mennesson v. France* and *Labassee v. France* (see Chapter 2) in upholding the rights of the child for private and family life under Article 8 of the European Convention. Every child has the right to a legal parent relationship with two parents.

The fact that parental status is assigned by the foreign decision to same-sex partners instead of a married couple cannot in itself result in a violation of public policy. According to the case law of the Federal Constitutional Court on successive adoption, it is rather to be assumed that the circumstances of a registered civil partnership can promote the upbringing of children just as much as those of a marriage. Accordingly, there is no sufficient basis for a differentiation between same-sex and different-sex intended parents in this respect.

Although the fact that opposite-sex intended parents may be fully genetic parents of the child may establish a closer relationship with the child, it does not preclude socially equal parenthood of life partners if the parenthood is intended to be permanent and is legally established.

An overall view of all the circumstances leads to the conclusion that the finding of a court on the basis of foreign law that there is a legal parent-child relationship between the child and the intended parents does not, in any event, contradict the essential principles of German law to such an extent that recognition of the relevant decision would appear to be intolerable in the end. Fundamental rights or human rights of the surrogate mother and the child also do not prohibit recognition in principle. Rather, the best interests of the child speak for rather than against recognition.

Surrogacy abroad has been carried out in a lawful manner and the child must now also be included in the consideration as a legal entity.

The human dignity of the surrogate mother may be violated if the surrogacy is carried out under circumstances that call into question the voluntary cooperation of the surrogate mother, or if essential circumstances remain unclear, such as information on the person of the surrogate mother, on the conditions under which she has agreed to carry the children to term, and on an agreement reached, or if fundamental procedural guarantees have been disregarded in foreign court proceedings.

A legal parent-child assignment is not without significance simply because the child can remain in the care of the intended parents even without one. This is because the best interests of the child also include the reliable legal assignment to the parents as the persons who continuously assume responsibility for his or her weal and woe.

The court rejected that adoption of the child would suffice. In addition to the difficulties associated with an adoption to be carried out in the country of birth, where the parenthood of the intended parents is already legally established, adoption entails additional risks for the child compared with an assignment made immediately at birth by virtue of parentage. This is because, even after the birth of the child, it would still be at the discretion of the intended parents whether they accept the child as their own or—for example because of the child's disability—refrain from their desire to have children. If, for example, the intended parents separate or she regrets her decision, it would in any case be possible for the genetically unrelated intended parent to permanently prevent legal parenthood from developing. Ultimately, the child would remain parentless in the country of birth and would not be able to enforce an assignment to the surrogate mother made in Germany. The intended parents, on the other hand, would be released from responsibility, even though they were the initiators of medically assisted conception and the child owes its existence to their decision.[41] The situation differs from adoption in that the child would not have been conceived and born without the surrogacy agreement. In contrast to adoptive parents, in the case of surrogacy, the intended parents undoubtedly play a central role in the subsequent identification of the child as persons (co-)responsible for its creation—persons, who, however, would not be reflected in a corresponding legal parental responsibility.

Italy

The Court of Cassation in 2019[42] refused to recognize a non-biological father as a parent. Two children had been born through surrogacy in Canada through two surrogacy journeys. The parents were an Italian gay couple. One man was the genetic father of both. The men had obtained an

41. At which one hears the words of *Johnson v. Calvert* ringing: "But for their acted-on intention, the child would not exist." 5 Cal. 4th 87, 93 (1993).

42. Cass., 8 maggio 2019, n. 12193/2019.

order in Ontario recognizing them as the parents. Canada is an altruistic surrogacy regime.

On their return to Italy, the men sought that the parentage of both children by both men be recognized.

The Court of Cassation refused to uphold the Ontario order. Its rationale was that surrogacy was prohibited in Italy as set out in Article 12.6 of Law No. 40/2004. The purpose of the law was a principle of public order, placed to protect the dignity of women. The court held that the foreign judicial measure required that the compatibility with public order

> must be evaluated in the same way not only as the fundamental principles of our Constitution and those consecrated in international and supranational sources, but also as the way in which they have been embodied in the ordinary discipline of the individual institutions, as well as the interpretation provided by constitutional and ordinary jurisprudence.[43]

It was seen that surrogacy intolerably offends the dignity of women and deeply undermines human relationships. The court left open the possibility of adoption of the child—a possibility that was not open to the couple in question, as it was not available to gay couples.[44]

Genetics

The nongovernmental organization International Social Service has adopted the Verona Principles (2021),[45] which in turn have been supported by the United Nations Committee on the Rights of the Child.

The Verona Principles purport to set out principles with surrogacy. On their face they are of deep concern as to whether a surrogacy arrangement in the United States, for example, will be recognized in another country. This is best typified in Principle 6:

---

43. *Id.* ¶ 12.3.

44. The difficulty with parental recognition in Italy was seen in *Re H* (Surrogacy: Step-parent adoption) [2023] EWFC 214, where a UK gay couple (one of whom was Italian) had undertaken surrogacy in Argentina but obtained a stepparent adoption order in the UK in order to enable the child to obtain Italian citizenship (rather than the usual route in the UK of a parental order).

45. INTERNATIONAL SOCIAL SERVICE, PRINCIPLES FOR THE PROTECTION OF THE RIGHTS OF THE CHILD BORN THROUGH SURROGACY (VERONA PRINCIPLES) (2021), https://bettercarenetwork.org/sites/default/files/2021-03/VeronaPrinciples_25February2021.pdf.

Best Interests of the Child

6.1 The best interests of the child shall be the paramount consideration in all decisions concerning legal parentage and parental responsibility related to a child born through surrogacy. The risk of short- and long-term harm to the child including but not limited to psychological and physical harm should also be considered.

[Comment: One could hardly argue with that approach.]

6.2 Protection of the best interests of the child precludes enforcement of contractual terms in surrogacy agreements purporting to transfer, establish, or relinquish legal parentage and parental responsibility.

[Comment: In other words, there can never be a binding contract.]

6.3 It is generally in the best interests of children born through surrogacy to have at least one genetically related intending parent.

[Comment: This issue of genetics appears to have greatly influenced several countries as to how surrogacy is permitted or recognized. An example of this approach is in South Africa. Section 294 of the Children's Act provides:

> No surrogate motherhood agreement is valid unless the conception of the child contemplated in the agreement is to be effected by the use of the gametes of both commissioning parents or, if that is not possible due to biological, medical or other valid reasons, the gamete of at least one of the commissioning parents or, where the commissioning parent is a single person, the gamete of that person.]

That genetic link requirement became the subject of a constitutional challenge in *AB v. Minister of Social Development.*[46]

The constitutional court held that the genetic link requirement serves the purpose of "*creating a bond between the child and the commissioning parents or parent. The creation of a bond is designed to protect the*

46. 2017 (3) BCLR 267 (CC).

best interests of the child to be born so that the child has a genetic link with its parent(s)."[47]

Psychological evidence before the court was that children of parents who used both male and female donor gametes through IVF enjoyed the same psychological well-being as children in the control group who had been conceived through intercourse. The evidence was disregarded.

The majority elaborated on the purpose. It held that one should consider the "*substance below the surface*," namely, "*clarity regarding the origin of a child is important to the self-identity and self-respect of the child.*"[48] In other words, the reason why the genetic link is required is to ensure that children know their genetic origins. AB intended to use male and female anonymous donors. If she had been allowed to proceed with her intended surrogacy agreement, her children would not know the identities of the donors. This according to the majority would compromise the children's self-identity and self-respect, and hence their dignity, and therefore would not be in their best interests.

In the second South African case, *Ex parte DW*,[49] a single and fertile man who did not have viable sperm intended to have children through surrogacy. He needed therefore to have a surrogate, egg donor, and sperm donor. He proposed to have sperm, consistent with *AB*, from an identity-release sperm donor in the United States. This would ensure that the children would in due course know their genetic origin. However, the KwaZulu-Natal High Court dismissed the application as it did not conform with section 24, namely that the gamete did not come from the intended father. The court said:

> I empathise with the applicant's desire to have a child, and would have helped him if I thought I could. Regrettably, I do not think I can.[50]

In the second constitutional challenge, *KB v. Minister of Social Development*,[51] *KB* and her husband could not conceive children through intercourse. As they could not contribute viable gametes, gametes from anonymous male and female donors were used to create embryos. One of these was transferred to *KB*'s womb and she fell pregnant. She then gave birth. There were complications with the birth. *KB* had to undergo a

47. *Id.* at 287.
48. *Id.* at 294.
49. [2022] ZAKZPHC 11.
50. *Id.* at 16.
51. [2023] ZAMPMBHC 12.

hysterectomy. *KB* and her husband intended to have more children using the remaining embryos and a surrogate. *KB* and her husband also have a child gestated by herself prior to the hysterectomy conceived by the same donor gametes that she now intends to use to further build her family through surrogacy. It remains to be seen whether *KB* is successful.

As seen in several of the cases discussed in Chapter 2, the European Court of Human Rights seems to pay much more attention when there is a genetic link, as opposed to when there is not. As seen in *A.M. v. Norway*,[52] for example, the woman who was the driving force to have a child through surrogacy due to her infertility was ultimately held not to be a parent—because of a lack of genetic link. Similarly in *Paradiso & Campanelli v. Italy*, the failure to have a genetic link between the intended parents and the child figured highly in why Italy removed the child from their care, and made it that much harder for them to have the child returned to them. Ultimately, they were unsuccessful.

Verona Principle 6.4 states:

> The best interests of children born through surrogacy should be promoted and protected at all times, including "when screenings and reviews of surrogacy arrangements prior to pregnancy are carried out." Such pre-surrogacy arrangements accomplish some of the purposes of a post-birth best interests of the child determination.

Verona Principle 6.5 states:

> A court or other competent authority of the State of birth shall, at a minimum, conduct a post-birth best interests of the child determination in proceedings concerning legal parentage and/or parental responsibility or if child protection measures are being considered in domestic and international surrogacy arrangements where:
>
> a. there have not been adequate pre-surrogacy evaluations and/or arrangements (see Principle on pre-surrogacy protections); or
> b. national laws provide that the surrogate mother is the legal parent at birth and a transfer of legal parentage is required; or
> c. there is a conflict between the surrogate mother and intending parents(s) or between the intending parents after birth in regard to legal parentage or parental responsibility; or

52. App. No. 30254/19 (Mar. 24, 2022).

d. there are unforeseen developments, particularly where neither the surrogate mother nor intending parents are able or willing to care for the child, or information has subsequently come to light that may affect the child's well-being, such as indications of sale, exploitation and trafficking or other illicit activity.
e. any other circumstances which may jeopardise the rights or best interests of the child.

This thinking is that there must always be a post-birth assessment of surrogacy, despite many jurisdictions where surrogacy is practiced having pre-conception orders, or recognition based on contract/biology, or by operation of law, or pre-birth orders, as set out in this chapter and as seen in Table 6.1. I have included in Table 6.1 all U.S. jurisdictions, to show the variety of ways that U.S. states deal with surrogacy.

Based on this model, automatic recognition of parentage at birth is deficient. Nevertheless, each of the Law Commissions of England and Wales, and Scotland, and New Zealand, have recommended auto-recognition of parentage upon birth. As seen in Chapter 2, the European Court of Human Rights is much more likely to accept parentage through a court order than by operation of law, but it still may not do so, as seen in *A.M. v. Norway.*

Table 6.1. Examples of Jurisdictions Where Intended Parents Are Recognized as Parents Automatically on the Birth of the Child/Post-Birth Orders Needed

Continent / Country / Province / State	Pre-Conception Order	Pre-Birth Order	Operation of Law	Contract	Post-Birth
North America					
Canada					
Alberta					Yes
British Columbia			Yes		
Manitoba			Yes		
New Brunswick					Yes
Newfoundland and Labrador					Yes
Nova Scotia					Yes
Ontario			Yes		

Continent / Country / Province / State	Pre-Conception Order	Pre-Birth Order	Operation of Law	Contract	Post-Birth
Prince Edward Island					Yes
Québec	No	No	No	No	Adoption
Saskatchewan					Yes
United States					
Alabama		Sometimes			Yes
Alaska	Yes				
Arizona		Sometimes			Yes
Arkansas		Yes			
California		Yes			
Colorado		Yes			
Connecticut		Yes			
Delaware		Yes			
District of Columbia		Yes			
Florida					Yes[53]
Georgia		Yes			
Hawaii					Yes
Idaho		Yes			
Illinois			Yes		
Indiana		Sometimes			Yes
Iowa		Both pre-and post-orders			Yes
Kansas		Yes			
Kentucky		Yes			
Louisiana		Yes			
Maine		Yes			
Maryland		Yes			

53. Florida is an example where a post-birth order is made (where there is a genetic connection with the child)—but the *Johnson v. Calvert* approach is embodied in the statute. The intended parents are taken to be the parents. FLA. STAT. § 742.16(7) (1993).

Continent / Country / Province / State	Pre-Conception Order	Pre-Birth Order	Operation of Law	Contract	Post-Birth
Massachusetts		Yes			
Michigan		Sometimes			Yes
Minnesota					Yes
Mississippi		Yes			
Missouri		Yes			
Montana		Yes			
Nebraska					Yes
Nevada		Yes			
New Hampshire		Yes			
New Jersey		Yes			
New Mexico		Yes			
New York		Yes			
North Carolina		Yes			
North Dakota		Yes			
Ohio		Sometimes			Yes
Oklahoma		Yes			
Oregon		Yes			
Pennsylvania		Yes			
Rhode Island		Yes			
South Carolina		Both pre-and post-orders			Yes
South Dakota		Yes			
Tennessee		Sometimes			Yes
Texas		Both pre-and post-orders			Yes
Utah		Yes			
Vermont		Yes			
Virginia	Yes + a confirmatory post-birth order				

Continent / Country / Province / State	Pre-Conception Order	Pre-Birth Order	Operation of Law	Contract	Post-Birth
Washington		Yes			
West Virginia		Yes			
Wisconsin		Both pre-and post-orders			
Wyoming		Yes			
Latin America					
Argentina	Unclear				
Buenos Aires			Yes		
Dominican Republic				Unclear	
Mexico					
Jalisco		Yes			
Mexico City		Yes			
Europe					
Georgia			Yes		
Greece	Yes				
Kazakhstan			Yes		
Russia			Yes, with surrogate's consent		
Ukraine			Yes		
United Kingdom			Proposed except N. Ireland		Yes
Asia					
Iran				Yes	
Israel	Yes, by state committee				
Kazakhstan			Yes		
Sri Lanka				Yes	
Oceania					
New Zealand			Proposed		Adoption

Verona Principle 6.6 states:

In international surrogacy arrangements where there is at least one State that does not permit the specific arrangement, a best interests of the child determination should be conducted additionally by a court or any other competent authority of the State where the intending parent(s) intend to reside with the child.

Verona Principle 6.7 states:

The best interests of the child determination shall be carried out on the basis of the best interests assessment, which in proceedings concerning legal parentage and/or parental responsibility in surrogacy cases should include but not be limited to the following considerations:

a. The parties' intentions when entering into the surrogacy agreement;
b. The child's genetic and gestational links to each of the parties to the surrogacy agreement;
c. All sibling relationships of the child;
d. The suitability of each of the parties to be a fit and proper parent and/or carer of the child;
e. The ability of each of the parties to facilitate the child's relationships with other parties;
f. The value of a stable family unit in the child's development;
g. The likely effect on the child including psychological and emotional impact, throughout the child's life, of the decision;
h. Any harm which the child has suffered or is at risk of suffering;
i. The likely effect of the decision on future generations;
j. The child's ascertainable wishes and feelings regarding the decision, taking account of the child's age and understanding;
k. The child's characteristics which are considered relevant, including age and sex;
l. The child's particular needs, including physical and health needs;
m. The child's emotional and/or physical attachment to each of the parties;
n. All circumstances in relation to the surrogacy arrangement;
o. Potential involvement of illicit practices;
p. Transparency in financial transactions; and
q. The role of intermediaries.

Birth Certificate and the Baby Bump

Many intended parents, and for that matter lawyers, take the view that the birth certificate is the be-all and end-all. If the intended parents' names are shown on the birth certificate, then they *must* be the parents.

That view is accurate in some countries such as China. In China, the view is taken that the birth certificate is inviolate. Who is shown on the birth certificate are the parents—and that is the end of the story. Once the details are written down, it appears that they are etched in stone.

However, in many countries, including the United States, the birth certificate is not proof of parentage (as it is in China) but something much less than that—evidence of parentage. Courts and officials often peer behind the birth certificate in order to determine, in accordance with national law, as to who are (and who are not) the parents of the child.

Two famous examples suffice to illustrate the point. The first is that of *Paradiso & Campanelli v. Italy* (see Chapter 3), where Italy relied on its presumptions about parents, based on genetics, to determine who were the parents—not what was stated in the birth certificate.

The other is the notorious Baby Gammy case.

What Really Happened in the Baby Gammy Saga

The Baby Gammy case burst upon the world in August 2014. For the next month or so, the world's media followed, wrote about, and broadcast the case. The media camped out en masse outside the home of the intended parents, an Australian couple, Mr. and Mrs. Farnell. One revelation followed another. I had a bit part to play. For some reason, although I was not part of the case, which involved Mr. and Mrs. Farnell undertaking surrogacy in Thailand, I was considered an expert by the media. In one month, I did innumerable media interviews. In one day, I did five separate national television interviews, plus radio and press. There was a feeding frenzy by the media, of the kind satirized by Evelyn Waugh in *Scoop* (1938). It was utterly crazy.

So was the story. Eventually the matter ended up in court.[54] The court made findings about truth, which at times were at variance with some of the stories that had been published in the media to that point.

Mr. and Mrs. Farnell were childless. Like most Australian intended parents seeking to undertake surrogacy (see Chapter 4), they went

54. *Farnell & Chanbua* [2016] FCWA 17.

overseas, in this case to Thailand. Given that restrictions had commenced in India, Thailand had become the go-to place for surrogacy.

There was very little, if any, checking by the Thai IVF clinic that ran the surrogacy program. Mr. and Mrs. Farnell did not say, nor were they asked, that Mr. Farnell had been convicted of numerous child sex offences.

The Thai surrogate, Mrs. Chanbua, always wanted to have a son. She did not tell, nor was she asked, by the Thai IVF clinic about this. Nor was she honest about her age. Mrs. Chanbua falsely increased her age, as otherwise she could not be a surrogate through that clinic.

Twins were conceived, from a double embryo transplant (as was common in Thailand then), composed of Mr. Farnell's sperm and eggs from an anonymous donor. One was a boy, who became known as Gammy. The other was a girl, Pypah.

It was discovered in utero that Gammy had Down syndrome. The doctor suggested that there be an abortion—not in Thailand, as it was against the law, but to go to China where anything was possible with money. The Farnells refused. They wanted their son.

Following the births, Mrs. Chanbua relinquished Pypah, but did not relinquish Gammy. Riots and shootings were happening in Bangkok then, just before there was a coup. Rather than litigate in Thailand and place their and Pypah's lives at risk, Mr. and Mrs. Farnell returned to Western Australia with Pypah.

After Gammy and Pypah were born, Mrs. Chanbua again advertised her services as a surrogate, but she did not pursue this when she found out international commercial surrogacy had been banned in Thailand, apparently as a result of the furore about Gammy, and the Thai baby farm. See Chapter 18.

For some mysterious reason, they then commenced court proceedings in Western Australia so that they could have parental responsibility of Pypah. I say "mysterious," as court proceedings of that kind were very rare. Australian intended parents on returning home just got on with their lives. It was also mysterious because what happened next was entirely predictable.

They served Mrs. Chanbua. She promptly sought an order to have Pypah live with her. Commencing the court proceedings was a case of waking the dog with the loudest bell.

Ultimately, the court was faced with six parties—the Farnells, Mrs. Chanbua, an independent children's lawyer, the Australian Human Rights Commission, the Western Australian Attorney General, and child protective services.

The court determined that Pypah should remain living with the Farnells. The court noted that it was likely they had undertaken commercial surrogacy overseas in breach of Western Australian law. Pypah was attached to the Farnells. They were the only people she knew. She was at home in Bunbury, a regional town, apparently loved, and spoke English. To move her to the care of Mrs. Chanbua to be with Gammy would have meant she was speaking a language she did not know (Thai), was cared for by someone she did not know, and was removed from the place where she was loved and settled.

As to the risk to Pypah remaining in the care of the Farnells, child protective services had undertaken a thorough assessment, including visiting the home under the literal glare of the world's media. Authorities had determined that there would be both scheduled visits, but also surprise, unscheduled visits, to make sure Pypah remained safe. The court was satisfied that as a result there was not an unacceptable risk to her.

The court made plain that it was not bound by the birth certificate nor by Thai law as to who was a parent. The child was in Western Australia—and therefore Thai law did not apply but Western Australian law applied. The court determined that the Farnells were not the parents of the child in accordance with Western Australian law.[55]

The court rejected intention as an element of who is a parent. That approach has since been rejected in Australia.[56]

The court agreed with the approach by UK courts, where courts are caught between the competing considerations of Parliament banning commercial surrogacy, and the need to protect the child's best interests:

> I feel bound to observe that I find this process of authorisation most uncomfortable. What the court is required to do is to balance two competing and potentially irreconcilably conflicting concepts. Parliament is clearly entitled to legislate against commercial surrogacy and is clearly entitled to expect that the courts should implement that policy consideration in its decisions. Yet it is also recognised that as the full rigour of that policy consideration will bear on one wholly unequipped to comprehend it let alone deal with its consequences (i.e. the child concerned) that rigour must be mitigated by the application of a consideration of that child's welfare. That approach is both humane and intellectually coherent. The difficulty is that it is almost impossible

55. Although that outcome, that they were not the parents, may not reflect the law now.

56. *Masson v Parsons* [2019] HCA 21.

> to imagine a set of circumstances in which by the time the case comes to court, the welfare of any child (particularly a foreign child) would not be gravely compromised (at the very least) by a refusal to make an order. Bracewell J's decision in Re AW . . . is but a vivid illustration of the problem. If public policy is truly to be upheld, it would need to be enforced at a much earlier stage than the final hearing. . . . In relation to adoption this has been substantially addressed by rules surrounding the bringing of the child into the country and by the provisions of the Adoption with a Foreign Element Regulations 2005. **The point of admission to this country is in some ways the final opportunity in reality to prevent the effective implementation of a commercial surrogacy agreement.** It is, of course, not for the court to suggest how (or even whether) action should be taken, I merely feel constrained to point out the problem.[57]

Not surprisingly, in light of the facts of the case, the court was scathing about commercial surrogacy:

> The decision should therefore not be interpreted as indicating any form of approval of commercial surrogacy. While I accept my orders may be seen as encouragement to other couples to beg forgiveness rather than seek permission, the outcome might have been very different had the dispute come before me much earlier in Pypah's life. At that point, it may well have been decided it was in her best interests to return to live with her birth mother and twin brother.
>
> The appalling outcome of Gammy and Pypah being separated has brought commercial surrogacy into the spotlight. Quite apart from the separation of the twins, this case serves to highlight the dilemmas that arise when the reproductive capacities of women are turned into saleable commodities, with all the usual fallout when contracts go wrong. The facts also demonstrate the conflicts of interest that arise when middlemen rush to profit from the demand of a market in which the comparatively rich benefit from the preparedness of the poor to provide a service that the rich either cannot or will not perform.
>
> This case should also draw attention to the fact that surrogate mothers are not baby-growing machines, or "gestational

57. *In re* X & Y (Foreign Surrogacy) [2008] EWHC (Fam) 3030 [24], *quoted in Farnell* [2016] FCWA 17, at 353.

carriers." They are flesh and blood women who can develop bonds with their unborn children. It is noteworthy that no evidence was provided about the long-term impact on mothers of giving up children they carried, and there was no evidence of the impact on the children themselves. Nor was there any expert evidence of the impact on the other children of birth mothers who would have seen their mother pregnant, and perhaps felt the baby move in her belly, only to find that the baby never came home from hospital. Did those children wonder who would be the next to be given away? And what of their feelings of grief and loss if they were misled into believing the baby had died?

I accept it is for others to decide whether the manifest evils associated with overseas commercial surrogacy can be overcome by importing the problem into Australia, even though such suggestions have been made as a result of what happened to "baby Gammy." It is also for others to determine whether even a "first world" country can provide a regulatory regime sufficiently robust to protect the interests of surrogate mothers and the children they bear. But can any regime anticipate the ingenuity of would-be parents? Who would have contemplated the facts in Dudley & Chedi,[58] where a couple commissioned one surrogate to carry two boys and, at the same time, commissioned another to carry a third boy, with both mothers being induced on the same day so that all three boys would share a birthday? This arrangement was entered into notwithstanding it constituted an offence in Australia under the existing regulatory regime.

The arrangement leading to the births of Pypah and Gammy would never have been put in place had it not been for the fact that a department of the Australian Government provided assurances that the children would receive citizenship and automatic entry to this country. Such assurances could not be provided if the citizenship laws were harmonised with all the other laws of this country. Effective law reform therefore does not have to involve the legalisation of commercial surrogacy to encourage would-be parents to buy locally-grown children. Equally, it could involve amendment of the citizenship laws to align them even more clearly with existing state laws. A fundamental policy decision is required.[59]

58. [2011] FamCA 502.
59. *Farnell & Chanbua* [2016] FCWA 17 at 755–59.

Gammy continued to be cared for by Mrs Chanbua. Mr Farnell died of an asbestos related disease in 2020.[60]

The Final Word: Venezuela

The outcome when these conflicting approaches—between procreative intent, and that of the surrogate as mother, and protection of the identity of the child—are not resolved, is an arbitrary approach, dependent on the whims and values of the judge concerned, as happens in Venezuela.

The Civil Code specifies that the mother is determined by who gave birth, irrespective of genetics. The constitution recognizes the fundamental right to know one's biological or genetic origin. The Supreme Tribunal of Justice mentions the concept of the intention to parent.

Therefore, judges are caught between that the surrogate is the mother, the genetic test, and the intention to parent being the tests of who is the parent of the child. It is no surprise that, depending on which approach a judge may take, who is a parent is uncertain.

Take Away

What might be seen as good practice in one country, and an efficient method of establishing parentage, might be frowned upon elsewhere. There remain two broad schools of thought about surrogacy—one seeking to uphold reproductive rights, and the other denying the existence of those rights, and recognition of surrogates as the mothers, and the rights of the child. As seen in Venezuela, a failure to resolve these approaches can result in a chaotic regulatory approach, with random outcomes.

It is essential for legal practitioners to talk to their colleagues overseas. The internet, or a general guide such as this book, will only get you so far.

60. *David Farnell, Father of Baby Gammy and Convicted Sex Offender, Dies*, News.com.au (July 16, 2020), https://www.news.com.au/lifestyle/real-life/news-life/david-farnell-father-of-baby-gammy-and-convicted-sex-offender-dies/news-story/5be57b260503c8445f18e168f6ab82e5.

Chapter 7

Issues for LGBTQIA+ Intended Parents

"Family law is a particularly sensitive legal area which is characterised by a plurality of concepts and values at the level of the Member States and the societies within them. Family law—whether based on traditional or more 'modern' values—is the expression of a State's self-image on both the political and social levels. It may be based on religious ideas or mark the renunciation of those ideas by the State concerned. To that end, however, it is in any event an expression of the national identity inherent in fundamental political and constitutional structures."

Court of Justice of the European Union, *Baby Sara* (2021)[1]

The challenges for singles and for LGBTQIA+ couples who seek to become parents through assisted reproductive technology (ART) are often very similar to those for heterosexual couples:

- For some at least, a history of trauma of tried that, didn't work, let's try again—and not succeeding
- The need of many to find an egg or sperm donor, or both
- The need of many to find a surrogate

LGBTQIA+ people have unique challenges in seeking to become parents through ART:

- Although some will have the history of trauma of tried that, didn't work—most haven't. Single men and gay male couples usually have a practical realization that not having a uterus means that they have no alternative but surrogacy in order to fulfil the dream

1. Case C-490/20, VMA v. Sofia Municipality, ECLI:EUC:C:2021:296, ¶ 77 (Apr. 15, 2021).

of parenthood. Most heterosexual couples[2] who come to the realization that they need to undertake surrogacy in order to reproduce, do so only as option D:

- Option A: natural conception, when that didn't work, they tried
- Option B: in vitro fertilization (IVF). After x cycles of IVF, and undertaking the rollercoaster of emotions of failed IVF cycles, they tried
- Option C: egg donation, but when that didn't work, they tried
- Option D: surrogacy

- How many gay male couples and single men view surrogacy in order to reproduce is very similar to women born without a uterus, because of Mayer-Rokitansky-Küster-Hauser (MRKH) syndrome—this is option A; there is no other option. As a practical issue, this can be undertaken without a history of trauma preceding it.
- They face discrimination, both in barriers to treatment, and barriers to parental recognition. I cover discrimination later in the chapter.

In broad terms, these couples fall into two groups:

1. Those who need a sperm donor, typically lesbian couples and single women. However, I have acted in cases where gay couples have needed a sperm donor because neither of the men had good-quality sperm.
2. An egg donor and a surrogate—typically this group would be single men and gay couples. However, I have acted in cases where single women have needed an egg donor, sperm donor, and surrogate, and where lesbian couples have needed a sperm donor, egg donor, and surrogate.

Discrimination

Step 1: Criminalization of Same-Sex Consensual Acts in the Home Country

Many countries actively discriminate against those citizens who are homosexual or are perceived to be so—trans and intersex people being swept up under the same banner. According to the International Lesbian, Gay, Bisexual, Trans and Intersex Association (ILGA), the jurisdictions that criminalize consensual same-sex sexual acts are 64, down from 113

2. Of course, this is a generalization. There are always exceptions, such as women who are cancer survivors, or those who have Mayer-Rokitansky-Küster-Hauser (MRKH) syndrome, who were born without a uterus.

in 1990.[3] Half that number is in Africa, and most of the rest are in the Middle East. They are:

Africa

- Algeria
- Burundi
- Cameroon
- Chad
- Comoros
- Egypt
- Eritrea
- Eswatini
- Ethiopia
- Gambia
- Ghana
- Guinea
- Kenya
- Liberia
- Libya
- Malawi
- Mauritania
- Mauritius
- Morocco
- Nigeria
- Rwanda
- Senegal
- Sierra Leone
- Somalia
- South Sudan
- Sudan
- Tanzania
- Togo
- Tunisia
- Uganda
- Zambia
- Zimbabwe

Americas[4]

- Grenada
- Guyana
- Jamaica
- Saint Lucia
- Saint Vincent and the Grenadines

Asia

- Afghanistan
- Bangladesh
- Brunei
- Oman

3. *Area 1: Legal Frameworks—Criminalisation of Consensual Same-Sex Sexual Acts*, ILGA World Database, https://database.ilga.org/criminalisation-consensual-same-sex-sexual-acts (last visited Mar. 26, 2024).

4. On April 22, 2024, the Eastern Caribbean Supreme Court decriminalized homosexual consensual sexual acts in Dominica, in *BG v. Attorney-General*, Claim No. DOMHCV2019/0149, https://www.humandignitytrust.org/wp-content/uploads/resources/JUDGMENT-DOMHCV2019.0149-BG-V-THE-AG.pdf.

- Indonesia—Aceh province
- Iran
- Iraq
- Kuwait
- Lebanon
- Malaysia
- Maldives
- Myanmar
- Pakistan
- Qatar
- Saudi Arabia
- Sri Lanka
- Syria
- Turkmenistan
- United Arab Emirates
- Uzbekistan
- Yemen

Europe

There are no countries in Europe that criminalize consensual same-sex sexual acts.

Oceania

- Kiribati
- Papua New Guinea
- Samoa
- Solomon Islands
- Tonga
- Tuvalu[5]

Those who may be the subject of persecution may be loath to live openly. They may have to live discreetly, and hide who they are.[6]

Even if it is lawful for them to have consensual same-sex sexual acts, there may be active discrimination against them in their home country in accessing ART or surrogacy because they are LGBTQIA+, or in becoming parents from having a child overseas, because of their sexuality or relationship status.

Step 2: Barriers to Treatment at Home

Barriers may exist in law, or exist in practice. Toleration of LGBTQIA+ people might be the norm, but acceptance is not. Countries that have not criminalized same-sex acts nevertheless have witnessed barriers against

5. *Area 1: Legal Frameworks—Criminalisation of Consensual Same-Sex Sexual Acts*, *supra* note 3.

6. For an excellent discussion of this phenomenon, see the High Court of Australia decision of *S395/2002 v Minister for Immigration & Multicultural Affairs* [2003] HCA 71, 216 CLR 473, 203 ALR 112, 78 ALJR 180.

same-sex couples having children—with reports to that effect from Poland, Russia, and China, for example.

A simple example of a barrier to treatment is in Hong Kong. While consensual same-sex sexual acts are not criminalized, Hong Kong's Human Reproductive Technology Ordinance does not allow access to ART for anyone other than for married couples.[7] As Hong Kong does not allow gay marriage, this limits ART only to heterosexual married couples.

A similar example is seen in Singapore. The government's licensing conditions on assisted reproduction services requires that treatment only be carried out on a married woman, with her husband's consent.[8]

Barriers at home that prevent couples from becoming parents through donation or surrogacy may cause those couples to pursue their journey overseas.

Step 3: Barriers to Treatment Abroad

When same-sex couples undertake international surrogacy (primarily affecting gay couples) or IVF (primarily affecting lesbian couples), consideration has to be given about who is to be recognized as the parent or parents back home, and how this will be achieved. The birth certificate might name both of them as parents, or only one of them, or in the case of surrogacy, one of them with the surrogate named as the other parent. Whichever option is chosen, then consideration must be given at the beginning of the journey whether a court in the surrogacy destination can make orders that meet the needs of the intended parents.

Not all overseas destinations are LGBTQIA+ friendly. Spain is friendly for lesbian couples seeking to be parents through IVF and sperm donation.

Many surrogacy destinations available to heterosexual couples are not available to LGBTQIA+ couples, as seen in Table 7.1.

---

7. Human Reproductive Technology Ordinance, No. 47 (2000), § 15(5).

8. Licensing Terms and Conditions on Assisted Reproduction Services Imposed under Section 6(5) of the Private Hospitals and Medicals Clinics Act (CAP 248) ¶ 5.2 (2011), https://www.moh.gov.sg/docs/librariesprovider5/licensing-terms-and-conditions/licensing-terms-and-conditions-on-assisted-reproduction-services.pdf.

Table 7.1. Availability of Surrogacy

Continent/ Country	Surrogacy Available for?				
	Opposite-Sex Couples	Same-Sex Couples	Single Men	Single Women	Trans/ Non-Binary/ Intersex
Africa					
Ghana	Yes	No	Sometimes	Sometimes	Doubtful
Kenya	Yes	No	Sometimes	Yes	Doubtful
Nigeria	Yes	No	Sometimes	Yes	Doubtful
South Africa	Yes	Yes	Yes	Yes	Yes
Uganda	Yes	No	Unclear	Unclear	Doubtful
Americas					
Argentina	Yes	Yes	Yes	Yes	Yes
Brazil	Yes	Yes	Yes	Yes	Likely
Canada[9]	Mostly	Mostly	Yes	Mostly	Mostly
Colombia	Yes	Yes	Yes	Doubtful	Doubtful
Mexico[10]	Yes	Yes	Yes	Yes	Unclear
United States	Yes	Yes	Yes	Yes	Yes
Uruguay	Yes	Possibly for female couples	No	Yes	Doubtful
Asia					
India	Yes	No	No	Yes	No, unless seen as single woman
Iran	Yes	No	No	No	No
Israel	Yes	Yes	Unclear	Unclear	Unclear
Kazakhstan	Yes	No	No	No	No
Thailand	Yes	No	No	No	No
Vietnam	Yes	No	No	No	No

9. Canada is a surrogacy destination and surrogacy friendly. Establishing parenthood varies province by province. For most intended parents, Québec is not surrogacy friendly, hence "mostly."

10. Mexico is a federation. Surrogacy is practiced in several states, but banned in several.

Continent/ Country	Surrogacy Available for?				
	Opposite-Sex Couples	Same-Sex Couples	Single Men	Single Women	Trans/ Non-Binary/ Intersex
Europe					
Georgia	Yes[11]	No	No	No	No
Greece[12]	Yes	No	No	Yes	No
Russia	Yes[13]	No	No	No	No
Ukraine	Yes	No	No	No	No
United Kingdom	Yes	Yes	Yes	Yes	Yes
Oceania					
Australia	Yes	Yes, except Western Australia—male couples excluded	Yes, except Western Australia and Australian Capital Territory[14]	Yes, except Australian Capital Territory[15]	Yes; only sometimes available in Western Australia
New Zealand	Yes	Yes	Yes	Yes	Yes

An issue for gay couples or single men undertaking surrogacy in the United States, for example, is who is shown on the birth certificate. Some states in the United States, such as California, are prepared to issue two birth certificates, for example:

- One showing both the surrogate and the genetic father
- The other showing both men as the parents, and not showing the surrogate

11. The Georgian Health Minister announced in June 2023 that international intended parents would be banned from accessing surrogacy from January 1, 2024. As of April 2024 that ban has not taken effect, as the bill to effect the ban has not been enacted.

12. Gay marriage has been legal in Greece since February 15, 2024. However, this change did not extend to allow single men or male couples to access surrogacy.

13. But not available to foreigners from 2022.

14. Under the Parentage Act 2004 (Australian Capital Territory), surrogacy is limited to couples. A government bill to allow singles to access surrogacy there was tabled in Parliament in 2023, but as of April 2024 has not been enacted.

15. Under the Parentage Act 2004 (Australian Capital Territory), surrogacy is limited to couples. A government bill to allow singles to access surrogacy there was tabled in Parliament in 2023, but as of April 2024 has not been enacted.

I was asked recently (late 2023) by a client, a single gay man, about which birth certificate takes precedent. It depends on how the country concerned considers the birth certificate. In a country, such as the United States, where the courts peer behind the birth certificate to determine parentage, it doesn't matter. In a country where the birth certificate is the final word on who is a parent, such as China, it may matter a lot. As always, intended parents should get good legal advice from lawyers in both countries.

In an ideal world, both the intended parents would be named on the birth certificate. We do not, of course, live in such a world. It is essential that a lawyer in the surrogacy destination who is acting for the intended parents speak to a lawyer in the home country (if that is possible) to minimize the risk to the intended parents or the child (of the intended parents being prosecuted, the child being denied entry, or the child being removed from their care), and to maximize the chances that the child can live with the intended parents in their home country.

Multiple Parents

A relatively recent trend has been the slow rise of multiple partners intending to become parents. Where there are three intended parents, this has been called a throuple. Issues that arise with more than two intended parents are:

1. Who is recognized on the birth certificate? If the child is born in Ontario, for example, more than two parents can be recognized by a pre-conception parentage agreement.[16] As with other aspects of international ART, it should not be assumed that because more than two are recognized in one part of a country that their parentage will be recognized in another part. See Chapter 10. In Manitoba, by contrast with the position in Ontario, there is a limit to two parents of a child.[17]
2. Intended parents may choose a destination that reflects all of them being recognized on the birth certificate as the parents, as opposed to one that does not.
3. Even if more than two parents can be recognized on the birth certificate in the surrogacy or ART destination, how many of them are recognized as parents back home?
4. If an intended parent is not recognized as a parent back home, are they liable to pay child support/maintenance for the child anyway?

16. Children's Law Reform Act, R.S.O. 1990, c C.12, s 9.
17. Family Law Act, C.C.S.M, c F20, s 16(4)(4).

5. If not, do they have some liability, such as for damages, if they fail to provide financially for the child?[18]
6. If an intended parent is not recognized back home, do they (or how might they) have rights of custody under the 1980 Hague Child Abduction Convention or parental responsibility under the 1996 Hague Child Protection Convention?
7. Is there a way (such as by agreement or court order) for all the parents to have custody rights/parental responsibility established in the home country? Can this be achieved quickly, simply, and cheaply?
8. For the lawyer in the home country—even if an agreement is not or may not be recognized under law, and an order is not possible, are the likely benefits of the parties entering into a likely unenforceable agreement about who has custody/parental responsibility greater than the likely risks in doing so (e.g., by documenting the deal, representations that lead to a party being estopped, or set out the parties intentions)? There may be ethical issues for lawyers preparing documents that are not binding for which they charge a fee.

It is common practice, for example, when a lesbian couple has a child in the United States, for there to be a second-parent adoption order so that the non-biological mother is recognized as a parent. However, it may not be wise to do so, depending on what the requirements of the home country are—for example, if it prevents the child entering the country—because female couples are not recognized. See Chapter 13. In those countries, only one woman is named on the birth certificate—the birth mother. The couple may be recognized by statute as the parents in the United Kingdom,[19] but they are not recognized as the parents when they either move to or travel to Italy.[20]

While it is sometimes assumed that allowing same-sex parties to marry will mean axiomatically that both become parents of the resulting children, that assumption is false. The law in every jurisdiction should be checked to see whether both parties are recognized as the parents. Table 7.2 shows a comparison of recognition of same-sex parenting in Europe. When reading Table 7.2, be aware of two decisions of the European Union Court of Justice concerning recognition within the European Union of children born to lesbian couples, discussed later.

18. Such as in *W v G* [1996] NSWSC 43, where the non-birth mother was not a parent, but was found liable in damages for equitable estoppel.

19. Human Fertilisation and Embryology Act 2008 § 42.

20. For example, Davide Ghiglione, *Italy Leaves Children of Same-Sex Parents in Limbo*, BBC (Mar. 18, 2023), https://www.bbc.com/news/world-europe-64967517.

Table 7.2. A Comparison of Recognition of Same-Sex Parenting in Europe

Jurisdiction	Recognition of Same-Sex Marriage?	Registered Partnership?	Second-Parent Adoptions?	Automatic Co-Parent Recognition?	Recognition of Trans Parenthood?
Albania	No[21]	No	No	No	No
Andorra	Some[22]	Yes[23]	Yes[24]	No[25]	No[26]
Armenia	No[27]	No[28]	No[29]	No[30]	No[31]
Austria	Yes	Yes	Yes[32]	Yes[33]	No[34]

21. No to all categories. Rainbow Eur., https://www.rainbow-europe.org/ (last visited Mar. 26, 2024).
22. Yes for civil weddings, but not for church weddings. Law of Person and the Family 202.
23. Law 34/2015, of November 27.
24. Law on Adoption and Other Forms of Protection of Unmatched Minors 1996, *amended by* Law on Person and the Family 2023.
25. Rainbow Eur., *supra* note 21.
26. *Id.*
27. *Id.*
28. *Id.*
29. *Id.*
30. *Id.*
31. *Id.*
32. Verfassungsgerichtsof [VfGH] [Constitutional Court], Oct. 9, 2012, B 121/11, 137/11.
33. Allgemeines Bürgerliches Gesetzbuch [ABGB] [Civil Code].
34. Rainbow Eur., *supra* note 21.

Jurisdiction	Recognition of Same-Sex Marriage?	Registered Partnership?	Second-Parent Adoptions?	Automatic Co-Parent Recognition?	Recognition of Trans Parenthood?
Azerbaijan	No[35]	No[36]	No[37]	No[38]	No[39]
Belarus	No[40]	No	No	No	No
Belgium	Yes[41]	Yes[42]	Yes[43]	Yes[44]	Yes[45]
Bosnia and Herzegovina	No[46]	No	No	No	No
Bulgaria	No[47]	No	No	No	No

35. *Id.*
36. *Id.*
37. *Id.*
38. *Id.*
39. *Id.*
40. No to all categories. *Id.*
41. Loi ouvrant le mariage à des personnes de même sexe et modifiant certaines dispositions du Code civil [Same Sex Marriage Act], M.B., Feb. 13, 2003.
42. Rainbow Eur., *supra* note 21.
43. Loi modifiant certaines dispositions du Code civil en vue de permettre l'adoption par des personnes de même sexe [Adoption (Same Sex) Amendment Act], B.S., May 18, 2006.
44. Loi portant établissement de la filiation de la coparente [Law Establishing the Parentage of the Co-Mother], B.S., May 5, 2014.
45. Rainbow Eur., *supra* note 21.
46. No to all categories. *Id.*
47. No to all categories. *Id.*

Jurisdiction	Recognition of Same-Sex Marriage?	Registered Partnership?	Second-Parent Adoptions?	Automatic Co-Parent Recognition?	Recognition of Trans Parenthood?
Croatia	No[48]	Yes[49]	Yes[50]	No[51]	No[52]
Cyprus	No[53]	Yes[54]	No[55]	No[56]	Unlikely[57]
Czech Republic	No[58]	Yes[59]	No[60]	No[61]	No[62]

48. *Id.*
49. Zakon o životnom partnerstvu [Life Partnership Act] 2014.
50. Decision of the High Administrative Court, April 2022, *discussed in* Jasmin Klarić, *Now It's Legal! High Administrative Court: Same-Sex Couples in Croatia Have the Right to Adopt Children*, TELEGRAM (May 26, 2022), https://www.telegram.hr/politika-kriminal/e-sad-je-pravomocno-visoki-upravni-sud-istospolni-parovi-imaju-pravo-posvojiti-djecu/.
51. RAINBOW EUR., *supra* note 21.
52. *Id.*
53. *Id.*
54. The Civil Union Act 2015, L. 184(I)/2015.
55. RAINBOW EUR., *supra* note 21.
56. *Id.*
57. ALINA TRYFONIDOU, EUROPEAN PARLIAMENT, CROSS-BORDER LEGAL RECOGNITION OF PARENTHOOD IN THE EU (2023), https://www.europarl.europa.eu/RegData/etudes/STUD/2023/746632/IPOL_STU(2023)746632_EN.pdf.
58. RAINBOW EUR., *supra* note 21.
59. O registrovaném partnerství a o změně některých souvisejících zákonů účinný [Registered Partnerships and other Amendments Act], Zákon č.115/2006 Sb.
60. RAINBOW EUR., *supra* note 21.
61. *Id.*
62. *Id.*

Jurisdiction	Recognition of Same-Sex Marriage?	Registered Partnership?	Second-Parent Adoptions?	Automatic Co-Parent Recognition?	Recognition of Trans Parenthood?
Denmark	Yes[63]	Pre-2012[64]	Yes[65]	Sometimes[66]	Soon[67]
• Faroe Islands	Yes	Yes	Yes, if married	No	No
• Greenland	Yes	Yes	Yes	Unclear	No
Estonia	No[68]	Yes[69]	Yes[70]	No[71]	No[72]
Finland	Yes[73]	No[74]	Sometimes[75]	No[76]	Yes[77]

63. Ægteskabsloven [Marriage Act], Law 256 of June 4, 1969.
64. *Id.*
65. Lov om registreret partnerskab [Registered Partnership Act], Law 372 of June 7, 1989.
66. Only by a pre-conception agreement between both women and the known sperm donor. Børneloven [Children's Act].
67. Amendments to the Children's Act, passed in 2022 and which would allow this, are yet to commence.
68. RAINBOW EUR., *supra* note 21.
69. The Registered Partnership Act 2014 has been enacted but not implemented.
70. Kooseluseadus [Registered Partnership Act 2014]; Perekonnaseadus [Family Law Act 2009].
71. RAINBOW EUR., *supra* note 21.
72. *Id.*
73. Marriage Act 234/1929, effective in 2015.
74. RAINBOW EUR., *supra* note 21.
75. Registered Partnerships Act 950/2001 § 9.
76. RAINBOW EUR., *supra* note 21.
77. Legal Gender Recognition Act 2023 § 4.

Jurisdiction	Recognition of Same-Sex Marriage?	Registered Partnership?	Second-Parent Adoptions?	Automatic Co-Parent Recognition?	Recognition of Trans Parenthood?
France	Yes[78]	Some[79]	Yes[80]	No[81]	No[82]
Georgia	No[83]	No[84]	No[85]	No[86]	No[87]
Germany	Yes[88]	No[89]	Yes[90]	No[91]	No[92]

78. Loi 2013-404 du 17 mai 2013 ouvrant le mariage aux couples de personnes de même sexe [Law 2013-404 of May 17, 2013 Opening Marriage to Same-Sex Couples].

79. Loi 1999-944 du 15 novembre 1990 relative au pacte civil de solidarité [Law 1999-944 of November 15, 1990 Relating to the Civil Solidarity Pact].

80. Loi 2013-404 du 17 mai 2013 ouvrant le mariage aux couples de personnes de même sexe [Law 2013-404 of May 17, 2013 Opening Marriage to Same-Sex Couples].

81. Rainbow Eur., *supra* note 21.

82. *Id.*

83. *Id.*

84. *Id.*

85. *Id.*

86. *Id.*

87. *Id.*

88. Bürgerliches Gesetzbuch [BGB] [Civil Code].

89. Rainbow Eur., *supra* note 21.

90. Bürgerliches Gesetzbuch [BGB] [Civil Code].

91. Rainbow Eur., *supra* note 21.

92. *Id.*

Jurisdiction	Recognition of Same-Sex Marriage?	Registered Partnership?	Second-Parent Adoptions?	Automatic Co-Parent Recognition?	Recognition of Trans Parenthood?
Gibraltar	Yes[93]	Yes[94]	Yes[95]	Yes[96]	No
Greece	No[97]	Yes[98]	No[99]	No[100]	No[101]
Hungary	No[102]	Yes[103]	No[104]	No[105]	No[106]

93. Civil Marriage Amendment Act 2016.
94. Civil Partnerships Act 2014.
95. *Id.*
96. Surrogacy Act 2021.
97. Rainbow Eur., *supra* note 21.
98. Nomos (3719/2008) Metarrhythmiseis pou aforoun then oikogeneia, to paidi kai then koinonia [Reforms Concerning the Family, Children, and Society], *as amended by* Nomos (4356/2015).
99. Rainbow Eur., *supra* note 21.
100. *Id.*
101. *Id.*
102. *Id.*
103. 2009. évi XXIX. törvény a bejegyzett élettársi kapcsolatról, az ezzel összefüggő, valamint az élettársi viszony igazolásának megkönnyítéséhez szükséges egyes törvények módosításáról (Act XXIX of 2009 on Registered Partnerships).
104. Magyarország Alaptörvénye [The Fundamental Law of Hungary], Alaptörvény.
105. *Id.*
106. Rainbow Eur., *supra* note 21.

Jurisdiction	Recognition of Same-Sex Marriage?	Registered Partnership?	Second-Parent Adoptions?	Automatic Co-Parent Recognition?	Recognition of Trans Parenthood?
Iceland	Yes[107]	Sometimes[108]	Yes[109]	Limited[110]	Yes[111]
Ireland	Yes[112]	No[113]	Yes[114]	Sometimes[115]	No[116]
Italy	No	Yes[117]	No[118]	No[119]	No[120]
Kosovo	No[121]	No	No	No	No

107. Hjuskaparlog nr 31/1993 (Law in Respect of Marriage No. 31/1993), Log um breytingar a hjuskaparlogum og fleiri logum um brottfall laga um stadfesta samvist (ein hjuskaparlog) nr 65/2010 (Amendment 65/2010).

108. Only those who are recognized prior to the recognition of same-sex marriage in 2010. RAINBOW EUR., *supra* note 21.

109. Hjuskaparlog nr 31/1993 (Law in Respect of Marriage No. 31/1993), Log um breytingar a hjuskaparlogum og fleiri logum um brottfall laga um stadfesta samvist (ein hjuskaparlog) nr 65/2010 (Amendment 65/2010).

110. Barnalog (Children's Law) No. 76/2003, Log um breytingar a hjuskaparlogum og fleiri logum um brottfall laga um stadfesta samvist (ein hjuskaparlog) nr 65/2010 (Amendment 65/2010).

111. *Id.*

112. Marriage Act 2015.

113. RAINBOW EUR., *supra* note 21.

114. Adoption Act 2010 § 33.

115. Children and Family Relationships Act 2015 § 5.

116. Ireland takes the traditional view of mater semper certa est (the mother is always certain). The person who gives birth for a donor conceived child is the mother: Children and Family Relationships Act 2015, s.5.

117. Legge 20 May 2016, n.26.

118. Corte coste n. 237/2019.

119. *Id.*

120. RAINBOW EUR., *supra* note 21.

121. No to all categories. *Id.*

Jurisdiction	Recognition of Same-Sex Marriage?	Registered Partnership?	Second-Parent Adoptions?	Automatic Co-Parent Recognition?	Recognition of Trans Parenthood?
Latvia	No[122]	No	No	No	No
Liechtenstein	No[123]	Yes[124]	Yes[125]	No[126]	No[127]
Lithuania	No[128]	No	No	No	No
Luxembourg	Yes[129]	Yes[130]	Yes[131]	No[132]	No[133]
Malta	Yes[134]	Yes[135]	Yes[136]	Yes[137]	Yes[138]

122. No to all categories. *Id.*
123. *Id.*
124. Registered Partnership Act 2010.
125. Rainbow Eur., *supra* note 21.
126. *Id.*
127. *Id.*
128. No to all categories. *Id.*
129. Civil Code art. 143.
130. Law of July 9, 2004.
131. Rainbow Eur., *supra* note 21.
132. *Id.*
133. *Id.*
134. Marriage Act, Cap. 255 (1975).
135. Civil Unions Act, 2014 (Act No. IX of 2014) § 9.
136. *Id.*; Civil Code, Cap. 16, art. 100B (last amended 2017).
137. Civil Unions Act, 2014 (Act No. IX of 2014) § 9; Civil Code, Cap. 16, art. 67 (last amended 2017).
138. Gender Identity, Gender Expression, and Sex Characteristics Act, 2015 § 3.

Jurisdiction	Recognition of Same-Sex Marriage?	Registered Partnership?	Second-Parent Adoptions?	Automatic Co-Parent Recognition?	Recognition of Trans Parenthood?
Moldova	No[139]	No[140]	No	No	No
Monaco	No[141]	No[142]	No[143]	No[144]	No[145]
Montenegro	No[146]	Yes[147]	No[148]	No[149]	No[150]

139. No to all categories. RAINBOW EUR., *supra* note 21.
140. Registered Partnership Act, 2010.
141. RAINBOW EUR., *supra* note 21.
142. *Id.*
143. *Id.*
144. *Id.*
145. *Id.*
146. *Id* .
147. Law on Life Partnerships of Persons of the Same Sex, 2020.
148. RAINBOW EUR., *supra* note 21.
149. *Id.*; *The Ministry of Interior of Montenegro Discriminates against Children Because of the Sexual Orientation of Their Parents*, LGBTI ERA (Mar. 2, 2024), https://lgbti-era.org/the-ministry-of-interior-of-montenegro-discriminates-against-children-because-of-the-sexual-orientation-of-their-parents/.
150. RAINBOW EUR., *supra* note 21.

Jurisdiction	Recognition of Same-Sex Marriage?	Registered Partnership?	Second-Parent Adoptions?	Automatic Co-Parent Recognition?	Recognition of Trans Parenthood?
The Netherlands	Yes[151]	Yes[152]	Yes[153]	Yes, by known donor or by the second parent recognizing the child administratively[154]	No[155]
North Macedonia	No[156]	No	No	No	No
Norway	Yes[157]	No[158]	Yes[159]	Yes[160]	No[161]
Poland	No[162]	No	No	No	No

151. Wet van 7 oktober 2015, Stb. 2015, 354 [Marriage Amendment Act].
152. Wet van 1 januari 1998 [Registered Partnerships Act].
153. Wet van 1 april 2001 [Adoption (Same Sex People) Act].
154. Wet van 25 november 2013, Stb. 2013, 480 [Legal Parentage of the Female Partner of the Mother Act].
155. Rainbow Eur., *supra* note 21.
156. No to all categories. *Id.*
157. Marriage Act, 1991, *amended in* 2008.
158. Rainbow Eur., *supra* note 21.
159. Childrens Act 1981, s.3
160. Childrens Act 1981, s.4.
161. Rainbow Eur., *supra* note 21.
162. No to all categories. *Id.*

Jurisdiction	Recognition of Same-Sex Marriage?	Registered Partnership?	Second-Parent Adoptions?	Automatic Co-Parent Recognition?	Recognition of Trans Parenthood?
Portugal	Yes[163]	Yes[164]	Yes[165]	Yes[166]	No[167]
Romania	No[168]	No[169]	No[170]	No[171]	No[172]
Russia	No[173]	No[174]	No[175]	No[176]	No[177]
San Marino	No[178]	Yes[179]	No[180]	No[181]	No[182]

163. Lei n. 9/2010 de 31 de maio [Law no. 9/2010 of 31 May].
164. Lei n. 23/2010 de 30 de agosto [Law no. 23/2010 of 30 August].
165. Lei n. 2/2016 de 29 de fevereiro [Law no. 2/2016 of 29 February].
166. Lei n. 17/2016 de 20 de junho [Law no. 17/2016 of 20 June].
167. Rainbow Eur., *supra* note 21.
168. *Id.*
169. *Id.*
170. Law No. 273/2004.
171. Rainbow Eur., *supra* note 21.
172. *Id.*
173. *Id.*
174. *Id.*
175. *Id.*
176. *Id.*
177. *Id.*
178. *Id.*
179. Regulation of Civil Partnerships, Law No. 147 of 20 November 2018.
180. Rainbow Eur., *supra* note 21.
181. *Id.*
182. *Id.*

Jurisdiction	Recognition of Same-Sex Marriage?	Registered Partnership?	Second-Parent Adoptions?	Automatic Co-Parent Recognition?	Recognition of Trans Parenthood?
Serbia	No[183]	No	No	No	No
Slovakia	No[184]	No	No	No	No
Slovenia	Yes[185]	Yes[186]	Yes[187]	No[188]	No[189]
Spain	Yes[190]	In some regions[191]	Yes	Yes, but only if married[192]	No[193]

183. No to all categories. *Id.*
184. No to all categories. *Id.*
185. Constitutional Court Decisions Nos. UI-486/20, Up 572/18, UI-91/21, Up 675/19 (2022).
186. Civil Partnership Act of 24 February 2017.
187. Constitutional Court Decisions Nos. UI-486/20, Up 572/18, UI-91/21, Up675/19 (2022). Supreme Court decision II IPS 462/2009 recognized a same-sex couple's adoption in New Jersey, although such an adoption was not then possible in Slovenia.
188. Rainbow Eur., *supra* note 21.
189. *Id.*
190. Law 13/2005 of 1 July 2005 Amending the Civil Code on the Right to Marry (B.O.E. 2005, 157).
191. Except in Murcia, Castilla La Mancha, Castilla y León, and La Rioja. Rainbow Eur., *supra* note 21.
192. Law 19/2015 of July 13 on Administrative Reform Arrangements in the Areas of Civil Registry Office and Administration of Justice art. 2 (B.O.E. 2015, 167).
193. Rainbow Eur., *supra* note 21.

Jurisdiction	Recognition of Same-Sex Marriage?	Registered Partnership?	Second-Parent Adoptions?	Automatic Co-Parent Recognition?	Recognition of Trans Parenthood?
Sweden	Yes[194]	No[195]	Yes[196]	Sometimes[197]	Sometimes[198]
Switzerland	Yes[199]	Yes[200]	Yes[201]	No[202]	No[203]
Türkiye	No[204]	No	No	No	No
Ukraine	No [205]	No	No	No	No

194. Äktenskapsbalken (Svensk författningssamling [SFS] 1987:230), *as amended by* SFS 2009:253.
195. Rainbow Eur., *supra* note 21.
196. Föräldrabalk [FB] [Children and Parents Code] 1949:381.
197. When the couple are married: *id.*
198. *Id.*
199. Schweizerisches Zivilgesetzbuch [ZGB], Code Civil [CC], Codice Civile [CC] [Civil Code] Dec. 10, 1907.
200. Partnership Law, 2004.
201. *Adoption*, ch.ch, https://www.ch.ch/en/family-and-partnership/adoption/adoption/ (last visited Mar. 26, 2024).
202. Rainbow Eur., *supra* note 21.
203. *Id.*
204. No to all categories. *Id.*
205. No to all categories. *Id.*

Jurisdiction	Recognition of Same-Sex Marriage?	Registered Partnership?	Second-Parent Adoptions?	Automatic Co-Parent Recognition?	Recognition of Trans Parenthood?
United Kingdom	Yes[206]	Yes[207]	Yes[208]	Yes[209]	No[210]
• Guernsey, Alderney, and Sark	Yes[211]	Yes	Yes	Not known	Not known
• Isle of Man	Yes	Yes	Yes	Not clear	Not clear
• Jersey	Yes	Yes	Yes	Not clear	Not clear
Vatican City	No	No	No	No	No

206. England and Wales: Marriage (Same Sex Couples) Act 2013; Scotland: Marriage and Civil Partnership (Scotland) Act 2014; Northern Ireland: Northern Ireland (Executive Formation etc.) Act 2019.

207. Civil Partnership Act 2004.

208. Human Fertilisation and Embryology Act 2008 § 54.

209. *Id.* § 42.

210. See the case of Freddie McConnell, discussed in this chapter. R (on the Application of McConnell) v. Registrar-General [2019] EWCA (Civ) 599 [86].

211. Guernsey: The Same-Sex Marriage (Guernsey) Law, 2016; Alderney: The Same-Sex Marriage (Alderney) Law, 2017; Sark: The Same-Sex Marriage (Sark) Law, 2019.

As seen in Chapter 2, in Iceland, a female couple were unable to establish parentage, when surrogacy had been undertaken in the United States and there was no genetic link between them and the child.[212] Adoption may have been open to them.

In other jurisdictions, a second-parent adoption order is not needed. This is because both women may be recognized as the parents if the conception came about when they were living in a marriage or marriage-like relationship, such as a de facto relationship or a civil partnership, as is the case in Manitoba, for example.[213] In Manitoba, the timing of the relationship is when the child is conceived, not the time of birth.[214] Depending on the words of the statute, there has been dispute whether the timing of the relationship is at the time of conception or at the time of birth. A non-birth mother who was in a relationship with the birth mother, but not in a marriage or similar relationship, may therefore not be found to be a parent.[215]

A second common element is that both parties consented to the treatment. One must always revert to the statute as to what is consent. It may prescribe, for example, that the party has executed certain forms. However, a more common requirement is that the form of consent is not prescribed.

As a 2023 English case, *S (Children: Parentage & Jurisdiction)*,[216] showed, consent could be seen in a number of ways:

> This question is the only one that must be answered in order to determine whether an individual is to be treated as the child's legal parent. A closer examination of the legislation and the case law enables the following further observations to be made, but they are not a substitute for the statutory question:
>
> (1) Whether a person did not consent is a matter of fact, taking account of all the circumstances. Assisted reproduction takes place in a wide variety of circumstances and the evaluation of whether consent has not

212. Fjölnisdóttir v. Iceland, App. No. 71552/17 (May 18, 2021).

213. Family Law Act, C.C.S.M., c F20, s 30.

214. *Id.* s 20(2).

215. For example, *Masson & Parsons* [2017] FamCa 789, when the relationship between the women was formative, and had not yet advanced to a de facto relationship; or *Wickham & Toledano* (No. 2) [2022] FecCFamC1F 32, where the whirlwind, tumultuous relationship of the parties was found not to be a de facto relationship on the day of conception.

216. [2023] EWCA (Civ) 897.

been given must be made in the context of the actual circumstances of the individual case.

(2) The relevant time is the time when the procedure is undertaken. There will be a natural focus on evidence about that moment in time, but evidence about earlier or later periods may contribute to the assessment of whether consent was given or not.

(3) The Act does not prescribe the form in which consent can be given. It may be in writing or oral or unarticulated. It may be express or implied from all the circumstances. Formal written consent is not a requirement of the parenthood provisions of the Act, though licensed clinics in England and Wales will not offer treatment without it. In other circumstances the absence of written or express consent may not be a strong indicator that a person did not consent. The assessment will by definition be taking place in the presence of a marriage or civil partnership and will inevitably take account of the nature of the adults' relationship.

(4) The Act does not require that consent or lack of consent is communicated but a lack of communication may be a relevant factor in determining whether consent exists.

(5) The Act does not equate a lack of consent with an objection or a stated withholding of consent.

(6) The Act does not require that the consent is limited to a specific form of assisted reproduction or to a specific time or place. If the nature of the consent is broad enough, it may encompass a variety of procedures in a range of circumstances.

(7) Awareness that a procedure is being undertaken is not the same thing as consent, though it is clearly a precondition to the possibility of consent having been given.

(8) Acquiescence in a procedure being undertaken is not the same thing as consent, but the court will be careful to distinguish acquiescence from consent that has not been expressly stated.

(9) The assessment of a lack of consent is an objective exercise, but as it concerns the state of mind of the

spouse or civil partner, that person's own account of their state of mind is of great importance and the court will need to have clear reasons for rejecting it. Such reasons may be found in the evidence of the gestational mother or elsewhere in the evidence.

(10) Finally, the Act does not limit the ways in which a state of mind can be formed. Whether a spouse or civil partner has or has not consented may be the result of a deliberate exercise of choice, but the law does not require consent to be given or not given in a decisive manner or on a single occasion: in some cases its presence or absence may be inferred from the circumstances.[217]

Two difficulties with consent to treatment when the relationship is a de facto or cohabiting relationship are:

1. The date of the de facto or cohabiting relationship. Did it exist at the time of the artificial insemination or implantation, or is at the time of the birth?[218]
2. Whether or not there was a de facto or cohabiting relationship. Proving a relationship based on indicia, when the existence of the relationship is disputed, can be very hard.

In 2023, the Italian Parliament criminalized Italian citizens extraterritorially for undertaking surrogacy overseas. Some comments about the law made plain that it is not aimed at heterosexual couples (who will continue to claim that the wife became pregnant overseas), but at gay male couples (who cannot).

Step 4: Traveling Overseas

Once all the legal planning has been put in place in Step 3 to enable a couple to become parents through donation or surrogacy overseas, it might seem a simple step for them to fly to their destination, either to become pregnant or to be at the birth of their child—and then return.

While that might sound like a simple step, getting there and back can be fraught with difficulty. The parents may seek a different route, rather than stopping off in the Middle East, for example. The parents should engage a reputable travel agent to plan their journey, to minimize this and other risks in getting there and back quickly, safely, and as cheaply as possible.

217. *Id.* at 45.

218. *E.g.*, *Wickham & Toledano* (No. 2) [2022] FedCFamC1F 32.

The Asian Two-Step

Many expatriates live in Asian hubs, like Hong Kong, Shanghai, Singapore, and Dubai. In all of these there are varying risks for LGBTQIA+ parents (and others) undertaking surrogacy abroad—both due to a policy against surrogacy, and due to homophobia.

It can be especially risky for a single man, or a gay couple, to undertake surrogacy in, say, the United States or Canada (who is not an American or Canadian citizen, but is a citizen of a third country) and then return "home" to the Asian city in which he or they have a residence visa or permit of some kind. This is because the citizenship of the child, being that of the parent, will not have been established by the time that the child moves from the country of birth to the country of residence.

The risk occurs if the residence country rejects the visa or permit. Hong Kong, for example, will not accept an intended parent as a parent if there is no genetic link. Parentage needs to be established based on DNA. All of these places will want to see a birth certificate in which the mother is named.

Authorities may be concerned about why a single (in their eyes) man is bringing his newborn into their country, but that the mother is not also coming. What is going on?

A much safer approach is to ensure that there is a two-step approach of going "home"—namely to leave the country of birth and travel to the country of citizenship of the parent. While there, hopefully briefly (which then calls for good advanced planning), obtain the citizenship of that country for the child, and then obtain the visa or permit to live at "home."

Why this approach is less risky is twofold:

1. If the visa or permit is rejected in the "home" city, the ability of the child to live in the country of the parent's citizenship has already been obtained, making a good backup plan.
2. It is less suspicious to government officials in the "home" country when the child applies for the visa or permit there having already secured the same citizenship as the parent, rather than having a different citizenship. The latter may result in questions being asked by officials concerned that the child may have been trafficked.

Trans Men Giving Birth

A more recent phenomenon is that of trans men giving birth. In essence, trans men who have not had "bottom" surgery stop taking hormones to enable them to become pregnant and give birth. After they give birth, they then go back to taking hormones.

Depending on where they live, they may be recognized as parent, father, or mother. However, in many jurisdictions, they would only be recognized as mother. It should be assumed in most of the developing world that they would be only recognized as mother. While this may make no difference to the birth certificate for a child born in a jurisdiction where the parent is recognized as parent or father, this could prove quite difficult if the parent and child migrate or travel and then get into trouble, having to rely on authorities for some reason.

Particularly for those who are migrating or are considering traveling to a country perceived as not being LGBTQIA+ friendly (e.g., much of the Middle East or Asia), then legal and practical advice should be obtained ahead of time before any travel or migration occurs.

Two examples are those of trans men who gave birth, one in England and one in Australia.

Freddie McConnell

Freddie McConnell is an Australian trans man living in England. He gave birth. However, there were issues as to the form of the birth certificate. Freddie did not want to be recognized as the mother but wanted to be recognized as the father or parent. He was unsuccessful.

Mr. McConnell argued:

> Having due regard to the complete facts of this case and the principles extolled in the jurisprudence of this court and the [European Court of Human Rights (ECtHR)], since the State permitted TT to undergo hormone treatment, live his life as a man for a significant part of his adult life and then, after he had gone through the required procedure and obtained a Gender Recognition Certificate, permitted him to undergo artificial insemination which led to the birth of YY, the State should reasonably be expected to accept the consequences and take all the measures needed to enable TT to live [a] normal [life], free from discrimination in any circumstances, under his new identity and with respect for [his] right to private and family life.[219]

The Registrar-General (RG) argued that the claim be dismissed:

i) The RG's duty in law is to register the claimant as YY's mother. Specifically, the RG does not have a power to register the claimant as YY's father or as his

219. R (on the Application of TT) v. Registrar-General [2019] EWHC (Fam) 2384 [69].

parent. Pursuant to section 12 of the [Gender Recognition Act (GRA) 2004], a [gender recognition certificate] does not affect the status of a trans-person as a mother or father to a child, even if the child is born after the issue of a [gender recognition certificate].

ii) As to the claim under the [Human Rights Act] 1998, the case raises complex issues of public policy about how best to protect the rights and interests of trans-people and their families in legislation. It is an area in which the European Court of Human Rights recognises that the United Kingdom should have a wide margin of appreciation, and one in which the decisions of the legislature should be accorded considerable respect.

iii) The RG and the Secretaries of State accept (for the purpose of the hearing of this claim only) that the legislative scheme interferes with the rights of the Claimant and YY under Article 8(1) of the [European Convention on Human Rights] and therefore requires justification under Article 8(2).

iv) The interference is justified by the need to (i) have an administratively coherent and certain scheme for the registration of births, and (ii) the rights and interests of others, notably but not exclusively, the right of a child to know—and have properly recognised—the identity of the person who carried and gave birth to him or her. This is an important and consistent principle that applies throughout birth registration legislation, including in relation to surrogacy, adoption and in relation to the children born by donor conception. The interference is proportionate, particularly having regard to the respect to be given to the legislature in this context, the measures introduced by legislation to protect against discrimination and harassment and maintain confidentiality, the absence of workable alternatives and given that there is no decision of the ECtHR requiring a trans-parent to be recorded as the parent of his or her child in his or her acquired gender.[220]

220. *Id.* [78].

It was further argued that Mr. McConnell carried and gave birth to the child as a result of intrauterine insemination (IUI).[221] He was therefore the mother for the purposes of parentage presumptions. He did not fall within the definition of "father" under the legislation, nor "parent." There was no legislative basis for him to be registered as father/parent.

The trial judge drew preliminary conclusions as to domestic law:

> i) At common law a person whose egg is inseminated in their womb and who then becomes pregnant and gives birth to a child is that child's "mother".
>
> ii) The status of being a "mother" arises from the role that a person has undertaken in the biological process of conception, pregnancy and birth.
>
> iii) Being a "mother" or "father" with respect to the conception, pregnancy and birth of a child is not necessarily gender-specific, although until recent decades it invariably was so. It is now possible, and recognised by the law, for a "mother" to have an acquired gender of male, and for a "father" to have an acquired gender of female.
>
> iv) Section 12 of the GRA is both retrospective and prospective. By virtue of that section the status of a person as the father or mother of a child is not affected by the acquisition of gender under the GRS, even where the relevant birth has taken place after the issue of a [gender recognition certificate].[222]

Treatment was provided to Mr. McConnell by clinics within the legislative scheme. He was therefore deemed a mother for the purposes of that law, too.

The trial judge stated:

> TT regards the term "mother" as being gender specific. His argument before this court in favour of "father" is also gender specific. Whilst, for the reasons that I have given so far in evaluating the domestic law, my preliminary conclusion ***as a matter of law*** is that the term "mother" is free-standing and separate from consideration of legal gender, thus in law there can be male mothers and female fathers, I fully accept that this is not TT's perspective

221. A form of artificial insemination.

222. *Id.* [149].

and is unlikely to be the perspective of others who, like TT, suffer from gender dysphoria. Whether or not there has been a breach of Art 8 must be assessed regarding the particular characteristics of the individual in focus, and in that regard to require him to be registered as "mother" is rightly seen by him as a frontal assault on the integrity of his acquired male gender. The requirement to register would, I accept, adversely impact upon TT's human dignity and his human freedom.

Separately, irrespective of how often this may happen, if an event occurs where YY's full birth certificate must be produced, this is very likely to be an occasion of exquisite embarrassment and confusion for both parent and child. More than that, even if such an occasion never arises, the fact that it might arise is a legitimate cause for significant anxiety and distress on the part of TT, and probably YY when he is older, to the extent that this on its own is an interference with their right to respect for private and family life.

Moving on, the requirement for registration as "mother" is, on the Government's case, made "in accordance with the law", namely the [Births and Deaths Registration Act] 1953 coupled with the GRA 2004 and pursues one of the legitimate societal aims identified by the government, namely of establishing a coherent registration system. There is, rightly, no challenge to these assertions.[223]

Furthermore:

The fact that a person's gender has become the acquired gender following the issue of a [gender recognition certificate] "does not affect the status of the person as the father or mother of a child", Parliament has made a social and political judgment as to how the competing interests should be accommodated. In doing so, it has afforded priority to the need for clarity as to parental status. There are, as I have recorded, sound child-focussed reasons in favour of striking the balance in that way. The fact that it is possible to identify other factors which might, in particular cases, be to the detriment of a child, does not mean that the outcome promoted by Parliament is not in the best interests of children or that their best interests have not been a primary consideration in striking the policy balance as it has been struck.

223. *Id.* [251].

> Further, in the context of "best interests", each of the alternative options put forward will present some difficulties for a child. For example, registration of a male parent as "gestational parent" invites the conclusion that the parent is trans-gender and registration as "father" leaves the child without a "mother".[224]

Mr. McConnell appealed. Among his other arguments was that Article 3 of the United Nations Convention on the Rights of the Child (CRC) (i.e., the best interests of the child) should be a primary consideration. The Court of Appeal held:

> In the present context, where we are concerned with a legislative measure, not a decision on the facts of a particular case, what Article 3(1) of the CRC requires is that the best interests of children generally should be taken into account as a primary consideration when striking a balance in legislation. In our judgement, that is precisely what Parliament has done in enacting a carefully crafted set of provisions which balance the rights of transgender people and others, including their children. The view that Parliament has taken is that every child should have a mother and should be able to discover who their mother was, because that is in the child's best interests. Others may take a different view and in time may be able to persuade Parliament to take a different view. What cannot be doubted is that Parliament has taken into account the best interests of children as a primary consideration.[225]

The Court of Appeal concluded:

> The legislative scheme of the GRA required Mr McConnell to be registered as the mother of YY, rather than the father, parent or gestational parent. That requirement did not violate his or YY's Article 8 rights. There is no incompatibility between the GRA and the Convention.[226]

Mr. Coonan

Mr. Coonan was a trans man living in Queensland, Australia. Like Freddie McConnell, he gave birth and wanted to be recognized, either as the

224. *Id.* [263].
225. R (on the Application of McConnell) v. Registrar-General [2019] EWCA (Civ) 599 [86].
226. *Id.* [89].

parent or the father on the birth certificate. Queensland law only allowed him to be recognized as the mother. Following the case, there have been amendments to Queensland birth registration laws,[227] whereby someone in the position of Mr. Coonan can choose whether he wishes to be known as a parent or father or mother, although at the time of writing those laws have not yet commenced.

The Tribunal concluded that Mr. Coonan was the mother for the purposes of the Queensland Act:

> [56] Section 10A of the [Births, Deaths, and Marriages Registration Act (BDMR Act)] provides some statutory limitations in determining this issue. Section 10A was inserted in the BDMR Act by the Surrogacy Act 2010 (Qld) which had, as one of its objectives, to amend the Status of Children Act 1978 (Qld) to extend the parentage presumption to the female de facto partner of a birth mother when the birth mother has undergone a fertilisation procedure to conceive the child with the consent of her female de facto partner and to make related amendments to the BDMR Act following amendments to the Status of Children Act 1978 for parentage presumptions.
>
> [57] To summarise s 10A:
>
> (a) If the child has one parent, then that parent must be registered as the child's mother or father.
> (b) If the child has two parents, then one of the child's parents must be registered as the child's mother or father.
> (c) There can be only one registered mother.
> (d) There can be only one registered father.
> (e) Not more than two people in total may be registered as the child's parents however described.
>
> [58] There is no definition of "parent", "mother" or "father" in the "dictionary" to the BDMR Act. However, "birth" is defined to be:
>
> > The expulsion or extraction of a child from its mother.

227. With the enactment of the *Births, Deaths, and Marriages Registration Act 2023* (Qld).

[59] In my view, it is clear from the definition of "birth" that a mother, under the Act, is the person who gave birth.

[60] This meaning of "mother", defined by reference to the role the person plays in the child's birth, is also reflected in the key provision, s 5, which requires that the "responsible person" notify the Registrar of the birth. The responsible persons do not include the "father" but are described in a hierarchical way as follows:

(a) a doctor present at the birth;
(b) if none, then a midwife present at the birth;
(c) if neither doctor nor midwife present, then a person, other than the mother, present at the birth;
(d) if the mother was alone at the birth, the mother; or
(e) if the mother dies or abandons the child—the person who takes physical custody of the child, for example, a person who discovers the child with the body of the mother.

[61] In my view, this list also makes clear that the mother is the person who gives birth, otherwise she could not be the person "alone at the birth". Further, it is clear from the list that a father is not someone the Act envisages can also give birth within the meaning of the BDMR Act, otherwise the section would not presume that only the mother can give birth. The section also makes clear that if a father is a "responsible person" it is only because he was a person "present at the birth" not the person giving birth. Further, the mother is assumed, but the father is not, by s 5(b)(iii), (iv) and (v) to be at the birth.

[62] The applicant accepts that ss 5 and 33 of the BDMR Act operate on the assumption that the mother gives birth and that "birth" is defined as the expulsion or extraction from the "mother" and that there is therefore no scope for the operation of s 32B of the Acts Interpretation Act 1954 (Qld) in this respect. However, the applicant submits that there is no such assumption in respect of "father" and that there is nothing in the BDMR Act to suggest that the person who gave birth,

who might ordinarily be the mother, but is recognised as of the male sex, could not be named as the father. The applicant submits that the Registrar, under ss 10 and 10A, need only be satisfied that the applicant is a parent of the child to identify him as such in the register, but he must be recorded as either the child's mother or father. The birth certificate, according to the particulars required by Schedule 2, does not require that each of the mother's and father's details be on the certificate, also recognising that a person may be registered as a parent only.

[63] In my view, this is a strained interpretation of the BDMR Act when viewed as a whole. It is not an interpretation which means the provisions are construed together to achieve a harmonious goal.

[64] The BDMR Act, as properly construed, does not, in my view, provide for a person being, at the same time, a child's mother and father. As the applicant gave birth to the child, the applicant must be the child's mother for the purposes of the registration of that child's birth. No-one else gave birth to the child. Because the applicant is the mother and must be registered as the mother, the applicant cannot be registered as the father.

[65] There is, in s 22 of the BDMR Act, express recognition that a person may undergo sexual reassignment surgery and that it may be noted in the person's entry in the register of births. "Sexual reassignment surgery" is defined to mean:

a surgical procedure involving the alteration of a person's reproductive organs carried out—

(a) to help the person to be considered to be a member of the opposite sex; or

(b) to correct or eliminate ambiguities about the sex of the person.

[66] Under s 24, a person is a person of the sex as reassigned, in effect, if they have undergone sexual reassignment surgery and the reassignment has been registered or the subject of a recognition certificate. Given that sexual reassignment surgery involves "the alteration of a person's reproductive organs," in my

view, it was not envisaged by the BDMR Act that a person who was male due to the application of s 24, could also be a "mother".

[67] However, having said that, the definition does not require the removal of the person's reproductive organs, only their "alteration" to help them to be considered a member of the opposite sex. In my view, given the beneficial nature of the provision and its purpose, a broad interpretation of the definition should be applied so that a person can be registered as having the reassigned sex of male despite having retained the ability to give birth. This is consistent with the approach adopted by the High Court in AB v State of Western Australia where it was held that an equivalent definition (though with different wording) did not require a particular level of success in achieving the gender of the opposite sex. Accordingly, under the BDMR Act, while perhaps not foreseen by the legislature when drafting the Act, it is possible under its provisions to be registered as male and at the same time, as a mother.

[68] This may be seen to give rise to a less than harmonious interpretation of the Act when read as a whole. Under the Act a person can be male under s 24 and yet, be registered as a "mother" for the purposes of his child's birth. That this can occur may, on one view, undermine the purpose of s 24. Having said that, it may be that the purpose of the sexual reassignment provisions is to recognise that a person's sex may be re-assigned and that this can be reflected in the person's entry in the register of births or adopted children register. In other words, that the reassignment of sex provisions only apply to the person's registered birth details and were not intended to affect whether that person is registered as a mother or father of their child. In other words, that the importance of recording who gave birth to a child takes precedence over a person's right to identify as male.

[69] It appears possible, at first glance, under the Births, Deaths and Marriages Registration Regulation 2015, Schedule 1, Part 5 to register as a "parent," but not as

> the father or mother. However, s 10A provides that the child's parent, or one of the child's parents, must be registered as the child's mother or father. In this case, it appears that the applicant could be registered as a "parent" but only if the other parent registered as either "mother" or "father". The other parent could not be the "mother" which would mean that the other parent could only register as the "father". As not more than one person may be registered as the child's father, it must follow that, while the applicant may conceivably register as "parent" in the circumstances described, he could not register as "father".
>
> [70] The Act does make provision for a person to apply to change a child's parentage but only in the case of adoption or surrogacy. Section 14(1) permits the Registrar to "re-register" a birth following an adoption, or where the person's parentage is changed by a parentage order under the Surrogacy Act 2010.
>
> [71] For all the above reasons, I have concluded that the BDMR Act does not concern itself with the role a parent wishes to take in raising the child. It uses as its reference point, the biological aspects of childbirth and the role a person takes in that process. It is not concerned with the role a person wishes to play in the upbringing of that child. I note that being registered as the "mother" or, as the person who gave birth to a child, does not prevent that person from being the father figure in that child's life.[228]

Anonymity Is Dead

Due to a lack of local donors, or an inability to access donors (due, for example, to discrimination based on sexuality or relationship status), or perceptions of choice or availability, many intended parents access sperm donation overseas.

Those who consider sperm donation or egg donation overseas are often presented with a sperm or egg donor who is to be anonymous. This might be because of local practice (as commonly occurs in the United

228. *Coonan v. Registrar of Births, Deaths & Marriages* [2020] QCAT 434.

States, for example) or by virtue of the law, such as in Spain where anonymity is mandated.[229]

In some European countries, as well as other jurisdictions such as Canada and Australia, there is an expectation that the child will in due course be able to find out the details of the donor, typically after they turn 18.

In several European countries, for example Switzerland,[230] as well as several Australian jurisdictions,[231] there has been retrospective transparency of donors right back to the beginning of whenever donation occurred, typically with sperm donors.

Anonymity is dead due to the removal of anonymity in the world in general. Aside from the rise of social media with apps such as Facebook, X (formerly Twitter), and Instagram—where much of our data is now put out publicly for the enjoyment of friends and family and often accessible by third parties, there are two main methods by which anonymity is dead:

1. **The rise of DNA databases**. The two most prominent examples in the United States are 23andMe.com and Ancestry.com. I have had a few cases where anonymous sperm donors have been located by the donor-conceived adults—in one case 40 years after the donation. The DNA test does not need to be done directly for that donor-conceived adult but by a relative or a relative of the donor. By putting two and two together, the donor is then able to be identified. Whatever data is in those databases now is likely to balloon in say 20 years' time when a child conceived today may first start making enquiries about how they were conceived. In

229. Law 14/2006, of 26 May, on Assisted Human Reproduction Techniques (B.O.E. 2006, 126).

230. Reproductive Medicine Act.

231. Retrospective transparency of donors first occurred in Victoria in 2017 with the commencement of the Assisted Reproductive Treatment Amendment Act 2016 (Victoria). In March 2024, South Australia enacted retrospective transparency of donors, after previously rejecting that. The Assisted Reproductive Treatment (Posthumous Use of Material and Donor Conception Register) Amendment Act 2024 (South Australia) commences on a date to be proclaimed. That date, as of April 2024, has not been proclaimed. In March 2024, the Australian Capital Territory enacted retrospective transparency of donors. Part 5 of the Assisted Reproductive Technology Act 2024 (Australian Capital Territory), which enables the change, is to commence on a date to be proclaimed, which if not proclaimed is to occur by default on March 28, 2025. As of April 2024, the date has not been proclaimed. As of May 2024, the Queensland government has tabled the Assisted Reproductive Technology Bill 2024, which proposes that there be a central donor registry and retrospective transparency to the commencement of sperm donation, which is estimated to be in the late 1970s or early 1980s.

a similar vein, if a sample of hair, for example, is undertaken by the intended parents with the child and as the subject of a DNA test with one of these databases, that information may be discovered. Whether it is wise to take that step prior to the child turning 18 and having full agency is another matter. Evidently it should be the child's ability to find out where they come from and not the parents' determination. The child should have full agency.

2. **Photo scraping apps**. Web scraping tools are now available so that if there is ever a photo of the donor or other data that can be scraped then sooner or later with the benefit of that data, the person is able to be identified. It may be as simple as a google reverse image search, which will positively identify the donor.

Finding a Sperm Donor

There remain barriers throughout the world to finding a sperm donor, often based on the relationship status of the intended parents and their sexuality. Typically, heterosexual married couples are able to find sperm donors a lot easier in many countries, due to the lack of access for singles or LGBTQIA+ couples because of discriminatory laws and practices.

That picture is changing, albeit slowly.

In Europe, many single women and lesbian couples travel to Spain because there is no discrimination and there are many donors available. However, all the donors there are anonymous, with implications subsequently for the child. In other destinations, donors are readily available, such as South Africa. There is no discrimination in South Africa as to gender, sexuality, or relationship status. South Africa requires the donor to be anonymous. However, in 2016 the South African Law Reform Commission recommended enacting laws in South Africa along the Australian lines—namely, that when the child turns 18, he or she can find out the identity of the donor. In practice, what this has meant is that egg donor agencies in South Africa require donors to consent if necessary to the disclosure of their details to the child in due course—in anticipation that the law will change and that therefore the agency will be compliant.

There appear to be fewer barriers in accessing sperm. Sperm is relatively cheap and accessible, primarily being supplied internationally from either the United States or Denmark.

In some countries, the import of sperm must be compliant with local requirements, which include full disclosure as to the child in due course, that there are caps on the number of donations, and that the donation not be commercial.

Egg Donation

One of the reasons that intended parents undertake surrogacy overseas is because they cannot obtain a local egg donor. Typically, if a woman gives birth via egg donation, she will be considered the mother. This is either based on the old principle of the mother is always certain (*mater semper certa est*) all because there is specific law in place, or because the woman or couple do not disclose that there was ever an egg donation.

The availability of egg donors is often extremely limited and, as a result, many intended parents from around the globe come to countries where egg donors are readily available, often in conjunction with surrogacy. Three of the leading countries where this practice occurs are:

1. The United States
2. Ukraine
3. Canada

In terms of LGBTQIA+ intended parents, of those three available countries, only two are available to them—namely, the United States and Canada—with Ukraine only being available to heterosexual married couples.

When intended parents come to a country for the purposes of egg donation, they may be committing an offense back home. Again, I will reference my country of Australia. Throughout Australia it is an offense to pay an egg donor for anything other than her reasonable expenses. The offense is punishable by up to 15 years' imprisonment. In six of the eight Australian jurisdictions, undertaking commercial egg donation overseas may be caught by a long-arm law (i.e., a law that provides that an offense is committed in that jurisdiction if the substantive elements of the offense are committed there, or the effect of the offense occurs there). Therefore, a couple living in Australia could, by entering into what Australians see as commercial egg donation (although it would be seen as good practice in much of the United States), be committing an offense punishable by up to 15 years' imprisonment.[232]

It should not be assumed that if the couple is coming to the United States for egg donation that they are in no legal peril at home.

While there is certainly some understanding of criminal laws by American colleagues concerning surrogacy from countries such as Australia, there is very little it would seem concerning egg donation.

232. *E.g.*, *Human Cloning and Other Prohibited Practices Act 2003* (NSW) s 16 (substantive offense); *Crimes Act 1900* (NSW) s 10C (long-arm law).

It is vital with these international journeys that there be lawyers at both ends of the transaction—namely, someone in the country in which they reside and someone where they are going (such as the United States).

HIV

There have been remarkable advances in the treatment of HIV, including the ability to facilitate IVF where one of the genetic parents has HIV. Care needs to be taken by intended parents undertaking an international ART journey where one or both of them is HIV-positive. They may be actively discriminated against in the country in which they live. They may not be able to ship their genetic material easily overseas. They may need, therefore, to travel overseas in order to provide their genetic material. Their ability to travel may be impeded by their HIV status.

The clinic that they believe may be able to assist them may not do so, either because the clinic has the ability to discriminate under its laws, or because the clinic does not have the technical ability to undertake HIV cases.

For those in Europe, there are barriers to using their sperm in IVF, or sending their sperm overseas. Following Brexit, the UK government in late 2023 signaled that it would amend the law to make it easier for same-sex intended parents who are HIV-positive to undertake surrogacy and reciprocal IVF. See Chapter 2.

Those with HIV should take extra care in their journey, just in case.

Coming Home Might Be the Hard Part

While international surrogacy journeys are extraordinarily complex, getting the child home and recognized as the parents' child is often the hardest part, as seen in the case of *UKM*, from Singapore.

UKM was a gay man who had a partner. UKM had Singapore citizenship, and his partner had U.S. citizenship. They considered adoption, "*but were advised by adoption agencies that because of their homosexual orientation, they would not be allowed to adopt in Singapore.*"[233] So they turned to ART. Surrogacy was banned in Singapore. Singapore criminalized homosexual sexual acts. Therefore, they undertook surrogacy in the United States. They paid $200,000 for their surrogacy journey, of which $25,000 was the surrogate's fee, which was deemed a reimbursement. In 2013 the men had a son through surrogacy in Pennsylvania.

233. *UKM v Attorney-General* [2018] SGHCF 18 [4].

UKM brought his son to Singapore. UKM then applied for Singapore citizenship for the son. This was denied. The child obtained an eight-month visa.

UKM then applied, as a single man, to adopt his son in Singapore. He did so in part because it would improve his chances of the child remaining in Singapore. Among his reasons for seeking to adopt was to remove the stigma of being a single parent in Singapore, and to formalize his legal status as father "*so as to give him a good start in life*," which may have included to ensure that the child was legitimate.

The Singaporean adoption authority carried out a three-year assessment. It appeared that the father, a pathologist, appeared to have the financial means to meet the child's basic needs and the home environment was comfortably furnished and child-safe. It also set out that the men were committed to parenting the child as two fathers and described the father's "*thoughts on how he would help the child to cope with possibly having to face social stigma in the future and to make sense of his unconventional family structure*."[234]

The officer recommended against adoption as it was "*contrary to public policy*" because same-sex marriage was not recognized in Singapore, and because UKM was "*seeking to form a family unit with his male partner*." The report also referred to UKM's homosexual "*lifestyle*."

Adoption was refused by the trial court, which said that UKM had, by undertaking surrogacy in the United States, walked "*through the back door of the system when the front door was firmly shut*."[235] The court considered that the payment for the surrogate was a payment for adoption, an offense in Singapore, which therefore contradicted the spirit of Singapore law. The trial court could have condoned the payment, but chose not to because the surrogacy arrangement "*promotes the idea of the child as a commodity and is drawn up to facilitate the severance of human ties so as to enable the creation of new ones as a fee to be paid to the surrogate, the physician and the lawyer*." Further, "*commercial surrogacy demeans and exploits human beings at various levels, especially women in poverty*."[236]

The trial judge found that an adoption order would serve only UKM's wishes and that "*the courts must never be used as a fait accompli*."[237]

234. *Id.* [14].

235. Sounding very much like the language of the Supreme Court of Iceland in *Fjölnisdóttir v. Iceland* (2021). *See* Chapter 2.

236. *UKM* [2018] SGHCF 18 [21].

237. *Id.* [186].

UKM appealed. He succeeded on appeal.[238] The High Court reversed the decision, saying that an adoption order would enhance the child's prospects of remaining in Singapore by entitling him to apply for citizenship on a different ground. With citizenship granted, care arrangements would be stabilized, giving caregivers peace of mind, and in turn contributing to the child's "*sense of security and overall emotional well-being.*" The countervailing public policy consideration against allowing adoption was not sufficiently weighty against the "*statutory imperative*" to promote the child's welfare. The court engaged in a two-stage inquiry. First, to determine what was in the child's welfare. Second, whether there were countervailing public policy considerations that defeated the claim based on the child's welfare, if established.

Take Away

1. While the rights of LGBTQIA+ people have gone backward in some parts of the world in recent years, slowly the rights of their children, at least in some parts, are being more and more recognized.
2. Intended parents and their children may have a journey in which rights, at the same time, are advancing and retreating.
3. The law in this space evolves fairly quickly. Lawyers should always work closely with their overseas counterparts, where possible from the beginning of the international ART journey, to reduce the risk for their clients.
4. Never make the mistake of assuming that the journey will be an easy one.
5. Care should be taken as to the country where the intended parents live, the country where they are going to, and, if their citizenship is different, their country of citizenship.
6. There are many fewer countries in which surrogacy is available for gay couples than heterosexual couples.
7. Care should be taken when one or both of the intended parents is HIV-positive.
8. If the parents move for work or travel, their parentage may not be recognized in the other country.
9. Sometimes the move "*home*" to those who are expatriates might involve a two-step process, so that they travel to the country of

238. *UKM* [2018] SGHCF 18.

the intended parent's citizenship first in order to obtain that citizenship for the child before returning "*home.*"

10. It should not be assumed that because surrogacy is available for gay couples that it is available for trans, intersex, or non-binary intended parents.

Chapter 8

Citizenship and Residence Are Not the Same

The concepts of citizenship and residence are often confused, as is the issue of a passport.

Unless we are stateless, every person is a citizen of a State. Citizenship is obtained in a number of ways, typically by location of birth (such as in the United States) or by blood (such as in Italy).

For an example of how the world looks differently at citizenship, one only need look at India.

When India Was Booming. . .

In the early 2010s, the surrogacy agreement would say that the child would be the child of the intended parents, and take the citizenship of the parents. Sometimes the agreement would also say that the child would not at birth be an Indian citizen, due to the effect of the Indian Citizenship Act 1955. Citizenship of a child born in India is acquired under that act when one or both parents are Indian citizens.[1] Citizenship is not acquired by place of birth.

Therefore, children born in India to international intended parents were born stateless. Application was then made by the parents for the child to acquire the citizenship of the parents. Parents (and therefore the children) ran into trouble when the parents' country refused to accept the child as a citizen.

Too often I have seen reference to intended parents under U.S. agreements that because they reside in a particular location, the assumption is made that they are also citizens in that location. To quote George Gershwin, "*It ain't necessarily so.*"[2] Never assume. *Always ask.*

---

1. Citizenship Act, 1955, § 3.
2. George Gershwin & Ira Gershwin, *It Ain't Necessarily So*, *on* Porgy and Bess (1935).

Matters get complicated when intended parents have multiple citizenships. Intended parents will have to make a decision about where they want to live and what citizenship their child should have. They should be making this decision right at the beginning of the matter, so that for any international surrogacy journey, planning can be done to ensure that the maximum number of citizenships for their child can be obtained. This should never be left to chance.

In the early 2010s, all my clients who had multiple citizenships wanted their children to have the lot. The most between one couple, from recollection, was six: Australia, the United Kingdom, New Zealand, Italy, Argentina, and Ireland. Their child was to be born in the United States, so the child would have ended up with seven.

The challenge of course with that approach is that as a lawyer you should be trying to contact colleagues overseas for the clients to obtain advice, so that there is a coordinated approach to ensure that the surrogacy journey is compliant in all places.

Our tendency, as practitioners, is to send emails to each other. We forget about use of the phone (or apps such as Zoom). I can't emphasize enough in this type of situation the benefit of using a dialogue communication, such as phone or Zoom, rather than a monologue with a long email thread where points gets lost.

At times when these matters get confusing and there are three professionals assisting the clients involved, get all three together in the one call, so that the levels of confusion melt away. More recently, in my practice at least, I've noticed that clients really haven't been wanting to have multiple citizenships for their child. They have worked out where they want to live—and just want that one.

Having to go off to talk to lawyers in different parts of the world, with increasing cost and complexity, has meant that if intended parents are going to be seeking that citizenship, they are going to do it later. If they make the decision at that point not to seek some other citizenship for their child straightaway, I then seek to document that to ensure there is no doubt as to the advice that they were given.

Of course, in some countries, most prominently in this space, India and China, the concept of dual citizenship is not recognized. The person is either a citizen of that country or they are not. They cannot hold dual citizenship. That is then an issue for a child born in a country where the child automatically attains citizenship by birth (such as the United States and Canada). It is essential that the intended parents obtain local advice early in the journey to make sure that the child's intended citizenship is not prejudiced by attaining other citizenship through birth.

India complicates matters further with its designation of Overseas Citizens of India (OCIs)—which typically are those people who have migrated from India and obtained other citizenship (and therefore had to give up their Indian citizenship). Being an OCI may enable them easier entry at the border and certain privileges in India. Surrogacy in India is restricted to Indian citizens. It is unclear to me whether OCIs are able to access surrogacy in India, but it appears from limited information that Indian authorities accept OCIs can undertake surrogacy. See Chapter 3.

Many countries restrict surrogacy within that country's borders to citizens of that country, or at least where one of the parties is a citizen of that country, for example Russia, Georgia (from January 1, 2024),[3] India, Thailand, and Vietnam.

Other countries have no difficulty with a person not being a citizen of that country but require them, if undertaking surrogacy there, to be resident or domiciled there—for example, Australia and the United Kingdom.

Too often clients of mine who wonder whether surrogacy is legal and then find out that there are offenses relating to surrogacy wonder how it applies to them when they are not citizens of Australia, but they are citizens of a foreign country. Of course, if they happen to be present in the jurisdiction, then the law typically will also apply to them. I explain it very simply that if you are driving down the road, the traffic rules apply, irrespective of whether you are a citizen or not.

As seen in Chapter 13, if adoption is the method to establish parentage, and the 1993 Hague Intercountry Adoption Convention applies, citizenship is not a prime consideration. One of the prime considerations is the habitual residence of the adoptive parents and of the child.

If someone is an expatriate resident in some Asian hubs, it is often best that the journey home with the child from being born overseas be via the parent's country of citizenship—so the child has the parent's citizenship. See Chapter 7.

Across the Ditch with Thee

As an in-house joke, the Tasman Sea, which separates Australia and New Zealand, is nicknamed the "ditch."

3. The ban was announced by the Health Minister, to take effect from January 1, 2024. As of April 2024, the bill to effect the ban has been tabled in Parliament, but not enacted.

Australian and New Zealand citizens can reside in each other's country as a matter of right, and as a result many do. Australian and New Zealand cross-border surrogacy journeys play out in a number of ways, as set out in the following examples.

Example One: The Two Sisters

As seen in the New Zealand case *In re Application by L*[4] (see Chapter 1), a sister in Australia was a surrogate for her sister and brother-in-law in New Zealand. With care, if a child is born in Australia to a couple living in New Zealand, the Australian surrogacy arrangement is likely to be lawful, but noncompliant (though that varies), with the result that the child has to get back to New Zealand before an adoption order can be made to reflect the parentage of the intended parents.

In reverse, the surrogate living in New Zealand should not give birth there, but fly to Australia to give birth. Because the process of surrogacy in New Zealand is by way of adoption, and the intended parents do not live in New Zealand (and therefore may not be eligible to have an adoption order made in their favor), there is a real risk that an adoption order will not be made.

The risk is to hope that the surrogate can get medical and airline clearance to fly to Australia—and not too early in the pregnancy (as that will cause great stress in her job and care arrangements for her children), but not too late.

At this point it should be noted that despite International Air Transport Association (IATA) rules about when those who are pregnant can fly, every airline has its own rules. It is good to know those differences keenly at the beginning of the surrogacy journey.

Example Two: Gay Kiwis[5] in Australia

Quite a few single gay New Zealanders live in Australia. They live in Australia as residents, but are not Australian citizens. A number of them have become parents through surrogacy in the United States.

When their child has traveled back to Australia with them, the child has obtained a visa to live in Australia as the dependent child of the parent. However, the child has done so as a U.S. citizen, and not a New Zealand citizen. The reason is twofold:

---

4. [2003] NZFLR 529.

5. An affectionate name for New Zealanders, named after their national bird, the kiwi, not the kiwifruit.

- The process of surrogacy in New Zealand is that of adoption, which is perceived by intended parents as being difficult and slow.
- Interviews of the intended parent would need to be carried out by Australian state authorities on behalf of New Zealand authorities. In several Australian states, commercial surrogacy overseas is a criminal offence. As seen in *In re Application by L*, those living in Australia do not want to engage with Australian state authorities.

Example Three: The Domestic Australian Surrogacy Journey

Jack and Jennifer, an Australian couple living in Australia, needed to undertake surrogacy in order to become parents. Their best friends Jewel and Jim offered to help—with Jewel as the surrogate. All lived in the same city.

The arrangement seemed straightforward. Jim was a New Zealander. He was therefore entitled to live in Australia, but not as a permanent resident. Jewel, as his spouse, was able to reside in Australia under a subsidiary visa. Jewel was a citizen of Zimbabwe.

When the child was born, Jim and Jewel were the parents under local Australian law. The child was immediately in the care of Jack and Jennifer and remained in their care throughout. The child upon being born in Australia was not an Australian citizen. Its citizenship was uncertain. Australian citizenship is determined from the citizenship of the parent. The child could only remain in Australia if Jim obtained a visa that the child was his dependent. Jim did not do so, in light of the pending parentage order.

Some weeks after the child was born, an Australian parentage order was made transferring parentage from Jim and Jewel to Jack and Jennifer. It was only at that point that the child gained Australian citizenship.

Obtaining a passport, of course, is different. Ordinarily, a passport or travel document of some kind cannot be obtained without first the person being a citizen. As has been seen in cases such as *Mennesson v. France*[6] (Chapter 2), being recorded in identity documents within the State has been a challenge for some, let alone having a passport issue.

Too often the intended parents (and some lawyers) think that the home journey requires only the obtaining of a passport. Somehow, they have just assumed that the child, being their child, will automatically hold their citizenship. The child may not. It's a simple point, but an essential

6. App. No. 65192/11 (Sept. 26, 2014).

one—the child typically needs to be a citizen of their country first before that child can obtain a passport of that country.

I am astonished at the number of times that intended parents have a disconnect between citizenship and passport. Their thinking is to *assume* that they are the parents because they are the genetic or intended parents—and therefore the child will automatically obtain the passport of their citizenship. It is essential that lawyers do not make that mistake of *assuming*. To do so is to fall into error.

Take Away

1. Always ask as to all the citizenships of all the parties.
2. If the party has multiple citizenships, planning may need to occur at the beginning of the journey to take that into account.
3. Just because a person lives in one country does not necessarily mean that they are a citizen of that country.
4. How does the child acquire citizenship?
5. Does the country of the intended parents recognize dual citizenships or not, and if the answer is not, then what?
6. If the intended parent is an expatriate undertaking surrogacy somewhere else—they should consider going to their country of citizenship on the way "home" so that the child has secure citizenship of the parent's country of citizenship, just in case.
7. Citizenship is needed before a passport is obtained.
8. Proposed extraterritorial surrogacy laws for Irish and Italian citizens may affect them, even if they do not live in Ireland or Italy.
9. Where possible, have your clients also retain a lawyer in that country or countries.
10. Where possible, liaise directly with that lawyer, so that the two of you do not act at cross-purposes.

Chapter 9

Finding an Overseas Lawyer

Why You Should Find a Lawyer

A theme of this book is always try to ensure that your clients retain a lawyer in the other place—someone who is an expert in the law of that place. Where possible, if there are complex issues, engage in active dialogue with that lawyer (such as the use of the phone), not monologue (emails). While letters and emails have their uses, active dialogue usually identifies the problems, and possible solutions, quickly and efficiently.

Self-evidently, this book is written in English. The joy of the English language, for those of us fluent in it, is that it is the prime language of the internet and international commerce. As a result, many foreign laws, written in foreign languages, are translated into English, often via official government translations.

The benefit of being an English speaker is that one can instantly absorb foreign statutes that have been translated into English, rather than rely on websites of lawyers, surrogacy agencies, or clinics that set out what they perceive to be the substance of the law. You can go to the primary source and, hopefully, understand it.

As a result, as an Australian lawyer, I have had the benefit of reading many American statutes such as relevant provisions of the California Family Code, as well as statutes relating to surrogacy, such as relevant provisions of the Russian Family Code, the Greek Civil Code, and the Health Code of Kazakhstan.

However, being able to read a foreign statute in English is not the same as understanding the law there. Quite simply, you are not admitted in the foreign jurisdiction and while you may have the benefit of the foreign law in English, and this is not always assured, you should not pretend for a second that you understand the context of the law there. While you may see that there is a law concerning surrogacy, you may have missed critical laws concerning adoption, regulation of health clinics, regulation of in vitro fertilization (IVF) clinics, and regulation of egg donation, to name but a few. To state the obvious to common-law lawyers: what is in the statute may not be the significant part that you need to look at. You may see only the tip of the iceberg, not the other 90 percent.

The only person who can truly be able to tell your client the state of the law in that place is a lawyer of that place.

You Need a Local

In 2010 I was in Memphis. I was in Beale Street and was watching some magical performers. I took some amazing shots, with the result that a local teenage girl wanted me to take photos of her. Why she wanted me to do that, I do not know. Her friends then suggested that they also have photos taken and I obliged.

The girl then asked me where I was from. I said I was from Australia. She then asked me what I did. I told her that I was a lawyer. She said, "*I need a lawyer. I'm in trouble with the county.*" I tried to explain to her that because I was a lawyer in Australia and not a local lawyer, I was unable to help her. Despite my statements, she could not be dissuaded, until her friend said, "*No, Lurlene, you need a local. He ain't a local.*"

To assume is to fall into error. The assumptions about finding a lawyer in another country are explained in Table 9.1.

Table 9.1. Assumptions about Finding a Lawyer in Another Country

Assumption	Why	Response
My clients don't need a lawyer in the other country.	This is a straightforward deal. Everyone knows how to do this. I've had clients from there before.	You aren't admitted there. You do not have expertise in the laws of that country. If something goes wrong, you will likely pay a significant deductible on your insurance—as the overseas laws are outside your area of expertise. You may miss a change in the law, or miss a subtle issue of practice known to locals. You may be committing an ethical breach.
I will find a lawyer in the other country.	Finding lawyers overseas is easy.	It may not be easy to find a lawyer—for that country or province.
The lawyer overseas speaks English.	Everyone speaks English.	Not necessarily. English is the third most spoken language, after Chinese and Spanish.

Assumption	Why	Response
I will find an ethical lawyer.	All lawyers are ethical.	Not all are.
I will find a lawyer who knows what they are doing.	Assisted reproductive technology (ART) is straightforward. Lots of lawyers do ART.	Not necessarily. While lots of lawyers might do ART where you come from, in much of the world it is a niche—and in some parts of the world *no lawyers* practice in this area.
If I find a lawyer from that country, they know the law across the country.	Laws are the same across the country.	Laws can be different across federations. You may need a lawyer in that state or province.

Experience has taught me that it is not always possible to find a lawyer overseas, or, for that matter, the right kind of lawyer—someone from the right place, who knows what they are doing, and is ethical. While surrogacy and ART may to you be an everyday part of your work, in many other parts of the world it is seen as controversial, novel, or a very niche area of business in which the lawyer in question has no expertise. In small countries, there are sometimes no laws at all about surrogacy ART, and there may be no IVF clinics. Surrogacy, at least in the gestational form, might be unknown. Even if you find someone you think may know something about the topic in question, for example an experienced family lawyer, they may have no idea whatsoever about ART, or may be disinclined to help because of the steep learning curve required of them, or because of their distaste in dealing with this, as they perceive it, controversial area.

That is not even considering that your clients might be a gay couple, for example. See Chapter 7. There may be great reluctance at the other end by a lawyer to assist, depending on the society.

How to Find a Lawyer Overseas. Let Me Count the Ways. . .[1]

The *first way* I would suggest is to be a member of the American Bar Association Family Law Section ART Committee and ask online. That has been remarkably helpful for me in finding lawyers overseas. The

1. Apologies to Elizabeth Barrett Browning, "How do I love thee?" (Sonnet 43).

news list is a remarkable resource. However, with all the ways mentioned, it has not always been successful.

The *second way* is that if you are a Fellow of the Academy of Adoption and Assisted Reproduction Attorneys (AAAA), ask through there or ask other Fellows. I found on occasion that this has worked too.

The *third way* is to ask colleagues. The more experienced colleagues with international ART experience, the better. Usually, they will be members of the American Bar Association Family Law Section ART Committee, or Fellows of AAAA, but they may not be. For example, to enable me to find a lawyer in Moldova, I asked an ART colleague I trust in Greece. She was able to give me the contact details of a colleague in Romania. The lawyer in Romania spoke the same language as someone in Moldova (Romanian) and was able to refer me to a lawyer in Moldova.

The *fourth way* is if you are a Fellow of the International Academy of Family Lawyers (IAFL), then this often works. Even if you are not a Fellow, you can go to the IAFL website to find a Fellow: www.iafl.com. On the right-hand side of the home page there is a search box to find family lawyers worldwide. You will start, at worst, by selecting the country in the top box, and sliding down the drop-down menu, until you find the country you are looking for. Once you have found the country, then click the green box at the bottom, "BEGIN SEARCH." That will take you to the names of the Fellows in that country.

That search function is often helpful. That search function is open to anyone and is not limited to IAFL Fellows.

Once you find a Fellow, click on their name. This brings up their profile. You will be able to see from their profile whether they have ever handled surrogacy or ART. Even if they have not, if they have handled parenting cases, that is better than a generalist lawyer.

However, some countries, for example Iran, are not in the drop-down menu. That is not the end of the line. Even if you have not been able to find a country, the IAFL has referral resources open to Fellows. Try to identify someone you know who is a Fellow and ask them if they can look for you.

The *fifth way* to find an international attorney is to go to the Family Law Committee of the International Bar Association and ask. The committee can be found at: www.ibanet.org/officer/officerList/3093.

You will find that several members of that committee or the Family Law Committee Advisory Board are also Fellows of the IAFL. A couple at least are members of the American Bar Association Family Law Section ART Committee.

The *sixth way* is if you are aware of some lawyers who practice across jurisdictions. For example, within China, some lawyers are admitted in

China as well as in Hong Kong or Macao. Nauru is a micro-country in the South Pacific, with a population of 12,000. There are no practicing lawyers. However, Australian lawyers have often appeared there.

If you are looking for lawyers in Latin America and are unable to find a local lawyer in Latin America, a good starting point may be with prominent ART lawyers in Florida, Miami being referred to of course as the capital of South America. The links between Florida and South America are deep, and you may be lucky to find such a lawyer.

The *seventh way* is to ask the local law society or bar association. Recently, for example, I managed to find an adoption lawyer in Fiji, by contacting the Fijian Law Society.

The *eighth way* is to contact the local consul or embassy. The U.S. embassy, or the embassy of your country, in each country (where there is representation) often has a list of trusted lawyers. However, these lawyers tend to be commercial lawyers, not specializing in family law, let alone ART. Alternatively, contact the nearest embassy or consul of that foreign country. They may be able to refer you to someone.

Even if you are referred to a commercial lawyer, that lawyer or law firm may be able to refer you to someone more suitable.

The *ninth way* is that surrogacy agencies that have programs in those countries or indeed links in those countries may be able to identify a lawyer for you. One must always take care with those referrals. The lawyer may have obvious (and sometimes not so obvious) conflicts.

The surrogacy agency may have some benefit in referring you to that lawyer. It is always, from your point of view, a case of buyer beware.

Don't Forget Ethics

Of course, if you manage to find an overseas lawyer, that is not the end of the matter. You should not assume that the overseas lawyer is necessarily ethical. Obviously if you have had a referral from someone you trust, then that is always a good sign. In most of the world, namely any place that is not a common-law country, lawyers are not officers of the court. I have found, sadly, widely divergent views about the laws in various places, and at times this divergence has depended on the ethics of the lawyer.

What If They Don't Speak English?

If you manage to find a local lawyer, and you are only fluent in English, try to find someone who speaks English. If the foreign lawyer speaks another language but not English, you will need to use an interpreter for any phone calls or Zoom/Teams calls that you have with that lawyer.

The sending and receiving of emails are easier because of translation tools such as Google Translate, but you must always take care.

Google Translate Is Not Perfect

In 2013 I was interviewed by a journalist from Xinhua, the Chinese news agency, about adoption laws in Australia. The journalist contacted me about a day before I was going overseas. He had a list of questions that he wanted to ask me. He was not based in my hometown. He suggested that he send the list through and then I record the answers and send them to him.

Because I was traveling to the United States, I suggested that I use the then revolutionary idea of recording it on my iPhone and using Dropbox to send the file back to him. On my third attempt, I managed to get the taping right and about an hour later had successfully uploaded the file to Dropbox (internet speeds were a lot slower then) and off it went.

Several weeks later, I was told that the link was live, and the story had been published. Lawyers around the world had been asked for their views. When I was given the link, it was to the Xinhua site, in Chinese. I then applied Google Translate to see what I had said (as I did not recall what I had said) and, to my consternation, it quoted me as saying that in Australia we had "*compulsory execution.*" I did not recall what I had said, but I knew I had not said that!

After a great deal of effort, I managed to find the original clip (which no longer had been translated twice—once from English into Mandarin and then via Google Translate from Mandarin to English. What I had said was quite different—namely, that in Australia our adoption laws meant that there was "*mandatory regulation.*"

Somehow the double translation had morphed my words of "*mandatory regulation*" of adoption to "*compulsory execution*"!

Again, Don't Assume!

In your dealings with the foreign lawyer, keep an open mind. What you may think is impossible to be done, may be able to be done. What you consider doable may in fact not be doable, or may be doable with such onerous conditions, or such a difficult pathway, or slow or costly, that it is not worth trying. When you get the advice from the foreign lawyer, you always have to look at it with a practical bent—is this thing ever going to fly?

Your duty to your client means that you need to second-guess to an extent what has been said and put yourself in your client's shoes as to having to undertake this journey, and whether this journey is worth it, how much it is going to cost, how long it is going to take, and what easier or more difficult steps are required to get there.

A Recent Example

A recent example is that of clients of mine contemplating a surrogacy journey in Mexico who were told by a lawyer there that to bring their baby home, they should apply for a Mexican passport for the child. The child being born there is entitled to Mexican citizenship. The process to obtain the passport, I was told, would take three months. Once the passport was obtained, then the child would have to apply to obtain an Australian visa.

By comparison, I knew from prior experience that a child born via surrogacy to an Australian citizen parent in Mexico should be able to obtain the birth certificate, Australian citizenship via the Australian embassy in Mexico, and then an emergency Australian passport home—in all of eight weeks. I was also concerned that the Australian government is keen for children born overseas through surrogacy to obtain Australian citizenship in the surrogacy destination before they enter Australia.

My advice? Take the latter option, not the former. Like most other intended parents, they want to go home with their baby as soon as possible.

You may have been told, for example, that because you act for a gay couple that surrogacy is not possible in that country—as that country has on its statute books criminal offenses for homosexual sex. The reality, however, may be that surrogacy is available there, albeit only to single men and with the surrogate, in some cases, remaining on the birth certificate, or in other cases, not.

If You Cannot Find a Lawyer Overseas. . .

If you cannot find a lawyer, then you must do second best, which is trawling through the statutes as best you can and, if the country is a common-law jurisdiction or has a constitutional court, try to find any significant decisions that you are able to lay your hands on. You must be as thorough as possible, but with the written caveat to your clients that you are flying blind. Therefore, any advice that you give is imperfect because you are not admitted in that jurisdiction, and therefore you do not know the laws of that jurisdiction. You are trying to do your best in the circumstances.

Beware of the ethical limitations imposed on you.

The American Bar Association's Model Rule of Professional Conduct 5.5 provides:

Law Firms And Associations

(a) A lawyer shall not practice law in a jurisdiction in violation of the regulation of the legal profession in that jurisdiction, or assist another in doing so.

(b) A lawyer who is not admitted to practice in this jurisdiction shall not:

  (1) except as authorized by these Rules or other laws, establish an office or other systematic and continuous presence in this jurisdiction for the practice of law; or

  (2) hold out to the public or otherwise represent that the lawyer is admitted to practice law in this jurisdiction.

(c) A lawyer admitted in another United States jurisdiction, and not disbarred or suspended from practice in any jurisdiction, may provide legal services on a temporary basis in this jurisdiction that:

  (1) are undertaken in association with a lawyer who is admitted to practice in this jurisdiction and who actively participates in the matter;

  (2) are in or reasonably related to a pending or potential proceeding before a tribunal in this or another jurisdiction, if the lawyer, or a person the lawyer is assisting, is authorized by law or order to appear in such proceeding or reasonably expects to be so authorized;

  (3) are in or reasonably related to a pending or potential arbitration, mediation, or other alternative resolution proceeding in this or another jurisdiction, if the services arise out of or are reasonably related to the lawyer's practice in a jurisdiction in which the lawyer is admitted to practice and are not services for which the forum requires pro hac vice admission; or

  (4) are not within paragraphs (c)(2) or (c)(3) and arise out of or are reasonably related to the lawyer's practice in a jurisdiction in which the lawyer is admitted to practice.

(d) A lawyer admitted in another United States jurisdiction or in a foreign jurisdiction, and not disbarred or suspended from practice in any jurisdiction or the equivalent thereof, or a person otherwise lawfully practicing as an in-house counsel under the laws of a foreign jurisdiction, may provide legal services through an office or other systematic and continuous presence in this jurisdiction that:
   (1) are provided to the lawyer's employer or its organizational affiliates, are not services for which the forum requires pro hac vice admission; and when performed by a foreign lawyer and requires advice on the law of this or another U.S. jurisdiction or of the United States, such advice shall be based upon the advice of a lawyer who is duly licensed and authorized by the jurisdiction to provide such advice; or
   (2) are services that the lawyer is authorized by federal or other law or rule to provide in this jurisdiction.

(e) For purposes of paragraph (d):
   (1) the foreign lawyer must be a member in good standing of a recognized legal profession in a foreign jurisdiction, the members of which are admitted to practice as lawyers or counselors at law or the equivalent, and subject to effective regulation and discipline by a duly constituted professional body or a public authority; or,
   (2) the person otherwise lawfully practicing as an in-house counsel under the laws of a foreign jurisdiction must be authorized to practice under this Rule by, in the exercise of its discretion, [the highest court of this jurisdiction].[2]

If you are a Fellow of AAAA, then the mandated ethical requirement on this point provides:

16. REPRESENTATION in ART MATTERS and AVOIDANCE of CONFLICTS of INTEREST:

2. Model Rules of Pro. Conduct r. 5.5 (Am. Bar. Ass'n 2024), https://www.americanbar.org/products/inv/book/438500107/.

(a) In every ART Matter in which a Fellow represents a Party, the other Party(ies) must also have independent legal counsel except:
  (1) in an uncontested process to establish parentage in which no actual conflict of interest exists or is likely to arise among the Parties to that proceeding, so long as the unrepresented Party is informed of a right to independent legal counsel;
  (2) A Fellow may represent (i) both Intended Parents, (ii) a Donor and Donor's spouse or partner or (iii) a Surrogate and Surrogate's spouse or partner provided that there is no actual conflict of interest and the potential conflict of interest has been disclosed and waived.

(b) A Fellow may represent a Party in an ART Matter if:
  (1) The representation is in accordance with all applicable laws and ethics rules pertaining to competence, the unauthorized practice of law, and multijurisdictional practice, including the laws and rules of the jurisdiction in which the Fellow is licensed to practice law and the laws and rules of any other jurisdiction in which the Fellow provides legal services [see comment 1]; and,
  (2) The Fellow is licensed in at least one of the following jurisdictions:
    A) the jurisdiction of the Child's expected birth;
    B) the jurisdiction in which at least one Party resides; or
    C) the jurisdiction in which the medical procedures in furtherance of the ART Matter are expected to take place.
  (3) A Fellow who is not licensed in one of the jurisdictions described in 16(b)(2) may provide legal services in a jurisdiction where that Fellow is not licensed to practice law if they are licensed in another US state and such legal services are undertaken as co-counsel with, or in consultation with, a lawyer licensed to practice law in that jurisdiction.

(c) A Fellow who represents any Party in an ART Matter shall ensure that any agreement between or among the

Parties in that ART Matter is drafted or reviewed by an attorney licensed to practice law in the governing jurisdiction as defined by that agreement's choice of law provisions.

(See comment 2: A Fellow is not required to ensure independent representation of a party that is a business entity, including but not limited to a law or medical practice, and that offers surrogate or donor matching and/or coordinating services)

(d) If the Fellow is advising a client as to the laws of a jurisdiction in which the Fellow is not licensed to practice law, the Fellow shall inform the client as to the Fellow's understanding of the laws of that jurisdiction, provided that the Fellow:

(1) Discloses to the client that the Fellow is not licensed to practice in that jurisdiction; and

(2) Advises the client of the benefit of obtaining advice from an attorney licensed to practice law in that jurisdiction.

(e) Except as provided in Section 16 (a) (1) and (2), a Fellow who represents a Party in an ART Matter shall not represent multiple Parties in drafting or negotiating the ART Matter.[3]

For those law firms that are also members of the Society for Ethics in Egg Donation and Surrogacy (SEEDS), there is also an applicable ethical standard, and, in bold, guideline:

> An Agency shall refer clients to all necessary legal, tax, medical, psychological, insurance, or other professionals for advice and provision of services in areas of expertise in which they are not licensed.
>
> ***Guideline: A Member must be licensed to practice law, tax, medicine, mental health, and/or insurance before providing advice on these issues. A Member is not qualified to give advice on any of these topics merely based on experience alone and must refer Participants to the appropriate third-party***

3. AAAA, Academy Code of Ethics for the Academy of Adoption and Assisted Reproduction Attorneys 16 (2022), https://adoptionart.org/wp-content/uploads/2022/05/ACADEMY-CODE-OF-ETHICS-Approved-May-2022.pdf.

professionals (see relevant SEEDS professional Member directories for some resources).[4]

Take Away

1. Never, during the whole of what at times seems an odyssey to find an overseas lawyer, and then testing from the client's perspective what the overseas lawyer says, ever lose sight of your overriding duty to your client.
2. Most of the time you will be able to find a lawyer overseas.
3. If you cannot find an overseas lawyer, ensure your advice complies with ethical obligations and is clearly documented.

4. SEEDS, Standards of Ethical Conduct for SEEDS Member Agencies 8 (2023), https://seedsethics.org/wp-content/uploads/2023/08/Final-Standards-with-Guidelines-and-intro-1.pdf.

Chapter 10

In Different Parts of the Same Country, Different Laws May Apply

I have said in other parts of this book not to assume. As the old saying goes, "to assume is to make an ass out of you and me." This is the classic example. Just because you have had clients from that country before, do not assume that the law that applies to the current clients who come from that country is the same.

Of course, the law may have changed, as it often does in this area, sometimes at what seems to be lightning speed. The country might be a unitary state, such as France or Italy. It may be, therefore, that the law is the same everywhere in that country.

However, a few countries are not unitary states, but are federations, of which the best known is the United States. As the United States demonstrates, the law concerning assisted reproductive technology (ART) in federations can vary within a country because it varies from state to state or from province to province within that country. The United States has 51 different versions of law concerning ART. Some have parallels, and some stand out on their own, such as Louisiana. The point is that each and every one of them is different to the others, which means that if you are an American attorney and you have an interstate matter, then you would typically rely on co-counsel from that other state to make sure that you get the result right.

The same applies in other federations. While most federations have federal laws that concern ART, some don't, and with some federations, there are both federal and state laws. They are all different.

Countries That Are Federations

Argentina

Argentina has provinces. While it is possible in other provinces to obtain pre-birth orders based on the practice of the courts, invariable advice from Argentine colleagues is instead to rely on laws passed by the capital area of Buenos Aires (CABA), which has an auto-recognition process for intended parents, based on laws enacted by CABA. There is no discrimination against single or same-sex couples.

Australia

Australia has a population of 27 million with six states and two territories. Who is a parent for the purposes of citizenship is determined under federal law (the Australian Citizenship Act 2005 (Commonwealth)). An overseas surrogate is considered by the administering Australian department to be a parent (as the surrogate is considered to be the natural parent, by having given birth) for the purposes of issuing a passport,[1] irrespective of overseas law or what is contained in the surrogacy agreement.

Parentage is determined for the purposes of family law under federal law[2] for children born overseas through surrogacy, except for some children in Western Australia. If a child in Western Australia is not considered a child of the marriage, and parentage was not established via adoption, then Western Australian law, not federal law, applies.[3] In all other states and territories,[4] federal law applies as to who is a parent for the purposes of family law.

Commonwealth law criminalizes entry into commercial egg, sperm, or embryo donor agreements. Those laws are unlikely to apply overseas. In addition, each state and the Australian Capital Territory (but not the Northern Territory) criminalizes those entering into commercial egg donor agreements. Under a separate statutory scheme, all eight jurisdictions have laws concerning banning the sale of human tissue, with some exceptions—which can apply to sperm, eggs, embryos, and (with the exception of Queensland) breast milk. In six of the eight jurisdictions (the exceptions being Victoria and Tasmania) it can be an offense committed overseas by someone in that jurisdiction in entering into a commercial sperm, egg, or embryo donor agreement, or human tissue agreement (including breast milk) (with the exception of Queensland concerning breast milk).

In three jurisdictions—Australian Capital Territory, New South Wales, and Queensland—it can be an offense for someone ordinarily

1. *Australian Passports Act 2005* (Cth).
2. *Family Law Act 1975* (Cth).
3. *Family Court Act 1997* (WA).
4. Australian Capital Territory, New South Wales, Northern Territory, Queensland, South Australia, Tasmania, and Victoria.

resident (or, in the case of New South Wales, as an alternative if the person is domiciled there—see Chapter 4) in engaging in commercial surrogacy overseas—the definition of which is under that state's or territory's law. In three other jurisdictions, Northern Territory, South Australia, and Western Australia, the relevant offense concerning commercial surrogacy can be committed overseas based on a local long-arm law. In two states, Tasmania and Victoria, no offense is committed overseas concerning surrogacy.

In all Australian jurisdictions, an offense may be committed overseas if a payment is made, and the form of surrogacy is by way of adoption.[5]

In all Australian jurisdictions, other than Tasmania and Victoria, an offense may be committed overseas by engaging in what is defined in the Australian jurisdiction as commercial egg, sperm, or embryo donation, by virtue of a long-arm law, punishable by up to 15 years' imprisonment.[6] Payment to the surrogate for breast milk may also be caught by these provisions, though not for residents of Queensland.[7]

Brazil

Surrogacy is permitted, by virtue of the Federal Medical Council. Commercial surrogacy is considered as a form of human organ trafficking.[8] Altruistic surrogacy is permitted[9] only in two cases: (1) when the intended mother can contribute an egg, however, she herself cannot carry a gestation to term or has a medical condition that puts her life at risk; or (2) when the intended parents are part of a same-sex marriage. The parties must sign a contract that establishes the child's parentage and the intended parents must warrant they will pay medical and related pregnancy expenses; additionally, they will be the parents listed on the birth certificate.

Those who have no diagnosed reproductive problems can take advantage of ART such as egg freezing and embryo creation. Limited classes of relatives can be a surrogate.[10] Reciprocal in vitro fertilization

5. *E.g.*, *Adoption Act 2009* (Qld) ss 301, 303.

6. *E.g.*, *Human Cloning for Reproduction and Other Prohibited Practices Act 2003* (NSW) ss 1 6; *Human Tissue Act 1983* (NSW) s 32; *Crimes Act 1900* (NSW) s 10C.

7. *Transplantation and Anatomy Act 1979* (Qld) ss 4, 40–42.

8. Constituição Federal [C.F.] [Constitution] art. 199(4).

9. Resolução CFM No. 2.121/2015, Diário Oficial da União [D.O.U.] de 24.9.2015.

10. Resolução CFM No 2.168/2017, Diário Oficial da União [D.O.U.] de 10.11.2017.

(IVF) for lesbian couples is allowed. Women up to 35 and men up to 50 can be donors, although doctors have a discretion for a higher age limit. Reflecting the challenges of older patients becoming pregnant, the number of embryos that may be transferred may be fewer according to the patient's age: up to 35 years, a maximum of two embryos; between 36 and 39 years, up to three embryos; and 40 years or older, a limit of four embryos. Surrogacy for gay couples is allowed. At least one of the intended parents must be a citizen of Brazil.

Canada

Surrogacy is regulated at a national level by the Assisted Human Reproduction Act and Assisted Human Reproduction Regulations, which criminalize payments of fees to gamete or embryo donors or to surrogates, and criminalize the payment of fees to match intended parents with surrogates.

Surrogacy agencies in Canada operate on the basis that they cannot charge a fee to match.

The recognition of parentage, however, is determined province by province. A parentage order is made post-birth. The process can take between two business days and several weeks, depending on the province. Four provinces, British Columbia, Ontario, Manitoba, and Québec, have an auto-recognition process so that the intended parents, provided that the relevant statutory criteria are met, are automatically recognized as the parents upon the birth.[11]

If you have foreign intended parents having children born in those provinces, the practice I usually take out of caution is to have an order made. Usually this is without difficulty, although on a number of occasions I have had to explain, for the benefits of a Canadian judge, why an order needs to be made when the statute mandates auto-recognition in any event. The reality is that orders on their face can be seen by officialdom of the home country as setting out who is a parent, without having to explain the nuances, the hills and dales, of the ART law of that particular province. As seen in Chapter 3, there may be benefits in having an order (as opposed to the statutory process) for some intended parents from Europe.

The differences between provinces is best illustrated in a Canadian case, *Re Family Law Act*,[12] in which a gay couple living in Québec had

11. For example, in British Columbia, the Family Law Act, S.B.C. 2011, c 25, s 29.

12. [2016] B.C.S.C. 22.

a child born through surrogacy in British Columbia. They could have availed themselves of the auto-recognition process in British Columbia, but had "*obtained a legal opinion from a Quebec lawyer advising that it is necessary to obtain a British Columbia court order to have their parentage of [the child] recognized in Quebec, where they reside.*"[13] They then sought a declaration from the court in British Columbia that they were the parents.

The court then made the order.

Québec

The law of Québec now recognizes surrogacy agreements, with the passage of Bill 12, 2023. Surrogacy is available to singles or couples, irrespective of sexuality.[14] If the child is born to a woman who is domiciled outside Québec, the Minister of Health and Social Services may intervene on the application for birth registration in Québec.[15] For filiation to be recognized for a child born outside Québec:

> [A]n application for recognition of a filiation established outside Québec must be filed together with the child's foreign act of birth or the decision establishing the filiation and the foreign legislation. It must also, if applicable, be accompanied by the certificate of compliance for the project issued by the Minister of Health and Social Services. An application to claim status must also be attached, if applicable.[16]

Ethiopia

The woman who gives birth is the mother, under the Family Code.[17] The father is her husband. Surrogacy is not criminalized in Ethiopia, although some women have been surrogates for foreign intended parents. There

---

13. *Id.* at 9.

14. An Act to Reform Family Law with Regard to Filiation and to Protect Children Born as a Result of Sexual Assault and the Victims of That Assault as Well as the Rights of Surrogates and of Children Born of a Surrogacy Project, R.S.Q., c 13, s 431.0.1.

15. *Id.* s 431.0.2

16. Civil Code of Québec, S.Q. 1991, s 541.27. *See also* s 541.26.

17. Tegen Mamaru Wondie, *Legal Protection against Surrogacy's Threat to Reproductive Human Rights of Women in Ethiopia*, 6 INT'L J. ACAD. MULTIDISCIPLINARY RSCH. 60 (2022), http://ijeais.org/wp-content/uploads/2022/3/abs/IJAMR220309.html.

does not appear an obvious way to recognize the intended parents as the parents.

Nevertheless, it is claimed that "surrogacy is a legal and regulated practice in Ethiopia."[18]

It would be expected that the only method of parental recognition therefore would be by adoption. To add to confusion, while the Ethiopian Embassy to the United States sets out criteria for adoption by surrogacy,[19] the Family Code was amended in 2018 to ban all intercountry adoptions.[20]

Germany

Parentage is determined under federal law.

Only the woman who bears the child can be regarded as the legal mother.[21] If she is married, her husband is the father. If the surrogate is unmarried, then with the surrogate's consent the genetic father can acknowledge paternity, and be recognized as the father.[22] Therefore, German citizens undertaking surrogacy overseas always seek a single surrogate. Surrogacy is illegal in Germany.[23] It is a criminal offense to perform IVF on a surrogate.[24] Surrogacy agreements in Germany are void as they are in breach of the Embryo Protection Act and therefore contrary to public policy.[25]

The differences about how someone becomes a parent through surrogacy under foreign law are illustrated by two decisions in Germany. In one, where the parents were the parents by operation of law of a child born in Ukraine, the surrogate was recognized as the mother. In the other,

18. Med Fertility Centre, *Do You Know What the Surrogacy Cost in Ethiopia Will Be in 2023?*, MEDIUM (July 18, 2023), https://medium.com/@medfertilityoffical/do-you-know-what-the-surrogacy-cost-in-ethiopia-will-be-in-2023-7cd3891a9244.

19. *Adopting an Ethiopian Child*, EMBASSY ETH., https://ethiopianembassy.org/adoption-an-ethiopian-child/ (last visited Mar. 26, 2024).

20. *Ethiopia: Federal Family Code Amended, Ending Intercountry Adoption*, LIB. CONG. (Mar. 26, 2018), https://www.loc.gov/item/global-legal-monitor/2018-03-26/ethiopia-federal-family-code-amended-ending-intercountry-adoption/.

21. Bürgerliches Gesetzbuch [BGB] [Civil Code], §1591.

22. Staatsangehörigkeitsgesetz [StAG] [Nationality Act], July 22, 1913, § 3, para. 1, no. 1, § 4, para. 1.

23. Adoptionsvermittlungsgesetz [*AdVermiG*] [Adoption Placement Act] §§ 13b, 13c, 14.

24. *Gesetz zum Schutz von Embryonen* or *Embryonenschutzgesetz* [*ESchG*] [Embryo Protection Act] § 1, para. 1, no. 7.

25. Bürgerliches Gesetzbuch [BGB] [Civil Code], §§ 134, 138; Oberlandesgericht Hamm [OLG] [Higher Regional Court Hamm] Dec. 2, 1985, Docket No. 11 W 18/85, 39 Neue Juristische Wochenschrift [NJW] 781,783 (1986).

where the parents were declared to be the parents by a foreign court, they were recognized by the German court.

The Federal Court of Justice determined[26] in 2019 that a surrogate to a child born in Ukraine to a German heterosexual married couple was the mother for the purposes of German law—because only the woman who bears the child is the mother under German law. The child had been conceived from an embryo from the intended parents' gametes. The intended father was held to be a parent under German law.

In a case that is significant, as to whether the 1993 Hague Intercountry Adoption Convention applies to international surrogacy arrangements, the court held that the child's habitual residence was in Germany. This was because all parties to the surrogacy agreement agreed that the child would go to Germany with the intended parents immediately after the birth and remain there permanently.

Under Ukrainian law, the intended parents are the parents through surrogacy by operation of law. Under the Ukrainian Family Code,[27] if the intended parents are a heterosexual couple, one of whom has a genetic connection with the child, then they become the parents by operation of law on the birth of the child.

By contrast, the same court determined[28] in 2014 that where a foreign court has declared that the intended parents are the parents, and the surrogate had no genetic connection with the child, and there is a genetic connection between the intended parent and the child, then the intended parent is a parent for the purposes of German law, and the surrogate is not.

The intended parents in that case were a German-Swiss gay couple who lived in Berlin. They were registered life partners. There was no violation of public policy, notwithstanding that surrogacy is illegal in Germany. One of the men was the genetic father. The men undertook surrogacy in California with a single surrogate. A California court declared that both the men were the parents. Both were recognized by the Federal Court of Justice as the parents.

---

26. Bundesgerichtsof [BGH] [Federal Court of Justice] Mar. 20, 2019, Docket No. XII ZB 530/17, ECLI:DE:BGH:2019:200319BXIIZB530.17.0.

27. Law No. 2947-II, art. 123.

28. Bundesgerichtsof [BGH] [Federal Court of Justice] Dec. 10, 2014, Docket No. XII ZB 463/13.

India

Surrogacy is regulated federally. Under the Surrogacy (Regulation) Act, 2021, commercial surrogacy is banned.[29] Surrogacy is available to legally married Indian men and women aged 21 and 18 and older, respectively, "of Indian origin," or to single women, provided that it is altruistic surrogacy, not commercial. Pre-approval for the medical necessity must be given by a District Medical Board, as well as a pre-approval order being made by a magistrate. There are other restrictions—for example that traditional surrogacy is not permitted.

Typically, approval will not be given unless the couple are aged 26 to 55 for the husband and 23 to 50 for the wife.

India does not recognize dual citizenship. Indians who migrate overseas and then take up foreign citizenship then disclaim Indian citizenship. They are then recognized as Overseas Citizens of India (OCIs). While they are not citizens, they have benefits that foreigners do not have.

It is unclear if OCIs would be considered "Indian man and woman" and "of Indian origin" for eligibility. However, limited data, as seen in Chapter 3, might indicate that Indian authorities consider that OCIs are eligible to undertake surrogacy in India.

LGBTQIA+ people and single men are excluded from access.

Malaysia

There is no specific law issued by the federation or by the states concerning surrogacy. However, sharia law in Malaysia bans any Muslim from undertaking surrogacy. Some surrogacy occurs in Malaysia, by those who are not Muslim. Kelantan and Terengganu states are stricter in their application of sharia law than other states.[30] There is no basis for the transfer of parentage in Malaysia, so the surrogate will remain on the birth certificate as the mother. There can be difficulty accessing IVF in Malaysian clinics for LGBTQIA+ people or singles, as clinics tend to only provide access to heterosexual couples, although there is no law to that effect.

Mexico

There is no overarching framework of law concerning surrogacy in Mexico. Determination of parentage, and therefore regulation of surrogacy, is a state responsibility, however subject to the constitution. Regulation of

29. The Surrogacy (Regulation) Act, 2021, § 3.

30. *Malaysia*, SMARTRAVELLER.GOV.AU, https://www.smartraveller.gov.au/destinations/asia/malaysia (last updated Dec. 8, 2023).

IVF clinics is exclusively a matter for federal law by virtue of Article 3 of the General Health Law, as to the sanitary control of organs, tissue, and cells. Artificial insemination of a woman without her husband's consent is a federal offense.[31] Children have a right to know their affiliation and origin as far as possible and provided that this is consistent with their best interests.[32] The law recognizes their right to preserve their identity, including as to family relationships, and the right to live as a family.[33]

Querétaro, Coahuila, and San Luis Potosí[34] explicitly do not recognize surrogacy contracts. Tabasco has permitted surrogacy since 1997. Traditional surrogacy is permissible in Tabasco.[35] In 2016 the state banned surrogacy to foreigners, and restricted surrogacy to a contracting mother and father, thereby seemingly excluding singles and LGBTQIA+ intended parents.

However, this restriction was removed by the Supreme Court in 2021,[36] which ruled that the restriction was a breach of human rights, and that foreigners had the same right to protection as Mexican citizens.

Sinaloa also regulated surrogacy, but also included restrictions that surrogacy is only available to married, heterosexual Mexican couples.

In 2017 the Supreme Court recognized family life of same-sex couples. Same-sex marriage has been legalized across Mexico by the end of 2022.

In 2018 the Supreme Court held[37] that a gay couple in Yucatán were the parents of a child born through surrogacy based on their intention, the consent of the surrogate set out in the surrogacy agreement, and the rights of the child. It held that the right to procreation was recognized through access to ART to same-sex married couples. The concept of family is not identified or limited to a single type of family, but in the context of a democratic state of law in which respect for plurality is part of its essence, it must be understood that the constitutional norm is referring

31. Ley General de los Derechos de Niñas, Niños y Adolescentes [LGDNNA] art. 466, Diario Oficial de la Federación [DOF] 4-12-2014 [General Law on the Rights of Children and Adolescents].

32. *Id.* art. 19.

33. *Id.* art. 22.

34. Código de Familia, art. 243.

35. Código Civil Tabasco, art. 380.

36. Suprema Corte de Justicia de la Nación [SCJN], 129/2019 (decided June 8, 2021). For a summary, see Press Release, Supreme Court of Justice of Mexico, SCJN Concludes Analysis of an Amparo Filed by a Legal Entity against Various Provisions of the Civil Code of Tabasco on Assisted Gestation and Surrogacy (June 8, 2021), https://www.internet2.scjn.gob.mx/red2/comunicados/noticia.asp?id=6468.

37. Suprema Corte de Justicia de la Nación [SCJN], 553/2018.

to the family as a social reality; therefore, it protects all its forms and manifestations as an existing reality. The right to decide freely about the number and spacing of their children includes the right of all people to organize, in accordance with the law, their life according to their own options and convictions.

Like most Mexican states, Yucatán had no regulation of children born through ART, nor regulating surrogacy, and no specific parentage laws concerning ART or surrogacy.

The most popular surrogacy locations are Mexico City and the states of Jalisco and Quintana Roo (Cancún).

In practice, surrogacy in Mexico is complicated. Pre-birth orders are made in both Jalisco and Mexico City, by which both intended parents are recognized as the parents, and the surrogate is not. However, some attorneys claim that, despite the 2018 case, that a pre-birth order is not possible, and that the surrogate—as the mother—must be and remain on the birth certificate, and that the other parent on the birth certificate is the genetic father. Other attorneys obtain post-birth orders in Mexico City in favor of the intended parents.

The quality of IVF in Mexico varies greatly. As clients or IVF auditors have reported to me about IVF in other developing countries,[38] using the wrong sperm has occurred in Mexico.[39] I recommend obtaining advice from a reputable Mexican ART attorney as to which clinic to use.

Nepal

Nepal is a federation, but by virtue of a permanent injunction issued by the Supreme Court of Nepal in 2016, followed by legislation, surrogacy is not permissible in Nepal, except for infertile heterosexual, married Nepalese couples, and illegal for single men or women, transgender couples, and foreign nationals.[40]

---

38. India, Thailand, and Cambodia.

39. Client reported.

40. U.S. Embassy Kathmandu, *Surrogacy Services Are Banned in Nepal*, U.S. Embassy Nepal (June 4, 2021), https://np.usembassy.gov/surrogacy-services-are-banned-in-nepal/.

Nigeria

Only Lagos state regulates ART,[41] but it does not regulate surrogacy. The other 35 states and the Federal Capital Territory have not regulated ART. Nigeria is not LGBTQIA+ friendly.

Clients of mine have undertaken surrogacy in Nigeria. Parentage was transferred through a process of adoption. The Nigerian judge insisted that Australian processes for surrogacy by which the surrogate and the intended parents were assessed be followed. A report was prepared by an Australian psychologist, by which a thorough assessment of the parties was undertaken prior to conception.

In 2022, a United States–based Nigerian couple, relatives of a traditional surrogate, accused their Nigerian surrogate of absconding with twin boys. The surrogate claimed that she had been abandoned by the couple while she was pregnant and had been shortchanged by them with expenses. She had had to pay the medical bills for herself and the babies, which then caused her to decide not to relinquish. She claimed that she had acted under duress to be the surrogate. The couple claimed that the surrogate had refused to return to the Dutch embassy for her visa appointment. The case is an example of a lack of laws regulating surrogacy.

Nigeria has alarming maternal mortality rates. Implantation of multiple embryos is also the norm there. See Chapter 19.

Pakistan

The Federal Shariat Court in 2015 ruled[42] that surrogacy was illegal under sharia law. ART between husbands and wives, not involving donor gametes or surrogacy, was lawful.

A male doctor, who had a wife from Pakistan, who lived in the United States, said that he had advertised for a surrogate in Pakistan. He said that he then paid her a fee. They went through a ceremony of marriage. She was a traditional surrogate. They undertook IVF.

The doctor said that he and the surrogate had an oral agreement. A girl was born. The surrogate refused to relinquish the girl. The doctor sued to enforce the agreement.

---

41. Oolasunkanmi, *Lagos Restates Commitment to Improving Assisted Reproductive Technology Practice*, Lagos State Gov't (Nov. 18, 2019), https://lagosstate.gov.ng/lagos-restates-commitment-to-improving-assisted-reproductive-technology-practice/.

42. Siddiqi v. Naheed, (2017) Sh. Petition No. 2/1 of 2015.

The "surrogate" claimed that the whole story of surrogacy was false, that she was married to him. The girl was born out of wedlock, and he is required to pay for the upkeep of the child.

The court did not determine which version was true.

The Chief Justice stated:

> The above stated situation has created serious problems for the poor developing countries. In most of the developed countries surrogacy is either not permitted or illegal or extremely expensive. As a result most of the developed countries have turned towards the poor undeveloped countries for arranging surrogate mothers.
>
> All the underdeveloped countries, where poverty is order of the day, are on high risk of becoming markets for surrogacy.[43]

Further:

> This exploitation becomes worst when it is seen that people in the developed countries come to third world countries like India, Pakistan and Thailand where the rates are cheap, no medical protection is provided and other related facilities are also not available. If this process is allowed, it would be a new exploitation of the poor third world countries by the developed European as well as American countries.[44]

The Chief Justice recommended changes to the law, including making egg and sperm banks illegal, and for doctors who engage in surrogacy to lose their license.

Russian Federation

The Russian Family Code specifically recognizes surrogacy by heterosexual married couples.[45] Despite that stated restriction, single intended parents and male couples have undertaken surrogacy in Russia. The Russian Family Code applies across the country. In December 2022 laws were enacted to ban international intended parents undertaking surrogacy in Russia. The changes restrict surrogacy to heterosexual married couples, where one of them is a Russian citizen, or single Russian

43. *Id.* at 14.
44. *Id.* at 19.
45. Semeĭnyĭ Kodeks Rossiĭskoĭ Federatsii [SK RF] [Family Code] art. 51.4.

women.[46] Russia allows dual citizenship for citizens of Turkmenistan and Tajikistan only.[47]

South Africa

Surrogacy in South Africa is governed by the Children's Act, which is a federal act. Surrogacy is limited to at least one of the intended parents being domiciled in South Africa. Surrogacy must be altruistic and not commercial. Surrogacy is available irrespective of sexuality or gender to singles or couples. There must be a genetic link by at least one of the intended parents with the child. Parental recognition occurs by a preconception court order.

Gamete donation is anonymous, but in practice donors acknowledge that they consent to the child being able to find out their details after the child turns 18, if needed. The South African Law Reform Commission has proposed laws to that effect.

In the past, Caucasian South African egg donors have supplied their eggs by traveling to the United States, India, Malaysia, and Australia. In 2016, the medical director of one IVF clinic in South Africa told me that the clinic was seeing three to five Australian heterosexual couples needing an egg donor per business day.

The United Arab Emirates

The United Arab Emirates (UAE) is an elective monarchy governing a federation of seven emirates.

Federal Decree Law No. 17 of 2023 amending the Federal Decree Law No. 7 of 2019 eliminates the ban on surrogacy for heterosexual married Muslim and non-Muslim couples using their own gametes. Gamete donation is prohibited for any ART. That law permits embryo freezing,[48] which previously had been banned. Egg freezing has been allowed since 2021.

The law also grants access to ART to unmarried non-Muslim heterosexual couples.[49] Those couples must provide a declaration specifying which one of them will establish the child's parentage. The declaration

---

46. *Putin Bans Surrogacy for Foreigners*, Moscow Times (Dec. 19, 2022), https://www.themoscowtimes.com/2022/12/19/putin-bans-surrogacy-for-foreigners-a79738.

47. *Citizenship in Russia—Updated Guide for 2024*, LawyersRussia (Jan. 24, 2024), https://www.lawyersrussia.com/citizenship-in-russia.

48. Federal Decree Law No. 17 of 2023, art. 10.

49. *Id.* art. 8.

requires approval by the relevant authority in the spouse's country of nationality and the child's anticipated citizenship.

The requirements for the surrogacy arrangement are:

- The surrogate must be aged between 25 and 35, and be either a UAE citizen or resident.
- The arrangement must be made through a licensed IVF clinic.
- The surrogate must be medically and psychologically fit to carry a child.
- The surrogate must not have a criminal record.
- Regulatory consent is required to proceed.

The law grants each emirate the authority to regulate medically assisted reproduction through local legislation.[50] Where those laws do not have specific provisions, the regulations in Federal Decree Law No. 7 of 2019 apply.

Posthumous use is not permitted.

Homosexual acts are criminalized.

In 2019, the Personal Status Court ruled in an unusual case.

A 37-year-old Indian woman, who had been married to an Indian man, 38, for 15 years, could not have a child. In 2016, the woman discovered that her husband had not only used a surrogate in India but also registered the infant in her name without her knowledge or consent, following which the wife asked for divorce.

Her lawyer told the court that in return for granting her divorce and alimony, the husband forced the wife to sign a document approving the surrogacy procedure.

The woman filed for divorce in India but it was declined. A girl was born in March 2016.

The woman said in case documents, "*I didn't know that he had registered the child under my name in the birth certificate. He used the womb of another woman and the egg of another woman without my permission for fertilisation. I was forced to sign the agreement to get my divorce and alimony.*"

The wife's lawyer submitted, "*Although the Indian law can be applied in several cases in the UAE, it cannot in this specific case because surrogacy is against the laws and public morals of the country (UAE) where the case is being heard.*"

50. *Id.* art. 2.

Dubai's Personal Status Court ordered that the child be referred for a DNA test, but the husband failed to follow the order after which the court ruled in favor of the wife.

The wife's lawyer said, "*As per the court's judgement surrogacy was ruled forbidden according to UAE's Islamic principles which are part of the country's laws and public morals.*"[51]

Intended parents have successfully brought children born through surrogacy abroad to live in the UAE, either while the parents were resident there, or upon their parents migrating to the UAE.

The United States

The United States is a wonderful example of the complexity of a federal system. For example, an order in California concerning the birth of a child through surrogacy may be recognized in another state or it may not be. Each state has different rules.

By way of example, Oregon is a pre-birth state, arising from court decisions. Nevertheless, in one case that I had in Oregon, the court made a pre-birth order and also made an adoption order whereby the intended parents adopted the child who was already theirs. The reasoning by the court was simple—the pre-birth order was not recognized in Texas. As a work-around, the court came up with the solution of the adoption order to fix that problem—so that the child's parentage was clear.

Venezuela

While Venezuela is defined as a federation, in reality, it is a unitary State. Judges in Venezuela carry out a balancing act of conflicting law, leaving it uncertain whether parentage will be recognized. The surrogate, being the birth mother, is recognized as the mother. However, the constitution recognizes the fundamental right to know one's biological or genetic origins. Decision No. 1456 of the Supreme Tribunal of Justice mentions the concept of procreative will.

Example of the Issue

I have lost count of the number of times where American lawyers have told me that they have had a client from, say, Melbourne, and clearly the laws that apply in Melbourne apply to this couple (who come from Sydney).

---

51. Ali Al Shouk, *Indian Woman in Dubai Divorces Husband Over Surrogate Child*, Gulf News (Nov. 19, 2019), https://gulfnews.com/uae/indian-woman-in-dubai-divorces-husband-over-surrogate-child-1.67931148.

Sadly, Australian law when it comes to surrogacy is remarkably complex.

A couple who live in Melbourne, which is the capital of the Australian state of Victoria, and presumably are not domiciled in New South Wales, have only one potential criminal issue concerning undertaking surrogacy overseas. If they engage in adoption overseas, they have to be careful not to pay a fee to the birth parent because otherwise they may commit a criminal offense in Victoria. However, they won't commit any criminal offense concerning eggs, sperm, or embryo donation overseas.

Victorian criminal law, with rare exceptions, such as adoption, does not extend beyond the borders of Victoria. Similarly, no matter how much they may pay the surrogate, intended parents do not commit a criminal offense in Victoria by doing so overseas. Victoria makes it an offense to pay anything other than prescribed expenses for a surrogate mother (and these prescribed expenses are rather narrowly defined—but in any case, do not include a fee)—but the Victorian law again only applies in Victoria and does not apply overseas.

A couple living in Sydney, the capital of New South Wales, are not so lucky. Not only is there an adoption offense applicable in New South Wales as applying overseas, but there are several other offenses that apply:

1. If they enter into a commercial (as defined in New South Wales) egg, sperm, or embryo donor agreement, they could be committing an offense punishable by up to 15 years' imprisonment—based on long-arm laws.
2. If they enter into a commercial (as defined in New South Wales) egg, sperm, or embryo donor agreement, or commercial agreement for human milk, they could be committing an offense in New South Wales punishable by up to six months' imprisonment—which applies by virtue of long-arm laws.
3. If they enter into or offer to enter into a commercial surrogacy arrangement (as defined under New South Wales law) they could be committing an offense punishable by a fine of up to A$110,000 or two years' imprisonment or both. The offense is committed by anyone who is ordinarily resident (a question of fact) in New South Wales or anyone who is domiciled in New South Wales.

The most absurd example of this difference in laws concerns the twin cities of Albury/Wodonga. Albury is on the north bank of the Murray River. It is in southern New South Wales. Directly opposite Albury is

Wodonga, which is on the south bank of the Murray River. Wodonga is in northern Victoria. A couple living in Albury will be subject to these extraterritorial or long-arm laws concerning surrogacy. A couple living in Wodonga (with the exception of the adoption law) won't.

The distance between the two towns is four miles.

At the other end of New South Wales, the northern border of the state abuts the southern border of Queensland. Part of the border is in the middle of Griffith Street. Griffith Street on its northern side is in Coolangatta, Queensland. On its southern side, Griffith Street is in Tweed Heads, New South Wales. Those who live on the northern side and pay for the supply of human milk in their surrogacy journey are unlikely to be committing any offense. Those on the southern side may well do so.

A Simple Explanation of Domicile

"Domicile" is of Latin origin to do with home—as is "domestic." In broad terms, it is the jurisdiction that is the permanent home of a person. Under the common law, there are two types of domicile—domicile of origin and domicile of choice. If they are different, then the latter prevails. Not everyone has a domicile of choice, but everyone will have a domicile of origin. An example is a man who is single, and not keen to pay income tax. He chooses to move from country to country, not staying in any country for more than three months. While he has no domicile of choice, he has a domicile of origin.[52]

The classic definition of "domicile" is from the House of Lords in *Udny v. Udny* (1869):

> Time is always a material element in questions of domicile, and, if there is nothing to counteract its effect, it may be conclusive upon the subject. But in a competition between a domicile of origin and an alleged subsequently acquired domicile, there may be circumstances to shew, that however long a residence may have continued, no intention of acquiring a domicile may have existed at any one moment during the whole of the continuance of such residence. The question in such a case is not, whether there is evidence of an intention to retain a domicile of origin, but whether it is proved, that there was an intention to acquire another domicile. As already shewn, the domicile of origin remains till a new one is acquired animo et facto. Therefore a wish or desire expressed

52. This is not an absurd example. I had a client like this once.

> from time to time to return to the place of the first domicile, or any looking to it as the ultimate home, although wholly insufficient for the retention of the domicile, may yet amount to material evidence to rebut the presumption to acquire a new domicile arising from length of residence elsewhere.[53]

When considering domicile, be aware that statute may have changed the common-law definition.

Take Away

1. As seen elsewhere in this book—don't assume you know the law and practice overseas.
2. Do not assume that the law is the same throughout every country.
3. Your perception of the law based on past experience may simply be wrong because your clients have come from a different part of that country.
4. Do not put your clients unnecessarily at risk of committing criminal offenses or in some way prejudice them in being able to return home with their babies.
5. Where possible, consult with a local lawyer so that you can give the right advice.

53. [1869] 2 Paterson 1677, 1685 (per Lord Chelmsford).

Chapter 11

Insurance for International Parent Journeys

"As an athlete, I understood the value of my health insurance. I knew that in my profession, injuries were common and could happen at any time."

Magic Johnson

Putting Insurance into Perspective

It is recommended that intended parents ensure that they have all types of insurances that are available to assist them in the process.

Insurance at its heart is a useless product—until the day that it is needed. The person whose house was flooded, for example, will feel a little more at ease knowing that flood insurance will make good much of their loss.

Many intended parents worry about the legal process on their international surrogacy journey. And so they should. As seen in other chapters of this book, the legal process can at times be extraordinarily complex, difficult to navigate, and contradictory.

While that legal process always appropriately must be a worry, to my mind, for those who travel to the United States for surrogacy there are at least two bigger worries:

1. **The exchange rate**. There is nothing quite like seeing that your budget for the journey has increased by a third due to nothing that you have done other than to be present when the exchange rate has dropped. Intended parents always have to plan for exchange rate variations with international journeys. Trying to hedge is always helpful. I certainly don't profess to provide financial advice, as I have neither the expertise nor the authorization, but I do suggest that intended parents obtain advice from experts. All

intended parents undertaking international assisted reproductive technology (ART) should be aware of exchange rate risks.

2. **Insurance costs**. If healthcare costs are not properly covered, and something goes wrong, the costs can be ruinous.

Beware of the Drop!

"*How could the cost of your U.S. surrogacy journey be so high?*" I asked. The couple had not finished their surrogacy journey. Instead, they were halfway through, and had already spent as much as others had done through completion.

> Well, we signed with the surrogacy agency when the exchange rate was $0.81, but when it came time to pay, the exchange rate was $0.60.

I immediately understood. Thanks to exchange rate fluctuations, the cost of their surrogacy journey had increased by a quarter. They had not budgeted for the increase. Luckily, the intended parents had the funds to pay the difference. Some don't.

The Premature Twins

A couple had twins born very early in Texas. The children needed a very long time in hospital before they could be released and then they were medevaced across the United States. The couple had adequate insurance. The cost to the insurance company was estimated to be in the order of $5 million. Imagine having to pay for that without having insurance.

A feature in recent years with U.S. surrogacy journeys has been that far fewer twin pregnancies are occurring. Instead, when intended parents are seeking to have two children at once, they are much more inclined to have a parallel journey—two surrogates at about the same time bearing a child for them.

Parallel journeys bring their own complexity—openness and honesty with both surrogates about the other journey. The belief by intended parents that there will be two children born at the same time inevitably is challenged by the reality that the two pregnancies start at the same time, or finish at the same time. That risk is reduced if the obstetrician decides to induce the births—whether or not it is in the surrogate's interest.

An example of a parallel journey is that of the Dudleys, aka the Dennises.

The Dudleys, aka the Dennises

A feature of most family law cases in Australia is the use of pseudonyms to protect the privacy of those involved.

In one case the same intended parents, husband and wife, were identified as the Dudleys,[1] and in the other as the Dennises.[2]

After ten years of infertility, the couple underwent surrogacy in Thailand, at the beginning of the great boom for surrogacy there, before the boom ended with law changes in 2014. See Chapter 3.

The plan was to have two children, via parallel surrogacy journeys. Two embryos, composed of the husband's sperm and eggs from a donor, were created. One each was implanted in each surrogate.

A Thai doctor induced both women to give birth on the same day. Three children were born, as one of the embryos had split.

One Australian judge recognized the husband as the father of one of the children. The other judge found that he was not the parent of the other two children.

That judge in turn referred them for prosecution, one of two couples[3] he referred on the same day. Both couples had the misfortune to have come from Queensland, the first place in the world to criminalize its residents for engaging in commercial surrogacy overseas. See Chapter 4. Neither couple was prosecuted.

Insurance for International Intended Parents for United States Journeys

Intended parents coming to the United States will likely obtain many forms of insurance:

- That of protection of the egg donor
- Health insurance for the egg donor and surrogate
- Life and accident insurance for the surrogate
- Newborn insurance

Insurance may vary greatly. Affordable Care Act insurance may be available for the surrogate, or it may not. Insurance rates may vary, state by state, or even county by county, as they do in California. There is often an assumption of international intended parents that there is universal

1. *Dudley & Chedi* [2011] FamCA 502.
2. *Dennis & Pradchaphet* [2011] FamCA 123.
3. The other was *Findlay & Punyawong* [2011] FamCA 503.

healthcare in the United States as there is at home (which there isn't), and that the cost of that insurance across the United States will be the same. The United States is one market after all, right? It's not.

For example, if the surrogate is in Hawaii, the surrogate will almost certainly have Hawaii Medical Service Association insurance, the dominant insurer in that state.

While the surrogate may have health insurance, the terms of it may not cover surrogacy.

While not insurance, some hospital chains are insistent that a proportion of the surrogate's earnings be the subject of a lien. The hospital wants to make sure it is paid!

As an outsider reading retainer agreements, I have been struck by one clause commonly seen in retainer agreements for:

- Egg donor agencies
- Surrogacy agencies
- In vitro fertilization (IVF) clinics
- U.S. attorneys

And the clause? A disclaimer of all-care, no-responsibility for whether the insurance is the right insurance. There is no guarantee that the insurer will pay out. No one wants to be liable if the insurance is required and is not paid out.

To minimize risks, in addition to the agency or lawyer who is giving them advice on their journey (including assistance as to which insurance policy to obtain), intended parents should always obtain a second opinion, such as from an experienced insurance broker in this field. The broker is not a lawyer, but will have a sense of what insurance is available, including its costs and limitations. Armed with that information, the intended parents can then make an informed choice.

Oh, Canada!

While Canada has a universal healthcare scheme, intended parents need to have newborn insurance. When the surrogate gives birth, she does so as a Canadian citizen and resident. In other words, birthing costs are met by the Canadian taxpayer.

However, if the child has medical needs, and the child is to live overseas, the cost of the child's care will not be met by the Canadian taxpayer. While the child, by birth, is a Canadian citizen, because the child will be residing overseas, universal healthcare costs are not available.

Intended parents need to ensure they have newborn health insurance for the child. There is a waiting period for that insurance, which in the past has been up to 12 months. There have been media reports of intended parents who did not have that insurance, and then found themselves liable for bills up to C$250,000.

And Elsewhere?

For those who undertake surrogacy internationally, they may find there is no available insurance. Where possible, they should talk to the local surrogacy agency and to their local lawyer to see what insurance, if any, is available, what it costs, and what it covers.

Take Away

1. Insurance for intended parents coming to the United States is remarkably complex.
2. Intended parents should always obtain a second opinion, just in case.
3. Newborn insurance is needed in Canada.
4. Insurance elsewhere may be touch and go, and may not exist.

Chapter 12

Who Is a Parent?

"Parent" is a legal construct. With heterosexual couples, it seems pretty clear and is consistent with the way the Western world has seen parentage since the sixth century. The underlining thinking about who is a parent in the Western world was set out by the Emperor Justinian: the mother is always certain[1]—because she is the one who gave birth. The search from that time onward has always been about who is the father.

The great difficulty of course in more recent years with the rise of in vitro fertilization (IVF) and egg and sperm donation is that life has become more complicated. IVF and surrogacy mean that someone potentially other than the woman who gave birth is the mother, and that the woman who gave birth therefore is not the mother. Thus, there are confusing elements about who is a parent.

Before the rise of IVF was the rise of sperm donation, commencing in the 19th century. It was generally seen that the husband of a woman who gave birth was the parent, even though he was not the genetic parent. However, the rules about this are not consistent.

A woman who gave birth who was single was generally seen as the mother, consistent with the maxim, but then an issue arose as to whether the man was a parent or merely a sperm donor.

Much of the time, this has been tackled by statute law which has provided that in some circumstances the man is or is not a parent.

If the woman had a female partner, then matters became more complicated. Was the partner a parent? Statute law in many places has provided that she is. However, recognition of that relationship of parent and child is not assured. In many places the partner is not recognized as a parent, due to underlying homophobia. Many women in this circumstance, although recognized at home as a parent, are recognized abroad as a parent. If the couple are to move abroad or to travel, she is not seen to be a parent under the law.

1. Or in the Latin maxim, "mater semper certa est."

Care must be taken for women in this circumstance to ensure that their rights—and the rights of the child—are protected. Sometimes there is simply no protection available under the law in the other place.

Sometimes, if there is a second-parent adoption or stepparent adoption somewhere—either in the first jurisdiction or even in another jurisdiction, then that relationship of parent and child with the partner is recognized. Sometimes it is not.

A feature of the law, as always, is the old phrase "the devil is in the details." It is important to be across the details.

An example of an approach that can be taken before there was statute law reform, is that from Australia.[2] A lesbian couple had children. One of the women underwent IVF (which necessarily involved the consent of her partner) and gave birth to two children.

The relationship was an abusive one. Subsequently, the women split up and underwent a financial settlement. During the course of the breakup, the non-birth mother in effect thumbed her nose at the birth mother, saying that she was not responsible for the children, much like the character of Nelson Muntz from the television show "The Simpsons," "*ha ha!*" She wasn't covered by child support legislation and therefore said that she had no financial liability for the children.

The court found that the couple intended to have the children together and, therefore, the non-birth mother was liable in equitable estoppel as to the costs of raising the children. Damages were awarded.

Being a parent is essential. Being a non-parent may not affect the daily care of the children, in that the couple wake up every day and care for the children, feed them, change them, bathe them, and so on—but if a person is not recognized at law as a parent, then aside from the potential deep psychological impact that has on them and on the child, the other impact it can have is a substantial legal impact.

A person wishing to be seen as a parent may be concerned about the impact that nonrecognition might have in areas such as:

1. Medical treatment for the child
2. Registering with any health insurance fund or State health insurance scheme
3. Applications for things such as passports or schools that require a birth certificate specifying the child's parents
4. Rights for a child arising upon the death of a parent, including rights to an intestacy and retirement benefits

2. *W v G* [1996] NSWSC 43.

5. The ability of a child to be referred to as a child in a will
6. Complications in relation to recognition as to entitlements and liabilities for child support or child maintenance, and recognition of a child's rights to entitlements on injury or death of a parent in schemes of workers' compensation
7. Recognition if the child is abducted under international conventions such as the 1980 Hague Child Abduction Convention or the 1996 Hague Child Protection Convention[3]

John and Jim

John and Jim were international intended parents who underwent surrogacy in California. A pre-birth order was made recognizing them as the parents. The birth certificate from California said that they were the parents. After the child was taken home, the nongenetic father, Jim, was not recognized as a parent. The reason he was not recognized was because he was not the genetic father. The country in which they lived was a country that was a signatory to the 1980 Hague Convention.

An argument ensued between John and Jim. John was a dual passport holder. He took the child, without notice, back to his home country to live. There was no question on the face of his actions that it was an abduction that would ordinarily be actionable under the 1980 Hague Child Abduction Convention.

However, Jim was not recognized as a parent where they lived under the 1980 Child Abduction Convention. Therefore, John's actions in unilaterally taking the child overseas permanently were not under the convention. This is because Jim had no rights of custody under the 1980 Hague Convention, and it was not a child abduction as defined under that convention. Instead, Jim had no choice but to litigate based on best interests in John's home jurisdiction, without having a presumption of the return of the child as dictated by the 1980 Hague Convention.

Just because law in the United States, such as California, identifies that someone is a parent by virtue of intention does not mean that someone internationally is identified as a parent by virtue of intention.

As seen in several European cases in Chapter 2, intention does not necessarily mean that someone is a parent. Often genetics is considered the critical means by which someone is identified as a parent.

3. I am grateful to Judge Watts in *Dudley & Chedi* [2011] FamCA 502 for most of this list.

In a country such as the United States, a birth certificate is considered as evidence of parentage, but not proof of parentage.

In a country such as China, however, the birth certificate is *proof* that someone is a parent.

Therefore, one should take extreme care if a child is born through surrogacy in the United States, for example with a gay couple who reside in China. The immediate inclination is that both men would be recognized on the birth certificate. Given ingrained homophobia in China, to take that approach may prejudice the parentage, and deprive the child of the right of having Chinese citizenship and therefore being able to live in China. It is a common practice, where available in the U.S. jurisdiction, that several birth certificates are issued, one of which only identifies one of the men as a parent. It may be that the surrogate is also identified as a parent. This is because of the firm view that the woman who gave birth is identified as the mother and should be shown as the mother. It is not uncommon in that circumstance for there to be a legal fiction that is, in essence, that the intended father and the surrogate were in some kind of relationship that then resulted in the birth of the child. To disclose that the intended father was gay may result in prejudice to him, his partner, and the child.

Taking that approach means that the child may be able to live in China but may inevitably prejudice the recognition of the other parent who was on the face of it a non-person concerning the child. Reality of course is otherwise.

Children born in China via surrogacy and going to live overseas can be the subject of great grief. Because of the view in China that the birth certificate is sacrosanct as to who is a parent, there is no flexibility as to looking behind the birth certificate. It is an offense in China for doctors to undertake surrogacy, but it is not an offense for intended parents to engage in surrogacy. As a result, intended parents engage in surrogacy in China, organized by some doctors, but the identity of the surrogate is kept hush-hush from the intended parents. They are none the wiser as to the identity of the surrogate.

Because the parents do not know the identity of the surrogate, and some countries insist on establishing the identity of the surrogate so as to establish the identity of the child—consistent with Article 8 of the United Nations Convention on the Rights of the Child, the child has a right to an identity—then those applications for citizenship can be prejudiced because the surrogate is never able to be identified. Therefore, the identity of the child is never able to be finally determined. I have seen cases where children have remained in China, effectively stateless, for five years with their overseas citizenship not determined.

The Different Ways of Becoming Parents through Surrogacy

As also seen in Chapter 6, there are different ways to establish parentage:

1. By birth—under the maxim that the birth mother is a parent
2. By court order or common law establishing that the intended parents are the parents, based on statute or procreative intent, for example California and Mexico
3. By a pre-conception order, the effect of which is that upon birth the intended parents are the parents, for example Greece, South Africa, and Israel
4. By operation of law, such as in Georgia, Ukraine, Kazakhstan, Buenos Aires, or for lesbian couples, such as in the United Kingdom who have conceived via assisted reproductive technology (ART) to which they consented
5. By contract, such as in Iran
6. By contract/self-declaration, as in Sri Lanka
7. By transfer of parentage, such as the United Kingdom and Australia
8. By adoption, such as in New Zealand

While it was once thought that the genetic father of a child conceived through sexual intercourse was automatically the father—and he may be deemed the father in many places—more recent case law from Canada and South Africa, for example, has made intent an element even in these cases.

Depending on local law, intent or genetics may be determinative of who is a parent. They may also be irrelevant. Quite simply, there is a myriad of approaches. Extreme care should be taken with any international ART journey so that there is clear identification at the commencement of the journey about who will be a parent at the end.

Take Away

1. At the beginning of the journey, identify how or if parentage is to be established.
2. Always liaise with your opposite number.

Chapter 13

Interplay of Adoption and Surrogacy

Not all the world recognizes adoption, let alone has any laws concerning surrogacy. Nevertheless, in some places, adoption is the form of becoming a parent. Despite their different characteristics, there can be a clear overlap between adoption and surrogacy. Sometimes, this has resulted in the conflation of surrogacy and adoption.

International Architecture

As I have said elsewhere in this book, there is no international architecture that directly relates to surrogacy. The Hague Conference on Private International Law (HCCH) has worked on a project concerning a possible convention regarding international surrogacy arrangements and private international law concerning parentage since 2011. However, there is yet no convention or protocol concerning that. There is no United Nations convention concerning surrogacy.

There are local conventions such as the American Convention on Human Rights and the European Convention on Human Rights that impact on surrogacy journeys, which I have discussed in Chapters 1 and 2. Although there is no international convention concerning surrogacy, there is one concerning adoption: the 1993 Hague Intercountry Adoption Convention.

1993 Hague Intercountry Adoption Convention

This convention recognizes adoptions that have occurred in a signatory country A, typically for a child who is habitually resident in that country, by an intended parent or intended parents in signatory country B—where they are habitually resident in that second country.

Adoption as the Method of Establishing Parentage

Adoption is the method of recognition of surrogacy in some U.S. jurisdictions, for example sometimes in Tennessee, Florida (including where there is no genetic link), and second parent adoptions in Hawaii, Iowa, and Minnesota.

The evident question to be asked is if the method of establishing parentage through surrogacy is by adoption, and international adoptions are covered by the 1993 Hague Convention, are those surrogacy parentage matters covered by the 1993 Hague Convention, the United States being a convention State?

The answer that has been put to me by former American Bar Association Family Law Section Artificial Reproductive Technologies (ART) Committee Chair Steve Snyder from Minnesota is that the approach taken by the U.S. State Department is not to include the second parent adoption or adoptions through surrogacy under that convention. Therefore, an adoption compliance certificate, which is required for compliance with that convention, will never issue.

If the expectation of the foreign jurisdiction is that given there was an adoption of some kind then there needs to be compliance with the convention, then this poses a difficulty for the intended parents on their journey home.

Adoption currently is the form of regulation of surrogacy in New Zealand. I say currently, because as of April 2024, there have been reports by the Law Commission of New Zealand suggesting that this model be done away with and that there be auto-recognition of intended parents in noncontentious surrogacy cases and, where needed, judicial orders recognizing the intended parents as parents.[1]

A New Zealand case from 2003[2] demonstrates both the limitations of application of the 1993 convention and making surrogacy illegal. That case, discussed in Chapter 1, shows that the habitual residence of a child born through surrogacy is that of the intended parents.

Because adoption is the method of establishment of parentage in New Zealand, then the adoption process involving pre-approval assessments by State officials needs to occur before the surrogacy journey can properly get underway. This also applied to international surrogacy arrangements for New Zealanders. As seen in Chapter 8, some New Zealanders living in Australia who become parents in the United States through

1. New Zealand Law Commission, Issues Paper 47, Review of Surrogacy (2001); New Zealand Law Commission, Report 145, Review of Surrogacy (2022). A private member's bill was introduced in response, Improving Arrangements for Surrogacy Bill 2021. That bill was referred to committee. The subsequent 2023 election resulted in a change of government. The view of the government as to surrogacy reform is unclear.

2. *In re Application by L* [2003] NZFLR 529.

international surrogacy journeys have chosen to bring their child back to Australia as an American citizen, rather than seek adoption approval through the New Zealand courts. The New Zealand process is perceived as being too onerous for those who are citizens, but not living there.

Similarly, in the case of *Baby Sara*,[3] decided by the European Union Court of Justice in 2021, discussed in Chapter 2, the habitual residence of a child born through ART in Spain was that of the lesbian couple.

As recognized by the American Bar Association:

> Surrogacy is a form of procreation through the use of assisted reproduction typically involving "a contract between intended parents and a gestational carrier intended to result in a live birth." The legal position of intended parents creating their own child through a surrogacy arrangement should be viewed as distinct from the legal position of adoptive parents seeking to raise someone else's existing child as their own. . . .
>
> Surrogacy is a medical solution to infertility, whether the infertility is physiological or social (based on relationship status), and is, therefore, a method of reproduction. Adoption is the transfer of legal responsibility over an existing child from one party (or the state) to another.[4]

The intertwining of the two comes about in a number of ways:

- Traditionally, adoption has been much more common than surrogacy—until recently. Recently has seen the decline of adoption, and the rise of surrogacy. The former is attributed to a number of factors, including changes in society (and attitudes) enabling single mothers to continue parenting, payment of social security benefits, the rise of once-poor countries—that has resulted in fewer children being adopted, and those being adopted within that country rather than overseas, and some impact of the 1993 convention.
- Because adoption has been more common, and long-standing, laws have long evolved concerning adoption—but have not evolved to the same extent concerning surrogacy.
- Given the similarities between the two, it has been convenient for legislators and sometimes courts to regulate surrogacy through the prism of adoption.

---

3. Case C-490/20, VMA v. Sofia Municipality, ECLI:EUC:C:2021:296, nn.24, 87 (Apr. 15, 2021).

4. American Bar Association Policy 112B, at 3 (2016). The author was the principal advocate and a co-author of the policy.

- The traditional view is that the mother is always certain, and therefore a move to someone else being a parent results in a transfer of parentage, which traditionally occurred via adoption.
- Therefore, the view has been taken at times that the payment of the surrogate equates to the sale of the child, as is prohibited with adoption. This argument was made by Anna Johnson in *Johnson v. Calvert*,[5] and rejected by the Supreme Court of California (see Chapter 6), but nevertheless this argument continues to be made.
- In female same-sex relationships, often a stepparent or second parent adoption has been used to protect the parentage of the child by recognizing the parentage of both parents, as legislators have at times failed locally, interstate, or internationally to enact laws to recognize both as parents.

As seen in some European cases, such as *K.K. v. Denmark*[6] (see Chapter 2), the prohibition of surrogacy comes from the regulation of adoption—in that case, under the Adoption Act. Surrogacy is conflated with adoption. In the words of the American Bar Association:

> Surrogacy and adoption are different processes and should not be conflated. . . . [S]urrogacy and adoption are separate and distinct ways for people to achieve parenthood. . . . Most, if not all societies permit adoption in some form, while many jurisdictions ban gestational surrogacy in one way or another. Regulating these two processes in similar fashion is inappropriate.[7]

Nevertheless, these separate and distinct ways are often conflated.

An Example of U.S. Surrogacy/Adoption

Recently, clients of mine underwent surrogacy in Iowa. There was no problem for the genetic parent in that he was recognized as the parent. The difficulty for the nongenetic parent came about because in Iowa for the nongenetic parent to be a parent, there is a process of second parent adoption.

This in turn requires the surrogate to consent to the adoption. The immediate reaction to that might be: *big deal*; because that's the way it's done. However, for this couple, to have the nongenetic parent recognized by virtue of a second parent adoption in Iowa spelt trouble at home.

5. 5 Cal. 4th 87 (1993).
6. App. No. 25212/21 (Dec. 6, 2022).
7. American Bar Association Policy 112B, at 3 (2016).

In every Australian jurisdiction, no doubt in much of the Western world, it is an offense to pay a woman for the sale of her child via adoption. Every Australian jurisdiction not only seeks to outlaw that practice in Australia, but, so far as it can be controlled in Australia, to *any* overseas adoption.[8] See Chapter 4. The reason that this would apply to overseas adoptions makes sense because of history in Australia. In the past, a number of children were made available in developing countries, including India, for adoption in Australia. Subsequently, adoption orders were made. Several children in India who were adopted by Australians had been sold in order to enable the adoptions to occur. As it turns out, although the Australian adoptive parents and authorities were completely innocent, the same could not be said of the actors concerned in India.

The Iowa adoption meant that because the surrogate had been paid expenses and would be paid expenses relating to the adoption, there was a risk that the offense back home would have been committed.

There was to be a subsequent adoption in Florida where there was not the same issue—because the surrogate was not considered a parent in Florida. Therefore payments to her were irrelevant to the adoption. Therefore, the Australian adoption criminal provisions did not apply.

While it may seem an arcane point as to whether an Iowa or Florida adoption occurred, the former may have resulted in an offense being committed, but the latter did not.

Even worse than the sale of Indian children was the case of Peter Truong and his partner Mark Newton. Mr. Truong was an Australian citizen. Mr. Newton was an Australian/U.S. citizen. They lived between Australia and the United States. In 2005 they went to Russia and said that they had engaged in either surrogacy or adoption, and that Mr. Newton was the biological father of the baby boy.

Subsequently, they went to the media in Australia to say how wonderful it was as a gay couple to have become parents via surrogacy in Russia.

It was all a lie. A man in Christchurch, New Zealand, put his computer in for repair. At that point, the lie was exposed. The man's computer was full of child porn. Mr. Truong and Mr. Newton had in fact bought a child for about $6,000. There never was any adoption, nor surrogacy. The purpose of their purchase was to sexually abuse the boy and also to make him available to a pedophile network, Boy Lovers Network. That was a forum for men who described sexual abuse of boys between the ages of two and ten as a form of consensual love between man and boy. One video showed the boy performing sex acts on Newton with a disturbing level of sophistication when he was not even two. When the boy turned

8. *E.g., Adoption Act 2009* (Qld) ss 301, 303.

five, Newton videoed himself engaged in sexual activity with him on more than a dozen different occasions in one month alone.

When Truong and Newton were in Los Angeles in 2011, they were arrested. The boy was taken into protective custody. Truong had faced a maximum 40-year sentence in the United States, but with a plea deal, he was allowed a minimum of 24 years' imprisonment.

The child's birth papers were falsified to list Newton as his biological father. Truong was sentenced to 30 years' jail. Newton had earlier been sentenced to 40 years' jail.

Female Couples

As discussed earlier, second parent adoptions are commonly used in the United States to establish parentage for both women who are a couple. That second parent adoption may not be recognized overseas. Care must be taken if that couple intend to migrate as to what is the status of the other parent in the other country. In some countries, the other parent will be recognized as a parent due to comity laws or specific statutory recognition, such as in the United Kingdom or Australia. In many countries the other parent will not be recognized as a parent of the child—and disclosure may cause great difficulties for the couple and child. See Chapter 7.

Developing Countries

In many developing countries, there are simply no laws about surrogacy ART at all. Instead, reliance is had upon adoption laws both

1. as a means of seeking to establish parentage (though this is patchy, as some countries do not have any familiarity with gestational surrogacy, such as island nations in Oceania—including Fiji, Papua New Guinea, Samoa, and Vanuatu—while others use adoption regulation as the means of establishing parentage, such as Ghana, Kenya, and Nigeria), and
2. to establish that criminal offenses have occurred. A payment to a surrogate for expenses (let alone a fee) might be considered the criminal act of purchasing a child.

These adoption laws in turn have their quirks as to who can undertake the adoption. Typically, adoption will only be open to heterosexual married couples. Sometimes adoption will be open to heterosexual unmarried couples. Sometimes adoption will be open to single intended parents (but commonly not those in same-sex relationships) and there can be restrictions on access, particularly for single men with girls.

In many post-colonial countries these adoption laws were written during the colonial era—and have not been updated. It can be difficult finding the current laws.

In Chapter 9 I recount how I had found a Fijian lawyer through the Fijian Law Society, concerning an adoption matter. Her advice was invaluable. I had tracked down Fijian adoption laws from the Pacific Islands Legal Information Institute (PacLII),[9] and then came across Fiji Consolidated Legislation—1985 revised edition, and then Fiji legislation indexes. Somehow, I had seen that there was both an Adoption of Infants Act 1944 and an Adoption Act 2020. I was unclear which applied. I would have guessed that the 1944 act had been repealed by the 2020 act. The latter said so, after all.[10] But I did not know.

My newfound colleague explained to me. The 1944 act remained in force. Though enacted in 2020, the 2020 act had not yet commenced. The 2020 act implemented the 1993 Hague Convention, but practitioners were concerned about its implementation in practice, with the result that the Fijian government had not yet proclaimed its commencement. The 2020 act was expressed to commence on a date to be proclaimed. What is simple for legislators to write can then be very difficult for practitioners to find out as to when, or if, an act has been proclaimed—and typically involves potentially hours of searching through government gazettes to find the needle in the haystack. Trying to find the location of government gazettes on the web can in turn be looking for that haystack in some enormous field.

Surrogacy in Kenya

The method of surrogacy regulation in Kenya is by adoption.

A child is not available for adoption unless the child is at least six weeks old and has been cleared by the National Council for Children's Services indicating the child is available for adoption.[11]

An adoption order may be made upon the application of a sole applicant or jointly by a heterosexual married couple.

The applicant or at least one of the joint applicants must be at least 26 and must be at least 21 years older than the child but should not have attained the age of 65. However, those age requirements are not mandatory where the applicant is a relative of the child.

9. PacLII, www.paclii.org (last visited Mar. 26, 2024).
10. Adoption Act 2020, § 60.
11. The Children Act (2001) Cap. 141 pt. XIV.

An adoption order cannot be issued unless the court is satisfied that there are special circumstances that justify making an adoption order, such as a sole male applicant in respect of a female child, a sole female applicant in respect of a male child, an applicant who is 65 years or older, and a sole foreigner female applicant.

A risk in a developing country, where the model of surrogacy regulation by default is that of adoption, is that because there is a post-birth transfer of parentage and because any agreement with the surrogate is not binding, that the surrogate can change her mind and withhold the transfer of parentage. There are reports from Kenya where surrogates have attempted to extort the intended parents—which is clearly open on that model.

Kenya criminalizes same-sex consensual acts. See Chapter 7.

A similar process of surrogacy occurs in other African countries, such as Nigeria and Ghana.

Surrogacy in Nigeria

Clients of mine underwent surrogacy in Nigeria. They did so because they had migrated from there. See Chapters 19 and 10. As seen in Chapter 19, it is estimated that in late 2023 in one clinic in Nigeria, one in ten patients come from Europe and North America.

A feature about that case that was different was that if they had undertaken surrogacy back in Australia, there was an expectation that before they entered into the surrogacy arrangement there would have been presigning counseling and assessment by a social worker or psychologist. The social worker or psychologist would then have written a report carrying out an assessment to assist in decision-making as to whether all the parties were suitable to undertake surrogacy. That report would be provided to the parties, their lawyers, the in vitro fertilization (IVF) clinic, and ultimately the court.

The court in Nigeria ordered that such a report be obtained. It was prepared by an Australian psychologist/fertility counselor. Obtaining the report involved counseling and interviews with both the intended parents (who resided in Australia) and the surrogate (who resided in Nigeria). The thorough report recommended that surrogacy proceed. There was a need for surrogacy, and all were entering into the arrangement with informed consent.

The surrogacy journey was able to proceed and subsequently an adoption order was made.

Nigeria criminalizes same-sex consensual acts. See Chapter 7.

Surrogacy in Ghana

Clients of mine, a heterosexual married couple, migrated from Ghana to Australia.

Their first child was born through an Australian surrogacy journey with help from a relative from Ghana who had moved to Australia.

That journey took about six years. Conceptually, it was a straightforward arrangement. However, migration laws made the journey extremely convoluted. My clients and I had considered if their surrogate had traveled to the United States or Canada to become pregnant there, and then for her to return home to Ghana. My clients would travel from Australia and bring the baby home to Australia. However, that was not possible. The surrogate would not be able to enter the United States. As Ghanaians are perceived by other nations to be poor, it is therefore hard for its citizens to obtain visas to visit other countries.

After that surrogacy journey was completed, they wanted to become parents again. Another migrant from Ghana offered to be their surrogate for their second journey. This started as an Australian surrogacy journey. All the parties lived in Australia.

However, halfway through the pregnancy, the surrogate migrated from Australia to Ghana. She went home. She did so without notice to my clients, and therefore without their consent. The first that they knew that she was going was after she had gone.

The fact that they had an Australian surrogacy arrangement was beside the point. The surrogacy arrangement could not be enforced in Ghana.

On its face, the law of Ghana was of no assistance either. Because the process had been undertaken in Australia, then the process of surrogacy in Ghana, which is via adoption, could not be followed.

The child was born in Ghana. The child was genetically that of the intended parents. The intended parents approached Ghanian authorities. On the face of it, they would not be recognized as the parents, which attached to the birth parents, but was in this case a single woman. Nor were they eligible to apply to adopt. Nevertheless, Ghanian officials were prepared to register the couple as the parents for the purposes of Ghanian law. Full disclosure had been made by the couple to Ghanian officials of their plight.

Their case is an example that black-letter law interpretation is not always strictly enforced in appropriate cases in some places. It is always important to engage where possible with a local lawyer.

Ghana criminalizes same-sex consensual acts. See Chapter 7.

Bringing the Baby Home

As *KK v. Denmark* (2023) (see Chapter 2) demonstrated, an overseas surrogacy journey might be regulated at home under adoption laws.

After the child has come home, it might be possible for there to be a second parent adoption, to enable the parentage of the second parent to be recognized, as discussed in *Fjölnisdóttir v. Iceland*,[12] a decision of the European Court of Human Rights. See Chapter 2.

If the intended parents are undertaking a surrogacy journey overseas, but using adoption as the method to establish parentage, they should be beware. Their parentage may not be recognized back home, unless the specific procedures of the 1993 Hague Convention or bilateral arrangements have been met.

Several countries publish information on their websites about adoption criteria that need to be met for the child to come "home." This information should never be used as a substitute for local legal advice. However, despite best efforts, sometimes no local legal advice can be obtained.

For example, the website of the U.S. Embassy in Fiji[13] covers adoption of children by U.S. citizens in Fiji, Kiribati, Nauru, Tonga, and Tuvalu.

Nauru consists of one island, which has a population of 10,000. I discovered a few years ago, when clients of mine brought a case against the government there, that it has no private practising lawyers, which is not surprising, given its size. The U.S. government on its site says that there are practising lawyers in Nauru. I would be most surprised if this were now true. The people giving advice in Nauru were law clerks.

Nevertheless, the site notes that Nauru is not a 1993 Hague country. It then states, helpfully:

> Below is the limited adoption information that the Department has obtained from the adoption authority of Nauru. U.S. citizens interested in adopting children from Nauru should contact the Magistrate Court of Nauru to inquire about applicable laws and procedures. U.S. citizen prospective adoptive parents living in Nauru who would like to adopt a child from the United States or from a third country should also contact Nauru's Magistrate Court. See contact information below.
>
> Nauru's adoption legislation does not permit the adoption of Nauruan children by non-Nauruans. However, the judiciary

12. App. No. 71552/17 (May 18, 2021).

13. *Adoption*, U.S. Embassy Fiji, Kiribati, Nauru, Tonga & Tuvalu, https://fj.usembassy.gov/adoption/ (last visited Mar. 26, 2024).

has determined that this legislation conflicts with certain obligations Nauru has undertaken with respect to the Convention on the Rights of the Child. The courts have permitted the adoption of Nauruan children by married couples in which only one of the adoptive parents is of Nauruan origin. There have been no applications for adoptions in which neither prospective adoptive parent is of Nauruan origin and it is unclear whether Nauru's courts would permit an adoption in such a case.

There are no adoption agencies in Nauru.[14]

The overseas birth might be recognized back home for some purposes but not others. Here I again return to my home country of Australia, with the example of Bill and Ted, which illustrates the complexity of some international surrogacy journeys. The method of establishing parentage via surrogacy in Hawaii is by post-birth orders, which includes a second parent adoption order in favor of the non-biological parent.

Bill and Ted Do Surrogacy in Hawaii

Bill and Ted are an Australian gay male couple, from Sydney, New South Wales. They undertake a surrogacy journey in Hawaii.

They create some embryos in Hawaii, using Bill's sperm and eggs from a donor. The donor receives a fee of $10,000.

They then enter a gestational carrier agreement with a surrogate, who is paid $25,000 plus expenses. Under the agreement, the surrogate agrees to provide breast milk and be compensated $250 per week.

A Hawaiian court recognizes Bill as a parent, and terminates the parental relationship of the surrogate.

The court makes a second parent adoption order in favor of Ted. The birth certificate shows Bill and Ted to be the parents of baby Georgina.

If extreme care is not taken by them, Bill and Ted may have committed a series of offenses back home:

The first possible offense

It is an offense in Australia under federal law to give or offer valuable consideration for the supply of a human egg, human sperm, or human embryo, punishable by up to 15 years' imprisonment.[15] There is an exception for reasonable expenses.

14. *Id.*
15. *Prohibition of Human Cloning for Reproduction Act 2002* (Cth) s 21.

The law is expressed to apply to overseas trade and commerce.[16] However, it is unlikely to apply to this transaction, based on the intention of Parliament.

The second possible offense

It is an offense under New South Wales state law to give or offer valuable consideration for the supply of a human egg, human sperm, or human embryo, punishable by up to 15 years' imprisonment.[17] There is an exception for reasonable expenses. The law can apply overseas under a long-arm law[18] if *part* of the elements of the offense occurs in New South Wales, or the *effect* of the offense occurs in New South Wales.

The third possible offense

It is an offense under New South Wales state law to enter into a contract for the sale or supply of human tissue, punishable by up to six months' imprisonment.[19] An egg falls within the definition of "tissue." This offense can also apply overseas by virtue of the long-arm law.

The fourth possible offense

It is an offense under New South Wales state law[20] to enter into or to offer to enter into a commercial surrogacy arrangement as defined under that law, punishable by a fine of up to A$110,000 or two years' imprisonment or both. The offense has specific extraterritorial effect to anyone who is ordinarily resident or domiciled in New South Wales, and can also be committed overseas due to the long-arm law.

The fifth possible offense

Breast milk also falls within the definition of "tissue."[21] An offense might be committed relating to the supply of the breast milk. This offense can also apply overseas by virtue of the long-arm law.

---

16. *Id.* s 4.

17. *Human Cloning for Reproduction and Other Prohibited Practices Act 2003* (NSW) s 16.

18. *Crimes Act 1900* (NSW) s 10C.

19. *Human Tissue Act 1983* (NSW) s 32.

20. *Surrogacy Act 2010* (NSW) ss 8, 9, 11.

21. How breast milk is treated is another example of how different parts of the same country may not be the same. *See* Chapter 10. Queensland, unlike other Australian states and territories, which continue to criminalize the commercial supply of breast milk under their definition of "tissue," has from 2022 excluded breast milk as tissue. *Transplantation and Anatomy Act 1979* (Qld) s 4. This arose out of concern that there was uncertainty as to whether or not breast milk was tissue. The likelihood or at least uncertainty of criminalizing the commercial supply of breast milk led to

The sixth possible offense

As covered under the Iowa discussion later, there is also an adoption offense in New South Wales that can apply with clear extraterritorial effect. It is unlikely to apply to the journey in Hawaii.

Does the 1993 convention apply?

For the 1993 Hague Intercountry Adoption Convention to apply to Georgina's adoption, five steps are required when an adoption order is made:

1. Both countries are Parties to the convention. Both the United States and Australia are Parties to the convention.
2. The adoption occurs in the sending country where the child is habitually resident (and the intended parents are habitually resident in the receiving country) *or* the adoption occurs in the receiving country where the adoptive parents are habitually resident (and the child is habitually resident in the sending country).
3. In this case, Bill and Ted are habitually resident in the receiving country. Therefore, it is necessary for Georgina to be habitually resident in the sending country. Given the approach in the New Zealand case *In re Application by L*[22] (see Chapter 1), the child may be habitually resident in New South Wales, Australia, because she did not have time to be habitually resident in Hawaii, and her habitual residence would ordinarily be that of her parents, in this case, Bill and Ted, in New South Wales. It is uncertain, therefore, if the convention applies.
4. The sending country must issue an adoption compliance certificate. The State Department does not issue adoption compliance certificates for second parent adoptions arising from surrogacy. Therefore, the provisions of the convention do not arise.
5. Even though both countries are Parties to the convention, Australia will not easily recognize an adoption under the convention from the United States, because the United States is not a bilateral adoption partner country.

An Australian federal law[23] recognizes Ted as a parent, as Georgina was adopted by him under the law of any place, in this case Hawaii. That same law takes up as domestic law the provisions of the 1993 convention.[24]

Australian states legislate about adoption. The New South Wales Adoption Act[25] makes plain that an overseas adoption does not have effect for the purposes of the law of New

---

the perception that there was a shortage of breast milk, particularly for babies born prematurely.

22. [2003] NZFLR 529.

23. *Family Law Act 1975* (Cth) s 4.

24. *Id.* s 111C; *Family Law (Hague Convention on Intercountry Adoption) Regulations 1998* (Cth).

25. *Adoption Act 2000* (NSW) s 105.

South Wales unless that adoption falls within the ambit of that act. Overseas adoptions are only recognized if:

- The adoption is in New South Wales of a child by parents from a convention country[26]
- The adoption is in New South Wales by parents habitually resident in New South Wales of a child from a convention country[27]
- The adoption occurred in a convention country of a child from that country[28]
- The child was adopted in a country that has a bilateral relationship with Australia, outside the convention, concerning adoptions[29]—the only two jurisdictions that meet that description are South Korea and Taiwan[30]
- The adoption occurred in a country that was not a convention country or a bilateral country, and the adoptive parents had either resided in that country for a year or more, or were domiciled there[31]

The only one that applies is that Ted must have undertaken the adoption in Hawaii, on the basis that he was habitually resident in New South Wales and Georgina was habitually resident in Hawaii, and an adoption compliance certificate issued in the United States. Leaving aside any views about habitual residence, because the State Department does not issue the adoption compliance certificate, Ted's parentage is not recognized under New South Wales state law.

Therefore, the appointment by Ted, as a parent,[32] of a testamentary guardian may be invalid. Any bequest in his will may also be at risk.

Despite how it might appear, Ted is a parent in New South Wales. The Australian Constitution[33] makes plain that where there is a conflict between a federal law and a state law, the latter gives way. Therefore, as Ted is a parent under the federal law, he is a parent of Georgina in New South Wales.

But what if Bill and Ted had undertaken surrogacy in Iowa, instead?

Bill would be recognized as a parent in Iowa through both pre- and post-birth orders. Like Hawaii, Ted as the second parent is added by a second parent adoption.

---

26. *Id.* s 106.
27. *Id.* s 107.
28. *Id.* s 108.
29. *Id.* s 113.
30. *Family Law (Bilateral Arrangements-Intercountry Adoption) Regulations 2023* (Cth).
31. *Id.* s 116.
32. *Guardianship of Infants Act 1916* (NSW) s 14 (the parent (including a mother or father) of a minor may by deed or will appoint any person to be guardian of the minor after his or her death; "parent" is not defined).
33. *Australian Constitution* s 109.

Unlike Hawaii, the surrogate must consent to the second parent adoption. The adoption would appear not to be within the ambit of the 1993 convention (Articles 4(c)(3), 4(d)(4), 16(c)), which requires that the consent to adoption "*ha[s] not been induced by payment or compensation of any kind.*"

In addition to the question of parentage back home, which is the same if they had undertaken surrogacy in Hawaii or Iowa, there is the additional complication of undertaking surrogacy in Iowa (but unlikely for Hawaii) of possibly committing an adoption offense back home.

Section 177(2) of the Adoption Act 2000 (New South Wales) contains an offense that has extraterritorial reach:

> (2) A person who is resident or domiciled in this State who—
>
> (a) makes any payment or gives any reward of any kind to a birth parent for relinquishing a child adopted from outside Australia or for consenting to an adoption under this Act, or
> (b) gives or takes any improper financial gain in relation to an adoption, is guilty of an offence.
>
> Maximum penalty—25 penalty units or imprisonment for 12 months, or both.

Not only do Bill and Ted have to make sure that they do not commit offenses relating to egg donation, the supply of breast milk, and entering into a commercial surrogacy arrangement under New South Wales law[34] (as it is one of the four places in the world that has extraterritorial offenses for surrogacy[35]), but they also have to make sure they do not commit the adoption offense as well.

Take Away

1. If you have clients who are heading overseas to live, do not assume that a U.S. adoption will be recognized overseas. They should obtain advice from lawyers in the overseas country about whether the adoption will be recognized.
2. Because of its difference with adoption, surrogacy may or may not be treated as adoption.

34. *Surrogacy Act 2010* (NSW) ss 8, 9, 11.

35. Australian Capital Territory, New South Wales, Queensland, and Hong Kong. In 2023, the Italian House of Delegates passed a bill to criminalize Italian citizens from undertaking surrogacy overseas. As of April 2024 that bill is being considered by but has not passed the Senate. As of April 2024, Irish politicians are also considering criminalizing overseas surrogacy.

3. Habitual residence of the child may follow that of the intended parents. If habitual residence of the child is that of the intended parents, then the 1993 Hague Convention will not apply.
4. Adoption authorities, such as the U.S. State Department, may decline to issue adoption compliance certificates, even if the adoption appears convention-compliant, with the result that the convention is not applicable.[36]
5. If you have clients from overseas and the local process of recognition of parentage through surrogacy is via adoption, there may be issues with the 1993 Hague Intercountry Adoption Convention and issues of criminality for the couple back home.
6. If the method of parentage establishment overseas is via adoption, check whether the other country is a 1993 Hague country. The status table showing which countries are signatories (and, therefore, by not being listed, which are not) can be found on the HCCH website.[37]
7. If you have clients who are going to a developing country for the purposes of surrogacy, then the process of parentage might be via adoption. Because a post-birth adoption process is chosen, then they may find themselves at risk if the surrogate changes her mind.
8. Sometimes while the recognition of parentage is not able to be done by statute law, in practice recognition in that country can occur. While this might favor single and LGBTQIA+ intended parents, it is more likely to favor heterosexual couples.
9. Even if parentage is recognized there, there is no guarantee that it is recognized here.
10. Extreme care should be taken, as with every international ART, to make plain before the journey starts, that no criminal offense is likely to be committed, and that the baby can return home with the intended parents.
11. As always, intended parents should obtain expert legal advice at both ends—and both lawyers should liaise with each other, so that there is unanimity of vision to ensure a smooth surrogacy journey.

---

36. The requirement for the certificates is under Article 17.

37. *Status Table: 33: Convention of 29 May 1993 on Protection of Children and Co-operation in Respect of Intercountry Adoption*, HCCH, https://www.hcch.net/en/instruments/conventions/status-table/?cid=69 (last updated Mar. 14, 2024).

Chapter 14

Deep Pockets and Short Arms

A joy about the way surrogacy is practiced in the United States and Canada is the perpetual requirement for there to be a trust account or an escrow account. Whether the money is being paid to an egg donor agency or a surrogacy agency or an attorney, much of the money invariably ends up in a trust account or escrow account—to be protected, to ensure that there is enough to pay for the relevant expenses, such as for the egg donor and the surrogate.

Well, I *say* always. That is certainly the common practice. There have been relatively rare occasions when agency owners have not used trust or escrow accounts, or that they have said that they did, but lied. See Chapter 18.

It is a question of when not if intended parents become parents through surrogacy. The combination of a high-quality embryo being implanted into a woman who is highly fertile (as surrogates tend to be) means that there is a very high chance that the surrogate will become pregnant quickly. Of course, it doesn't always work like that. Many surrogacy journeys are more complex. There are four reasons that intended parents won't get there and become parents:

1. They die.
2. They give up.
3. They need a donor but are not prepared to use a donor.
4. They don't have enough money.

If your clients are going overseas for surrogacy, then it's absolutely essential that if you are giving them advice about the process, that you have an idea about the cost.

While you may not be an expert on exchange rates, if you are advising clients about what the cost of the journey is or comparing costs, make sure you convert as best you can into local currency so they have some realistic figure and make generous allowances for the fact that the intended parents have to travel to that foreign country and spend a considerable amount of time there paying for a mortgage at home and rent abroad, car hire, meals—the whole of their direct costs for their surrogacy journey.

A Passage to India

In the early 2010s when India was a surrogacy hub, I was confronted by a number of Indian surrogacy promoters over numbers. They did not like my numbers. I was told that the numbers I was quoting to Australian intended parents for their journey in the order of $45,000–$52,000 were way off the mark, and that I did not know what I was talking about. I was told that surrogacy in India, through their clinic, cost between $22,000–$24,000.

The promoters only included their costs, and did not take into account the whole of the journey for the intended parents.

I was met with silence when I said something like:

> What you're saying about your costs are no doubt right. But my clients don't live in Mumbai/Delhi/Chennai—they live in Sydney/Melbourne/Brisbane. They have to get to India first. That means they have to fly there and pay for the flights—and come home. Once they get there, they are there for a couple of months and have to pay for accommodation, taxis, food, car hire, and all the rest. When you add it all up, the total is about $45,000.

Many intended parents forget about those hidden costs—exporting their genetic material overseas, then having to travel overseas, and staying overseas before they can come home: paying for accommodation, car hire, food, and necessities on top of their usual running costs at home. All of those costs have to be allowed for in the journey.

For some reason or another Australia has been the subject of a series of surrogacy inquiries that relate to the nervousness of Australian politicians to do something substantial about surrogacy reform but being pressed to do so. At each of these inquiries, there are complaints by Australian surrogates that they have intended parents who leave them short, as I said in the chapter heading—with deep pockets but short arms. Their expenses are simply not met.

The model used in the United States and Canada where the surrogate's expenses are paid into a trust or escrow account is marvelous. The surrogate is protected. Her expenses are met. In many other countries, either surrogacy agencies don't exist (and surrogates as a result are left short-changed) or the agency only meets part of the expenses.

Extreme care must be taken by intended parents in going to risky countries with poor human rights frameworks, poor legal frameworks concerning insurance and the like, and poor governance generally. Further allowance should be made by those intended parents, in addition to whatever they might have budgeted, just in case there are some unexpected expenses for the surrogate along the way.

As I said in Chapter 11, there needs to be protection against exchange rate movements. The U.S. dollar, as the world's reserve currency, has been particularly volatile. Are the other payments under the surrogacy agreement in U.S. dollars or in some other currency such as Canadian dollars or euros? The choice of currency can make a difference. Intended parents have to have a realistic budget and should always allow for extra, just in case.

There can be unexpected expenses that arise in extraordinary circumstances—just ask those who had to get their surrogates out of Ukraine after the invasion. All those whose airlines charged like wounded bulls at the commencement of the pandemic. Having barriers created around the world because of the pandemic greatly increased costs for those parents.

March 2020

A couple had undertaken surrogacy in the United States. They already had a toddler. Their newborn had just been born at a time when the world went mad. Borders started shutting. Airlines ceased flying.

The couple needed to get home. The only seats available on Qantas were business class, at a cost of $34,000. They looked like they were going to get stuck—between delays by the State Department in issuing a passport, and Australian authorities in issuing a visa for the child—and miss that Qantas flight. No more flights were available if they missed that flight.

They made a tentative booking on the only other airline with available seats: Qatar Airways, only available in business, flying back via the Middle East. The cost: $31,000.

Luckily, the State Department issued the newborn's passport, and Australian authorities issued the visa. They were able to fly on Qantas. While they had been gouged by one airline, they were not gouged by two. The family were able to come home safely.

The extraordinary cost of the flight was not included in their budget.

Moving Genetic Material

Moving genetic material internationally has been a challenge. Prior to the pandemic, the standard model was for a courier to carry the genetic material on the plane as hand luggage and then take it to the clinic at the other end.

The pandemic upended all of that. Suddenly, genetic material had to be carried as cargo, with the risk that it may not arrive at the other end, and at significantly inflated rates. Between Australia and the United States, for example, there was one flight a day, operated by United. Every other airline had stopped, even venerable Qantas, which celebrated its 100th year in 2020. Qantas had not stopped flying international flights during World War II, but it did during the pandemic.

With only one trans-Pacific flight per day, the cost of flying a container of sperm or embryos across the Pacific increased to as much as $4,500, three times the previous cost. Gradually those rates have decreased, but, nevertheless, they remain significant.

Before shipping the sperm, eggs, or embryos, your clients need to take care. Is the recipient clinic at the other end regulated and accredited? Are there any barriers against export of genetic material?

Do any tests need to be undertaken at each end to comply with the recipient clinic's requirements, such as in importing into the United States, so that Food and Drug Administration (FDA) requirements are met? Many in vitro fertilization (IVF) clinics in the United States that I have dealt with are not familiar with importation of genetic material. Only some are. This is not a criticism. If the clinic has focused on creating embryos in their IVF lab, to primarily American clientele, they may never have had the need to consider FDA requirements for imported material. It should never be assumed that the clinic knows about FDA requirements.

If the embryos are composed of donor eggs or sperm, is there, in effect, a restriction on the sending clinic to send them overseas?

Does the sending clinic have an objection to sending genetic material overseas for the purposes of surrogacy? Some do.

Is there a law in the country where the intended parents live that restricts the sending of genetic material overseas? In two Australian states, for example—Victoria and Western Australia—export of donor gametes or embryos comprising donor gametes cannot be exported except with regulatory approval, which would not be given for commercial surrogacy.

Is there a risk of a practical barrier to the material being sent? It is not a pleasant conversation to have with clients who say that their material was "lost" in transit. All their hopes and dreams might be in that package, and now their genetic material is gone. Is the carrier reliable? Is the transit point to point, or does it have to clear customs after a significant delay, or does it have to transit to some other destination?

Is it easier and cheaper to create embryos over there? Often the question must be posed at the very beginning of the matter (if you're lucky to be involved at the beginning). It may simply be easier, quicker, and cheaper to create the embryos in the country where the intended parents wish to undertake surrogacy than doing so at home.

In some countries, there is a government subsidy for IVF. That subsidy may be capped or it may be not available for surrogacy. As part of the budgetary exercise, there may need to be a comparison done as to what is the cost of creating embryos locally as opposed to shipping those embryos overseas, and the cost of shipping them, compared to the cost of creating the embryos from scratch overseas.

As always, every case will be different. While not common, loss of genetic material when it is shipped occurs occasionally. This is devastating for the intended parent. Doctors always recommend, where there is an option, not to cause genetic material to be sent.

In budgeting for the journey, intended parents will consider whether to create embryos at their local IVF clinic (including with donor material) and then exporting, or to create embryos overseas. Part of their consideration is the cost. Part is convenience, and availability. One barrier that they may not have considered is that when using donor gametes, the creating clinic might be resistant to export. This is because to do so might render the clinic in breach of the traceability requirements with the sperm or donor bank that supplied the donor gametes to that clinic.

The temptation then, if the intended parents are undertaking a surrogacy journey, is to move the surrogate around instead of the genetic material. It has been commonplace, for example for Canadian surrogates to travel to U.S. IVF clinics to become pregnant—because the perception of some intended parents is that the quality of IVF in the United States is higher, or the availability of egg donors is greater than that in Canada.

Similarly, I have seen a U.S. surrogate travel to Canada for implantation without any drama. The child was successfully born and orders made in the United States subsequently. However, when moving further afield, there can be difficulties either moving the surrogate or moving the genetic material. I will give an example.

Case: Unexpected Inability to Transport Embryos Due to Regulations

An Australian same-sex couple created embryos in the United Kingdom. They lived in the United Kingdom. A family member in Australia agreed to be the surrogate. To enable the import into Australia, there had to be:

1. Noncommercial donation. This had been complied with. The United Kingdom had similar rules to Australia.
2. A cap on the number of donations. The United Kingdom had similar rules there too.
3. The ability for the child to find out the identity of the donor if the child wanted after the age of 18. Again, that could be complied with.
4. Given the Australian state that the export was occurring to, local law required that the donor be identified to the Australian clinic (but not to the intended parents). The UK donor and UK clinic refused. The intention was for the embryos to move from the United Kingdom to Australia. Instead, the plan changed to the Australian surrogate traveling to the United Kingdom to become pregnant. Luckily, under the law of the Australian state, that was possible.

Take Away

1. Where possible, give your clients a ballpark estimate of the entire cost of their journey.
2. This then gives them some idea of what is realistic, what options they have available to them, and where they might undertake surrogacy.
3. There may be barriers in moving genetic material overseas. Some of these barriers are hidden. Some are from the sending country, and some in the receiving country.
4. Where possible, intended parents should be encouraged to create genetic material overseas, so as to minimize the potential loss of their genetic material.

Chapter 15

The First—and Last—of Life's Certainties

"[N]othing is certain except death and taxes."

Benjamin Franklin[1]

These days it is said that Ben was wrong, and that there are three certainties—the third being change. That statement is apt for the assisted reproductive technology (ART) world, which is at the forefront of scientific, medical, and societal change. Bringing up the rear, as ever, is the law.

But I digress. The point of this chapter is to be aware of estate planning for intended parents. None of us think that we are going to die, while knowing that we are. Most of my divorce or ART clients do not have wills when they seek to get divorced, or seek to have a family. I always ask, and I always insist that they get advice and have wills prepared. I am not an expert financial planner—but I refer them to someone who is.

From my experience, U.S. and Canadian ART attorneys are good at ensuring that the intended parents through surrogacy have an appointment of a testamentary guardian concerning an international surrogacy arrangement. However, too often the attorneys fail to raise with their clients, let alone seek to ensure, that their clients have up-to-date wills to protect the child, or other estate planning.

It's basic stuff, but often forgotten.

As I was writing this chapter, I reflected on clients I recently met for the first time—whose child is due soon in the United States. Their U.S. lawyer has prepared the appropriate guardianship documents required in the United States. So far, so good. However, they do not have wills—even though their surrogate is several months pregnant! No one, they said, has raised it with them, until I did. Nor had they checked whether they

1. *Benjamin Franklin's Last Great Quote and the Constitution*, Nat'l Const. Ctr. (Nov. 13, 2023), https://constitutioncenter.org/blog/benjamin-franklins-last-great-quote-and-the-constitution.

had life insurance, let alone adequate life insurance—or who the named beneficiaries were—nor whether they had made a binding nomination of beneficiary for their retirement savings.

During the first meeting with new clients, I always ask about whether they have wills and, if so, whether they are up to date, and about their life insurance and retirement savings. Every lawyer who practices ART should do so.

The Merry Widow

I once acted in property settlement proceedings for a wife.[2] She had applied to court for 60 percent of the marital property—which was all in the name of the husband. He had been, according to her, an abusive, controlling man. Not very pleasant, but rather successful at business.

On the Friday afternoon before court on the Monday morning, the husband, his lawyer, my client, and I all met to try to cut a deal. It was unsuccessful. I asked him about the ownership of a 50-foot yacht. The response from the husband was telling: "*It's owned by a man in Sydney.*"

I was young and green, and I knew that I was young and green. But I also knew a liar when I heard one. The answer was not, "*John Banks of Cherry Tree Lane,*" but "*a man in Sydney.*" No deal was cut. We left, knowing that on Monday morning the court process would be underway.

My client phoned me before court Monday morning, "*I'm not coming to court.*" Rather intemperately, I cut her off. I told her, "*You have to come. You are required to be there.*" My client responded, "*You know that 50-foot yacht owned by the man in Sydney? My husband died on that on Saturday.*" While sad that her husband had died (of natural causes), she was delighted that he had a practice of carrying around his briefcase with him at all times—including on that yacht. In that briefcase was his will—which he had not changed since they had separated. My client was named executor and sole beneficiary.

Many years of family law practice since, many clients have come to me from other lawyers. I have always asked in that first interview (as I do in the first interview with ART clients) as to whether they have a will. In the case of family law clients, I also ask whether their ex is the sole beneficiary. Doing so has confirmed what that case taught me—many, even particularly good, family lawyers don't ask their clients about their wills, and forget to ensure wills are prepared.

---

2. In Australia, financial disputes about property are a separate cause of action to divorce.

Basic ART practice is that intended parents ensure that they make arrangements in case they die. Therefore, they have wills in place, including the appointment of a testamentary guardian for the child, proper life insurance arrangements in place, including identification of the beneficiary, retirement savings arrangements in place, including, again, the identification of the beneficiary, and in more complex matters, for wealthier individuals, that appropriate complex estate planning is in place—just in case they die during the course of the surrogacy journey or shortly after the child is born.

Two Days before Christmas

One year, two working days before Christmas, in a casual conversation with clients who were about to go to the United States for surrogacy, I was told the names of the testamentary guardians that they were to appoint under their Australian wills. A quick check on the file discovered that the name of the testamentary guardian appointed under the U.S. guardianship appointment was someone else! There needed to be urgent immediate communications between the lawyer in the United States and me to make sure that the guardian who was appointed was the same person.

The clients had had a change of mind about who they wanted appointed but had not communicated with everyone concerned about that change. The documents were rectified prior to Christmas.

Estate planning is essential in the surrogacy process and is often overlooked. I am always astonished at the number of clients who do not have wills—even clients who are practicing lawyers.

The Will Prepared by a "Surrogacy Lawyer"

Jenny, 41, wanted to become a mom. Briefly in a relationship with Julie, at Julie's suggestion Jenny had a double embryo transfer. Jenny soon split up from Julie. Julie was a crazy, violent narcissist who engaged in coercive control toward Jenny, pulling Jenny toward her, then pushing her away.

Eventually, Jenny got away. About a month later, she gave birth to twins.

Jenny had been sure to see a lawyer who touted themselves as a specialist surrogacy lawyer. It was not me. That lawyer prepared a will, which said that if Jenny had a partner, the partner would decide what was to occur with the embryos. If she did not have a partner, Jenny's sister had to decide. There was no appointment of a testamentary guardian.

Three days after the births, Jenny died of preeclampsia. Her dying wish was that her children be cared for by her sister and sister's partner, and not by Julie. There was a real chance that Julie was a parent.[3] Accordingly, it was necessary to file urgent court proceedings about the children before Jenny's funeral was held. Julie's response in her court materials was, predictably, "*I am the mother.*"

The court found otherwise.[4]

While court might have been necessary once Julie had heard about the births, there was no certainty that there ever would have been a court case. The failure to appoint a testamentary guardian in the will guaranteed a lengthy, stressful, and expensive court case. Jenny's sister could not grieve for her sister for eight months after the death—until the court case was over. She worked full time to support four children under two (as she and her partner already had two children under two), while her partner and friends and family helped care for the children.

Good estate planning might have averted much of that pain, stress, and cost.

Death Duty

It may seem a basic step to prepare a will, but there can be implications. We are lucky in Australia that a generation or two ago, all estate duties or death duties were abolished. From our point of view, it does not seem especially important about where wills are prepared and executed. However, Australians would not like to have estate duties imposed on them. Those who live in jurisdictions that have estate duties need to take care about what jurisdiction applies to their will. It would be awful that if they have estate duty in, for example, the United Kingdom, and they executed a will in, for example, the United States, that their estate would be subject to a double dose of duty.

---

3. As with other countries, such as the United Kingdom, if lesbian couples in Australia consent to the ART procedure, the non-birth mother can be recognized as the parent upon the birth of the child. A prime issue in the court case was not whether or not the two women were in a relationship (they were), or whether or not Julie had consented to the artificial conception procedure (she had), but whether or not on the day of the artificial conception procedure they were in a de facto relationship (a necessary step to determine that Julie was a parent). The court concluded that they were not, and that therefore Julie was not a parent.

4. *Wickham & Toledano* [2022] FedCFamC1F 32. I acted for the successful sister and her partner.

More likely there would be ongoing litigation as to which duty would apply—at an enormous cost and delay to the estate and pain to the executors and beneficiaries—with a likely negligence claim against the lawyers who allowed that to happen.

The Wife Gets It

Anthony Shaffer and Diane Cilento were a power couple—he a successful playwright and she a successful actor, best known for her previous marriage with Sean Connery.

Shaffer was a UK citizen. Cilento was an Australian. They had met on set in Scotland. They then moved to far north Queensland. They married in Australia.

At the time of moving to Australia, Shaffer was keen to ensure that he had moved to Australia for tax purposes. He was well aware that death duties had been abolished. This abolition formed part of this decision to move.

Nevertheless, Shaffer continued to travel frequently around the world, including to England. When Cilento traveled to visit him in England, she found that another woman's belongings were in his home.

Shaffer died.

An English court found that Shaffer was domiciled in Queensland, Australia, not in England.[5] This finding had two practical effects—the estate was a lot larger, as death duties were not payable in Queensland but were payable in England, and the claim by the English mistress for a share of the estate was defeated.

Who Is a Parent?

Once the child has gone home, any thoughts of who is a parent of the child—and I use the term "parent" in its legal sense—are often forgotten in the joy of parenthood and the busyness of life. It is essential, however, for the parents to ensure that their estate planning is up to date when they return home—especially if they are not the legal parents.

As *Mennesson v. France*[6] demonstrated (see Chapter 2), the potential impact on a child from the death of a parent can be enormous. The child may not inherit on the death of the "parent."

5. Morgan v. Cilento [2004] EWHC (Ch) 188.
6. App. No. 65192/11, ¶ 81 (Sept. 26, 2014).

Just because someone is recognized in the country of birth as a parent does not mean that the person will be recognized as a parent in his or her country of residence. The "parent" may not be recognized back home as a parent. The child may be considered illegitimate. If care is not taken with estate planning, the child may be disinherited.

Family lawyers may be more concerned about theoretical risks, such as the abduction of the child and whether the 1980 Hague Child Abduction Convention applies (whether the party is recognized as a parent in the jurisdiction and therefore has rights of custody under that convention—or not), than what might be seen as an esoteric discussion about estate planning. Still, estate planning must be undertaken to minimize the child's risks of being disinherited through inattention.

The old, wonderfully named English case *Occleston v. Fullalove*[7] is an illustration of the need to take care in the preparation of a will. James Occleston was a widower when he went through a ceremony of marriage in Switzerland with his late wife's sister, Margaret Lewis. The marriage was not recognized in England. His will provided that his estate would be given for his reputed children and all other children or reputed children that he might have or be reputed to have with Margaret. At the time of the execution of his will, Margaret was pregnant. After the child was born, the child was acknowledged by James as his own.

The Court of Appeal found that the child could inherit, despite the rule against illegitimacy. In the words of Lord Justice James:

> If the will in this case were read and considered merely for the purpose of ascertaining the testator's intention, the language being construed however strictly according to the ordinary grammatical meaning of the words used by him, it seems to me beyond all doubt that the testator intended the Appellant as one of the objects of his bounty. He meant the children born of the body of the particular woman to take, with this qualification, that they should be children of whom he should have acquired the reputation of being the father. If the case had been the case of a child en ventre sa mere at his death, there might have been a great, perhaps an insuperable, difficulty in attributing reputation of paternity in the male, while there was nothing but signs more or less visible of a possible or probable parturition expected of and by the female. But in this case it appears to me the very case

7. [1873–1874] LR 9 Ch App. 147.

contemplated and provided for by the testator so far as he could by law provide for it.

Between the date of his will and the time of his death a child was, with his knowledge, born of the body of the woman while she was Fullalove, living with him as his wife. After the birth, the cohabitation continued, and the child was in the most formal manner recognised by him by his registering the birth as the birth of the child of himself and his concubine, described by him in the register as his wife, and therefore, so far as he could, treating the child as legitimate. This evidence is to my mind absolutely conclusive that at the time when the will came into operation, when on his death it was opened and read, the Appellant did strictly and completely fulfil the description of a "child which he was reputed to have by the said Margaret Lewis."[8]

Take Away

1. Have a checklist to ensure that your client is informed of estate planning.
2. Where possible, liaise with your international counterpart to ensure estate planning is undertaken, and is consistent.
3. Just because the "parent" has returned home may not make that person a parent. Careful estate planning should be undertaken to protect the child.
4. No one wants a child to be born on the other side of the world as a penniless orphan, or to leave a mess to be cleaned up by the late parents' families.
5. Eventually, someone will allege that the lawyer who was retained failed in the duty of care—and sue. Make sure you put in steps to ensure that person is not you.
6. Ensure your retainer agreements are clear as to what you will do and what you won't.

8. *Id.* at 159–60.

Chapter 16

Gamete Donors Come in One of Three Forms

Gamete donors come in one of three forms: known, open identity (e.g., after the child turns 18), or anonymous.

There are those, such as John Pascoe, former Chief Justice of the Family Court of Australia, who maintain that it is everyone's right to know where they have come from.

Intended parents must determine at the commencement of their journey what type of donor they are going to have. In some countries, for example Spain, Mexico, Colombia, and Ukraine, gamete donors are anonymous. The implications for the child can be that the child never knows who the donor was. There are few more painful experiences than listening to donor-conceived adults describe the pain they feel every day because their parents decided to have them and they do not know where they came from. They are unable to find their genetic origins.

Intended parents need to be aware that if they choose an anonymous donor (whether by design or by default) the risk is theirs, potentially for the rest of their lives. Their offspring may not want to know or may be apathetic about their origins, but if their child does want to know where he or she has come from and learns that the parents had the option of making a choice, but chose otherwise, then the pain may well be visited upon them.

The United States has had a default model with donation being from anonymous donors, but, increasingly, donors have been either known or open identity. Those in Canada, Australia, and the United Kingdom, for example, are either known or open identity.

A risk in having a known donor is that there is confusion between the parties about whether the donor is a parent or a donor—as seen in cases in Canada, South Africa, and Australia.

The trend to open-identity donation, as seen, for example, in Greece in 2022, has come about because of the demands of donor-conceived adults.

South Africa has anonymous gamete donation, but the practice of all the egg donor agencies in South Africa is that donors sign up with the prospect that one day they may be known to the child. The reason for that approach is because the South African Law Reform Commission in 2016 proposed laws along the lines of the Australian laws—namely, that once the child turns 18, the child will be able to find out where he or she came from.

In several European countries, such as Switzerland and Austria, and the Australian states of Victoria and South Australia, the anonymity of donors has been stripped back to the beginning of donation. Both Queensland and the Australian Capital Territory are considering taking similar steps.

True anonymity is dead. With three tools that are available to intended parents or indeed the child, it is clear that anonymity is over:

- Ancestry.com database
- 23andMe.com database
- Image scraping, such as Google reverse image search

Even if the gamete donor does not show up today, the issue is whether the donor shows up in say 20 years' or even 40 years' time. As seen in the massive explosion of data that many of us have posted on social media in the past 20 years, the idea that this data will remain hidden in 20 years' time seems fanciful.

It is a confronting experience for a lawyer when talking with someone who has been an anonymous donor whose identity has been established many years later by the donor-conceived adult—when the donor was all along promised anonymity.

Take a photo of an egg or sperm donor and put it through a Google reverse image search and almost certainly you will be able to find out who that person is.

Whether it is wise for the parents to do so is another matter. For them to discover who the donor is without the child having agency over that process at a time when the child is old enough to understand the implications, is another matter entirely. Nevertheless, those tools exist now and it is likely that the information on the databases will increase exponentially.

Where intended parents undertake their journey may determine whether the donor is anonymous or not. Similarly, the desires of the intended parents about whether the donor is anonymous or not will be influenced by where the journey is undertaken.

Take Away

1. Some jurisdictions mandate that anonymity is the norm.
2. In reality, anonymous donors are no longer anonymous.
3. Intended parents should consider the implications on their child of having an anonymous donor.
4. A local lawyer should be familiar with local laws concerning donation.

Chapter 17

Protecting the Surrogate

The number one risk for any surrogate, which everyone wants to avoid, is death. The good news is that, according to the United Nations, maternal mortality rates declined by 34 percent worldwide between 2010 and 2020.[1]

The world map[2] divides the world into five colors:

- Very low—fewer than 100 maternal deaths per 100,000 live births
- Low—100–299
- High—300–499
- Very high—500–999
- Extremely high—greater than 1,000

Most surrogacy destinations, including Latin America and Europe, are in the very low category. However, the very low category greatly varies in the maternal death rate. For example, Australia is rated at three deaths per 100,000 live births, New Zealand at seven, China at 28, the Russian Federation at 14, France at eight, the United Kingdom at ten, Germany at four, Canada at 11, Mexico at 59, the United States at 21, Brazil at 72, Argentina at 45, and Colombia at 75. Countries with low maternal mortality rates are located in South America—Bolivia at 161, Venezuela at 259, Guyana at 112—and many of the countries in South and Southeast Asia, such as India at 103, Vietnam at 124, and Indonesia at 173, and in the Sahel and South of Africa, such as Senegal at 261, Angola at 222, South Africa at 127, and Ethiopia at 267.

The high countries from 300–499 maternal deaths per 100,000 live births are all located in Africa, such as Mauritania at 464, Niger at 441, Zimbabwe at 357, and Madagascar at 392.

---

1. World Health Organization et al., Trends in Maternal Mortality: 2000 to 2020 (2023).

2. Which can be found at *Maternal Mortality*, UNICEF (Feb. 2023), https://data.unicef.org/topic/maternal-health/maternal-mortality/.

The very high band of countries, with the exception of Afghanistan at 620, are all in the Sahel, for example Kenya, a surrogacy destination, at 530, and the Democratic Republic of the Congo at 547.

The few extremely high countries are all located in Africa, being Nigeria, a surrogacy destination, at 1,047, Chad at 1,063, and South Sudan, the highest, at 1,223.

Even North Korea is a low country at 107.

What is the practice of assisted reproductive technology (ART) in that overseas clinic and that country? Is the practice to minimize risk by undertaking single embryo transfers, or are multiple embryo transfers the norm? If so, is it a double embryo transfer or even higher? I am aware from a UK colleague of a recent matter where a Uganda clinic had a four embryo transfer.

The Verona Principles in Principle 7 set out a protective checklist for surrogates:

> 7.1 Confidence in the integrity of the circumstances surrounding their surrogacy arrangement is of great importance to the child's rights. The surrogate mother should be in a position to make independent and informed decisions free from exploitation and coercion.
>
> 7.2 Free and informed decision making in all legal, social, financial and medical matters by the surrogate mother shall be supported pre surrogacy arrangements, throughout the pregnancy and post birth. Conditions shall be provided and ensured that enable the surrogate mother to exercise self-determination. Surrogacy should be permissible only when the surrogate mother inter alia:
>
> a. is legally an adult;
>
> b. has experienced as an adult, at least one prior birth which was not a surrogacy arrangement;
>
> c. is competent and has the cognitive ability to make decisions, give consent and exercise autonomy and self-determination.
>
> [Comment: While it is common practice for U.S. surrogacy agencies to require the surrogate to have previously given birth, this is not the requirement everywhere.
>
> Some years ago, I acted in such a case. A friend of a gay couple who wanted to be parents offered to be

their surrogate. She was aged 38, single, and a lesbian. She had never been pregnant.

I approached the case with trepidation. The motivation of the would-be surrogate was similar to that of egg or sperm donors. She never wanted to be a mother, but was keen for her friends to become parents—and to help them do so. She was especially keen that they were a gay couple and that she was a lesbian, so that together they would be making a rainbow baby.

My concerns were:

- As she had not experienced pregnancy before, that this journey might be other than she had expected (and potentially highly risky).
- She was single, so she did not have the support of a partner, which given the other elements increased potential risks for her.
- Her age. What if, on having this child, and discovering that something went wrong, that this was her only chance at parenthood, and she decides not to relinquish.

There was extremely thorough medical and psychological screening undertaken, with a regime of social and psychosocial supports for the surrogate during and after the journey.

Despite my trepidation, the journey was blissful, joyous, and uneventful. After the child was born, I called one of my clients on his cell phone. The surrogate answered! He was driving. She was accompanying him and the baby to the doctor for the child's injections. The surrogate had accomplished her dream to help her friends become parents, and to enable a rainbow baby to be born.]

Consent in legal matters

7.3 Consent to legal arrangements shall be free and independent, including:

a. informed and free from all forms of coercion and fraud;

b. all information provided shall be explained and provided in writing in her own language and presented in a way that she understands; and

c. the surrogate mother shall be allowed sufficient time to consider legal matters and discuss during independently conducted psycho-social assessments and counselling.

[Comment: Whilst it is common in jurisdictions that permit surrogacy, such as the United States, Canada, the United Kingdom, Australia, New Zealand, and South Africa, for the surrogate to have independent legal advice, that's not true of everywhere. In several surrogacy destinations, such as Ukraine, common practice is that the surrogate does not have independent legal advice. It is self-evident that a surrogate will be protected better if she has independent legal advice before entering into the surrogacy arrangement.]

Consent in medical matters

7.4 To support self-determination and autonomy, the informed medical consent procedure between the surrogate mother and medical professionals performing each medical procedure, should occur prior to each procedure and include, as a minimum:

a. effective access to independent medical advice and/or a second opinion;

b. informed consent for each procedure that is free from all forms of coercion and fraud;

c. the provision of information and education about the medical procedure, lifestyle restrictions and short and long-term risks, as well as possible complications in a language the surrogate mother understands and in a way that she understands;

d. the number of embryos implanted and donor information;

e. the right to maintain control over her own body including to refuse, restrict or request a medical procedure;

f. the right to decide on birth conditions including labour, delivery and persons to be present; and

g. information on post-birth implications related to the surrogate mother's future health and on subsequent births.

7.5 In addition to paragraphs 7.3 and 7.4, the consequences of the consent and arrangements with the agency or clinic facilitating the procedure if their operation is permitted in national law should be clearly set out with respect to:

a. financial arrangements;
b. selection of intending parent(s) by the surrogate mother with the opportunity to meet intending parents and any other children in the family to inform her decision;
c. each medical procedure and pregnancy and birthing arrangements; and
d. transfer of legal parentage and/or parental responsibility.[3]

Bollywood Actresses

It really is no surprise that India has legislated to tightly control surrogacy, not only from foreigners but within India. At the height of the Indian surrogacy boom, an Indian promotor of surrogacy when asked by me as to how many of their surrogates had C-sections, said: "*80 percent.*" That number could not accord with good medical care and informed consent, but would appear to accord with the needs of clients.

If you have a part to play as to whether a surrogate is giving birth, it is a basic requirement to ensure that she goes to the best possible hospital that she can. What is the quality of that hospital? I have seen it debated many times by U.S. lawyers to ensure that the hospital in which the U.S. surrogate gives birth is of a certain standard. Intended parents who go overseas have no idea as to what is the standard of the maternity hospital. Aside from maternal mortality rates, is the hospital welcoming for surrogacy? Will the surrogate be treated with respect and with care?

Principle 8 of the Verona Principles provides:

3. International Social Service, Principles for the Protection of the Rights of the Child Born through Surrogacy (2021) [hereinafter Verona Principles], https://bettercarenetwork.org/sites/default/files/2021-03/VeronaPrinciples_25February2021.pdf.

8.1 Confidence in the integrity of the circumstances surrounding their surrogacy arrangement is of great importance to the child's rights. Intending parent(s) should be in a position to make independent and informed decisions free from exploitation and coercion.

8.2 Free and informed consent in all legal, medical, social and financial matters shall be sought from the intending parent(s) prior to any surrogacy arrangements and following all screening and preparatory processes. Such consent should be recorded in writing and preserved. Surrogacy should be permissible only when the intending parent(s) inter alia:

a. have been screened and assessed;
b. understand the psychosocial issues that impact on a child born to surrogacy and all parties involved;
c. are at an age to parent a child to independent adulthood;
d. has/have provided consent in the required legal form, and expressed or evidenced in writing in their own language, free from all forms of coercion and fraud;
e. have agreed to responsibilities identified in these principles including nominating guardians, providing medical insurance and financial support, especially when unforeseen circumstances arise.

8.3 Intending parents and the child should have appropriate opportunities to know the surrogate mother, her immediate family and community for the benefit of the child.[4]

It is common in countries where surrogacy regularly occurs but is underground, such as China, for the intended parents not to ever meet or know the surrogate.

Principle 9 provides:

9.1 Confidence in the integrity of the circumstances surrounding their surrogacy arrangement is of great importance to the child's rights. Donors should be in a

4. *Id.*

position to make independent and informed decisions free from exploitation and coercion.

9.2 In States where human reproductive material is used for surrogacy, transparent and comprehensive information should be provided to the donor including on medical complications, intended use of material, retention and accessibility of identifying information, to ensure pre- and post-surrogacy protections have been respected and that there is informed consent.

9.3 Free and informed consent and agreement in all legal, financial and medical matters shall be sought from the donor. Such consent should be recorded in writing in the donor's own language and preserved. Donations intended for surrogacy should be permissible only when the donor inter alia:

a. is an adult;
b. is competent and has cognitive ability to make decisions;
c. has provided written and signed agreement in accordance with applicable national law, together with certification that they have understood that agreement;
d. has effective access to independent legal and medical advice;
e. has received independent counselling from a qualified practitioner with respect to the future impact of the surrogacy arrangement such as:
    i. importance of limiting the number of donation(s);
    ii. disclosure of identifying information; and
    iii. any potential relationships that may result.[5]

Principle 10 provides:

10.1 States recognise the primary responsibility of parents for the upbringing and development of the child, and therefore have the obligation to provide appropriate assistance to parents in regard to these responsibilities. The best interests of the child will be the parents' basic concern.

5. *Id.*

10.2 States that permit surrogacy may have different rules regarding legal parentage and parental responsibility including related to:

a. the establishment of legal parentage at birth, by operation of law, bearing in mind that in the vast majority of States, a surrogate mother has legal parentage at birth;

b. transfer of legal parentage;

c. requirements about genetic relations, if any, to the child with either the surrogate mother and/or intending parent(s).

10.3 States that do not permit but nevertheless encounter surrogacy should ensure that there is a legal framework governing parentage and parental responsibility applicable to children born through surrogacy. This framework shall ensure that the child has legal parent(s) at birth.

Determination of legal parentage at birth, by operation of law

10.4 Where the surrogate mother is a legal parent by operation of law at birth, a court or other competent authority should determine the post-birth wishes of the surrogate mother after an appropriate reflection period. If the surrogate mother wishes to:

a. relinquish and/or transfer legal parentage and parental responsibility, an expeditious post-birth legal and safe mechanism should be available.

b. retain legal parentage and/or parental responsibility, then a court or other competent authority should expeditiously conduct a post-birth best interests of the child determination.

10.5 Where the surrogate mother is not a legal parent by operation of law at birth, an expeditious procedure that comes into effect after an appropriate reflection period, should be provided by which the surrogate mother post birth:

a. has access to a suitably qualified neutral third party as part of informed consent procedures;

b. freely confirms or revokes her consent that the intending parent(s) have exclusive legal parentage;

c. provides her consent without any financial consequences as to either payments or reimbursements related to the surrogacy arrangement.

10.6 States may provide intending parent(s) with exclusive legal parentage and parental responsibility by operation of law at birth only if the following two conditions are met:

a. the surrogate mother confirms consent post-birth (see para 10.5 above)

b. a post-birth best interests of the child determination is not required under these Principles (see paras 10.8, 10.9 & 10.10 below).

Transfer of legal parentage

10.7 A court or other competent authority of the State of birth shall, at a minimum, expeditiously conduct a post-birth best interests of the child determination in proceedings concerning legal parentage and/or parental responsibility or where child protection measures are being considered in domestic and international surrogacy arrangements where:

a. there have not been adequate pre-surrogacy arrangements; or

b. there is a conflict between the surrogate mother and intending parents(s) or between the intending parents after birth in regard to legal parentage or parental responsibility; or

c. there are unforeseen developments, particularly where neither the surrogate mother nor intending parents are able or willing to care for the child, or information has subsequently come to light that may affect the child's well-being, such as indications of sale, exploitation and trafficking or other illicit activity.

10.8 In international surrogacy arrangements where there is at least one State that does not permit the specific arrangement, a best interests of the child determination should be conducted additionally by a court or any other competent authority of the State where the intending parent(s) intend to reside with the child.

10.9 If the surrogate mother either revokes consent or fails to confirm consent, then a court or other competent authority should conduct a best interests of the child determination with particular attention to a psycho-social assessment of both parties.

10.10 States shall prohibit, as constituting the sale of children, any termination or transfer of legal parentage and/or parental responsibility, or promise to terminate or transfer legal parentage and/or parental responsibility, in exchange for remuneration or any other consideration.

Parental responsibility

10.11 Courts and competent authorities should provide such interim orders as to parental responsibility as are necessary, including for the period immediately after birth.

10.12 Neither a surrogate mother nor intending parent(s) should be forced to maintain parental responsibility, for forced parenting is generally contrary to the best interests of a child. States may however require intending parent(s) to:

a. have some degree of financial responsibility even in the absence of legal parentage or other exercise of parental responsibility;

b. provide advance provision for the surrogacy arrangement and/or maintenance of the child for a reasonable period, especially in international surrogacy arrangements where there is often a large disparity between the economic situation of the parties.

10.13 Courts and competent authorities may use alternative dispute resolution procedures designed to assist the parties in resolving their conflicts. By this or other means, courts and other competent authorities should seek to avoid destructive ongoing conflicts that could be harmful to the child and should seek to maximize opportunities for positive ongoing relationships important to the child's identity.[6]

6. *Id.*

Principle 10 follows the thinking of the former United Nations Special Rapporteur[7] that the surrogate is at all times the mother and that she can only relinquish parentage after the child is born. The idea of a mechanism such as a contract (e.g., Iran), pre-conception orders (e.g., Greece, Israel, and South Africa), pre-birth orders (e.g., in much of the United States), or operation of law (e.g., Buenos Aires, Ukraine, and Kazakhstan) that means upon the birth of the child that the intended parents are the parents, seem to have escaped the drafters.

Principle 10 talks of parental responsibility, not parental rights, or custody and guardianship. The language is taken in part from the United Nations Convention on the Rights of the Child, but also from the 1996 Hague Child Protection Convention. See Chapter 1.

Principle 11 provides:

> 11.1 Every child should be able to enjoy and exercise their right to preserve their identity (nationality, name and family relations) with appropriate assistance and protection. The child's ability to preserve their identity, including their genetic, gestational and social origins, has an on-going, lifetime impact on the child and future generations, in particular from the perspective of the child's right to identity, health and cultural rights.
>
> 11.2 States have a duty to ensure that every child born through surrogacy has the opportunity to access information concerning their identity, including genetic, gestational and social origins. This should include access to information as an adult. States should assist in this process.
>
> 11.3 Surrogacy arrangements should only involve surrogate mothers who provide verified and accurate identifying information about themselves, and who agree that their identifying information may be transmitted to persons to whom they gave birth.
>
> 11.4 Human reproductive material in surrogacy should only be used from persons who provide verified and

7. *Report of the Special Rapporteur on the Sale and Sexual Exploitation of Children, Including Child Prostitution, Child Pornography, and Other Child Sexual Abuse Material*, U.N. Doc. A/HRC/37/60 (Jan. 15, 2018). *See Surrogacy*, UNITED NATIONS, https://www.ohchr.org/en/special-procedures/sr-sale-of-children/surrogacy (last visited Apr. 30, 2024).

accurate identifying information about themselves, and who agree that their identifying information may be transmitted to persons with whom they have a genetic connection.

11.5 In instances where children are born through surrogacy, open surrogacy arrangements should be encouraged, in order to provide a safeguard for protection of identity rights and access to origins. States should therefore encourage education about the benefits of post birth contact between the child born through surrogacy, surrogate mother, intending parent(s) and extended family, persons providing reproductive material where such opportunities exist.

11.6 States should ensure rigorous collection and storage to preserve in perpetuity identity information relating to all surrogacy arrangements. States should clarify under what conditions identity information will be stored and kept up-to-date, who can access this information, and when and how this information can be accessed. This should include preservation of data when changes occur, such as when intermediaries close down.

11.7 States that permit surrogacy should establish and maintain registers and national records containing information about the genetic and gestational origins of children born through surrogacy, to which children can seek access, in accordance with the age and maturity of the child and subject to conditions set out in national legislation. States should appropriately train persons collecting, storing and facilitating identity information in the context of surrogacy.

11.8 Consistent with the best interests of the child, intending parent(s) undertaking surrogacy should ensure, from the earliest opportunity, the collection and preservation of all available information relevant to the child's identity, including all aspects of their origins.[8]

Some jurisdictions maintain a State-operated central registry (e.g., New South Wales), where a child born through donation or surrogacy

8. Verona Principles, *supra* note 3.

or both, will as an adult be able to find out the identity of any gamete or embryo donors, and of their surrogate.

Principle 12 provides:

> 12.1 Irrespective of the circumstances of their birth, a child's birth should be expeditiously notified to, and registered by, the appropriate competent authority in the State of birth. Every child "shall be registered immediately after birth" and such registration should be without any discrimination related to the circumstances of birth.
>
> 12.2 States must register the birth of all children born on their territory, including those born to a foreign parent or if the parents are unknown.
>
> 12.3 The notification and registration of the birth should be as complete as possible including in States which permit surrogacy arrangements or [States of destination] which subsequently register the child in their national registries. Identifying information should include date and place of birth, the surrogate mother, intending parent(s) and information relating to persons providing human reproductive material if any. Medical clinics, providers and/or registries of human reproductive material should make all identifying information available to national registries.
>
> 12.4 States should ensure that there is a national register that records identifying information. States should devise a procedural framework to ensure that such identifying information is recorded and preserved in accordance with applicable data protection law. States may also consider establishing a separate registry for children born through surrogacy.
>
> 12.5 Certification of the birth should be issued for all children born through surrogacy. This should not lead to any discrimination for reasons of the child's birth or other status. The certification of a birth is closely linked to the fulfilment of many other rights, inter alia, to a name, nationality and identity, the enjoyment of the highest attainable standard of health and education.
>
> 12.6 The right to privacy of children born through surrogacy is important. In many States, a birth certificate must be presented to register for official services in

order to fully access their rights to education, health and economic, social and cultural rights. In addition to a birth certificate, States may consider providing a supplementary document with identifying information to the child born through surrogacy.

12.7 Birth records should be updated upon a subsequent change of legal parentage while preserving the original records and the history of those changes.

12.8 All persons should be able to access their own birth records. States should ensure that a child born through surrogacy or their representative has access to such information, under appropriate guidance and counselling in accordance with his or her age and maturity.

12.9 Information on the child, intending parent(s), surrogate mother or any person providing human reproductive material should only be disclosed to competent authorities and other persons with legitimate interest(s) in accordance with applicable data protection law.

12.10 Registers of providers of human reproductive material and other relevant registries shall preserve such information and complement the use of birth notification, registration and certification.[9]

Principle 13 provides:

13.1 Irrespective of the circumstances of their birth, all children have a right to a nationality. The right to acquire a nationality requires States to prevent statelessness of children as part of the right to identity.

13.2 A State's application of nationality law should be without any discrimination related to circumstances of birth, including surrogacy. The policy of States regarding the nationality of a child born through surrogacy should be guided by the overriding importance of avoiding a situation in which a child is stateless.

13.3 States shall act in an expeditious manner when determining nationality.

13.4 With a view to reducing the risk of statelessness of children born through surrogacy arrangements and facilitating their access to a nationality:

9. *Id.*

a. If legal parentage is established or recognised by a State, that State should apply its provisions on the acquisition of nationality under the same conditions as any other child born to that legal parent. Where this is not possible, the State(s) of nationality of an intending parent(s) is encouraged to provide the necessary assistance to ensure the child obtains such nationality; failing which,
b. States should grant their nationality at birth to a child born on its territory in cases where the parents are unknown or do not have that State's nationality, and the child would otherwise be stateless; failing which,
c. States of which the surrogate mother is a national should grant their nationality if the child would otherwise be stateless; failing which,
d. Other States connected to the surrogacy arrangement should consider the discretionary grant of nationality if the child would otherwise be stateless.

13.5 The granting of nationality for the child does not automatically imply the recognition of legal parentage between the child and intending parent(s).

13.6 If the law of a State entails a loss of nationality as a consequence of any change in legal parentage, such loss should be conditional upon possession or acquisition of another nationality.

13.7 States should provide that revocation or annulment of legal parentage will not cause the permanent loss of the nationality acquired by the child, if the child is habitually resident on their territory for a specific period of time.

13.8 States should take measures, where necessary and appropriate, to grant without delay a visa and/or discretionary status to the child to remain in and/or travel from the State of birth pending any determination of legal parentage and/or nationality, in the best interests of the child.

13.9 States should devise a procedural framework during the determination of nationality and train relevant professionals including immigration officials and border guards in the application of this principle.[10]

Principle 14 provides:

14.1 States shall prohibit surrogacy arrangements that constitute or promote the sale of or traffic in children as defined by international law, including the [Convention on the Rights of the Child (CRC)] and the [Optional Protocol on the Sale of Children, Child Prostitution, and Child Pornography (OPSC)]. States should create safeguards to prevent the sale of children in the context of surrogacy.

14.2 Sale of children includes "any act or transaction whereby a child is transferred by any person or group of persons to another for remuneration or any other consideration." Sale therefore occurs in a surrogacy context when these three elements concur:

a. transfer ("a child is transferred by any person or group of persons");

b. payment ("remuneration or any other consideration"); and

c. exchange ("for"—payment for transfer).

14.3 Transfer exists in all completed surrogacy arrangements, because such includes physical and/or legal handover of the child. If for any reason, the surrogate mother is not considered a legal parent at birth, handover of the child by the surrogate mother still constitutes a transfer.

14.4 Commercial surrogacy by definition includes payment, and therefore meets at least two of the three elements of sale of a child: payment and transfer. Commercial surrogacy constitutes the illicit sale of children where such payment is made "for" (in exchange for) transfer. In commercial surrogacy, payment is made as a minimum for gestational services; the question is whether payment includes payment for transfer.

14.5 One approach to commercial surrogacy views payment for gestational services and payment for transfer as an inseparable whole envisioned from the

10. *Id.*

beginning and hence views all commercial surrogacy as constituting, or unduly risking, the sale of a child. States that view commercial surrogacy as constituting or unduly risking the sale of children should prohibit commercial surrogacy.

14.6 Another approach to commercial surrogacy views it as possible, under certain circumstances, to separate payment for gestational services from payment for transfer, in which case there is no payment for transfer and hence no sale of a child.

14.7 Accordingly, States that permit commercial surrogacy shall ensure, at a minimum, that all payments are separate from the determination or transfer of legal parentage and parental responsibility. Measures should include that:

a. the surrogate mother at birth retains the right to decide whether or not to consent to transfer of legal parentage and parental responsibility;
b. any remuneration or any other consideration provided to the surrogate mother (or anyone on her behalf) be made in advance of any post birth transfer of legal parentage and parental responsibility to the intending parent(s) or post-birth confirmation of the surrogate mother's consent, and be non-refundable (absent fraud);
c. all payments and reimbursements are reported and properly regulated by law; and
d. intermediaries are properly regulated by law.

14.8 Surrogacy purporting to be altruistic and non-commercial may nonetheless result or unduly risk the sale of children when:

a. there is a provision of unregulated, excessive or lump sum "reimbursements" or consideration in any other form; or
b. there are reimbursement categories like "pain and suffering," which can be similar to payment in commercial surrogacy; or
c. reimbursement occurs which cannot be separated completely from the establishment or transfer of legal parentage and/or parental responsibility. (See para. 7).

14.9 Sale of children occurs where legal parentage is assigned or transferred based primarily on contractual provisions (see Principle on legal parentage). Written agreements describing the intentions of the parties as to legal parentage and/or parental responsibility do not violate the prohibition of sale of children, as long as they are understood to be non-binding.

14.10 Sale of the child may occur if "remuneration or any other consideration" is promised or paid to obtain exclusive legal parentage and parental responsibility for intending parent(s).

14.11 Activities of intermediaries can constitute or lead to the sale of the child:

a. due to the intermediaries' creation and control of commercial surrogacy markets and networks;

b. if the intermediaries exercise such control over the surrogate mother and/or child as to be responsible for transferring the child for remuneration or any other consideration.

c. intermediaries and other professionals involved in surrogacy arrangements receive remuneration for services rendered which are excessive, according to the standards of comparable work in the same profession where the work is performed.

14.12 States shall likewise prohibit surrogacy arrangements that constitute or promote the trafficking and/or exploitation as defined by international law, including the CRC, Palermo Protocol and [Association of Southeast Asian Nations (ASEAN)] Convention Against Trafficking in Persons, especially women and children. States should create safeguards to prevent the trafficking and/or exploitation in the context of surrogacy.

14.13 States generally should prohibit commercial surrogacy where it is not possible to reliably separate payment for gestational services from illicit payment for transfer of the child including, but not limited to, where:

a. there may be unregulated exchanges of payments for children;

b. the surrogate mother is a genetic parent of the child;

c. payment is only made if/when child is transferred to intending parent(s);
d. the intending parents for the child were not identified prior to pregnancy;
e. there may be unregulated or under-regulated intermediaries;
f. the legal system does not accord the surrogate mother the right, after birth, to either provide consent or revoke consent to the transfer of legal parentage and parental responsibility to the intending parent(s).[11]

The thinking remains that compensating surrogates is wrong, and amounts to the sale of children. Based on that thinking, it would seem that judges in the United States and other countries have been complicit (when making orders either pre-birth or post-birth establishing the intended parents' parentage in such cases) in the sale of children. The principles seem to defy the reality that surrogacy often works well when the surrogate is compensated, when there is a solid human rights framework, and with judicial oversight, if needed.

After all, knowing that there is a risk of death or injury in helping someone else achieve their dream of parentage, who would volunteer to be a surrogate, unless they have a particular connection with the intended parents, such as friend or family or an affinity with the concept of surrogacy, such as being a midwife, or unless they are compensated in some way?

Principle 15 provides:

15.1 States shall take all appropriate measures to prevent improper financial or other gain in connection with surrogacy.

15.2 States that permit surrogacy should require transparency and accountability in any financial transaction, relating to surrogacy by, inter alia:

a. requiring the keeping of written accounts which clearly identify each fee and cost incurred for each different service, ideally outlined in a standard list of services to be covered, connected with each surrogacy arrangement;
b. requiring that such written accounts be made available to the court or other competent authority

11. *Id.*

for purposes of monitoring individual surrogacy arrangements as well as for the purpose of oversight of persons, intermediaries and others involved in surrogacy arrangements.

15.3 Intermediaries and other service providers should not receive remuneration which is unreasonably high in relation to services rendered, according to the standards of comparable work done where the work is performed.[12]

Principle 16 provides:

16.1 The actions of intermediaries in surrogacy arrangements may impact the rights of the child born through surrogacy. Regulation of intermediaries is therefore of prime importance.

16.2 In States where surrogacy is permitted, all intermediaries should be subject to authorisation and regulation by a designated competent authority. A designated competent authority also should ensure regular monitoring and evaluation of ongoing compliance on the part of intermediaries with appropriate regulatory standards. Criteria for authorization and ongoing compliance should cover, inter alia:

a. financial and administrative probity;
b. relevant competencies;
c. legality of contractual arrangements; and
d. ethical standards of overall operations.

16.3 States should prohibit the surrogacy-related operations of intermediaries who fail to comply with regulatory standards or fail to cooperate with regular monitoring and evaluation of ongoing compliance.

16.4 States encountering surrogacy should monitor the activities of intermediaries acting within their jurisdiction and offering services prohibited in their State. If such States do not have specific surrogacy laws, including related to intermediaries, States should consider legislation to prohibit intermediary activities due to potential risks, including the sale of children.

12. *Id.*

16.5 Intermediaries should uphold these Principles as applicable to their activities. Intermediaries should not offer or advertise services where such services are prohibited by law.

16.6 Intermediaries should be required and appropriately trained to collect, store, and facilitate identity information in the context of surrogacy in order to uphold the child's right to identity and access to origins. Identifying information shall be handled in accordance with applicable data protection law.

16.7 Intermediaries and other service providers involved in surrogacy arrangements should not receive remuneration which is unreasonably high in relation to services rendered, according to the standards of comparable work where the work is performed.

16.8 Where an intermediary is not authorized to provide surrogacy services in the country where it is operating and/or is involved in the sale or trafficking of a child, appropriate sanctions and liability should be imposed on the intermediary.[13]

It is always a challenge when being asked by a client about ethical surrogacy agencies overseas. We can either decline to advise (which might be an abrogation of our duties) or advise, but with the usual caveats that agencies are not licensed, and for the client to undertake due diligence. One must always be concerned as to sharks in the water. See Chapter 18.

There is an assumption in this principle that all surrogacy agencies must be State-licensed. I am not aware of any that are State-licensed in any country, except in an incidental way. Some U.S. surrogacy agencies, for example, are licensed incidentally but not directly, because of who controls or owns them. Although anyone it seems can own a surrogacy agency, if the agency is owned by a lawyer, a nurse, or a doctor, for example, then that lawyer, nurse, or doctor may have certain ethical or statutory requirements about how they conduct themselves, which then has an incidental effect as to the operation of the agency.

As has been seen in the United States, when an agency owner has engaged in stealing clients' funds or trafficking surrogates or children (or both), that owner is prosecuted, and if found guilty, imprisoned. Those

13. *Id.*

actions in and of themselves are a strong incentive for other owners to act ethically. See Chapter 18.

The principles assume that it is just for the State to regulate, ignoring the benefits of civil society actions. In the United States, for example, those actions have included those of the Society for Ethics in Egg Donation and Surrogacy (SEEDS), the American Bar Association Model Act Governing Assisted Reproductive Technology (2008), and the Academy of Adoption and Assisted Reproduction Attorneys. See Chapter 9.

Principle 17 provides:

> 17.1 States that permit surrogacy and/or encountering surrogacy should ensure that child protection systems are able to respond to sudden unexpected developments, such as situations where:
>
> a. there is a conflict with respect to child-care arrangements;
>
> b. neither a surrogate mother nor an intending parent(s) are able or willing to care for the child;
>
> c. illicit practices are revealed that are linked to a surrogacy arrangement;
>
> d. situations of emergency; and
>
> e. changes in social, political and legal conditions
>
> 17.2 In the event of an unexpected development and consequent increased vulnerability of the child born through surrogacy, States should act expeditiously to:
>
> a. ensure that the competent authority in the State where the child is present is notified immediately;
>
> b. activate immediate measures to provide suitable care to ensure physical, emotional and psychological well-being of the child;
>
> c. encourage the use of mediation services in circumstances where there is disagreement with respect to legal parentage and/or parental responsibility. Where there is no agreement, the court or other competent authority should consider providing appropriate orders;
>
> d. ensure that psycho-social reports are prepared to assist with best interest determination;
>
> e. if neither the surrogate mother nor the intending parent(s) is able or willing to parent the child, competent authorities should make guardianship

orders and/or other care arrangements relating to the child consistent with the UN Guidelines for the Alternative Care of Children. Opportunities for appropriate kinship care should be considered before envisaging placements in other suitable care settings, and siblings born of the surrogacy arrangement should be placed together. Placement in residential care facilities should be avoided.

f. When the child's sole or main carer may be the subject of deprivation of liberty as a result of preventive detention or sentencing decisions, non-custodial remand measures and sentences should be taken in appropriate cases wherever possible, the best interests of the child being given due consideration.

g. keep records of all decisions made in relation to the child, and ensure these are available to the child.

17.3 When illicit practices are linked to surrogacy arrangements (see Principles on best interest and on prevention and prohibition of sale of children and trafficking):

a. the child's best interests should be the paramount consideration in determining legal parentage and/or parental responsibility and if there is evidence of involvement by any party in illicit practice(s) such involvement, including its possible long-term consequences, should be taken into account;

b. sanctions should primarily be focused on intermediaries involved and authorisation, if any, should be withdrawn for improper conduct.

17.4 Regardless of legal parentage and/or nationality, States may determine that intending parent(s) are responsible for child maintenance, welfare and health.

17.5 States should have policies which allow for timely decision-making in relation to the child's best interests, and ensure that child protection systems are implemented expeditiously.[14]

14. *Id.*

Rome and Casablanca

In April 2024, the Pope called for all surrogacy to be banned, finding it "deplorable," as it was exploitative of the surrogate and child:

> The Church also takes a stand against the practice of surrogacy, through which the immensely worthy child becomes a mere object. On this point, Pope Francis's words have a singular clarity: "The path to peace calls for respect for life, for every human life, starting with the life of the unborn child in the mother's womb, which cannot be suppressed or turned into an object of trafficking. In this regard, I deem deplorable the practice of so-called surrogate motherhood, which represents a grave violation of the dignity of the woman and the child, based on the exploitation of situations of the mother's material needs. A child is always a gift and never the basis of a commercial contract. Consequently, I express my hope for an effort by the international community to prohibit this practice universally."
>
> First and foremost, the practice of surrogacy violates the dignity of the child. Indeed, every child possesses an intangible dignity that is clearly expressed—albeit in a unique and differentiated way—at every stage of his or her life: from the moment of conception, at birth, growing up as a boy or girl, and becoming an adult. Because of this unalienable dignity, the child has the right to have a fully human (and not artificially induced) origin and to receive the gift of a life that manifests both the dignity of the giver and that of the receiver. Moreover, acknowledging the dignity of the human person also entails recognizing every dimension of the dignity of the conjugal union and of human procreation. Considering this, the legitimate desire to have a child cannot be transformed into a "right to a child" that fails to respect the dignity of that child as the recipient of the gift of life.
>
> Surrogacy also violates the dignity of the woman, whether she is coerced into it or chooses to subject herself to it freely. For, in this practice, the woman is detached from the child growing in her and becomes a mere means subservient to the arbitrary gain or desire of others. This contrasts in every way with the fundamental dignity of every human being and with each person's right to be recognized always individually and never as an instrument for another.[15]

15. Declaration of the Dicastery for the Doctrine of the Faith "Dignitas Infinita" on Human Dignity 42, 48–50 (Apr. 8, 2024) (citations omitted), https://press.vatican.va/content/salastampa/en/bollettino/pubblico/2024/04/08/240408c.html.

In March 2024, the Papal Nuncio to the United Nations hosted an anti-surrogacy event in New York City[16] entitled "Too High a Cost: End Surrogacy Now—Preventing the Exploitation and Commodification of Women and Children."

The Pope's statement occurred two days after an anti-surrogacy meeting at a Vatican-aligned university in Rome, with the Holy See's participation, calling for the abolition of surrogacy:

> Convinced that "the contract by which one or more principals agree with a woman to carry a child or children for them for delivery at birth, regardless of its designation and terms," the participants called on States, through this text, to condemn surrogacy "in all its forms and under all its forms, whether paid or not, and to adopt measures to combat this practice."[17]

The statement echoed the 2023 Casablanca Declaration for the Universal Abolition of Surrogacy, made by a group of self-appointed experts calling for surrogacy to be banned. The declaration states:

> We, signatories of this Declaration,
>
> **Aware of**
>
> - the suffering of the people who may not conceive
> - the attractiveness of the reproductive technologies
> - and of the international issue of an efficient protection for human dignity
>
> **Convinced** that the contract through which one or several orderers agree with a woman that she will carry one or several children for the purpose of their delivery upon birth, regardless to the name and terms and conditions of such contract, here below called surrogacy,
>
> - violates human dignity
> - and contributes to the commodification of women and children
>
> **Require** from the States the prohibition of surrogacy in every modalities and kinds, whether remunerated or not, and the implementation of measures to fight such practice.

16. Too High a Cost: End Surrogacy Now—Preventing the Exploitation and Commodification of Women and Children (Mar. 20, 2024), http://webtv.un.org/en/asset/k15/k15dezq9ig.

17. Olivier Bonnel, *International Conference in Rome Demands Abolition of Surrogacy*, Vatican News (Apr. 5, 2024), https://www.vaticannews.va/en/world/news/2024-04/international-conference-in-rome-demands-abolition-of-surrogacy.html.

For this purpose, we make the following recommendations to the States:

- Prohibit surrogacy on their territory
- Deny any legal validity to contracts bearing the undertaking from a woman to carry and deliver a child
- Punish individuals and corporations acting as intermediaries between the surrogacy mothers and the orderers
- Prosecute individuals who have recourse to a surrogate mother on their territory
- Prosecute their nationals who have recourse to a surrogate mother outside their territory
- Act in favor of the implementation of a legal instrument bearing global prohibition of the surrogacy.

Attached to this Declaration, is a proposal for an international Convention, freely available to the States wishing to commit themselves in such process.[18]

The proposed convention states:

The signatory States to this Convention,

Aware of

- The suffering of the people who may not conceive
- The attractiveness of the reproductive technologies
- And of the international issue of an efficient protection for human dignity

Convinced that the contract through which one or several orderers agree with a woman that she will carry one or several children for their delivery upon birth, whatever name and terms and conditions of such contract, here below called surrogacy,

- Violates human dignity
- And contributes to the commodification of women and children

Denounce surrogacy in any modalities and kinds, whether remunerated or not.

Undertake to fight against such practice to protect and preserve human dignity and women's and children's rights, through the implementation of effective measures, including by:

- Prohibiting surrogacy on their territory

18. Declaration of Casablanca 2023 for the Universal Abolition of Surrogacy (Mar. 3, 2023), https://declaration-surrogacy-casablanca.org/wp-content/uploads/2023/03/Declaration-of-Casablanca.pdf.

- Denying any legal validity to contracts bearing the undertaking from a woman to carry and deliver a child
- Punishing individuals and corporations acting as intermediaries between the surrogacy mothers and the orderers
- Prosecuting individuals who have recourse to a surrogate mother on their territory
- Prosecuting their nationals who have recourse to a surrogate mother outside their territory.

No State has signed the convention. However, since the declaration was made, Italy has proposed a ban on international surrogacy for Italian citizens, with a bill that as of April 2024 had been passed by the House of Deputies but was still to be debated by the Senate. See Chapter 4.

In April 2024, following the Pope's statement, I was presenting in a webinar celebrating 40 years of egg donation, following the first child born via egg donation, which was in Australia in 1983. This comment was made by a Vatican functionary in the question and answer session:

> Embryos outside the uterus with all the complications that it entails is a nightmare like slavery was. It is in everyone's best interests that these practices disappear as soon as possible.[19]

Take Away

1. Surrogacy is not just a legal transaction. It is a fundamental human experience.
2. The person who is taking the biggest risk, including potentially with her life, is the surrogate.
3. All steps should be taken where possible to ensure that the surrogate is protected, and that she is able to enter into the surrogacy arrangement with informed consent.

19. 40 Years of Egg Donation and Counting: What Have We Learned? What Happens Next?, Progress Educational Trust event (Apr. 24, 2024), comment by Francisco José Ballesta, Faculty of Bioethics, Pontifical Athenaeum Regina Apostolorum, Rome.

Chapter 18

Always Be Aware of the Sharks in the Water

Food purity laws are a marvelous 19th century innovation. They mean that when we spend a small amount of money at the shop to buy milk, for example, we know that it's pure. Not everywhere has food purity laws, but most places do. We know that when we buy milk, it won't poison us. The production and sale of milk is highly regulated.

By contrast, surrogacy is often not regulated at all.[1] The assumption from a Western point of view is that in vitro fertilization (IVF) clinics will be highly regulated. It's assumed that the manner of regulation will be unique to that particular country. Other countries have no regulation whatsoever. It should never be assumed that IVF clinics have adequate regulation, let alone any regulation. The quality control of an IVF clinic might be excellent. The regulation of the IVF clinic might be excellent. But it should never be assumed.

Surrogacy often works hand in hand with IVF clinics. While traditional surrogacy has been with us since time immemorial, the growth of surrogacy internationally has worked in conjunction with the growth of IVF clinics. Sometimes there is quite significant regulation of IVF clinics and sometimes there is significant regulation or prohibition of surrogacy—and sometimes they are in sync. Sometimes they are not.

I want to give some examples of what I've described as sharks in the water. If you are referring your clients overseas or they have decided to go overseas for their fertility or surrogacy journey, do not assume that those who are treating your clients are honest and reasonable.

Those who are desperate to have children, what has been described as "baby lust," are happy at times to spend tens or hundreds of thousands of dollars on their journey to become parents. Inevitably there will be sharks in the water feeding on this desperation. While their focus won't

1. And yet the Verona Principles seek that agencies be regulated by the State. *See* Chapter 17.

just be on what are perceived as rich Westerners seeking to become parents, that target market is certainly worthwhile focusing on for those who want to make money.

I want to give some examples of this.

Lack of Regulation of IVF Clinics

Recently, an Australian clinic, at the direction of clients of mine, wanted to send their embryos to an African clinic. The African clinic apparently had great reviews and was seen as high quality.

As is common in developing countries, there was no legal framework in the particular African country regulating IVF clinics. Instead, the IVF clinic maintained on its website that it was a Member of the European Society of Human Reproduction and Embryology (ESHRE). ESHRE is one of the leading IVF groups in the world, focused on Europe, in parallel to the other big group, the American Society for Reproductive Medicine (ASRM).

The Australian clinic sought to have confirmation about the regulation and certification of compliance by the African clinic. Ultimately, it was determined that the African clinic had not been accredited by ESHRE for three years. Accordingly, the Australian clinic did not send the embryos to the African clinic.

Theresa Erickson

Theresa Erickson is an example of greed, international assisted reproductive technology (ART), and a country where there is effective action taken to protect human rights. Theresa Erickson was a prominent California, internationally renowned, ART attorney. She had her own firm. She also had a television show. She had referred clients to me. She certainly appeared to be all aboveboard. However, she was arrested by the Federal Bureau of Investigation (FBI). In 2011 Erickson pleaded guilty, admitting that she and her conspirators used numerous gestational carriers to create an inventory of unborn babies that they would sell for more than $100,000 each. They did this by sending women to become implanted with embryos, including in Ukraine. If the women who had now become gestational carriers sustained their pregnancies into the second trimester, the conspirators offered the babies to prospective parents by falsely representing that the unborn babies were the result of legitimate surrogacy arrangements that had fallen through because the original intended parents had backed out. They also drafted fraudulent "*assumption*" agreements for the intended parents to sign, which reinforced the lie that original intended parents had existed but had simply backed out.

Erickson admitted to lying to the California Supreme Court by fraudulently representing in court documents that these post-pregnancy agreements were legitimate surrogacy arrangements, which allowed her and her co-conspirators to make more than $400,000 in profit for the sale of parental rights. She admitted that she prepared and filed with the Superior Court of California, County of San Diego, declarations and pleadings that falsely represented that the unborn babies were the products of legitimate surrogacy arrangements—ones that involved agreements between intended parents and the gestational carriers entered into prior to the embryo being transferred. With these fraudulently obtained pre-birth orders, the intended parents' names were placed on the babies' birth certificates through surrogacy and the conspirators would be able to profit from their sale of parental rights.

Erickson and her co-conspirators risked the health of at least one surrogate in order to profit from a fraudulent surrogacy, instead of a legitimate adoption.

For example, in 2010 a gestational carrier who was living in a Midwest state that did not allow surrogacy received orders from her doctor to be on bed rest due to premature labor contractions. In response, Erickson told the woman:

> I really think that you need to get out to California as soon as possible in order to avert an adoption.[2]

Erickson was arrested by the FBI. She was sentenced to a $70,000 fine, five months' imprisonment, and nine months of home confinement. She was subject to three years of supervised release.

Co-conspirator Hilary Neiman, a Maryland attorney also specializing in ART, was sentenced to 12 months' imprisonment, with five months in prison and seven months of home confinement, a $20,000 fine and $133,000 in forfeiture, and three years of supervised release.

The third co-conspirator, Carla Chambers, was sentenced to five months' imprisonment, seven months of home confinement, $180,000 in forfeiture, and three years of supervised release.

---

2. Press Release, FBI San Diego Division, Prominent Surrogacy Attorney Sentenced to Prison for Her Role in Baby-Selling Case (Feb. 24, 2012), https://archives.fbi.gov/archives/sandiego/press-releases/2012/prominent-surrogacy-attorney-sentenced-to-prison-for-her-role-in-baby-selling-case.

Human error exists in IVF clinics in the United States and Western countries. However, when it comes to international ART, human error appears to be more common in IVF clinics that are unregulated or have minimal regulation. If the expectation under the law is that there is a genetic link between your client and the child in order to establish citizenship, then this can cause extraordinary problems for your client.

The expectation in Australia, for example, is that ordinarily if there is a country where an order for surrogacy is not made, the relevant officials look very carefully about whether or not there is a genetic link with the child. The expectation is in the unregulated countries that there must be a genetic link out of concerns as to child trafficking.

As examples of this problem, an Australian/Spanish couple underwent surrogacy in Thailand, when Thailand was extremely busy with surrogacy, before the *Baby Gammy* case/international baby farm (see "The Thai Baby Farm" section in this chapter) in 2014.

This couple provided their sperm with the intention of seeing who had better quality sperm. They were advised by the clinic that the better quality sperm was from the Australian man. They then authorized the clinic to only use the Australian man's sperm for the creation of embryos.

The child was born. The Australian man was named on the Thai birth certificate as the father.

A subsequent DNA test showed that the Australian man was not in fact the father. The Spanish man was. This caused enormous complications in obtaining Australian citizenship. Because of this complication, rather than immediately seeking Australian citizenship, and returning to live in Australia, the couple decided with the child to seek Spanish citizenship first and then while in Spain seek Australian citizenship. Spain was then in recession. The couple went through some considerable difficulties economically because of the recession and then having to wait several months in order to obtain Australian citizenship.

Australian citizenship was ultimately obtained, but after quite some deal of difficulty.

A gay couple went to India for surrogacy at a time when India was booming with international surrogacy. The couple were an Australian man and a man from another country. As it was their desire to obtain Australian citizenship, only the sperm of the Australian man was provided. The child was born. In compliance with Australian citizenship requirements, a DNA test was undertaken. The child was not the child of the Australian man. In essence, the clinic had used sperm from someone else. Who that person was remains unknown. Ultimately, Australian citizenship was able to be obtained, but there was a great delay in the couple being able to obtain Australian citizenship.

A gay couple underwent surrogacy in India, again during the surrogacy boom there. Their plan was to have twins. As part of the baby guarantee often given in developing countries, two or more embryos are commonly implanted.

They were excited to see that twins had been conceived. Both of the men were white skinned. When the twins were born, one was evidently white skinned. The other appeared to be an Indian baby. The Australian couple took the white child, but not the Indian child. The clinic's DNA test undertaken of the "*Indian*" child was that neither of the Australian couple was the genetic father of that child. The explanation by the Indian clinic was that the surrogate and her husband had sex during the pregnancy, which caused the conception of that child.

Commentary by fertility doctors, not from India, was that more likely there was a laboratory error and that an embryo belonging to an Indian couple had been used in error by the clinic.

The child went on to be cared for by the surrogate and her husband.

The Thai Baby Farm

At the same time as the Baby Gammy scandal, there was another scandal in Thailand: the first surrogate baby farm.

At least 13 children had been born via Cambodian and Thai surrogates in parallel journeys under the supervision of Thai IVF fertility specialist Dr. Pisit. All of them had been fathered by then 24-year-old Mitsutoki Shigeta, the son of a Japanese .com billionaire, who was single.

The fact that a young secretive and single man would want so many babies raised immediate concern by Thai authorities over his motives. Thai police began investigating Mr. Shigeta for possible human trafficking. The surrogacy agent he had first used, Georgia-based New Life, headed by Mariam Kukunashvili, stopped dealing with him when he told her how many children he planned to father. He wanted more than 1,000 babies and planned 10–20 surrogacies every year or more.

Mr. Shigeta's Thai lawyer explained that his client simply wanted a large family. Given his wealth, there would be no problem looking after the children properly.

Thai authorities had identified two other children born in Cambodia, and four in Japan already fathered by Mr. Shigeta. After three years, in 2017, a Thai court awarded Mr. Shigeta custody of the remaining 13 who had been living in a state children's home. He had not come back to Thailand to visit them—perhaps either fearing publicity or possible prosecution, but Thai officials said his mother had visited them every two days. The court ruled that as Mr. Shigeta was the biological father of the children and that there was no evidence of ill-intent or trafficking, nor of a criminal record, and that the surrogate mothers had made no claim to them, it could find no reason not to award him custody. It found that he had established bank accounts specifically for them in Singapore, had paid for helpers to assist in looking after them, and was preparing a home for them in Japan, along with schooling.

He had also bought a property in Thailand in which to look after the children during a planned transition period where they would get to know the nannies who would care for them in Japan. Thai officials visited Japan and said that they were reassured by the evident affection showed for him by his four children already living there. They would continue to monitor the 13 who expected to move to Japan in the near future.

Following the Baby Gammy scandal and the baby farm, Thai passed laws strictly limiting surrogacy to Thai couples and banning commercial surrogacy altogether with up to ten years' imprisonment. The business moved over the border to Cambodia for a while but in 2016, that country outlawed surrogacy, with the business largely moving to Laos, which also borders Thailand.

In the words of Mariam Kukunashvili:

> Ethically, we don't understand how one can share love, time and affection among 300 or 1,000 babies. Sometimes wealthy people with no parental experience assume that bringing up children just means hiring dozens of nannies, and paying bills.
>
> You cannot outsource parenthood entirely to nannies, as this can cause psychological problems in the children and adults.[3]

The Georgian Baby Farm

That lesson was evidently lost on Kristina Ozturk, 24, a former stripper originally from Moscow, who wanted 105 biological children. She met her hotel-owner husband Galip Ozturk, 57, while she was holidaying in Georgia. Between March 2020 and July 2021, they had spent €168,000 to surrogates. In 2020/2021 they had had 21 babies in Georgia via

3. Jonathan Head, *"Baby Factory" Mystery: Thailand's Surrogacy Saga Reaches Uneasy End*, BBC (Feb. 25, 2018), https://www.bbc.com/news/world-asia-43169974.

surrogacy. Mrs. Ozturk insisted that she was still a "*hands-on mother*" despite spending $96,000 every 12 months on 16 live-in nannies.

Mrs. Ozturk, who also lived with a six-year-old daughter, Vika, from a previous relationship, said:

> I'm with the kids all the time, doing all the things that mums normally do.[4]

The couple's nannies worked a rolling schedule of four days on, two days off, and all live in, with bedrooms near the youngsters and their own kitchen. When asked on her social media account if each nanny was "*assigned a particular child*," Mrs. Ozturk said:

> No, there are no bindings. During the day—of course, a specific one is responsible for a specific child. But during the week the nannies change.[5]

When asked if she was able to spend quality time with each of her many children, Mrs. Ozturk replied:

> Many times I've been asked how I have enough for each child, whether I devote time alone to each. Yes. We have a special bond with every child. I wish every parent to be able to spend all their time with their children, because this is the most important thing in life.[6]

Their babies as of October 2021 were Mustafa, 19 months; Mariam, 18 months; Ayran, 18 months; Alisa, 18 months; Hasan, 17 months; Judi, 17 months; Harper, 16 months; Teresa, 16 months; Huseyin, 16 months; Anna, 15 months; Isabella, 15 months; Ismal, 14 months; Mehmet, 14 months; Ahmet, 14 months; Ali, 13 months; Kristina, 13 months; Sara, 12 months; Lokman, 12 months; Galip, 11 months; Olivia, 9 months; and Judy, 3 months.

Mr. and Mrs. Ozturk's plans went awry in June 2022 when he was arrested following a police raid. Mr. Ozturk was detained on charges related to money laundering and falsifying documents.

---

4. Alexandra Feiam, *"I'm 26 and Already Have 22 Biological Kids—I Won't Stop Until I Reach 105,"* Kidspot (Oct. 27, 2023), https://www.kidspot.com.au/news/im-26-and-already-have-22-biological-kids-i-wont-stop-until-i-reach-105/news-story/6f3444f517fea553c24d35db07e69991.

5. *Id.*

6. *Id.*

Mr. Ozturk had fled to Georgia in 2018 after being sentenced to life imprisonment in relation to a 1996 murder in his home country of Türkiye. He had been convicted of ordering the murder of a man named Kuvvet Köseoğlu.

In February 2023, Mr. Ozturk was sentenced to eight years' imprisonment by a Georgian court on drug charges.

In March 2023, Mr. Ozturk announced that he was appealing the conviction and sentence.

After Russia had announced in June 2023 that it was banning foreigners from undertaking surrogacy in Russia, the Health Minister of Georgia announced that on January 1, 2024, Georgia would be legislating to then ban any foreigners undertaking surrogacy in Georgia.

The news from Georgia illustrates the point—that countries with poor human rights protections and lax laws and procedures concerning surrogacy result in lurches between anything goes to nothing happens, therefore being a case of the risk of here today, stuck tomorrow.

Countries that have previously had booming surrogacy industries and then screeched to a halt, seemingly overnight, with no surrogacy, or extremely limited access to surrogacy, have been:

- India: starting in 2012 and then further lurches by administrative process in 2014 and 2016 resulting in laws passed in 2021 greatly restricting surrogacy
- Nepal: 2016
- Thailand: 2014
- Cambodia: 2016
- Mexico: 2016
- Georgia: (with more notice) 2023

While the United States and other Western countries that allow surrogacy are not immune, if you have clients who wish to undertake surrogacy in developing or post-Soviet countries, you must warn them about:

- Quality of IVF
- The risk of being there today and stuck tomorrow

They need to know. They won't want to hear that information as they are often blinded by the possibility of now becoming parents for a price that they could afford (and ignore obvious red flags), and as it is sometimes called, they have baby fever, but nevertheless they need to know that while the surrogacy journey in that country may have worked for everyone else, for them to be stuck is a truly traumatizing and expensive process.

Rudy Rupak

I cannot ever claim to be an expert in this field, but when I met Rudy Rupak at a surrogacy conference in Australia, I immediately was struck that he appeared to me to be like the archetypal 1970s California porn film director. His long black hair was slicked back, tied, and oily. He wore a heavy gold chain with a gold bar at the end above his open-necked shirt, showing his hairy chest. He had a handlebar moustache and many gold rings and jewelry on his fingers. I had an instant dislike for him.

He was promoting surrogacy in Mexico. As it turns out, after he was exposed by the *New York Times* and the Australian Broadcast Corporation, the extent of his crimes was clear.

Rudy Rupak ran an operation called Planet Hospital. It was in essence an international surrogacy agency. He worked in conjunction with an IVF clinic in Cancún and undertook surrogacy in the Mexican state of Tabasco.

His surrogacy agency was a Ponzi scheme. In essence, he fleeced intended parents of their funds and often didn't deliver.

Even worse, he trafficked poor Colombian women to Mexico to be surrogates.

After his media exposure, Rudy Rupak was arrested by the FBI and in 2017 was sentenced to two years in custody and subject to a $10,000 fine.

He was also to pay compensation to his victims. His company originally promoted and coordinated international and medical tourism focused on cosmetic surgery and organ transplants but in 2006 expanded into surrogacy. It started in India and then moved to Thailand, then followed by Mexico.

Mr. Rupak would undercharge clients to induce them to work with the company. Once they had committed time and resources, he would require additional payment. He created a fake website and email address and then sent emails claiming to be a physician for a fertility clinic but offered excuses as to why the surrogacy services had not been provided.

Rupak had scammed victims out of at least $250,000.

In the words of the U.S. attorney:

> The defendant betrayed the trust placed on him by people desperate to have a child. By preying on their vulnerable emotions, he was able to extract more money on the false promise that he was doing everything possible to help them obtain a baby. To

use the dream of parenthood as leverage for obtaining fraudulent proceeds is intolerable and heartbreaking.[7]

Greg Blosser

Mr. Blosser ran a Maryland agency called the Surrogacy Group. All looked good. Unbeknownst to his clients, Mr. Blosser had not deposited their funds in an escrow account, but had stolen them instead. Several intended parents, on learning that their surrogate was pregnant, were then horrified that the preserved money to pay the surrogate was no longer there. It had vanished. Intended parents then had the extraordinary ordeal of coming up with replacement funds—that they were bound to pay the surrogate, but for which they had not budgeted.

Mr. Blosser was jailed after he had stolen $1.1 million from 44 victims who lived in Maryland, Australia, North Carolina, Germany, and Virginia.

Take Away

1. Those who are desperate to have children may be taken advantage of by dishonest players.
2. Care should be taken when dealing with overseas agencies and clinics. They may be legitimate. They may not be.
3. Wherever possible, try to find a reputable lawyer in the overseas jurisdiction, who may be able to give guidance about who to avoid.

7. Press Release, U.S. Attorney's Office for the Southern District of California, International Surrogacy Clients Defrauded in Racketeering Scheme (Aug. 7, 2017), https://www.justice.gov/usao-sdca/pr/international-surrogacy-clients-defrauded-racketeering-scheme.

Chapter 19

Success, but at What Price?

Part of the duty of lawyers to their clients is to enable their clients to make informed choices about where to undertake their fertility journey. Your clients may well have the right to choose to undertake surrogacy in a developing country of their choice, for example, but if you get the opportunity, they ought to be told about what possible risks there might be in going there. A lawyer advising about assisted reproductive technology (ART), even one experienced in international ART, does not hold the same professional qualifications as a fertility doctor. However, they can and should be alert to red flags:

- When presented with the agency agreement (if you are lucky enough to be asked before the clinic or agency is engaged), do you know the agency and its reputation? If not, look them up and ask colleagues.
- Does the agency agreement mandate the surrogate to have a C-section? Some years ago, I saw such an agreement for an agency in Ukraine specify that the surrogate must have a C-section.[1] My advice was not to sign—as the surrogate will have lost all bodily autonomy. An Indian surrogacy agent some years ago boasted, in response to a question from me at a seminar,[2] that her agency had a C-section rate of 80 percent, and that all the surrogates were "*very happy*" with that. This was done, she said, to ensure that her clients, many of whom were Bollywood stars, could minimize the inconvenience of when they collected their children. At the time that Cambodia shut down surrogacy in 2016, I was told by an industry insider that Chinese travel agents were demanding, and succeeding, in determining when Cambodian surrogates were to give birth—to fit in with the travel plans of the Chinese intended parents.

1. And many that did not.
2. From recollection at the Surrogacy Australia seminar, Melbourne, circa 2013.

- Does the surrogacy agency boast of a baby guarantee? I will discuss this later in the chapter.
- What is the practice in that country or of that clinic of multiple embryo transfers?
- What is the maternal death rate in that country?
- How many in vitro fertilization (IVF) cycles does the individual clinic undertake?
- Are the intended parents going to meet the surrogate, and get to know her?
- Do the intended parents and the surrogate speak the same language?

Surrogacy agencies across the world promote, to a greater or lesser degree, success rates. At their worst, it is a baby guarantee. Some U.S. and Canadian clinics, for example, guarantee that there will be a baby born, but only after a series of rigorous requirements have been met on the part of the intended parents, such as their age, quality of the embryo, use of preimplantation genetic testing,[3] and so forth.

That is not always the case elsewhere. Intended parents have been presented with contracts guaranteeing a baby at the end of their surrogacy journey. How is this achieved? One way has been to implant multiple embryos. In Ukraine and Georgia, for example, it has been widespread practice for two embryos to be implanted, in the hope that one child is born. Of course, the more embryos that are implanted, the greater the risk that multiple children will be born. The more children who are born, the greater the risk that the children will be born underweight and preterm—and therefore the higher the chances that the children will have, at least before reaching puberty, developmental delays.

This is demonstrated by data from the Centers for Disease Control and Prevention (CDC), as seen in Table 19.1.

3. Commonly called PGT, but sometimes called preimplantation genetic screening (PGS) or preimplantation genetic diagnosis (PGD).

Table 19.1. Birth Outcomes for Singles and Multiples in the United States, 2020[4]

Number of Children Born	Preterm (%)	Low Birth Weight (%)
Singleton infants from single fetus pregnancies	17.8	7.9
Singleton infants from multiple-fetus pregnancies	27.0	16.2
Twins	62.4	51.0
Triplets or more	87.9	86.8

The more children who are born, the greater the risk to the pregnant patient. Best practice by IVF clinics now dictates that, except for older patients, there should only be a single embryo transfer.[5]

The Six-Embryo Baby

In about 2013, clients of mine underwent their second surrogacy journey in India. Their first surrogacy journey had not worked. The IVF doctor was also the agent. They had not met their first surrogate. Nor were they aware as to how many embryos had been implanted in the first journey.

A child was born on their second surrogacy journey. Six embryos were implanted. There had been no discussion by the IVF doctor with the intended parents about what risks there would be in implanting six embryos, as opposed to one.

I asked my client, "*What about selective reduction?*" My client responded, "*What's that?*" I explained what it was. The IVF doctor had not explained what it was. In all likelihood, the IVF doctor had not told the surrogate about the risks of implanting six embryos or what was involved with selective reduction. It is unlikely that she gave informed consent.

It is likely that there was no selective reduction—just that the quality of the IVF was so poor that six embryos were implanted in the hope that one would take, which it did.

In some places, the practice of IVF clinics is, with rare exception, only to have single embryo transfers, such as in Australia and New Zealand. Double embryo transfers occur for older patients. Both countries

4. CDC, 2021 Assisted Reproductive Technology: Fertility Clinic and National Summary Report (2023).

5. *See, e.g.*, Ahmad Badeghiesh et al., *Effect of Double Embryo Transfer Derived from Autologous Frozen Oocytes on Multiple Pregnancy Rates and Presentation of Success Rates Stratified by Age at Retrieval*, 22 J. Turkish-German Gynecological Ass'n 168 (2021).

have very low maternal mortality rates. Table 19.2 demonstrates the use in 2021 of Australia and New Zealand clinics of single embryo transfers.

Table 19.2. Number of Embryos Implanted, Australia and New Zealand, 2021[6]

One Embryo (%)	Two Embryos (%)	Three or More Embryos (%)	Singletons Born (%)	Twins Born (%)	Three or More Born (%)
93.6	6.4	0.1	97.0	2.9	0.1

The low rate of twins, and thus risk, is attributed to single embryo transfers. Similarly, the practice in Canada is to require single embryo transfers. In the words of the Canadian Clinical Practice Guidelines:

> It is universally agreed that high-order multiples (triplets or more) are associated with adverse outcomes and are considered an undesirable outcome of IVF. . . . It is also well-established that IVF twin pregnancies are associated with a higher incidence of adverse maternal, fetal and neonatal outcomes when compared to singleton gestations, primarily due to increases in preterm birth. In 2007 in Canada, of all singleton births resulting from ART, the total perinatal mortality rate was 1.3%, preterm delivery under 37 weeks was 14.3%, under 32 weeks was 2.3%, and birth weight less than 2500 [grams (g), about 5.51 pounds] was 10.3%. For twins, the perinatal mortality rate was 3.2%, delivery less than 37 weeks was 67.5%, under 32 weeks was 11.3%, and birth weight less than 2500g was 53.5%. Given the increased morbidity and mortality associated with any multifetal pregnancy, the aim of IVF treatment should be the birth of a healthy singleton.[7]

---

6. Jade E. Newman et al., University of New South Wales, Sydney, Assisted Reproductive Technology in Australia and New Zealand 2021 (2023).

7. Jason Min & Camille Sylvestre, Canadian Fertility and Andrology Society, Guidelines on the Number of Embryos Transferred (2013) (citations omitted), https://cfas.ca/_Library/clinical_practice_guidelines/CFAS_CPG_Embryo_Transfer_2013.pdf.

Europe

When one then looks at European data, there appears to be the practice in northern and western Europe to have single embryo transfers, but in eastern and southern Europe, more use of double embryo transfers, including in surrogacy destinations such as Ukraine, Greece, and, as of 2023, Georgia,[8] as seen in Table 19.3, notwithstanding the clear risks.

Table 19.3 also shows how much or how little IVF is done in various countries in Europe. Spain, popular for donor cycles, had more than 23,000 transfers. Albania, by comparison, had 66. Greater than one in four cycles in Serbia resulted in twins being born. By comparison, one in 37 cycles in Sweden resulted in twins being born. The figures demonstrate the differences in how IVF is practiced in these different European countries.

8. As of April 2024, a bill had been introduced, but the ban had not been implemented. Reports from Georgia in May 2024 suggest that the government is not proceeding with the ban.

Table 19.3. A Comparison of IVF Clinics and Embryo Transfers Across Europe, 2019[9]

Country	IVF Clinics	IVF + ICSI[10] Transfers	1 Embryo (%)	2 Embryos (%)	3 Embryos (%)	4 Embryos (%)	Births	Twins (%)
Albania	10	66	1.5	98.5	0	0	26	26.9
Armenia	6	544	26.1	52.4	21.5	0	211	16.1
Austria	30	5,714	73.3	26.6	0.1	0	1,640	0
Belarus	8	2,135	32.9	59.2	7.9	0	449	12.2
Belgium	18	12,048	72.5	24.5	2.7	0.3	2,604	5.7
Federation of Bosnia-Herzegovina, part	9	71	76.1	19.7	4.2	0	26	3.8
Bulgaria	36	0	0	0	0	0	0	0
Czech Republic	46	10,151	79.9	19.9	0.2	0	2,033	5.7
Denmark	19	8,492	83.1	16.5	0.4	0	1,695	3.5
Estonia	6	1,500	57.6	40.3	2.1	0	389	9.8
Finland	16	2,564	95.7	4.3	0	0	680	0
France	103	40,432	60.8	36.6	2.4	0.1	10,182	8.9
Germany	139	53,737	34.4	62.6	3.0	0	12,936	18.1
Greece	41	7,284	23.5	61.0	13.2	2.2	1,741	20.0

9. Jesper Smeenk et al., *ART in Europe, 2019: Results Generated from European Registries by ESHRE*, 38 HUM. REPROD. 2321 (2023), https://doi.org/10.1093/humrep/dead197.

10. Intracytoplasmic sperm injection. *See* Chapter 5.

Country	IVF Clinics	IVF + ICSI[10] Transfers	1 Embryo (%)	2 Embryos (%)	3 Embryos (%)	4 Embryos (%)	Births	Twins (%)
Hungary	14	0	0	0	0	0	1,354	16.8
Iceland	1	299	100	0	0	0	82	0
Ireland	9	977	50.7	46.9	2.5	0	324	11.1
Italy	189	28,731	44.8	46.7	7.8	0.7	5,151	12.3
Kazakhstan	23	4,193	51.9	46.5	1.6	0	1,414	12.6
Latvia	6	380	83.4	16.6	0	0	122	5.9
Lithuania	7	1,386	56.1	29.5	14.4	0	256	11.0
Luxembourg	1	499	55.7	44.4	0	0	115	4.3
Malta	4	0	0	0	0	0	5	0
Moldova	5	0	0	0	0	0	0	0
Montenegro	5	481	29.7	49.1	21.2	0	148	23.6
The Netherlands	15	0	0	0	0	0	0	0
North Macedonia	2	1,734	35.9	62.2	1.8	0.1	488	14.8
Norway	11	0	0	0	0	0	0	0
Poland	44	8,884	66.9	32.9	0.1	0	2,137	6.1
Portugal	25	3,692	54.0	45.6	0.4	0	941	9.9
Russia	299	58,120	61.1	38.5	0.3	0	13,758	12.5
Serbia	18	1,511	23.5	31.8	41.8	3.0	380	28.7
Slovakia	12	0	0	0	0	0	0	0
Slovenia	3	2,578	61.8	38.1	0.1	0	686	7.3

Country	IVF Clinics	IVF + ICSI[10] Transfers	1 Embryo (%)	2 Embryos (%)	3 Embryos (%)	4 Embryos (%)	Births	Twins (%)
Spain	244	23,132	52.8	46.2	1.0	0	6,020	11.0
Sweden	19	8,587	88.8	11.2	0	0	2,485	2.7
Switzerland	28	3,207	72.2	26.5	1.2	0.1	808	7.7
Türkiye	167	7,796	58.7	41.3	0	0	2,388	11.6
Ukraine	50	5,747	41.3	53.9	4.8	0	2,042	15.8
United Kingdom	86	30,879	68.6	29.7	1.7	0	0	0
All		**344,452**	**55.4**	**39.9**	**2.6**	**0.2**	**75,716**	**11.9**

United States

The CDC does not report how many double or triple embryos are implanted, as seen in Table 19.4.

Table 19.4. Singles and Multiples Born through U.S. IVF Clinics, 2021[11]

Reporting Clinics	Cycles	Births	Multiple Live Births (%)
453	413,776	79,942	4.6

Latin America

Latin America, especially Argentina, Colombia, and Mexico, have become popular surrogacy destinations. Most Latin American countries undertake ART. As seen in Table 19.5, the number of cycles is large in Argentina, Brazil, and Mexico. Although Colombia has become a popular surrogacy destination, it had comparatively fewer cycles as of 2019.

Table 19.5. IVF Clinics and Number of Cycles in Latin America, 2019[12]

Country	IVF Centers	Total Cycles	Estimated Births from ART
Argentina	28	21,409	3,562
Bolivia	3	690	236
Brazil	63	46,745	8,545
Chile	11	5,425	1,481
Colombia	15	3,337	1,292
Dominican Republic	2	223	93
Ecuador	7	1,358	407
Guatemala	2	431	141
Mexico	40	15,884	5,352
Nicaragua	1	140	21
Panama	4	1,163	375
Paraguay	1	418	84
Peru	13	8,069	1,686
Uruguay	2	1,432	451
Venezuela	4	194	109
All		**106,918**	-

11. CDC, *supra* note 4.

12. Fernando Zegers-Hochschild et al., *Assisted Reproductive Technologies in Latin America: The Latin American Registry, 2019*, 26 JBRA Assisted Reprod. 637 (2022), https://doi.org/10.5935/1518-0557.20220034.

Most embryo transfers were multiple in Latin America in 2019, as seen in Table 19.6.

Table 19.6. Embryo Transfers and Twins in Latin America, 2019[13]

No. of Transferred Embryos	Embryo Transfers (%)	Singleton Births (%)	Twin Births (%)	Triplets or More (%)
1	36.2	97.9	2.1	0
2	53.8	78.3	21.5	0.2
3 or more	10.0	73.8	21.5	4.6

Africa

IVF is thriving in Africa. As seen in Table 19.7, clinics in Egypt, Tunisia, South Africa (which pioneered IVF in Africa), and Nigeria are busy.[14] In many countries, the clinics are quiet, and presumably relatively inexperienced. As of 2023, two promoted surrogacy destinations are Kenya and Uganda. In 2019, the one reporting Kenyan clinic only undertook 137 procedures. The other ten clinics did not report, possibly because they did not keep statistics, or did not want to report their outcomes. Similarly, the one reporting Ugandan clinic only underwent 262 procedures. Fewer than one in three Nigerian clinics provided data. If data is not provided, it is impossible for consumers such as intended parents to understand the quality, or otherwise, of the clinic.

Table 19.7. Number of African IVF Clinics and Procedures, 2019[15]

Country	Total Number of Centers	Participating Centers	Total Procedures
Benin	2	1	6
Burkina Faso	1	1	23
Cameroon	4	1	123
Cote d'Ivoire	1	1	455
Egypt	103	11	23,158
Ethiopia	2	1	373
Ghana	17	5	366

13. *Id.* at 638 tbl.1.

14. Paversan Archary et al., *Assisted Reproductive Technologies in Africa: The African Network and Registry for ART, 2018 and 2019*, 46 Reprod. BioMed. Online 835 (2023).

15. Zegers-Hochschild et al., *supra* note 12, at 642.

Country	Total Number of Centers	Participating Centers	Total Procedures
Kenya	11	1	137
Libya	NA	2	310
Mali	1	1	187
Mauritius	4	1	182
Nigeria	70	18	3,268
South Africa	21	19	8,663
Sudan	12	2	24
Togo	2	1	242
Tunisia	11	2	7,306
Uganda	4	1	262
Zimbabwe	2	1	100
Total	**268**	**70**	**45,185**

Table 19.8 shows the number of singleton and multiple births through ART in African clinics in 2018 and 2019. The rate of multiple embryo transfers is not known. However, there is a high rate of triplets being born in Africa,[16] which is indicative of double or more embryo transfers being the norm. Nigerian IVF clinics have now, as of 2023, aimed to ensure that double embryo transfers, not triple or more, are the norm, even though it is acknowledged that the lowest risk is to have single embryo transfers.[17] A higher number is used than single due to the cost to the patients.[18]

At least at one clinic in Nigeria, one in ten patients come from Europe or North America. One in 50 are estimated to come from other African countries.[19]

Table 19.8. Singleton, Twins, and More Births via ART in Africa, 2018 and 2019[20]

Type of Embryo Transfer	Single Births (%)	Twin Births (%)	Triplets or More (%)
Fresh	76.9	20.9	2.2
Frozen	79.5	20.5	0

16. Dr. Paverson Archary, ART in Africa Webinar (Nov. 8, 2023).
17. Dr. Ibrahim Wada, ART in Africa Webinar (Nov. 8, 2023).
18. *Id.*
19. *Id.*
20. Paversan Archary et al., *Assisted Reproductive Technologies in Africa: The African Network and Registry for ART, 2018 and 2019*, 46 Reprod. Biomed. Online 835 (2023).

Asia

Asia does not have one repository of data for IVF clinics. ART registry reports from developing countries are scanty.[21] Data from Thailand from 2014 shows the practice of using double embryo transfers with a high rate of multiples being born.[22]

But All IVF Clinics Are the Same, Aren't They?

As Chapter 18, Always Be Aware of the Sharks in the Water, makes plain, not all agencies and IVF clinics are the same.

A few years ago, a couple who had migrated from Africa wanted to send their embryos to an IVF clinic in their home country.

According to the clinic's website, the clinic was accredited by the European Society of Human Reproduction and Embryology (ESHRE).

The sending clinic could only establish that ESHRE accreditation had expired three years before and had not been renewed.

The sending client refused to send the couple's embryos to the African clinic because the sending clinic could not verify that the African clinic remained accredited.

Maternal Mortality Rates

Every pregnancy and childbirth carry with them the risk of death. Maternal mortality rates give a broad guide to maternal care (or the lack of it) in that country. Maternal mortality rates are low in developed countries. Intended parents going overseas for surrogacy may see the risk of maternal death for their surrogate to be nonexistent, because maternal mortality rates at home are so low.

The data has some surprises. It was half as risky to be pregnant in Ukraine in 2020, for example, than in the United States. Some African countries in which surrogacy is practiced—Kenya, Nigeria, and Uganda, for example—are very risky places to be pregnant. In Kenya there were 7,700 maternal deaths and a one-in-52 lifetime risk of death through

21. Charoenchai Chiamchanya & Kamthorn Pruksananonda, *Development of Assisted Reproductive Technology Services in Thailand between 2008 and 2014 before the New Law: Results Generated from the National ART Registry, Royal Thai College of Obstetricians and Gynecologists*, 13 ASIAN BIOMED. 189 (2020), https://doi.org/10.1515/abm-2019-0060.

22. *Id.*

being pregnant and giving birth. In Nigeria, it was estimated that there were 82,000 maternal deaths in 2020, and a one-in-19 lifetime risk of death, among the worst in the world. In Uganda, there were 4,700 deaths and a one-in-66 lifetime risk of death.

Although intended parents often minimize the risk to surrogates, all of us know the risk of being stuck by lightning. According to the CDC, the chance of being hit by lightning in any given year in the United States is one in a million.[23]

The World Health Organization (WHO) and other agencies have estimated current (as of 2020) maternal mortality rates,[24] as seen in Table 19.9. The estimates are not precise. The WHO and other agencies have provided a listing for every country. For length, Table 19.9 only shows selected countries.

Between 2010 and 2020, all areas of the world have experienced a decrease in maternal mortality, except North America, where there has been an increase from 510 maternal deaths in 2010 to 810 in 2020. Anecdotal reports indicate that this increase has been in the United States, not Canada, and appears to relate to women of color, and women who live in rural areas.

While it is often assumed that a surrogate in a developed country will necessarily have access to close and high-quality maternity healthcare, that assumption may not be correct. Access to high-quality maternity healthcare should be checked.

---

23. *Lightning Strike Victim Data*, CDC, https://www.cdc.gov/disasters/lightning/victimdata.html (last reviewed Sept. 16, 2022).

24. WHO ET AL., TRENDS IN MATERNAL MORTALITY 2000 TO 2020: ESTIMATES BY WHO, UNICEF, UNFPA, WORLD BANK GROUP, AND UNDESA/POPULATION DIVISION (2023).

Table 19.9. Maternal Mortality Rates by Selected Countries, 2020[25]

Country	Maternal Mortality Ratio	Number of Maternal Deaths	Lifetime Risk of Maternal Death (1 in)
Australia	3	9	19,000
Austria	5	4	14,000
Belgium	5	5	12,000
Brazil	72	2,000	800
Cambodia	218	710	170
Canada	11	41	6,500
China	23	2,800	3,100
Colombia	75	550	780
Cyprus	68	9	1,000
Czech Republic	3	4	17,000
Denmark	5	3	12,000
France	8	54	7,300
Georgia	28	14	1,700
Germany	4	34	13,000
Ghana	263	2,400	100
Greece	8	6	9,400
India	103	24,000	470
Iran	22	270	2,600
Ireland	5	3	12,000
Israel	3	5	11,000
Italy	5	19	21,000
Japan	4	36	22,000
Kazakhstan	13	57	2,400
Kenya	530	7,700	52
Mexico	59	1,200	820
The Netherlands	4	7	13,000
New Zealand	7	4	8,200
Nigeria	1,047	82,000	19
Russia	14	200	5,300

25. *Id.* I have tried to illustrate risks in some current or former surrogacy destination countries and those in which intended parents may live. Their perception of maternal mortality risk, based on where they live, may be different to where they are considering surrogacy.

Country	Maternal Mortality Ratio	Number of Maternal Deaths	Lifetime Risk of Maternal Death (1 in)
Singapore	7	3	13,000
South Africa	127	1,500	300
Spain	3	12	28,000
Thailand	29	190	2,500
Uganda	284	4,700	66
Ukraine	17	56	5,800
United Kingdom	10	67	5,800
United States	21	770	2,700

Take Away

1. While ART lawyers are not fertility doctors, they can provide advice to clients about obvious risks. Lawyers can ask questions, which in themselves help inform clients about what to look for and what to avoid. Lawyers can assist clients with due diligence.
2. Due diligence is the responsibility of the clients—which should be reflected in correspondence from the lawyer or, even better, also in the retainer agreement as to scope of work.
3. Lawyers do not want to have it on their conscience that they blindly let their clients go to a high-risk country that resulted in the death of a woman who was the surrogate, with the potential of leaving her family destitute, and the clients traumatized.
4. Lawyers should use their expertise to help guide clients to minimize risks to themselves and others.
5. Access by the surrogate to high-quality maternity healthcare should not be assumed but, where possible, verified.
6. While the data is not always available, as this chapter demonstrates, often the data is publicly available, if you care to look. Do not assume that you are comparing apples and apples. It may be a case of comparing chalk and cheese.

Chapter 20

What Does the Future Hold?[1]

"Change is the law of life. And those who look only to the past or present are certain to miss the future."

John F. Kennedy

If I knew the answer to the question in the title, I would be wealthy! What is certain is that change in this area is constant. Those who practice assisted reproductive technology (ART) law are dealing with being at the forefront of science, medicine, society, and, leading the rear, the law. Much of the time, to be at the forefront of this new world is a blessing, but sometimes it is a curse—as what was seen as the known landscape disappears into the rearview mirror.

I will touch on some possible trends.

Increased International Regulation

As the world becomes smaller, increased international regulation becomes more and more inevitable. Certification of in vitro fertilization (IVF) labs with quality schemes worldwide is the norm, to comply with regulatory or membership bodies, such as the American Society for Reproductive Medicine.

It is likely that the push by nations to have international regulation of parental recognition is to continue. What form it will take, and how recognition will be achieved, remains unclear.

Fertility Rates

Fertility rates are slipping around the world. This is not just an issue for the United States. This means inevitably an increased reliance on ART of

1. *Fertility Rate, Total (Births per Woman)*, World Bank, https://data.worldbank.org/indicator/SP.DYN.TFRT.IN (last visited Mar. 26, 2024).

some kind in order to reproduce. Those who wish to become parents do so increasingly later in life.

Almost every country, and certainly every region, and every economic grouping of countries by category results, according to the World Bank, has a declining fertility rate.[2]

South Korea, for example, has the world's lowest fertility rate at 0.8 children per woman. The replacement rate to maintain the population level is 2.1 children per woman.

In response to these plummeting rates, governments have encouraged that more babies be born. Measures in some countries have included subsidies for IVF. Given reports of a demographic cliff in China in particular, it is likely that international demand for ART and surrogacy will in the short to medium term increase, rather than decrease, as intended parents use whatever tools are available to achieve parentage.

The rise of ART has occurred at the same time as the decline in adoption, a long-term trend that is likely to continue.

Sunlit Uplands[3]

Despite backward steps in some countries, such as at the time of writing in Uganda, overall there has been a greater liberalization of laws and practices involving LGBTQIA+ people. This has commenced with decriminalization, as seen in Singapore, for example, in 2022, and then an acceptance of LGBTQIA+ people. This is a gradual, and not inevitable, process.

LGBTQIA+ people will likely increasingly over time want to form relationships and have children. As the number of those who want to become parents increase, then demand on current limited supplies will increase. Those limited supplies are the number of sperm donors, egg donors, and surrogates.

Shortages?

Economist Thomas Robert Malthus predicted two centuries ago that there would be a shortage of food to feed the world's population.[4] That shortage has still not happened, but it may happen in the future. It is very hard to predict what may occur.

---

2. *Id.*

3. Churchill's memorable term from his June 18, 1940, speech "Their Finest Hour."

4. Thomas Robert Malthus, An Essay on the Principle of Population (London, J. Johnson 1798).

It is possible in the future, as demand increases, the reaction will be what the world saw in the COVID pandemic and arising from the Russian invasion of Ukraine in 2022:

1. Shortages of sperm, with the result that single women and lesbian couples have made do with known donation to a greater degree. Known donation brings its own risks—
   (a) Whether adequate medical checks are undertaken to minimize transmission of sexually transmitted infections, such as HIV or syphilis, and inheritable conditions such as cystic fibrosis
   (b) Whether the donor is a parent. This has been complicated further by some sperm donors traveling internationally to donate[5]
   (c) No cap on donations,[6] as would have otherwise occurred through sperm banks or IVF clinics
2. Whether the donor has provided his correct identity[7]
3. Shortages of egg donors, and a resultant increase, in the United States at least, in the compensation payable
4. Greater preparedness to use egg banks

5. *E.g.*, Sammi Taylor, *60 Minutes: "Arrogant" Sperm Donor Labelled Potential Danger*, 9NEWS (Feb. 17, 2019), https://www.9news.com.au/national/60-minutes-joe-donor-sperm-ivf-pregnancy-children/bb45b667-9494-4684-8295-64945eb8f3b8; *Adam Hooper: Australian Sperm Donor on His Nationwide NZ Tour*, NEWSTALK ZB (June 7, 2022), https://www.newstalkzb.co.nz/on-air/heather-du-plessis-allan-drive/audio/adam-hooper-australian-sperm-donor-on-his-nationwide-new-zealand-donation-tour/.

6. *See, e.g.*, Cindy Lever, *Australia's Most Prolific Sperm Donor Has Fathered 23 Children in a Year*, KIDSPOT (Oct. 15, 2020), https://www.kidspot.com.au/birth/conception/ivf/australias-most-prolific-sperm-donor-has-fathered-23-children-in-a-year/news-story/4d163b3b0e64c8aeda1a96d25daf35b2; Cindy Lever, *"Some People Fish . . . I Masturbate": Australia's Oldest Sperm Donor, 72, Who Has Fathered 21 Children "That He Knows About" Was Banned from Clinics Due to His Age and Now Helps Lesbian Women Start Families*, DAILY MAIL AUSTL. (Dec. 25, 2020), https://www.dailymail.co.uk/news/article-9087093/Meet-Australias-oldest-sperm-donor-fathered-50-kids.html.

7. E.g., Brett Lackey, *Sperm Donor Who Used Fake Names to Father Up to 60 Children Is Exposed after Parents at an LGBTQI Community Event Realised Their Kids All Looked the Same*, DAILY MAIL AUSTL. (Feb. 19, 2023), https://www.dailymail.co.uk/news/article-11764815/Sperm-donor-fathers-60-children-using-fake-names.html.

5. Shortages of surrogates, with long matching times, and an increase in the United States and some other countries with compensation payable
6. New availability for sperm, eggs, and surrogates through accessing riskier donor and surrogacy destinations, some of which are new
7. As fertility rates slip, the availability of current donor and surrogacy destinations should not be assumed
8. Gradual, although not inevitable, decriminalization of homosexual acts, and acceptance of LGBTQIA+ people, will mean sooner or later more LGBTQIA+ people worldwide will seek to become parents. What was seen as the impossible dream is now seen as destiny. For lesbian couples, this will likely mean an increase in demand for donor sperm. For gay couples, this will likely mean an increase in demand for surrogates.
9. Within the IVF lab, continued innovation

Greater Recognition of the Rights of Donor-Conceived Individuals

Another trend internationally has been the increasing demands of donor-conceived adults that they have a right to find out where they came from—and that those conceived in the future also have those rights. This trend has arisen with the rise of data banks such as ancestry.com and 23andMe.com, which in real time have rendered anonymity dead.

The fight to have recognition of these rights will likely mean greater retrospective access to donor records, and greater regulation of donation, including more rigorous capping of the number of donations. It should not be assumed that the current availability of donors will remain.

Take Away

1. ART is at the forefront of scientific, medical, and societal change. The law, as ever, lags behind.
2. It is extremely hard to make predictions about the future, as change has been, and continues to be, rapid.
3. One must live in hope that the Hague Conference on Private International Law (HCCH) will at long last enact a convention regulating international surrogacy arrangements that will give effect to children's right to have their parentage recognized across state borders.

4. LGBTQIA+ people will continue to push to be allowed access to treatment or will travel overseas to access treatment when resources allow. There has been considerable pushback against LGBTQIA+ people, especially in Africa, which will inevitably flow on to their desire to be parents.
5. The decision by the United States Supreme Court in *Dobbs v. Jackson Women's Health Organization* (2021) has led to availability (or otherwise) of abortion being part of the landscape to be considered when planning international surrogacy journeys into the United States.
6. Similarly, the decision by the Alabama Supreme Court in *Le Page v. Center for Reproductive Medicine* (2024) when the Court accepted that embryos were unborn children has caused uncertainty, and in some quarters alarm, about the availability of IVF in parts of the United States and reinforced efforts by some to uphold fetal personhood.
7. Donor conceived adults will continue to press for their rights to be recognized. In late 2023, donor conceived adults in Australia called for the continuation of criminalization of cross-border surrogacy because of its connection with anonymous donor conception. From one state in Australia having retrospective transparency for gamete donation to there likely being four by the end of 2024, change has happened suddenly.
8. The use of artificial intelligence (AI) is resulting in immediate changes and challenges in IVF laboratories. As of 2024, AI is now used in one European IVF clinic to determine the quality of eggs from donors. AI is now commonly being used to assess the quality of embryos.
9. From a request by a patient in Adelaide, Australia, followed by experimentation on animals, starting with mice, and then followed by the first uterine transplant in Sweden, uterine transplants have occurred in nine countries. Some patients will continue to seek uterine transplants as opposed to ART. Whether each uterus is further donated when the rejection period for the transplant expires remains to be seen.
10. Sex selection is banned in many countries. Intended parents who wish to undertake sex selection and have the means to do so will travel to perceived friendlier jurisdictions for that purpose.
11. Intended parents through surrogacy, when denied the ability to become parents at home, access surrogacy overseas in jurisdictions

that they perceive as welcoming. Some of those jurisdictions will change, as they have changed since 2010.

12. Like other intended parents, widows seeking to use their late husbands' sperm[8] have it exported to friendly jurisdictions, where it can be used to enable them to have children.
13. Following the attack by Hamas on Israel of October 7, 2023, there has been a large increase in the number of posthumous use applications in Israel—and they are mainly made by the deceased's parents.
14. The first child born in the United Kingdom through mitochondrial donation, in 2023, only occurred after a strict regulatory pathway was followed before approval to treat was given. Australia has started down the same pathway, with approval for research to occur, with the intention of replicating the United Kingdom approach. In the meantime, there have been an estimated 60 births[9] via mitochondrial donation in an unregulated country, Albania.
15. More countries are likely to criminalize overseas surrogacy journeys. These gestural laws are likely not going to be enforced and will likely make a mockery of the law, as has happened with each one of these legislated so far around the world.

---

8. Outside Israel, posthumous reproduction is primarily by widows, not widowers or other family members.

9. Estimate given to the author by Dr. Uliana Dorofeyeva, 2023.

Index

J

K

L

T